ISRAEL

Walking In Holy Footsteps
VOLUME 1

By
WINIFRED WHITE JOHNSTON &
HAROLD JOHNSTON

ISRAEL
WALKING IN HOLY FOOTSTEPS VOLUME 1
by Winifred White Johnston & Harold Johnston

Printed in the United States of America

ISBN 9781498468718

Unless otherwise indicated, Scripture quotations taken from the King James Version (KJV)–*public domain*.

Scripture quotations taken from the Holy Bible, New International Version (NIV). Copyright © 1973, 1978, 1984, 2011 by Biblica, Inc.™. Used by permission. All rights reserved.

Pictures are from the Israel Government Tourist Office and are used by permission.

www.xulonpress.com

Winifred "Winkie" Johnston
Harold Johnston

Dedication

To Our Parents,

Phillip Guy White, Jr. and Eunice Sullivan White of Fitzgerald, Georgia

George Dexton Johnston and Sara Frances Turner Johnston of Augusta, Georgia

Who guided our lives in the manner of Christ and led us to likewise raise our children in the same manner,

Harold G. "Hal" Johnston, Jr., born 1968 and Eunice Ann Johnston, born 1970

Preface

It was a real joy and a blessing to research and write this book. We learned a lot about the country of Israel through this journey. We hope that you, too, will enjoy reading this book. We have included many picture photos, maps, Bible quotations, magazine articles, and book summaries to add to the enjoyment of your walk through Israel. This first volume contains all kinds of historical, biblical, and contemporary information about Israel that we gathered and organized with pictures.

In our second volume, *Israel, Walking Through Israel, Volume 2,* we share our personal insights, photos, and travel observations about the land, the people, and the biblical insights from our trip.

Table of Contents

Acknowledgments

Wethank Esquire William Lawrence Fletcher and Mrs. Kimberly Fletcher Bowden for their valuable assistance.

We are indebted to Greg Deloach who planned a very fun and educational trip to Israel and was a big help to us along the way.

Introduction

M any of the events in the Bible happened a long time ago in Israel. Jerusalem, Haifa, Bethlehem, and Nazareth are familiar to many because of being discussed in the Bible in ancient times. At the same time Israel as a modern country is a very new nation developed in 1948. Israel is the only nation in the world where Judaism is the major religion and where most of the population is Jewish. The food of Israel is a blend of Middle Eastern and European dishes with a Jewish flavor added to the dish.

We have shared our feelings about Israel where we went walking in holy footsteps. Three modern world religions trace back to this Holy Land. The Holy Land is where Jews, Christians, and Muslims have holy sites in the same general locations. All three trace back to Abraham. It is like a family feud involving all three.

Israel is located on the narrow region connecting Asia and Africa. The official name is the State of Israel. The capital is Jerusalem. The State of Israel is 22,072 square kilometers; the population is 7.4 million people. The religious distribution is 75.6 percent Jews, 16.6 percent Muslim, 1.6 percent Christian, and 1.6 percent Druze. The official languages are Hebrew and Arabic. The currency is the New Shekel. The government of Israel is a Parliamentary Democracy. The Quality of Life Classification is placed twenty-fourth in the world.

The State of Israel is diversified in climate with snow on the mountain tops in the north alongside dry wildernesses in the southern part. You also find desolate areas around big populated cities. Due to three monotheistic religions and cultures, Israel has many holy and ancient sites to explore. It is recommended to visit during September-November and April-June.

Israel is a land of modern buildings and roads and there are many ancient Holy sites that are thousands of years old. Archaeologists have uncovered valuable information about the way of life centuries ago.

Ishmael was the oldest son of Abraham through the hand maid Hagar. Ishmael's descendants became the Muslims. Isaac was the second son of Abraham and Sarah and Isaac's descendants became the Jews. Christians trace the linage of Jesus back to Isaac and Abraham. Muslims believe the land of Israel belongs to them because Ishmael was the oldest son and oldest sons usually inherit the land, but the Jewish Bible contains an agreement from Jehovah God that Isaac was "the son of promise" and would therefore inherit the land of Israel.

The main problem to lasting peace between Jews and Muslims is they both claim the same land. Neither side will agree to give up any of their land therefore the country cannot be divided so that each will have part of the land and live in peace.

Muslim extremists have a goal of wiping out the existing Jewish population which causes constant friction in the land.

Some Important Dates in the History of Israel

BC
164: The Maccabees seized Jerusalem
63: Pompey's victory established Roman rule
40: Herod the Great appointed King
4: End of Herod's reign and approximate time of Jesus birth

AD
29: Christ's crucifixion and resurrection
66: First Jewish Revolt began
70: Titus destroyed Jerusalem and the Temple
73: Masada captured and destroyed
132: Second Jewish Revolt began
135: Bar-Kokhba defeated: Second Revolt ended
312: Constantine legalized Christianity
325: Queen Helena began extensive church building
395: Byzantines regained control of Palestine
614: Chosroes II of Persia began reign in Palestine
628: Byzantines regained control of Palestine
638: Omar led Moslems to power in Palestine
969: Egyptians began their rule of Palestine
1071: Seljuk Turks invaded Palestine
1099: Crusaders invaded, began 200-year rule
1187: Saladin defeated Crusaders
1250: Mamelukes came to power
1291: Last Crusaders driven from Palestine

1517: Ottoman Turks began 400-year rule
1799: Napoleon's unsuccessful attempt to invade Palestine
1897: World Zionist Organization founded
1909: Tel Aviv, first Jewish city established
1917: British seized Palestine and declared Balfour Declaration
1939: Britain's white paper limited Jewish advancement
1947: United Nations voted to partition Palestine and Dead Sea Scrolls discovered
1948: State of Israel declared; War of Independence
1949: Israel admitted to United Nations
1956: Sinai War with Egypt
1967: Six Day War; Jerusalem reunited
1973: Yom Kippur War
1976: Raid on Entebbe to rescue hostages
1977: Egyptian President Anwar Sadat visited Jerusalem
1979: Peace Treaty between Israel and Egypt signed
1982: Invasion of Lebanon by Israel
1984: Golan Heights annexed by Israel
1988: West Bank and Gaza Strip Uprisings

(Source: David R. Barnhart, *Israel: Land of Promise and Prophecy*)

Part One:

Background on Israel

CHAPTER 1

PREPARATION AND ANTICIPATION

D o not take too much luggage. Take the shirts, fold the sleeves in and roll down neatly from the top toward the base. Roll your pants, coats, and other things into bundles. In the summer you will need lightweight short sleeve shirts, but bring a sweater or jacket due to cool nights in desert and the mountains can be chilly at night. In winter you will need warm clothes, though it is warm enough in winter to swim in the Dead Sea. In both the winter and summer you will need sunscreen, a sun hat, and dark glasses.

Some tour leaders suggest taking $500 a couple. Charge cards can be used in most stores. Some places have access to ATM machines. On our tour we need cash only for lunches and small purchases. We bought a Dynex 1875 Watt International Converter Kit because if you don't buy a converter for your computer to be used overseas you can fry your computer. The Israeli power supply is single phase 220 volts at 50 Hertz. Most power sockets in Israel have three pin holes, but many of them will work with double-pin European plugs. Visitors who want to use shavers, traveling irons and other small appliances may need both transformers and adaptor plugs.

WiFi is industry standard and available at most hotels, fast food restaurants, museums, and visitor's centers.

There is a two-lane customs transit system that are red and green at Ben Gurion Airport. Green light is for tourists with nothing to declare. These articles do not need to be declared: personal clothes, shoes, cosmetics, alcoholic beverages one liter for hard liquor and two liters for wine, tobacco, presents, cameras, television sets costing up to $200, food that is three kilograms, binoculars, jewelry, musical instruments, camping or sporting equipment, and bicycles. Failure to declare taxable items is an offense with punishments of fines, prosecution, or have the goods confiscated. It is against custom regulations to import without a license plants, guns, raw meat, raw materials, counterfeit currency, and knives.

Some Hebrew words that may come in handy:

Shalom for hello or good-bye.
What time is it? is *Ma Ha'sha'a?*
Right say *Yemin* and left is *Smol*
"The bill or check, please" is *Cheshborn, bevakasha.*

Tips and Bargaining

It is customary to give a 12 percent tip primarily in restaurants. In hotels, one tips the bellhop or any other service provider. Taxi drivers are generally not tipped.

Bargaining is acceptable in the open-air markets and is part of the experience and doing so can lower the price. Storekeepers are legally required to display prices and for the most part are not open to bargaining. This is also true of restaurants and public transportation. Passengers are advised to ask cab drivers to turn on the meter, thus avoiding unnecessary haggling.

Shekels can be converted back to foreign currency at Ben Gurion Airport and banks up to US $500 or its equivalent in other currencies. Any remaining shekels over this amount that were acquired during a single visit to Israel (up to a maximum of US $5,000) can be reconverted with bank receipts proving the original conversion of the foreign currency.

Tourists may bring cash, traveler's checks, credit cards or State of Israel bonds. Foreign currency may be exchanged in airport, banks, post office, and most hotels. A passport is required in many places when exchanging travel's checks. Rates are not the same and banks also charge a commission. It is a good idea to have many U.S. dollar bills in the Old City of Jerusalem because merchants like them.

Storeowners and service providers are not required to accept foreign currency and may give change back in shekels even if payments are made with foreign currency. Tourists who pay with foreign currency may be exempt from VAT (Value Added Tax) on certain items.

The Storeowners must be registered to the Ministry of Tourism program for refunding tourist VAT payments. These registered merchants must give qualified customers a special invoice for the tourist to give to airport officials. The invoice and the item purchased must be in a sealed sack. To receive a VAT refund, keep all receipts and purchases in a bag and take it to the change place at Ben Gurion and receive a VAT. There is no VAT refund for food, drinks, tobacco, electrical appliances, cameras or other photography.

It is important for tourists to know that Jews cannot eat dairy and meat together. Both Jews and Muslims cannot eat pork at any meals. The falafel and schnitzel are available everywhere. If you are in Israel on a Friday night, it is their Sabbath and many Jewish restaurants are closed. Jews are not allowed to cook on the Sabbath.

Jews born in Israel are called "sabras" named after the cactus plant that has a prickly fruit on the outside but is sweet on the inside. There are three basic groups of Jews in Israel: Ashkenazim, Sephardim, and Oriental. The Ashkenazim are Jews with European, American, and South African backgrounds. Some Ashkenazim Jews speak Yiddish which is a language combination of Hebrew and German. The ultra-orthodox are called Hassidim and like to wear long black coats and fir trimmed hats. The Sephardim are Jews from Spain, Portugal, and North Africa. The Sephardim speak Ladino, a combination of Hebrew and Spanish. Today mainly older Sephardim Jews speak Ladino. The Oriental Jews are from countries of the Middle East and are influenced by Arab customs.

Religious Jews have views and habits from ultra-liberal to ultra-orthodox. Ultra-orthodox wear side locks and clothes style of a century earlier. Many ultra-orthodox female Jews shave their heads and wear a kerchief to cover them. An ultra-orthodox group, the Neturei Karta does not recognize the state of Israel and believe the Messiah is coming soon to develop a nation.

Festivals

The first festival in Israel begins in September or October with the Jewish New Year (Rosh Hashanah). Ten days later is Yon Kippur, the Day of Atonement in which no food is eaten for twenty-four hours. This is the day that the High Priest was allowed to go through the veil and into the Most Holy Place in the Tabernacle which was the Holy of Holies. Next the High Priest poured the blood of the bull and the goat on the altar over the Ark of the Covenant. That act made atonement for the children of Israel (Leviticus 17:11). Hebrews chapters 9 and 10 emphasizes that the blood of the bull and goat was foreshadow of the blood of Jesus with which we are forgiven once and for all.

To the Messianic Jews this celebration is a fun time of thanking and worshiping Jesus (*Yeshua*) for His sacrifice and for forgiving our sins. The Messianic Jews reflect on the prophecy yet to be fulfilled which is the turning of the Jewish people to Messiah *Yeshua*. (Zechariah 12:10). In Revelations 1:7 we learn, "Behold He is coming with the clouds, and every eye will see Him, even those who pierced Him; and all the tribes of the earth will mourn over Him. So it is to be. Amen." Romans 11:26 states that at the return of the Messiah, "all Israel will be saved."[1]

This festival is followed by eight days of harvest festival called the Feast of the Tabernacles (*Slukkot*). During this feast, Sukkahs are built as a temporary structure made out of lumber, grass or other natural items. They are decorated by tree branches, leaves, flowers, vegetables or fruit. The people eat and sleep in the sukkahs for seven days as they reflect the days of Exodus when they had nothing in the wilderness and God supplied their every need. He fed them supernaturally with manna, water from a rock, and made their clothes last for forty years (Leviticus 23:34, 40-44).

Sukkot has the tradition of "the waving of the lulav." Lulav is gathering of branches made from Palm branch, Myrtle, Willow, and the Etrog (Leviticus 23:40). The branches are held up and waved before the Lord to testify of His beauty and to show that He is everywhere and all gifts come from God. During the time of Jesus, the priests in Jerusalem marched from the Pool of Siloam to the altar at the Temple in Jerusalem carrying a pitcher of water. They poured the water on the

---

[1]   Rabbi K.A. Schneider. Fall Feasts of the Lord 2013. Discovering Jewish Jesus. Newsletter August 2013.

altar to thank God for the coming winter rains. The priests pouring water on the altar was called the day of Hoshana Rabbah. During this celebration Jesus cried out, "If anyone is thirsty, let him come to Me and drink. He who believes in Me, as the Scripture said, From his innermost being will flow rivers of living water" (John 7:37-38). When Jesus proclaimed this, He was revealing that He was the Messiah. Zechariah 14:16 teaches us "any who are left of all the nations that went against Jerusalem (during Armageddon), will go up from year to year to worship the King, the Lord of hosts, and to celebrate the Feast of Tabernacles."[2]

The Festival of Lights (around Christmas) is called Hanukah. The candles on a menorah are lit one by one for eight days. In early spring is a Purim, the Feast of Esther. After working hours, many people wear costumes and go to parties in the streets. People celebrate by eating cookies filled with poppy seeds or prunes. These treats of special cookies are called Haman's Ears or Haman's pockets after the mean man in Esther, one of the books of the Bible.

The Day of Trumpets is also known as Rosh Hashanah Head of the Year, and is celebrated as the Jewish New Year. The custom is to say, "*Lshanah tovah*" which means "May it be a good year." The people like to eat apples dipped in honey to represent God's provision and sweetness that He will give to us in the coming year.

Another name for this celebration is Yom T'rooah and it is mentioned in Leviticus 23:24, There are two scriptures that tell us that the Lord, Himself, blows the shofar (trumpet). The first passage is in Exodus 19:13 when the children of Israel prepared themselves to go up to Mount Sinai to meet the Lord. The second passage is in 1 Thessalonians 4:16-17, "For the Lord Himself will come down from heaven with a rousing cry, with a call from one of the ruling angels, and with God's shofar; those who died united with the Messiah will be the first to rise; then we who are left still alive will be caught up with them in the clouds to meet the Lord in the air."[3]

---

[2] Rabbi K.A. Schneider. Fall Feasts of the Lord 2013. Discovering Jewish Jesus. Newsletter August 2013.

[3] Rabbi K.A. Schneider. Fall Feasts of the Lord 2013. Discovering Jewish Jesus. Newsletter August 2013.

Archaeology in Israel-Notable sites

Israel is only one fourth the size of the state of Maine. It is 265 miles (424 kilometers) long at the eastern end of the Mediterranean Sea. Israel is one of the smallest countries in the world. The climate of Israel is like California except that Israel is at higher levels where it is often cold enough to snow. Israel has hot dry summers and short mild winters. The rainy season of Israel is from November to March.

Ashkelon excavations began in 1985 under the leadership of Lawrence Stager. This site has 50 feet of rubble from Philistine, Phoenician, Persian, Hellenistic, Roman, Byzantine, Islamic, and Crusader. They discovered a silvered bronze statuette of a bull calf that is probably from the Canaanite era. Over a hundred fireplaces and hearths were found. Archaeologists believe that this site was used by pastoral nomads for meat processing. Ashkelon is a coastal city in the South District of Israel on the Mediterranean coast and is thirty-one miles south of Tel Aviv and eight miles north of the Gaza Strip.

Beit Alfa is located at the bottom of the northern slopes of the Gilboa Mountains near Beit She'an. It is now part of the Gilboa Mountains near Beit She'an. It is now part of a national archaeological park managed by the Israel Nature and Parks Authority. The Beth Alpha synagogue was found in 1928 and 36 Byzantine coins. Archaeologists believe that the synagogue was a two story building with a courtyard, a vestibule, prayer hall, the bema which is a raised platform used when the Torah is read, and benches. The Torah Shrine within the Aspe faced southwest toward Jerusalem. The northern entryway had two inscriptions in Aramaic and Greek. The Aramaic inscription indicates the synagogue was built during the time of the Roman Emperor, Justin (518-527) and was funded by communal donations. The Greek inscription thanks artisans Marianos and his son Hanina. On either side of the inscriptions are a lion and a buffalo who were the synagogue's symbolic guardians. There was a northern panel that depicts the Binding of Isaac (Genesis 22:1-18). It tells the story in picture form. The central panel has a zodiac wheel.

Misliya Cave is southwest of Mt. Carmel and was excavated by anthropologists and archaeologists beginning in 2001. They discovered artifacts that may be from the earliest known prehistoric man.

Beth She'arim is a Jewish town 20 km east of Haifa in the southern foothills of the Lower Galilee. They found many rock-cut ancient tombs. This is part of the Belt She'arim National Park. Archaeologists found a large sheet of glass and a very old glassmaking furnace.

Tel Gezer is an archaeologic site that covers about 30 acres. Some inscribed boundary stones were found verifying the mound as Gezer. This is the first positive identified biblical city. Gezer is mentioned in the Hebrew Bible and the Amama letters. The Amama are collections of correspondence on clay tablets. The correspondence was between the Egyptian administration and its representatives in Canaan. There are 382 known tablets. The biblical references describe it as one of Solomon's royal store cities. Major discoveries were a soft limestone tablet named the Gezer calendar with the agricultural chores connected with each month of the year. This calendar is written in paleo-Hebrew script and is one of the oldest known examples of Hebrew writing dating back to the 10th century BCE. They also discovered a six-chambered gate similar to the ones found at Hazor and Megiddo, and ten monumental megaliths. A megalith is a large stone used to build a monument.

Mamshit, an UNESCO world heritage site is where the largest hoard of coins ever found in Israel was discovered. It was a total of 10,500 silver coins in a bronze jar dating back to the third century. Mamshit is ten acres with entire streets intact and many restored Nabatean buildings with open rooms, courtyards, and terraces. Archaeologists think that most of the buildings were built in the late Nabatean period in the 2nd century CE after the Nabatean kingdom was joined to Rome in 106 CE. Mamshit was an important station on the Incense Road going from the Idumean Mountains to Hebron and Jerusalem. Mamshit was a trade post on the route from Petra to Gaza. During the Roman occupation, trade subsided and the residents began to raise and breed Arabian horses which brought great wealth to the people. Two shirts were discovered in Mamshit. The Western Nine Church had a mosaic floor with colorful geometric patterns, birds, and a fruit basket, but is not open to the public. The Eastern Church has a lectern on small marble pillars and can be seen at the site.

Old Acre, an UNESCO World Heritage Site has been excavated since the 1990's. A major discovery was an underground passageway leading to the 13th century Knight's Templar.

Tel Rehov means wide place and was an important Bronze and Iron Age city in the Jordan Valley about 3 km west of the Jordan River. They discovered items relating to beekeeping in this Israelite-Canaanite city. The beehives, made of straw and unbaked clay, were found in orderly groups of 100 hives. The Bible refers to Israel as the land of the milk and honey. Many thought that meant just honey from dates and figs. These discoveries indicate that it may have been commercialized honey making of bee honey and beeswax. The beehives provided evidence that an advanced honey-producing beekeeping industry 3,000 years ago in the city. Archaeologists believe the population was about 2,000 during this period. The bees' DNA were tested and identified the bees as subspecies found today only in Turkey.

Tel Be'er Sheva, an UNESCO World Heritage site, is the first fortified settlement that dates to 1000 BCE. Major discoveries include an elaborate water system, a huge cistern carved out of rock beneath the town, and a large horned altar which has been reconstructed using several stones.

Gath is located half-way between Jerusalem and Ashkelon and is identified as a Canaanite and Philistine Gath. The Philistines ruled over five cities of Gaza, Askelon, Ashdod, Ekron, and Gath. The Bible considers them the worst enemy of Israel. The Philistines worshiped Baal, Astarte, and Dagon.

Masada, a UNESCO World Heritage Site is in the South District of Israel on top of an isolated rock plateau on the eastern edge of the Judean Desert overlooking the Dead Sea. Archaeologists found many wall paintings of King Herod's two palaces. A synagogue has been identified and restored. An ostracon is a piece of stone or pottery that has a few scratched in writing or other forms of writing that gives clues to the time period. Inside the synagogue an ostracon with the inscription *me aser kohen* which means "tithe for the priest" was found and two pieces of a broken scroll. They even found eleven small ostracons and one reads *ben Yair* which may be a short form for Eleazar ben Yair, the commander of the fortress. Ruins of a Byzantine church dating from the fifth and sixth centuries have been excavated at Masada.

Tel Arad is west of the Dead Sea about ten kilometers west from modern Arad. Archaeologists found a garrison-town known as The Citadel built during the time of King David and King Solomon.

Tel Dan is a mount that was a city in ancient times. The major discovery in Tel Dan was a stele with an inscription in Aramaic in the late ninth century BCE by an unknown king who wrote about his victories over the king of Israel and his ally, the king of the house of David. This was the first time David was mentioned outside of the Bible.

Tel Hazor is the largest archaeological site in Israel. The upper Tel is 30 acres and the lower Tel is 175 acres. It was declared a World Heritage Site by UNESCO as part of the Biblical Tels. Other Tels were Megiddo, Hazor, and Beer Sheba.

Canaanite Hazor was an Egyptian vassal state during 18th century BC and 13th century. Some 14th century documents from the El Amama archive in Egypt tell about the king of Hazor in Amarna letters called Hasura swearing loyalty to the Egyptian Pharaoh. According to the Book of Joshua, Hazor was the seat of Jabin a Canaanite king that led a Canaanite confederation against Joshua who won the battle by burning down Hazor. The Book of Judges states that Hazor was the seat of Jabin, the King of Canaan, Sisera led a Canaanite army against Barak and was defeated Archaeologist Israel Finkelstein claims that the Israelites were a sub-culture within Canaanite culture and the Israeli conquest did not happen as the Bible detailed. In his view the Book of Joshua happened over several battles and centuries. One archaeological stratum dating about 1200 BC shows signs of a catastrophic fire and cuneiform tablets found at the site refer to a monarch Ibni Addi where Ibni may be the etymological origin of Yavin (Jabin). Israel Finkelstein claims the destruction of Hazor was the result of civil strife, attacks by the Sea People, or a collapse of civilization. Amnon Ben-Tor disagrees with Israel Finkelstein and believes the recently excavated evidence of violent destruction by burning verifies the biblical account. In 2012, a team led by Amnon Ben-Tor discovered evidence of a violent destruction by burning. The 3,400 year-old ewers holding burned crops.

Israelite Hazor archaeological remains suggest after its destruction by burning, the city of Hazor was rebuilt as a small village. According to the Book of Kings, Hazor, Megiddo, and Gezer Solomon fortified these cities. Omrides or the House of Omri refers to Omri and his descendants like Ahab. The Bible and archaeological remains prove Omrides or the House of Omri as kings of ancient Israel. Obelisk is a black limestone that gives names of the kings of Israel. The Assyrian obelisk list five kings bringing tribute and bowing before the Assyrian king. One of the kings listed is Jehu of the House of Omri. The second register from the top describes how Jehu brought or sent his tribute in or around 841 BCE. The caption written in Assyrian cuneiform can be translated: "The tribute of Jehu, son of Omri: I received from him silver, gold, a golden bowl, a golden vase with pointed bottom, golden tumblers, golden buckets, tin, a staff for a king and spears." In the obelisk, Jehu's name appears as Jehu, son of Omri.[4]

Dig Deeper into the Rich History of Israel

Study the feasts by reading the scriptures referred to in this chapter.

Day of Atonement: Leviticus 17:11
Feast of Tabernacles: Leviticus 23:34, 40-44
Day of Trumpets (shofar): Leviticus 23:24, Exodus 19:13, 1 Thessalonians 4:16-17

---

[4]   www.en.wikipedia.org/wiki/archaeology_in_israel

CHAPTER 2

JAFFA AND TEL AVIV

T he cities of Jaffa and Tel Aviv are joined together and mean "Hill of Spring." Christian legend indicates that Jaffa was named after Noah's son, Yefet, who built it after the flood.

Jaffa was originally assigned to the tribe of Dan. It did not become a part of Israel until King David captured it from the Philistines. King David made it the seaport for Jerusalem. King Hiram of Tyre sent famous cedars from Lebanon through the port of Jaffa for Solomon's Temple (2 Chronicles 2:16). Jonah sailed from Port of Jaffa for Tarshish when he was hiding from God and ended up in the belly of a large fish (Jonah 1:17). Peter was called to Joppa from Lydda when Tabitha (Dorcas) became ill and died. With God's help, Peter raised her from the dead (Acts 9:36-48).

Under the Main square in Jaffa, archaeological remains from the Hellenistic (3rd century), Roman (2nd century), and Byzantine (4th century) were discovered.

In 1099 Godfrey of Bouillon during the First Crusade took over Jaffa and made it the main sea supply route for the Kingdom of Jerusalem. In 1192 Saladin captured Jaffa, but soon Richard Coeur de Lion rescued it and added to its defense. In 1268 the Mamluk Sultan Baibars captured it and destroyed the harbor. In 1345 both the town and harbor were destroyed. Jaffa was captured by the Ottoman's in the 16th century and renamed the Sanjak of Gaza. Napoleon captured the city in 1799 and killed most people living there.

There is an 1804 painting commissioned by Napoleon Bonaparte from Antoine-Jean Gros to paint an activity during the Egyptian Campaign. The scene shows Napoleon during a striking scene in Jaffa in 1799. The purpose of the painting was to stop rumors after Napoleon ordered fifty incurable plague victims in Jaffa to be poisoned during his retreat from his Syrian expedition. This painting is a part of the collection of French paintings in the Louvre.

On September 18, 1804, Salon de Paris exhibited this painting between Napoleon's proclamation as emperor and his coronation at Notre-Dame de Paris on December 2. Dominique Vivant Denon, who accompanied Napoleon to the expedition to Egypt, was now the director on the Louvre and he advised the artist Gros on the painting. The painting is set in a mosque and you can see in the background the courtyard and minaret. The background has the walls of Jaffa, the breached tower, and the oversized French flag. Smoke from a fire or excessive cannon smoke can be seen all over Jaffa. On the left side of painting is a man dressed in richly dressed clothes who hands out bread. A servant with a bread basket walks with him. Behind them two black men carry a stretcher with a figure that may be a cadaver to an arcade opening out on a gallery full of the sick. On the right side is Napoleon with his officers touching the bubo, (a Greek word meaning a swollen gland found in infections such as bubonic plague or tuberculosis) of one of the sick men. In front of Napoleon is an Arab doctor caring for another sick man.

In the early 18th century, Jaffa grew into an urban center when the Ottoman government guarded the port and protected Jaffa from Bedouins and pirates. The biggest population growth was from 2,500 in 1806 to 17,000 in 1886. The history in Old Jaffa, the ancient 3,000 year-old city, was built during the Ottoman Empire. Its old stone houses and narrow alleyways now are displayed in the picturesque artists' quarter and tourist center.

Alexander the Great captured Jaffa and renamed it "Joppa" as it was known in the New Testament. Jaffa was the main port and point of entry for visitors during the Turkish era. The hotels were in poor condition and the highways were not good. The Turks demanded special fees to travel on roads. The port of Jaffa is now closed.

Jaffa's oldest existing mosque may be Al-Bahr Mosque, overlooking the harbor. This mosque was in a painting by Dutch painter, Lebrun, in 1675. Mahmoudia Mosque was built in 1812 by Governor Abu Nabbut of Jaffa. Outside the mosque is a beautiful waterfall. Nouzha Mosque on Jerusalem Boulevard is Jaffa's main mosque in modern times.

OLD JAFFA: SUNSET ON THE MEDITERRANEAN

photo courtesy of the Israeli Ministry of Tourism and solely for this photo only at www.goisrael.com

Jaffa is known for its export of famous Jaffa oranges that have a sweeter flavor than the Valencia variety. In the late 19th century Jaffa's oranges business was very good, exporting about ten million oranges a year. Jaffa had about four hundred orange farms each one having about a thousand trees. Jaffa was also known for its soap industry in the 19th century. Most of the newspapers and books printed were published in Jaffa.

American settlers moved to Jaffa and taught the Israelites modern agriculture. The American farm settlers brought in farm machinery in the 1850's and 1860's. Beginning in the 1880's real estate became important to the economy. Water for the farm land was plentiful due to wells between ten and forty feet deep.

The Old City of Jaffa has artists' studios, art galleries, jewelry, and interesting narrow alleys to explore. Old Jaffa has Arabic and Ottoman architecture, ancient excavations, and many places to explore.

Jaffa has many churches, such as the Greek Orthodox Monastery of Archangel Michael near Jaffa Port with Romanian and Russian Orthodox communities. St. Peter's Church is a Franciscan Roman-Catholic basilica and hospice built during the 19th century on the remains of a Crusader fortress. Napoleon may have stayed there. Immanuel Church was built in 1904 and has a Lutheran congregation with services in both Hebrew and English.

THE CLOCK TOWER AT JAFFAMG
Photo courtesy of the Israeli Ministry of Tourism and solely for this photo only at www.goisrael.com

TEL AVIV

Tel Aviv was the first modern Jewish city built in Israel. Tel Aviv is built on a 14 km strip on the Mediterranean seacoast. The Mediterranean Sea is part of the Atlantic Ocean and is bounded on the north by Europe, on the south by Africa, and on the east by Asia and it meets the Atlantic Ocean through the Strait of Gibraltar. In the Old Testament the west coast of the Holy Land was known as the "Hinder Sea" and sometimes called the "Western Sea" (Joel 2:20). The Bible also calls the Mediterranean Sea the "Sea of the Philistines" (Exodus 23:31). Another name for the Mediterranean Sea is the "Great Sea" (Numbers 34:6-7).

UPPER REACHES OF THE YARKON RIVER
photo courtesy of the Israeli Ministry of Tourism and solely for this photo only at www.goisrael.com

To the north of Israel is the Yarkon River and the Avalon River is to the east. The Yarkon River is in central Israel. The beginning of the Yarkon River is at Tel Afek, north of Petah Tikva. The river flows west through Gush Dan into the Mediterranean Sea. The Yarkon River is the largest coastal river in Israel (27.5 km). It became polluted in the 1950's and the Reading Power Station at the mouth of the river is blamed. In 1988 the Yarkon River Authority was appointed to clean-up the river and make parts of it suitable for sailing, fishing, swimming, and other activities. Bicycle and hiking paths were built. On July 14, 1997, four members of an

Australian delegation to the Maccabiah Games were killed and sixty injured due to the collapse of a temporary pedestrian bridge over the river.

Tel Aviv is governed by the Tel Aviv-Yaffo municipality. The population of Tel Aviv is 404,400 and a land area of 20 square miles. Many countries build their embassies in Tel Aviv because they do not recognize or accept Jerusalem as the capital. Tel Aviv was built in 1909 by the Jewish community of Jaffa. Jaffa and Tel Aviv merged into one city in 1950 two years after Israel became a state. Residents of Tel Aviv are called Tel Avivim. The city of Tel Aviv is known for its twenty-four-hour culture lifestyle, beaches, bars, restaurants, cafes, parks, shipping, and landmark neighborhoods. Tel Aviv is home to the Tel Aviv Stock Exchange, and research and development centers. The unemployment rate of Tel Aviv is 6.9 percent. The average income of Tel Aviv is 20 percent above the national average and has education standards that are above the national average. Tel Aviv University is the largest university in Israel and it is known for its teaching of physics, computer science, chemistry, and linguistics departments.

TEL AVIV: BAUHAUS PERIOD BUILDINGS (1) RESTORED

Photo courtesy of the Israeli Ministry of Tourism and solely for this photo only at www.goisrael.com

Tel Aviv has the world's most Bauhaus architectural buildings. The Bauhaus Center in Tel Aviv is dedicated to this architectural heritage. The Bauhaus Museum, designed by Ron Arad, opened in Tel Aviv in 2008. Steve Jobs liked the Bauhaus movement in Tel Aviv which was to unify art, craft, and technology. German Jews began the Bauhaus movement style for houses and furniture after they fled or were exiled by the Nazi regime in Germany. Israel's first skyscraper, Shalom Meir Tower, was built in Tel Aviv in 1965. The Bauhaus movement contributed to the field of modern furniture. Tel Aviv is also known for its international center of fashion and design and the "next hot destination" for fashion. Tel Aviv Performing Arts Center is home to the Israeli Opera. Many opera and classical music performances are held daily in Tel Aviv.

TEL AVIV PERFORMING ARTS CENTER (TAPAC) (1) ENTRANCE TO THE PLAZA
photo courtesy of the Israeli Ministry of Tourism and solely for this photo only at www.goisrael.com

Almost every day hundreds of thousands of workers, visitors, tourists, and partygoers visit Tel Aviv to enjoy restaurants, nightclubs, shopping, swimming, festivals, and a good time of relaxation. Tel Aviv has the second largest economy in the Middle East was named the third hottest city in 2011 and the ninth best beach city by National Geographic. Tel Aviv is also ranked as one of the top places to visit in the world. Tel Aviv has hot humid summers and cool rainy winters though most days during the year are sunny.

TEL AVIV CITYSCAPE AND SHORELINE AT SUNSET
Photo courtesy of the Israeli Ministry of Tourism and solely for this photo only at www.goisrael.com

Hayarkon Park is the most visited urban park in Israel and has 16 million visitors yearly. Other parks are Charles Clore and Dubnow Park. The city provides 19 percent of the city land as green spaces.

Tel Aviv is known as "the gay capital of the Middle East" and is known for its pride parade attracting over 100,000 people. Tel Aviv also hosts a yearly LGBT Film Festival. The film, The Bubble, by Eytan Fox features the gay community of Tel Aviv.

In 1906 Israel formed the Maccabi Tel Aviv Sports Club and competes in more than ten sports fields. Maccabi Tel Aviv, a world-known professional team that holds fifty Israeli titles, thirty-nine editions of the Israel cup, and has five European Championships. Maccabi Tel Aviv is the largest sports club in Israel and is part of the Maccabi association. Maccabi Tel Aviv participates in football, basketball, judo, swimming, and handball. There is a National Sports Center in Tel Aviv that is a collection of stadiums and sports facilities. The Olympic Committee of Israel is located in these facilities as well as the National Athletics Stadium with the Israeli Athletic Association.

The Hapoel Tel Aviv Sports Club is also in Tel Aviv and has more than eleven sports clubs including Hapoel Tel Aviv Football Club listing thirteen championships, eleven state cups, one Toto Cup, and were once Asian champions. It has both men's and women's basketball clubs.

There are two rowing clubs in Tel Aviv and the Tel Aviv Marathon is held every year and with as many as 18,000 runners.

The Tel Aviv Museum of Art displays the works of many famous artists. The Beth Hatefutsoth, located on the Tel Aviv University campus, tells the story of Jewish prosperity and persecution through centuries of exile. People interested in military history will enjoy the Batey Haosef Museum that specializes in Israel Defense Forces. The Israel Trade Fairs and Convention Center has more than sixty events yearly. The Tel Aviv Raw Art displays contemporary art. Eretz Israel Musuem is known for its archaeology and history exhibits about the land found in Israel.

TEL AVIV: DIASPORA MUSUEM (BETH HATEFUTSOTH)

photo courtesy of the Israeli Ministry of Tourism and solely for this photo only at www.goisrael.com

This museum opened in May 1978 to create a monument to the Jewish diaspora, past and present. This museum uses audio-visual displays to tell the history of Jewish communities throughout the centuries from the time of their expulsion from the Holy Land 2,600 years ago to modern times.

The Israel ballet is based in Tel Aviv. Suzanne Dellal Center for Dance and Theater has modern and classical dance. The campus has four performing places. In the summer many outside performances are scheduled. In 2010 the center was awarded the Israel Prize for contributing to dance.

Tel Aviv also has a good zoo, many cultural events, good shopping malls, museums, and specialties like the Neve Tsedekk Quarters that gives the pictorial history of tiles.

The Fredric R. Mann Culture Center is known as The Culture Palace and is home to the Israel Philharmonic Orchestra. Bob Dylan was a visiting performer during his 1993 European Tour in June. The Fredric R. Mann is the largest performing arts center in Tel Aviv. The Habima Theatre is the national theatre of Israel and one of the first to use Hebrew language. It is located in Habima Square in Tel Aviv. This theatre had roots first in Russia in 1918 under the direction of the Moscow Art Theatre. Joseph Stalin authorized the creation of this theatre. In 1926 the actors left Russia to tour the world. Their performances included plays from the Jewish folk tradition and were in Hebrew. Later most of the actors settled in New York or in Israel in 1928. Habima won the prize for theatre in 1958 and received being national since. The actress Hana Rovina starring as Leah'le in the historic Habima production of S. Ansky's The Dybbuk made it an icon and represents Jewish and Israeli theatre.

The Beit Lessin Theater shows contemporary American and European plays and original productions. The theater also has plays at the Eretz Israel Museum. In 2005 the theater won the Israeli Theater Prize. Opera and classical music performances are held daily.

Project Better Place

In 2008 Tel Aviv started a pilot plan to build charging stations for electric cars with five charging points with a goal of setting up 150. This is Israel's electric car project called "Project Better Place." Battery replacement areas will be located in Tel Aviv.

Tel Aviv is building the first line of a light rail system that is scheduled to open in 2016. Some of it will be at street level and some will be an underground tunnel. The underground tunnel will have ten stations including an interchange with Israel Railways services at Tel Aviv Central Railway Station and the 2000 Terminal.

Tel Aviv has a bicycle sharing system that began in April 2011. The name of the system is Tel-O-Fun, a bicycle sharing with the goal of having 150 stations of bicycles for rent. By October 2011 the system had 125 active bicycle stations with more than 1,000 bicycles. By April 2011 the city built 100 kilometers of bicycle paths.

Tel Aviv has a share taxis plan with some taxis following bus routes and display the same route number in their window. Fares are standardized and are comparable to or less expensive than bus fees. These taxis also operate on Fridays and Saturdays.

Israel in the News

The United States Embassy is located at 71 Hayarkon in Tel Aviv. During the Second Intifada in 2003, Mike's Place, located next door to the U.S. Embassy was attacked by a suicide bomber. The blast killed three civilians and wounded fifty. The Jerusalem Embassy Act passed by Congress in 1995 requires the U.S. to relocate its embassy to Jerusalem by December, 1999. The Jerusalem Embassy has allowed the delay of the move over safety concerns. Presidents Clinton, Bush, and Obama have delayed the move to Jerusalem. The United States has a Consulate General in Jerusalem with offices on 18 Agron Road and on 14 David Flusser Street.

Dig Deeper into the Rich History of Israel

The city of Jaffa is a major part of the history of Israel. Read these verses from biblical history:

2 Chronicles 2:16
Ezra 3:7
Jonah 1:17
John 1:3
Acts 9:36-48; 10:5-8, 23, 32; 11:5, 13

CHAPTER 3

CAESAREA

Caesarea was built in 22 BC by Herod the Great and named for Caesar Augustus. The Romans enjoyed the city for about 500 years with their palaces, temples, theater, hippodrome, and baths. The first Jewish revolt took place in 60 AD and many Jews were killed. In 640 it was taken over by Arabs; in 1101 by Crusaders; in 1187 by Saladin; and in 1191 again by Crusaders. Moslems destroyed the city in 1291. It is located between Tel Aviv and Haifa.

Caesarea played an important role in Bible times. A Gentile centurion named Cornelius (Acts 10) had his home here. (Read Acts 10.)

Paul spent over two years in prison in Caesarea before being sentenced to Rome. Paul made his appeal here to Roman rulers Festus and Agrippa. About Paul, Festus said to Agrippa, "Of whom I have no certain thing to write unto my lord. Wherefore I have brought him forth before you, and specially before thee, O king Agrippa, that, after examination had, I might have somewhat to write" (Acts 25:26).

In its beginning, Caesarea was a Phoenician town called "Strato's Tower". In 20 BC, Herod the Great spent 12 years with the best architects and engineers to build palaces, public buildings, a market place, a marble temple, an amphitheater, and a hippodrome. Engineers lowered large stones into the sea to make a semi-circular jetty 200 feet wide. After Herod's death, Caesarea became Roman. Pontius Pilate lived in Caesarea and left home for a trip to Jerusalem for Passover. During this time he sentenced Jesus to be crucified. The massacre of 20,000 Jews was the main cause of a Jewish revolt and destruction of

Jerusalem and the Temple. The wall and gate at Caesarea are from the era of the Crusades. The wall was built by King Louis IX of France. It was protected by a moat 30 feet wide with a slope of 30-45 feet above the base of the moat. In 1291 the Baybars destroyed Caesarea and the city was abandoned and buried by sand until 1956, when archaeologists began excavating. This famous city lay destroyed, deserted, and covered with sand for 665 years.

Caesarea was an important church center during the early centuries of the Church. In the second century, a big church council met here to discuss Easter and its customs. The date for Easter is the first Sunday after the full moon of the Paschal full moon that follows the northern hemisphere. Eusebius, a church father and historian, was born in Caesarea in 260 AD. Origen wrote many of his Christian works here in the third century and built a building to be used for Christian learning. In 1101, Crusader King Baldwin I claimed to have located the Holy Grail in Caesarea.

In 66 AD, a riot started between the Jews and the Syrians, and Rome chose to help the Syrians. About 20,000 Jews were killed in this riot. In 69 AD, Vespasian was made Emperor here by his soldiers.

In 1291 the Baybars destroyed Caesarea, and the city was abandoned and gradually was buried under the sand dunes. In 1956, archaeologists began to excavate Caesarea. Balbars of the Baybars was one of the commanders of the Muslim forces who defeated the 7th Crusade of King Louis IX of France.

The Crusaders' city of Caesarea was about 35 acres, whereas the Roman Caesarea was six times larger.

CAESAREA: ROMAN THEATER ON THE MEDITERRANEAN

photo courtesy of the Israeli Ministry of Tourism and solely for this photo only at www.goisrael.com

Roman theater remains were uncovered in 1961. It is now restored and used for programs and concerts. Archaeologists found a stone there inscribed with the name of Pontius Pilate. It was a big theater with seats going up an incline, and they had concerts here at that time. Some of the original seats are still there.

Bible Study with Tony W. Cartledge: Isaiah 5:1-7

Isaiah 5:1-7 illustrates a vineyard that does not produce good fruit because the people of Israel understood how that worked. The name of the song is the Vineyard of the Lord Destroyed. "Let me sing for my beloved, my love song concerning his vineyard: My beloved had a vineyard on a very fertile hill. He dug it and cleared it of stones, and planted it with choice vines: he built a watchtower in the midst of it, and hewed out a wine vat in it: and he looked for it to yield grapes, but it yielded wild grapes. And now, O inhabitants of Jerusalem and men of Judah, judge between me and my vineyard. What more was there to do for my vineyard, that I have not done in it? When I looked for it to yield grapes, why did it yield wild grapes? And now I will tell you what I will do to my vineyard. I will remove its hedge, and it shall be devoured; I will break down its wall, and it shall be trampled down. I will make it a waste; it shall not be pruned or hoed, and briers and thorns shall grow up. I will also command the clouds that they rain no rain upon it. For the vineyard of the Lord of hosts is the house of Israel, and the men of Judah are his pleasant planting; and he looked for justice, but behold, bloodshed; for righteousness, but behold, an outcry."

Some of the people may have cheered if they thought God was justified in His actions of trying to get His people back on track. Some may have felt guilty because they knew God was talking about them in the song. Some of the people may have been puzzled because sometimes they went to the temple for sacrifices and worship. And some did not worship Baal or Asherah as some did. God wanted justice but the people showed him bloodshed. After the song Isaiah explained why Israel was so rotten as the grape vineyard. Crooked farmers sometimes bought the land around them and used crooked means for getting poor farmers into debt and then grabbing their land when they could not pay. Isaiah predicted deserved judgment and destruction on the people of Israel and even the city of Jerusalem.

In Isaiah 27:6 hope is given for Israel. This verse reads, "In days to come, Jacob shall take root. Israel shall blossom and put forth shoots, and fill the whole world with fruit." Isaiah did not live to see this happen. Many Bible scholars believe that this was fulfilled in New Testament times when Jesus came to do what

Israel could not do. Jesus called men and women to take root in His grace, to find nourishment in His spirit, and to bear fruits of love to fill the entire world.[5]

CAESAREA: ROMAN BATHS, MARBLE FLOORS

photo courtesy of the Israeli Ministry of Tourism and solely for this photo only at www.goisrael.com

Caesarea was used as a fancy city by the Romans for five hundred years. They built palaces, temples, a theater, a hippodrome, and baths. They used plenty of marble and fancy decorations. The streets had many marble statues.

The Holy Grail is a dish, plate, stone, or cup. It is rumored that Joseph of Arimathea had possession of these vessels that were connected to the Last Supper and crucifixion of Jesus, as written in the book *Joseph d' Arimathie* by author Robert de Boron in the late 12th century. According to the book, Joseph insisted that he received this information from an apparition of Jesus. Robert de Boron writes that Joseph was thrown into jail and Christ visited him and explained the mysteries of the cup. When he was released from prison, Joseph took his in-laws and followers to England and started what was known as the Grail Keepers. Other writers wrote that Joseph used the Grail to get the blood of Jesus when he buried him and used it to trace a line of guardians to keep it safe in England.

Grail literature is divided into two groups: King Arthur's knights visiting the Grail castle, and the Grail's history in the time of Joseph of Arimathea. One theory is that the earliest stories were meant to promote the Roman Catholic sacrament of Holy Communion. The first Grail stories may have been celebrations of a renewal in understanding Holy Communion. Daniel Scavone, Professor Emeritus of history at the University of Southern Indiana, has a hypothesis which states that the Shroud of Turin was the real object that inspired the stories of the

---

[5]   Tony W. Cartledge, *Bible Study with Tony W. Cartledge: Isaiah 5:1-7.* Baptists Today News Journal, July 2013, 24-25.

Holy Grail. Most scholars today believe that both Christian and Celtic traditions contributed to the development of the legend.

There are cups in churches that some feel may be the Holy Grail. Saint Mary of Valencia Cathedral has an artifact, a Holy Chalice rumored to be taken by Saint Peter to Rome in the 1st century and then taken by Saint Lawrence to Spain in the 3rd century. The legend says that the monastery of San Juan de la Pena, located in Jaca in the province of Huesca, Spain, protected the chalice from the Islamic invaders of the Iberian Peninsula. Archaeologists believe the artifact is a 1st-century Middle Eastern stone vessel probably from Antioch, Syria (now Turkey). The history can be traced to the 11th century. The artifact has medieval alabaster, gold, and gemstones. Pope Benedict XVI on July 9, 2006, made it the official papal chalice for many popes.

Another vessel rumored to be the Holy Grail is an artifact that was received during the Crusades at Caesarea Maritima. After the fall of Napoleon, while it was being returned from Paris to Genoa, there was an accident on the road and it was revealed that the emerald was green glass.

There are many more possible Holy Grail artifacts and stories. No one but God knows the true facts. Humans can only make guesses that may be right or may be wrong.

Bible Study with Tony W. Cartledge: Isaiah 58:1-14

Justice is usually thought of in respect to court cases and trials to see if the person is guilty or innocent. Another way to think of justice is in respect to nations who have so many laws or polices that are unjust to other individuals. Individuals who believe in God are trained to respect the dignity and rights of all.

Chapters 56 through 66 are believed by many Bible scholars to be set in Jerusalem after the return from exile and more than 200 years after the ministry of Isaiah of Jerusalem. The later prophet of God responded in the same way as Isaiah. The temple had been rebuilt and Jewish religious rituals restored. Many families had returned from Babylon with wealth and took advantage of their poorer neighbors.

Fasting began in Israel as a way of expressing sorrow during times of grief. They ripped up their clothes and wore sackcloth, sprinkled ashes on their heads and did not eat food for a period of time. Over time some of the people displayed outward piety without inner conviction. God's concern was that the people fasted for their own interests and not to honor God. Some of the people even argued to the extent that physical violence occurred.

The prophet criticized the way the people treated the Sabbath. In Isaiah 58:13 God stresses honoring God and not fulfilling your own interests.[6]

CAESAREA: THE GATE OF THE CRUSADER CITY

photo courtesy of the Israeli Ministry of Tourism and solely for this photo only at www.goisrael.com

The wall and gate at Caesarea are from the era of the Crusades. The wall was built by King Louis IX of France. It was protected by a moat 30 feet wide with a slope of 30-45 feet above the base of the moat. In 1291 the Baybars destroyed Caesarea and the city was abandoned and buried by sand until 1956, when archaeologists began excavating. This famous city lay destroyed, deserted, and covered with sand for 665 years.

---

[6] Tony W. Cartledge, *Bible Study with Tony W. Cartledge: Isaiah 58:1-13*. Baptists Today News Journal, July 2013, 26-27.

CAESAREA: THE ROMAN AQUEDUCT

This photo courtesy of the Israeli Ministry of Tourism and solely for this photo only at www.goisrael.com

These aqueducts were built by the Romans to bring water into the town of Caesarea.

Herod the Great built a beautiful harbor at Caesarea for ships to anchor. He ordered huge stones to be lowered into the water to form a semi-circular jetty 200 feet wide. Philip the Deacon also preached in Caesarea: "But Philip was found at Azotus: and passing through he preached in all of the cities, till he came to Caesarea" (Acts 8:40).

The Importance of the Number 40

The number 40 is often marked by the power of God's spirit and God's revelation. Moses was on the mountain for forty days and nights to receive the Torah, or the Ten Commandments. The children of Israel wandered in the wilderness for forty years, which was considered one generation of Israelites. Jesus was tempted in the wilderness for forty days and nights. Jesus also appeared on the earth for forty days between His resurrection and ascension.

Forty years ago in the late 1960's, Time Magazine named a special event, "the Jesus Movement". Thousands of young people were believing in Jesus, and many of these young people were Jews. The organization Jews for Jesus was born, led by a veteran missionary Moishe Rosen. In September 1973 Jews for Jesus was incorporated. Their creativity and commitment led to a new movement to win Jews to Jesus. Some Jewish communities believed that Jesus was indeed the Messiah. For years, the Jewish communities ignored the information about Jesus. Now, however, the Jews who believed in Jesus could show them Jewish scriptures that pointed to Jesus and how prophecy was fulfilled. Now Jews for Jesus is registered in Israel as a non-profit organization. The Tel Aviv branch of Jews for Jesus is the largest in the world. Jews for Jesus has a "Behold your God, Israel" campaign. The Moishe Rosen Center for Training and Evangelism is operational.

The internet has helped Jews for Jesus spread the mission all over the world.[7]

Isaiah 59:20-21 states, "The Redeemer will come to Zion and to those who turn from transgressions in Jacob; says the Lord. This is My covenant with them; My Spirit who is upon you, and My words which I have put in your mouth, shall not depart from your mouth, nor from the mouth of your descendants, nor from the mouth of your descendants' descendants, says the Lord, from this time and forevermore."

Dig Deeper into the Rich History of Israel

The city of Caesarea is spoken of at various points in the New Testament, especially the early Church in the book of Acts. Read these verses about the journeys of different followers of Jesus from biblical history:

Philip: Acts 8:38-40
Peter and Cornelius: Acts 10:1-48
Paul: Acts 18:22, 25:1-26:32

---

[7] David Brickner, executive director for Jews for Jesus. Newsletter for Jews for Jesus, September 2013.

Chapter 4

Tiberias

The city of Tiberias is mentioned only once in the New Testament. Tiberias was built in 22 AD by Herod Antipas, son of Herod the Great. Herod built beautiful palaces, theaters, temples made of gold and marble, and public baths over the hot springs. The Jews did not like the city because it was built over an old cemetery. The city was named for Emperor Tiberias, ruler of Rome. The city was also known for its hot mineral springs. Tiberias is located on the west side of the Sea of Galilee and is 682 feet below sea level.

When Jerusalem was taken over by the Romans in 70 AD, Tiberias became the seat of the Sanhedrin, the Jewish high court. Jewish scholars like Rabbi Judah the Nasi collected the items for the Mishna. One of Nasi's disciples, Rabbi Johanan ben Nappaha, established a rabbinic school in 235. Ben Nappaha collected information for the Jerusalem Talmud.

The famous Jewish doctor Maimonides was a forerunner of modern medicine. He died in 1204 and is buried in Tiberias. There was a Bar Kokhba revolt in Jerusalem, and the emperor Hadrian expelled Jews from Jerusalem. As a result, Tiberias replaced Jerusalem as the religious and intellectual center for the Jews.

Tiberias today has thirty hotels. Many restaurants cook delicious fresh fish. Near the boardwalk are horse-drawn carriages for tours. The Hamal Tiberias National Park is located south of Tiberias. This park has seventeen hot springs with temperatures of 60 degrees Celsius that are mixed with 100 therapeutic minerals. It is believed that this site can heal people and has been known to people for about 2,000 years.

Interesting Places in Tiberias

In Tiberias is the Dona Gracia Museum to honor Gracia Nasi, who used her wealth to save Jewish refugees of the Spanish Inquisition. The museum is a castle that tells her story through visual aids.

Tiberias has one of the most important archaeological sites in Israel. For the last fifty years, archaeologists have been exploring and finding good information about the past, from the Chalcolithic through the Ottoman periods. In March 2009 at the ancient city center of Tiberias, Dr. Katia Cytryn-Silverman of the Hebrew University of Jerusalem directed a new project. She is responsible for cataloguing and studying Islamic material, such as the transition between the Byzantine and Islamic periods. Ms. Silverman showed that the ruins of one site were not a market but a congregational mosque dating from the early Islamic period. A Byzantine church was also recently discovered by the Israel Antiquities Authority. Ms. Silverman has discovered a mosaic floor, Arabic inscriptions, complete oil lamps, and hundreds of coins.

TIBERIAS: EXCAVATIONS OF THE ANCIENT CITY
photo courtesy of the Israeli Ministry of Tourism and solely for this photo only at www.goisrael.com

Yoel Ben David, Filling Tool Boxes

Yoel Ben David of Jews for Jesus led the London Jews for Jesus monthly meeting, "Havurah", where he taught from the books of Moses to learn to initiate a dialogue about some of the topics covered in the weekly *parsha*. The *parsha* is the weekly reading from the Pentateuch used in the synagogue. Readings from the prophets are included in the weekly meetings. Only one of the Messianic texts is ever mentioned and that is Isaiah 9:6.

Some Bible scholars believe that Luke 4:16-21 shows that Jesus was participating in a *parsha* when He read the scriptures in the Shabbat service in His home synagogue. Jesus chose to read Isaiah 61:1-2, which was not a normally assigned reading. Isaiah 61 reads, "The Spirit of the Lord God is upon me, because the Lord has anointed me to bring good news to the poor; he has sent me to bind up the brokenhearted, to proclaim liberty to the captives, and the opening of the prison to those who are bound; to proclaim the year of the Lord's favor, and the day of vengeance of our God; to comfort all who mourn." Jesus then announced that the scripture He read was fulfilled that day.[8]

In 1998, a large metal treasure was discovered in three buried large storage jars. Inside were candelabras, lampstands, scissors, bowls with old Arabic writing, and fifty-eight Byzantine coins. Some archaeologists think the items may have belonged to someone who hid his money and possessions when he heard about a Crusader invasion.[9]

Near the beach is a 2nd-century square building with colonnades, built by the Romans as an administrative building. Four centuries later it became a church. Nearby is a 4th-century bath house that was still in use 800 years later. A roof covers it to protect the floor mosaics of animals. The guests would enter the hallway and then to two rooms in the south side of the building. Small pillars show where the floor of the hot room was located. A row of simple shops has been excavated, showing that the shops did not have windows but had only doors. Archaeologists assume that it was once a large covered market. Nearby is the theater with only the outer wall remaining. The area ends in the old city gate. Archaeologists can tell that the stones were silted due to winter floods. The original shape of the gate was an arch sided with two round basalt towers. Tiberias received a new wall in the 6th century, built by the Byzantine emperor Justinian who used the gate for defense purposes.[10]

Rabbi Maimon, a Spanish physician, worked in the court of the Muslim ruler Saladin. Rabbi Maimon is also known as Maimonides or Rambam. Rabbi Maimon was one of the 12th-century famous rabbis of Egypt who died in 1204 in Cairo and is buried in Tiberias. There is a legend that Rabbi Maimon instructed his followers to load his dead

---

[8] Yoel Ben David, *Filling Tool Boxes*, Newsletter for Jews for Jesus, September 2013.

[9] www.jewishmag.com/57mag/tiberias/tiberias2.htm

[10] www.jewishmag.com/57mag/tiberias/tibe

body on a camel and bury him wherever the camel died. The camel chose to go to Tiberias. Next to Rabbi Maimon's tomb is another tomb of Rabbi Yohanan Ben Zakkai, who was Israel's sage at the time of the Roman destruction of Jerusalem. A legend says that Ben Zakkai faked his own death to escape Jerusalem in a coffin, jumped out of the casket in front of the Roman general Vespasian, and prophesied that Vespasian would become the next Caesar. When the prophecy came true, Ben Zakkai received a Jewish learning center for him and his students. His tomb is located on Ben Zakkai Street.[11]

SEA OF GALILEE: DEMON-STRATING OLD FISHING TECHNIQUES OFF TIBERIAS

photo courtesy of the Israeli Ministry of Tourism and solely for this photo only at www.goisrael.com

The Sea of Galilee lies 688 feet below sea level; is thirteen miles long and seven miles wide; and is 144 feet deep in places. Twenty-two species of fish live here. Here Peter caught the fish that had a special coin in his mouth (read Matthew 17:24-27).

Mount Berenice is the main mountain of Tiberias, named after Berenice, a great-granddaughter of King Herod. Berenice lived in Tiberias with her brother Agrippa II, governor of Galilee. The Jewish historian Josephus Flavius indicates that Herod Antipas built a gold-roofed palace here, but it has not been located yet. The ruins on the mountain's summit were tested by archaeologists but turned out to be a church.

Below the summit, under the caves, are the ruins of a large building believed to be the Great Study House of Rabbi Johanan ben Nappaha. He and his followers prepared the *Gemarah* which led to the end of the Jerusalem Talmud. The building dates from the third to the eighth centuries. Decorations in the white mosaic courtyard are three squares with red triangles. There is also a pool across from the double entrance

---

[11] www.wikitravel.org/en/Tiberias

to the building, with two pairs of steps. There is no evidence of the Jewish sages.

On the slope is a theater from the 2nd and 3rd centuries and an aqueduct with spring water from the Galilee mountains that gave Tiberias drinking water. On top of Mount Berenice is a wall with towers fifteen meters high, which were part of the city wall that emperor Justinian had built.[12]

The Church and Monastery of the Apostles is also located in Tiberias. Today it is a Greek Orthodox complex built on the site of a Byzantine monastery that the Persians destroyed in the 7th century. The buildings on the property today were built in the late 19th century but were restored in 1975. Three monks live on the site and sometimes admit tourists who ring the bell. There are four chapels beyond the walled courtyard, dedicated to Saint Peter, to the disciples, to Mary Magdalene, and to Saint Nicholas.[13]

Bible Study with Tony W. Cartledge: Ephesians 4:1-16

Ephesians 4:1-3 teaches, "I therefore, a prisoner for the Lord, urge you to walk in a manner worthy of the calling to which you have been called, with all humility and gentleness, with patience, bearing one another in love, eager to maintain the unity of the Spirit in the bond of peace." Paul was concerned about unity and wanted the people of the Ephesians to live, work, and worship together in unity. It is hard to have church unity when everyone has to be careful because of someone's temper.

Ephesians 4:4-6 teaches, "There is one body and one Spirit - just as you were called to the one hope that belongs to your call; one Lord, one faith, one baptism, one God and Father of all, who is over all and through all and in all." Faithful Jews regularly recite a prayer from Deuteronomy called the Shema and it begins with these words: "Hear, O Israel, the Lord your God is one!" (Deut. 6:4). The unity of the Body of Christ begins with the unity of its Creator.[14]

In excavations in Tiberias, many synagogues were uncovered and reconstructed and many mosaics were found, including a mosaic of

---

[12]   Jewish Magazine, July 2002 Edition, www.jewishmag.com/57mag/tiberias/tibe.

[13]   www.comwikitravel.org/en/Tiberias

[14]   Tony W. Cartledge, *Bible Study with Tony W. Cartledge: Ephesians 4:1-16*. Baptists Today News Journal, July 2012, 18-19.

two seven-branched menorahs (see picture) and a zodiac with symbols and inscriptions. The national park in Tiberias is open to the public and is located on the southern entrance across the street from the modern baths of Hammei-Tveriah. The site may have been written about in the Anastasi Papyrus of the 13th century BC, during the Ramses dynasty, as an ancient tourist site. In ancient times it was one of the cities in the Naphtali region, and according to Joshua 19:35 it was a fortified Canaanite city. It was located on the old trade route from Syria/Mesopotamia to Israel/Egypt. The town had the lake beside it and mountains on another side. As Joshua 19:35 says, "And the fenced cities are Ziddim, Zer, and Hammath."

HAMMAT TIBERIAS: PANEL FROM THE ANCIENT MOSAIC SYNAGOGUE FLOOR

photo courtesy of the Israeli Ministry of Tourism and solely for this photo only at www.goisrael.com

In the Hellenistic period, buildings were built on the site and were called "Emmaus of the Galilee". In the Roman/Byzantine period the Romans built large baths in the water, which many considered to have healing powers. According to Josephus Flavius, Hammat Tiberias is the place where the Romans under Vespasian camped in 67 AD before leading the fighting men to Gamla. Josephus wrote almost 2,000 years ago describing the military campaign of Vespasian and his son, Titus, during the crushing of the Jewish revolt of 67 AD. Josephus Flavius was a prisoner of Vespasian and probably was at Hammat Tiberias observing these things of which he wrote.

Tiberias is the city with the lowest elevation in Israel, at 200 meters below sea level. The water level of Lake Kinneret, also known as Sea of Galilee, is important news to the people because it is a main source of drinking water. It is also a big tourist attraction. Some of the beaches have soft sand and other beaches are rocky, narrow, or wide. The reason is that above the eastern and western shores are the Galilee mountains and the foothills of the Golan, and to the north is the wide Beit Tsida Valley with enormous amounts of water from the Jordan River and Golan streams. The south has the Jordan estuary which flows south toward the desert areas.

The Turkish Citadel was the highest point in old Tiberias. Another good site to visit is the Antiquities Museum that houses the Fishermen's Mosque that is now being renovated. The Jewish Court is the site for the three 19th-century synagogues in the heart of old Tiberias.[15]

ITAMAR GRINBERG JESUS BOAT GALILEE

A boat from the first century CE found on the lake, commonly called Jesus Boat in Kibbutz Ginosar.

photo courtesy of the Israeli Ministry of Tourism and solely for this photo only at www.goisrael.com

Tiberias also displays the "Jesus Boat" that is 2,000 years old. This boat was excavated from the Kinneret in 1985 and may have been used at the time of Jesus.[16]

Bible Study with Tony W. Cartledge: Ephesians 4:1-16

Ephesians 4:4-6 teaches that followers of Christ come to Him in different ways; we all share the same faith. We can all say that "by grace we are saved through faith." And we all have one kind of faith.

Ephesians 4:7-16 states, "But grace was given to each one of us according to the measure of Christ's gift. Therefore it says, 'When he ascended on high he led a host of captives, and he gave gifts to men.' He ascended, what does it mean but that he had also descended into the lower regions, the earth? He who descended is the one who also ascended far above all the heavens, that he might fill all things. And he gave the apostles, the prophets, the evangelists, the shepherds and teachers, to equip the saints for the work of ministry, for building up the body of Christ, until we all attain to the unity of the faith and of the knowledge of the Son of God, to mature manhood, to the measure of the stature of the fullness of Christ, so that we may no longer be children, tossed to and fro by the waves and carried about by every wind of

---

15   www.comwikitravel.org/en/Tiberias
16   Virtual Israel Experience, www.jewishvirtualibrary.org/vie/vietoc.html.

doctrine, by human cunning, by craftiness in deceitful schemes. Rather, speaking the truth in love, we are to grow up in every way into him who is the head, into Christ, from whom the whole body, joined and held together by every joint with which it is equipped, when each part is working properly, makes the body grow so that it builds itself up in love.

Paul does not stress the growth of the church in numbers, financial, or political areas. Paul stresses unity that is patterned after the values of Christ. Paul stresses a result of building up the body in love and working in unity.[17]

About six miles north of Tiberias is the Kibbutz Ginosar, the former home of a great statesman, Yigal Allon. He lived from 1918-1980 and is known for his leadership as commander of Israeli forces in important battles during the War of Independence. He was later elected to the Knesset and was Minister of Labor. The Kibbutz has a museum with information on Allon's life and the history of the Galilee region.

One of the Herods, Antipas, built Tiberias on top of an ancient cemetery. The Jews considered it unclean and did not want to live there. The historian Josephus states, "Many were necessitated by Herod to come thither out of the country belonging to him, and were by force compelled to be its inhabitants." He also admitted poor people to dwell in it and he even built them nice houses to live in at his own expense. Over time, the Jews forgot about the offense of building on top of an ancient cemetery and Tiberias became an important city to Judaism. It is not known if Jesus ever visited Tiberias. The building of Tiberias could not have been accomplished before 20 AD, toward the end of the ministry of Jesus. Almost by magic, the Romans built many fancy, elegant buildings.[18]

Tiberias has a hot summer Mediterranean climate that in addition to being hot is also semi-arid. The rainfall averages 15.75 inches per year. The summer temperatures have an average maximum of 97 degrees and an average minimum of 70 degrees in July and August. The winter temperatures range from 46 degrees to 65 degrees. Extreme temperatures have been from 32 degrees to 115 degrees.

[17] Tony W. Cartledge, *Bible Study with Tony W. Cartledge: Ephesians 4:1-16*. Baptists Today News Journal, July 2012, 18-19.

[18] Life in the Holy Land, www.lifeintheholyland.com/tiberias_history.htm

Tiberias has been damaged by earthquakes since the beginning of time. Recorded earthquakes have been known to have happened in the years 30, 33, 115, 306, 363, 419, 447, 631-632, 1033, 1182, 1202, 1546, 1759, 1837, 1927, and 1943.[19]

The earthquake of 1837 was a bad earthquake that shook the Galilee on January 1 with a magnitude of 6.25-6.5, but Nicolas Ambraseys argued the event may have been worse. The event was documented by the 19th-century missionary, archaeologist, and author William McClure Thomson. The earthquake hit in a part of the Ottoman Empire, but the area at that time was under control of the Egyptians who had seized it.

LOWER GALILEE: HORNS OF HATTIN, MEDIEVAL BATTLEGROUND ABOVE TIBERIAS

photo courtesy of the Israeli Ministry of Tourism and solely for this photo only at www.goisrael.com

The Horns of Hattin battle was fought on Saturday, July 4, 1187, between the Crusader Kingdom of Jerusalem and the forces of the Ayyubid dynasty. The Muslim armies under Saladin killed most of the Crusader soldiers and became the dominant power in Israel. They reconquered Jerusalem and several more Crusader cities. Two years after the Battle of the Horns of Hattin, the Third Crusade began. The battle shares its name with a nearby extinct volcano named Hattin.

Guy of lusignan had become king of Jerusalem in 1186 after the death of wife Sibylla's son King Baldwin V. The following is a first-hand account of events by the son of Saladin, al-Afdal:

When the king of the Franks (Guy) was on the hill with that band, they made a formidable charge against the Muslims facing them, so that they drove them back to my father (Saladin). I looked towards him and he was overcome by grief and his complexion pale. He took hold of his beard and advance, crying out, "Give the lie to the Devil!" The Muslims rallied, returned to the fight and climbed the hill.

---

[19]   Haim Watzman, *A Crack in the Earth: A Journey up Israel's Rift Valley*, Macmillan, 2007, 161.

When I saw that the Franks withdrew, pursued by the Muslims, I shouted for joy, "We have beaten them!" But the Franks rallied and charged again like the first time and drove the Muslims back to my father. He acted as he had done on the first occasion and the Muslims turned upon the Franks and drove them back to my father. He acted as he had done on the first occasion and the Muslims turned upon the Franks and drove them back to the hill. I again shouted, "We have beaten them!" but my father rounded on me and said, "Be quiet! We have not beaten them until that tent (Guy's) falls." As he was speaking to me, the tent fell. The sultan dismounted, prostrated himself in thanks to God Almighty and wept for joy.

The exhausted captives were brought to Saladin's tent, where Guy was given a goblet of iced water as a sign of Saladin's generosity. When Guy passed the goblet to his fellow captive Raynald, Saladin allowed the old man (Raynald was about 60) to drink but shortly afterwards said that he had not offered water to Raynald and thus was not bound by the Muslim rules of hospitality. When Saladin accused Raynald of being an oath breaker, Raynald replied, 'Kings have always acted thus. I did nothing more.' Saladin then executed Raynald himself, beheading him with his sword. Guy fell to his knees at the sight of Raynald's corpse but Saladin bade him to rise, saying, 'It's not the wont of kings to kill kings; but that man had transgressed all bounds, and therefore did I treat him thus. This man was only killed because of his maleficence and perfidy.[20]

---

[20] www.en.wikipedia.org/wiki/Battle_of_Hattin

TIBERIAS, ON THE SHORES OF THE SEA OF GALILEE (LAKE KINNERET) WITH HOTELS PROMINENT
photo courtesy of the Israeli Ministry of Tourism and solely for this photo only at www.goisrael.com

The name of the Sea of Galilee (Kinneret) in Hebrew comes from the word for "harp" and is even shaped like a harp. The Sea of Galilee has fish, carp, mullet, sardine, catfish, and combfish. The fish are still caught using nets. The Sea has nine cities around it, including Tiberias. When Jesus went to the Sea of Galilee area, it was the center of roads crossing in all directions. Years ago, there were many trees around the lake and many boats in the water fishing.

The 12 apostles were ordained on a mountain near the Sea. One day when Jesus was walking along the shore, he called three fishermen, Andrew, James, and John, to follow him and become fishers of men (read Mark 1:16-20).

Luke tells how Jesus and the disciples got so many fish in one catch that the boat began to sink (read Luke 5:4-7).

HAMMAT TIBERIAS: ANCIENT SYNAGOGUE FLOOR (ZODIAC, LIONS, AND INSCRIPTION)
photo courtesy of the Israeli Ministry of Tourism and solely for this photo only at www.goisrael.com

One synagogue in Tiberias dates back to the 3rd to 5th centuries AD and has a beautiful mosaic floor shown in the photo here. The mosaic floor contains a zodiac and the combination of Jewish and pagan symbols. In Hammat, Tiberias, the Emperor Trajan in 110 AD had a coin dedicated to the springs, with the image of Hygeia, the goddess of health, sitting on a rock enjoying the water. The springs were also mentioned by an Arab writer who lived during the Crusades.

The springs were also recommended for the patients of the Jewish sage Rambam.

The Khan was Tiberias' central square with a mosque at its center, used many years ago.[21]

Migdal is two miles north of Tiberias and is near where Mary Magdalene was born. During the time of the Second Temple, Migdal was a large city known for the fish salters and dyers who worked there. During the Jewish Revolt against Rome, Migdal was called Magdala Tarikheai, which means "Magdala of the fish salters" in Greek. Migdal was captured in 67 AD by Titus Flavius Vespasianus. Today, Migdal is an agricultural settlement in the Ginosar Valley.[22]

Several synagogue buildings from the 4th to mid-8th centuries were discovered in Hammath Tiberias and excavated by Professor Moshe Dothan in 1961-1965. He wrote *Hammath Tiberias, Early Synagogue, Volume 1,* which covers Hellenistic and Roman remains. The second volume reports on the items found that are dated to the Byzantine and Early Islamic times. These volumes elucidate the role played by the city of Tiberias in the Jewish life during that period of history.[23]

Because the Sea of Galilee is below sea level and close to mountains and hills, winds become strong, violent storms. Once, the disciples thought they were sinking, but Jesus stilled the storm (read Mark 14:22-33).

Bible Study with Tony W. Cartledge: Ephesians 4:25-5:2

Paul stresses that believers should abandon harmful and unhealthy lifestyles to take on the goodness and love of Christ. We should follow this suggestion because we are already followers of Christ, called to live up to our needs. Ephesians 4 has a baptism theme because when we are baptized we symbolically strip off the old life of sin and bury it in the waters of baptism. Paul taught that Christ has the power to change our hearts. Paul does not tell the followers of Christ to go and find some goodness somewhere and put it on but to live up to the goodness that is already in them as children of God.

[21]   www.comwikitravel.org/en/Tiberias

[22]   Virtual Israel Experience, www.jewishvirtuallibrary.org/vie/Tiberias.html.

[23]   Israel Exploration Society, Hammath Tiberias Synagogues, www.israelexplora-tionsociety.huji.ac.il/Hammath.htm.

Ephesians 4:26-28 teaches about anger which everyone has sometimes. Even Jesus became angry. The issue is not getting angry but how we manage it. Paul is saying it is okay to get angry as long as you do not let your anger lead you to sin. We can practice saying what needs to be said in a way that is kind and clear. Ephesians 4:26 says, "Do not let the sun go down on your anger." Ephesians 4:29 teaches us to speak in ways that benefit others. Ugly words can destroy self-esteem. Christ asks us to live obediently, empowered by the Spirit of God. Believers are not to be characterized by bitterness, slander or malice. The indwelling Spirit does not like spiteful words we use. We can learn to forgive each other. We can learn to be imitators of God "who lives in love" as Christ taught us to do.[24]

TIBERIAS: SMALL HARBOR AND RUINS ON THE SEA OF GALILEE (LAKE KINNERET)

photo courtesy of the Israeli Ministry of Tourism and solely for this photo only at www.goisrael.com

Tiberias is the capital of Galilee and one of the four Jewish holy cities. The post-Bible books of the Mishna and Talmud were written in Tiberias. The population of Tiberias is 40,000 people. Tiberias was built on the southern side and then expanded to the north over the last two millennia of history. The south has the hot springs of Tiberias and the old city of Hammat that is now in ruins. During Bible times, Hammat was a walled city. It had seventeen warm health springs at a temperature of about 60 degrees Celsius, and it was a spa for the Roman city of Tiberias.

---

[24] Tony W. Cartledge, *Bible Study with Tony W. Cartledge: Ephesians 4:25-5:2*. Baptists Today News Journal, August 2012, 20-21.

Bible Study with Tony W. Cartledge: Ephesians 5:15-21

Paul taught that followers of Christ are to make good use of every moment that God gives us. Verse 15 teaches to be wise rather than unwise. Paul says we should be good stewards of the life we have been given, aware that our time is limited. The NRSV Version says, "making the most of the time." The King James Version says, "We should redeem the time" we have in a world dominated by evil. These verses teach to live each day to the fullest, to live in the light, to make the most of every present moment while remembering we are citizens of heaven and eternity and to live as Jesus lived. This is what "redeem the time" means. Verse 17 stresses, "So do not be foolish, but understand what the will of the Lord is." Paul teaches to be wise is to seek understanding of God's will. Verse 18 teaches to avoid being drunk with wine, but filled with the Spirit of Christ. A purpose of our singing to each other and to God is giving thanks to God.[25]

The Tiberias Marathon is held once a year along the Sea of Galilee in Israel with about a thousand participants. The runners go around the southern tip of the Sea of Galilee. The race area is about 200 meters below sea level which makes it the lowest-altitude course in the world.

Bible Study with Tony W. Cartledge: Ephesians 6:10-20

Paul closes with instructions to prepare themselves daily for "spiritual battle." In verse 10 Paul teaches to "be strong in the Lord and in the strength of his power." Paul did not intend for believers just to pray for strength to get through the day but to pray for the strength to overcome evil, and to pray for our plans to walk worthily of our faith and imitate Christ by loving others as Christ loved us. In verses 13-17 Paul stresses believers' putting "on the armor of God" which will help believers to stand firm against the powers of evil. Paul names the first armor of God as "the belt of truth". This armor is first mentioned in Isaiah 11:5 which mentions the coming messiah that wears a belt of righteousness and faithfulness. Deception is a powerful weapon but truth can beat it. The second piece of armor is the breastplate of righteousness taught in Ephesians 6:14. Isaiah 59:17 teaches a prophetic image of divine justice in which God "put on righteousness like a breastplate."

---

[25]   Tony W. Cartledge, *Bible Study with Tony W. Cartledge: Ephesians 5:15-21*. Baptists Today News Journal, August 2013, 24-25.

Paul taught to wear on your feet, whatever will help you best preach the gospel. Make one's feet ready for battle. We must have our feet firmly planted in the word of God. The fourth thing in the Christian's armor is the "shield of faith" which protects against "flaming arrows" of evil. Verse 17 is about "the helmet of salvation and the sword of the Spirit". In Isaiah 59:17 God wore a helmet of salvation but in Ephesians 6:17 Paul describes God's gift of salvation as a helmet that gives the believer hope and confidence that God is with us. Paul calls for believers to "pray in the Spirit with all kinds of prayers and requests."[26]

There are places to stay in the Sea of Galilee area with camping areas on sandy beaches. There are also hostels, guest houses, and beach front hotels. There are water activities to enjoy like swimming, boating, and giant slides in water parks. Restaurants and grocery stores are plentiful. The most beautiful nature places are the Jordan Park, the Beit Tsida Nature Reserve, Khamat Gader, and Naharayim.

OLD TIBERIAS: A DEFENSIVE TOWER ON THE LAKE KINNERET
photo courtesy of the Israeli Ministry of Tourism and solely for this photo only at www.goisrael.com

In 54 AD, the emperor Claudius named the city Tiberias Claudiupolis. Herod also minted coins in Tiberias with his name on them. Herod used the coins to entice the Jews to live in Tiberias, but they refused because it was built over an old cemetery. It took Tiberias 110 years to find a religious way to overcome the problem, by moving the graves out to make the city "kosher". During the Jewish revolt against the Romans, the Jews in Tiberias opened its gates to Vespasian and it was spared from destruction. At the end of the 1st century AD, the Jewish population moved to Tiberias. The Sanhendrin moved here and helped Tiberias become an important city.[27]

---

[26]   Tony W. Cartledge, *Bible Study with Tony W. Cartledge: Ephesians 6:10-20*. Baptists Today News Journal, August 2012, 26-27.
[27]   www.biblewalks.com/Sites

ARCHAEOLOGICAL GARDEN AND RESTORED CRUSADER BUILDING

photo courtesy of the Israeli Ministry of Tourism and solely for this photo only at www.goisrael.com

TIBERIAS: ST. PETER'S CATHOLIC CHURCH

photo courtesy of the Israeli Ministry of Tourism and solely for this photo only at www.goisrael.com

Some of the remains of the early St. Peter's Church can still be seen. Today's church was built on the ruins of a Crusader church with windows that look like portholes in boats. The modern church has artwork symbolizing the four Gospels and the inscription, "Feed My Sheep."

Dig Deeper into the Rich History of Israel

The area of the Sea of Galilee, near the present-day city of Tiberias, was an integral part of the ministry of Jesus and His disciples in the New Testament, including where Jesus called His disciples to follow Him. Here are a few of the many biblical accounts which you will be enriched by reading:

Matthew 4:18-25
Matthew 17:24-27
Mark 1:16-20
Mark 5:35-41
Mark 14:22-33
Luke 5:4-7
John 21:1-23

CHAPTER 5

ISRAEL GOSPEL TRAIL

The Israel Gospel Trail is a forty-mile hiking trail that guides people over some of the same territory that Jesus and his disciples used regularly. On the trail is Migdal, the ancient town of Magdala and the hometown of Mary Magdalene. Farther north is Tabgha, where the Church of the Multiplication of Loaves and Fishes is located. Remember that Jesus fed many hungry people with a little bit of bread and five fishes. On the trail, hikers pass by the Mount of Beatitudes before heading to Capernaum.

Many tourists and believers take a boat across the Sea of Galilee. The boats go between Capernaum and Kibbutz Ginosar, the place of the discovery of a 2,000-year-old boat similar to the ones that Jesus used. Another boat route runs to ancient Tiberias.[28] The Gospel Trail was created by a group of international and local volunteers and the Society for Protection of Nature in Israel. They developed the first hiking guidebook written in English. The Gospel Trail is marked with large stone basalt rock towers to mark the way.[29]

Biblical Archaeology Society Staff, 12-01-2011: Israel inaugurates "Gospel Trail"

Israel's Ministry of Tourism this week inaugurated the new "Gospel Trail", a forty- mile route from the hometown of Nazarethto Capernaum where Jesus

---

[28]   *Gospel Trail in Israel lets you walk 40 miles in Jesus' Shoes*, www.theoaklandpress.com/ articles/2011/12/25/life/doc4ef3974b3.

[29]   www.gospeltrail.com.

focused on his mission in the Galilee. The route passes through important Christian holy sites as Cana, the Mount of Beatitudes, Magdala, and Tabgha. The trail can be made by car, bicycle or walking.

The Feast of Tabernacles in Israel is a major holiday and attracts many Christian tourists to Israel to participate in the activities. One year, six thousand Christians arrived in Israel from over 100 countries to participate in seminars, lectures, workshops, and the Jerusalem March. Tourism Minister Stas Misezhnikov welcomed thousands of Christians to the feast in a broadcast at the International Convention Center in Jerusalem.[30]

Genesis 13:17 says, "Go walk through the length and breadth of the land, for I am giving it to you." In the spirit of this verse, the Gospel Trail is good for both Christians and Jews. Jesus spent most of his life growing up in Nazareth, walking the countryside, and performing many miracles along the way from Cana to Tabgha. Sadly, only 60 percent of Christian tourists visit the Galilee, whereas more than 87 percent visit Jerusalem.[31]

The Gospel Trail begins at the Mount of Precipice in Nazareth, where Jesus was rejected by his townsmen who threatened to throw him over the mountainside (read Luke 4:14-29).

The Gospel Trail goes down the old "Pilgrims Path" 500 meters to the Jezreel Valley below, and continues along the Nazareth Range with beautiful views of Mount Tabor and Kafr Kanna. The trail continues by the Golani Junction to the Horns of Hattin site of the battle between Crusaders and Muslims. It continues past Magdala to Tabgha, the Mount of Beatitudes, ending at Capernaum and the Sea of Galilee. Another trail is the Jesus Trail that covers the same sites on similar trails. The difference between the two is that the Jesus Trail also goes through Arab villages.[32]

And Jesus went about all Galilee, teaching in their synagogues, and preaching the gospel of the kingdom, and healing all manner of sickness and all manner of disease among the people. And his fame went throughout all Syria: and they bought unto him all sick people that were taken with divers diseases and torments, and

---

[30] www.ynetnews.com/articles/0.734.
[31] www.travelujah.com
[32] www.travelujah.com.

those which were possessed with devils, and those which were lunatic, and those that had the palsy; and he healed them. And there followed him great multitudes of people from Galilee, and from Decapolis, and from Jerusalem, and from Judea, and from beyond Jordan. (Matthew 4:23-25)

Capernaum

Synagogues have a large hall for prayer. Behind that is the *D'bhir* or Holy of Holies. There are smaller rooms for study and other purposes. All synagogues have a *bimah* or *bema* which is a table from which the Torah is read, and a desk for the prayer leader. The name and use for *bema* is traced back to Ezra's reading of the Torah on a wooden pulpit:[33]

And Ezra the scribe stood upon a pulpit of wood, which they had made for that purpose; and beside him stood Mattithiah, and Shema, and Anaiah, and Urijah, and Hilkiah, and Maaseiah, on his right hand; and on his left hand, Pedaiah, and Mishael, and Malchiah, and Hashum, and Hashbadana, Zechariah, and Meshullam. And Ezra opened the book in the sight of all the people; for he was above all the people; and when he opened it all the people stood up. (Nehemiah 8:4-5)

CAPERNAUM 2: ANCIENT SYNAGOGUE NEAR SEA OF GALILEE.
Photo by Mordagan, courtesy of the Israeli Ministry of Tourism and is solely for this photo only at www.goisrael.com

Archaeologists identified one 1st-century house as the home of Peter. The rough walls were covered with inscriptions. Some excavators found graffiti, including the name of Peter, and other excavators found little legible writing.[34]

Archaeological evidence shows that the town of Capernaum did not begin until the 2nd century BC, which explains why it is only mentioned in the New Testament. Capernaum is only ten miles from

---

[33] www.en.wikipedia.org.
[34] www.en.wikipedia.org

Tiberias and the ruins can be reached by car or by boat. Capernaum is only two and a half miles from the Jordan River. The old city of Capernaum was abandoned about 1,000 years ago and rediscovered by archaeologists in the 1800's. In modern times, Capernaum is called Kefar Nahum in Hebrew and Talhum in Arabic. Capernaum was a crossroads on a route between Damascus and Caesarea Maritima on the Mediterranean Sea, and another route of traveling was from Tyre and Egypt. Customs taxes were collected from all travelers. Levi was a tax collector who became one of the disciples of Jesus. Levi's name was later changed to Matthew (read Luke 5:27-29).

After being selected as a disciple of Jesus, Matthew's name does not appear in the Gospel except in the lists of the apostles. The last notice of him is in Acts 1:13: "And when they were come in, they went up into an upper room, where abode both Peter, and James, and John, and Andrew, Philip, and Thomas, Bartholomew, and Matthew, James the son of Alphaeus, and Simon Zelotes, and Judas the brother of James."

Peter's house is where Jesus healed Peter's mother-in-law. Later the house was used as a house church. Centuries later, Christians built a church on the site, which was later destroyed by a conquest of Capernaum. Archaeologists have excavated the church and Peter's house. Stanisla Loffreda said:

Literary sources and recent archaeological discoveries make the identification of the house of St. Peter in Capernaum virtually certain. The house was built at the very end of the Hellenistic period (first century AD). Some peculiar features set apart this building from all the others so far excavated in Capernaum. Here, in fact, the pavements received floors of lime several times. Interestingly enough, many pieces of broken lamps were found in the thin layers of lime. One hundred and thirty-one inscriptions were found. They were written in four languages, namely: in Greek (110), Aramaic (10), Estrangelo (9), and Latin (2). The name of Jesus appears several times. He is called Christ, the Lord, and the Most High God. An inscription in Estrangelo mentions the Eucharist.

There are also symbols and monograms, namely: crosses of different forms, a boat, and the monogram of Jesus. The name of St. Peter occurs at least twice; his monogram is written in Latin but with Greek letters. In another graffito, St. Peter is called the helper of Rome, and a third inscription mentions Peter and

Berenike. This Peter, however, might be a pilgrim. On several hundred pieces of plaster, decorative motifs appear. The colors employed are: green, blue, yellow, red, brown, white, and black. Among the subjects one can distinguish floral crosses, promegranates, figs, trifolium, stylized flowers, and geometric designs such as circles, squares, etc. At the beginning of the fifth century, the house of St. Peter was still standing, but it had been previously changed into a church. This we learn from Eteria, a Spanish pilgrim, who wrote in her diary: "In Capernaum, the house of the Prince of the Apostles (St. Peter) became a church. The walls, however, (of that house) have remained unchanged to the present day.[35]

In the old days, caravans stopped at Capernaum to buy produce and dried fish. Archaeologists even found an old fish sales area where Peter and the other fishermen worked. The ruins of Capernaum were acquired by Franciscans in 1894. In New Testament times, the population was about 10,000 to 15,000. Capernaum now has a population of about 1,500.[36] In New Testament times, Jesus named Capernaum as his own: "And he entered into a ship, and passed over, and came into his own city" (Matthew 9:1). Jesus taught here and healed the man with an unclean spirit (read Mark 1:21-28). Jesus then entered the home of Peter and Andrew and healed Peter's mother-in-law of a fever (Mark 1:29-31). Jesus called Levi, Matthew, to leave tax collecting and follow him. Later Jesus went to supper at Levi's home (read Mark 2:13-17).

---

[35] www.christiananswers.net.
[36] Ibid.

CAPERNAUM: ANCIENT TOWN AND SYNAGOGUE

Photo courtesy of the Israeli Ministry of Tourism and is solely for this photo only at www.goisrael.com

In 1838, an American explorer, Edward Robinson, discovered the ancient town of Capernaum. In 1866, a British Captain, Charles William Wilson, found the remains of the synagogue. In 1894, Franciscan Friar Giuseppe Baldi of Naples found the ruins of the Bedouins. In addition to discovering the old town of Capernaum, Edward Robinson traveled with Reverend Eli Smith and together they wrote many books, such as *Biblical Researches in Palestine and Adjacent Countries* and many others. Robinson and his partner, Rev. Eli Smith, made many identifications of ancient places in Israel.[37]

The Chapel of Peter is found a short distance from Tabgha. This spot is believed to be a post-resurrection appearance site of Jesus. A small chapel was built there by the Franciscans in 1934. Inside the chapel are ruins of a 4th-century church with a flat rock by the altar. It is believed that Jesus used the rock as a table to fix breakfast for the disciples (see John 21:1-14).

The Capernaum synagogue is located near the lake and was designed so that praying Jews faced Jerusalem. This synagogue was destroyed in 70 AD along with the temple in Jerusalem. Years later, about 250-300 AD, a white stone synagogue was built.

Jesus often taught in this synagogue:

These things said he in the synagogue, as he taught in Capernaum (John 6:59).
And they went into Capernaum: and straightway on the Sabbath day he entered into the synagogue and taught (Mark 1:21).

Scripture also says that a Roman centurion built a synagogue here for the Jews.

---

[37] www.en.wikipedia.org.

After he had finished all his sayings in the hearing of the people, he entered Capernaum. Now a centurion had a servant who was sick and at the point of death, who was highly valued by him. When the centurion heard about Jesus, he sent to him elders of the Jews, asking him to come and heal his servant. And when they came to Jesus, they pleaded with him earnestly, saying, "He is worthy to have you do this for him, for he loves our nation, and he is the one who built us our synagogue." (Luke 7:1-5)

Later this same centurion's servant was healed from severe palsy by Jesus (read Matthew 8:5-13). A centurion is a title for a Roman officer in command of 100 men. The centurions mentioned in the New Testament are praised in the Gospels and in Acts.[38] Cornelius, the first Gentile convert, was a centurion (Acts 10:1). A centurion also watched the crucifixion of Jesus (Matthew 27:54 and Luke 23:47), and when he saw it, he said, "Truly this man was the Son of God."

Jesus also healed the daughter of the ruler Jairus in Capernaum (Read Matthew 9).

CAPERNAUM (ON THE SEA OF GALILEE): ANCIENT OIL PRESS

Photo courtesy of the Israeli Ministry of Tourism and is solely for this photo only at www.goisrael.com

Miracles of Jesus in Capernaum

In the synagogue at Capernaum, a paralyzed man's family let the man down through the roof and Jesus healed forgave and healed him (read Mark 2:1-12).

---

38   www.christiananswers.net.

JORDAN RIVER VALLEY, THE BIBLICAL "GEON HAYARDEN"

Photo courtesy of the Israeli Ministry of Tourism and is solely for this photo only at www.goisrael.com]

The Jordan River forms the eastern border of Israel. John the Baptist baptized Jesus in this river. A first-century AD historian, Flavius Josephus, views the activities of John the Baptist as authentic and agrees with the Biblical gospels of the event. The baptism of Jesus was a dynamic way to celebrate the beginning of his public ministry. John the Baptist preached a "baptism with water" and proclaimed a baptism of repentance for the forgiveness of sins: "And he went into all the region around the Jordan, proclaiming a baptism of repentance for the forgiveness of sins" (Luke 3:3, ESV). John the Baptist declared himself to be a forerunner to One who would baptize with the Holy Spirit and with fire. In so doing, he prepared the way for the baptizing of Jesus and the beginning of his ministry.

Open Doors by Sylvia Barnhart

Revelation 3:20 says, "Behold, I stand at the door, and knock; if any man hear my voice, and open the door, I will come in to him, and will sup with him, and he with me." Christ stands at the door seeking to enter. He brings promises but will not enter unless He is invited. He knocks and invites you to open your heart's door and enter into fellowship with Him. Isaiah 22:22 teaches, "Our Lord has the keys of the kingdom of heaven, and He has given those keys to us." Matthew 16:19 says, "He tells us to knock and keep on knocking. Doors that are closed to us will be opened." Matthew 7:7 says, "Our Savior continuously opens and closes doors for His beloved children, and no power in heaven or earth can ever prevail against Him!

The Bible makes it clear that God has chosen to partner with us in the expansion of His kingdom. God stressed that all power, dominion, and authority have been given to Him as the Risen Son of God, and that we are to go forth in the power of His name.

Romans 10:13-15 teaches us, "Everyone who calls on the name of the Lord will be saved. How then, can they call on the one they have not believed in? And how can they hear without someone preaching to them? And how can they preach unless they are sent? How beautiful are the feet of those who bring good news!"

Isaiah the prophet taught, "Here am I, send me!" Jesus has the power when you take the Good News through the streets of our cities, to be standing there holding the door wide open for you.[39]

BAPTISM IN THE JORDAN RIVER(AT YARDENIT) (3)

Photo courtesy of the Israeli Ministry of Tourism and is solely for this photo only at www.goisrael.com

John answered them all, saying, "I baptize you with water, but he who is mightier than I is coming, the strap of whose sandals I am not worthy to untie. He will baptize you with the Holy Spirit and fire." (Luke 3:16, ESV)

Jesus came to the Jordan River to be baptized by John the Baptist. The baptismal scene has the heavens opening, a dove-like descent of the Holy Spirit, and a voice from Heaven, saying, "This is my beloved Son with whom I am well pleased."

Focus on Israel: Israel Facing Unprecedented Dangers

Tourism in Israel is very good this year and hotel space can be difficult to find. Israel appears to be peaceful and safe but danger lurks. The Jewish state is surrounded by political instability, rebellion, Islamic terrorism, and threats of nuclear annihilation. A British newspaper stated that Saudi Arabia now has missiles on a launch pad aimed at Iran

---

[39] Sylvia Barnhart, *Open Doors*. Abiding Word Ministries: The Vine and Branches, Volume 28 Midsummer 2013, Issue 4, 8-9.

and Israel. Russia has threatened to send Syria their advanced S-300 ground-to-air missiles. Israel has promised to strike Syria's arsenal if the weapons are sent. Iran is still pushing ahead on its missile program in spite of the threats from the Obama administration. A recent Pentagon report contained information that by 2015 Iran will have missiles capable of reaching the United States.

In Lebanon, Hezbollah, a terrorist group, has more missiles than the government in Lebanon. The Hezbollah Army has the power to come and go at will. Hezbollah has sent thousands of fighters into Syria to support Assad's government. There are thousands of rockets aimed at Israeli cities and Israel's enemies will use them when the opportunity comes. In Jordan, over a half million refugees from Syria have arrived and are putting a strain on the country's economy. A large group of Syrian rebel forces is trying to take over the area near the Golan Heights, which is near the border of Israel. These Syrian rebel troops say that when they are finished fighting Assad, they will fight Israel.

Egypt is also a threat to Israel. Saudi Arabia and the United Arab Emirates send billions of dollars to Egypt. The Obama Administration is also sending billions to Egypt. Simultaneously, the United States is putting pressure on Israel to resume peace talks. Much of the Middle East resembles descriptions found in Ezekiel 38 and 39. Who knows what lies ahead? But God is still on His throne.[40]

GALILEE: THE ANCIENT SYNAGOGUE AT KORAZIM (1)
Photo courtesy of the Israeli Ministry of Tourism and is solely for this photo only at www. goisrael.com

Korazim, Bethsaida, and Capernaum were condemned by Jesus for rejecting him. In ancient times, Korazim was known for its good wheat. The ruins of Korazim are spread over twenty-five acres, and they are

---

[40] David H. Barnhart, *Israel Facing Unprecedented Dangers*. Abiding Word Ministries: The Vine and Branches, Volume 28 Midsummer 2013, Issue 4, 16.

divided into five parts with a synagogue in the middle. The synagogue was built with black basalt stones and decorated with Jewish motifs. There is a ritual bath surrounded by public and residential buildings.[41]

Kursi is the site of the ruins of a Byzantine Monastery. Today, one can still see a large wine press and portions of a mosaic tile floor. At the base of the hill, Jesus cast out demons from a man and sent them into a herd of pigs (read Luke 8).

Other names for Korazin are Karraza, Chorazin, Kerazeh, and Korazim. The synagogue there is of a typical Galilean style with a basilical shape, with three hallways separated by two rows of pillars. There are three doorways, of which the center one is the largest. There are benches around the interior walls and a stylobate to support the weight of the arches. The seat of Moses was discovered in the 1920's.[42] Jesus respected this seat of authority (Read Matthew 11:20-24).

Nazareth

Nazareth is the largest city in the North District of Israel and is even known as the Arab capital of Israel. Most of the population is Arab, with 69% Muslim and 30% Christian. Nazareth is called the childhood home of Jesus. In modern Nazareth, there are about thirty churches and monasteries, mosques, and ancient synagogues.

About 2,000 years ago, Nazareth was a small Jewish village. The Church of the Annunciation is the tradition spot for the home of Mary and Joseph. Right next to the Church of the Annunciation is the Church of Saint Joseph, rumored to be the site of the carpentry shop of Joseph.[43]

"He settled in a city called Nazareth so that what was spoken through the prophets might be fulfilled: He will be called a Nazarene" (Matthew 2:23, CEB).

"When Mary and Joseph had completed everything required by the Law of the Lord, they returned to their hometown, Nazareth in Galilee" (Luke 2:29, CEB).

---

[41] www.goisrael.com.

[42] www.bibleplaces.com

[43] www.goisrael.com/tourism

"Jesus went to Nazareth, where he had been raised. On the Sabbath he went to the synagogue as he normally did and stood up to read" (Luke 4:16, CEB).

Jesus was called "Jesus of Nazareth" although he was born in Bethlehem. The disciples of Jesus were called Nazarenes.

"The multitudes said, 'This is the prophet, Jesus from Nazareth of Galilee'" (Matthew 21:11).

"And when he heard that it was Jesus of Nazareth, he began to cry out and say, 'Jesus, thou Son of David, have mercy on me'" (Mark 10:47).

"And he saith unto them, 'Be not affrighted: ye seek Jesus of Nazareth, which was crucified: he is risen; he is not here: behold the place where they laid him'" (Mark 16:6).

"Philip findeth Nathanael, and saith unto him, 'We have found him, of whom Moses in the law, and the prophets, did write, Jesus of Nazareth, the son of Joseph.' And Nathanael said unto him, 'Can there any good thing come out of Nazareth?' Philip saith unto him, 'Come and see'" (John 1:45-46).

"Then Peter said, 'Silver and gold have I none; but such as I have give I thee: in the name of Jesus Christ of Nazareth rise up and walk'" (Acts 3:6).

"For we have heard him say, that this Jesus of Nazareth shall destroy this place, and shall change the customs which Moses delivered us" (Acts 6:14).

"And I fell unto the ground, and heard a voice saying unto me, 'Saul, Saul, why persecutest thou me?' And I answered, 'Who art thou, Lord?' And he said unto me, 'I am Jesus of Nazareth, whom thou persecutest'" (Acts 22:7-8).

Archeological excavations by Bagati since 1955 show that Nazareth was a small agricultural village with only a dozen or so inhabitants during Old Testament times. The pottery artifacts show a continuous settlement during the years 900-600 BC. After those years, it was a tiny settlement until the year 200 BC. Since then, Nazareth has been inhabited. Most of the artifacts are caves, cisterns, and grain storage bins. When oil mills and millstone artifacts were found, the archeologists knew agriculture had been important in its history. During the first twenty years of his life, Jesus had plenty of time to walk on the mountain ranges, and to think about the history of his people.[44]

The Roman Catholic Church of the Annunciation in Nazareth was built over the traditional house of Mary. This church was dedicated in 1964 by Pope Paul VI and was completed in 1969. The lower level contains the ruins of Mary's house. The upper level is the main church. Each mosaic portrays Mary in it. One mural shows Christ standing with Peter on Mount Zion, and Mary sitting while praying for her children. Some scholars believe that the angel Gabriel may have appeared to Mary at the site of the Church of the Annunciation. Nearby is the Church of Saint Joseph, built over the traditional site of Joseph's carpenter shop.

Focus on Israel: Israeli Official Calls for the Rebuilding of the Temple

Uri Ariel, Israeli Minister of Housing and Construction, calls for the rebuilding of the Temple: Uri made this request during a speech at an archaeology conference and suggested the Temple be rebuilt on the site where the Dome of the Rock and the al-Aqsa Mosque now stand. Ariel said, "We've built many little, little temples but we need to build a real Temple on the Temple Mount."[45]

Focus on Israel: Artifacts from Destruction of Jerusalem in 70 AD Discovered

Four artifacts that may date back to the siege of Jerusalem in 70 AD were found by the team from the Israel Antiquities Authority. Three cooking pots and a small ceramic oil lamp were found in a small cistern. Dr. Eli Shukron explained, "This is the first time we are able to connect archaeological finds with the famine that occurred during the siege of Jerusalem at the time of the Great Revolt. The complete cooking pots and ceramic oil lamp indicate that the people went down into the cistern, where they secretly ate the food that was contained in the pots without anyone seeing them, and this is consistent with the account provided by Josephus who witnessed the sack of Jerusalem."

---

[44] www.inisrael.com.
[45] *The Times of Israel,* July 12, 2013.

Josephus, a first-century Roman-Jewish historian, wrote in his book, The Jewish Wars, "These concealed the food they possessed, for fear it would be stolen by the rebels, and they ate it in hidden places in their homes. As the famine grew worse, the frenzy of the partisans increased with it. For as nowhere was there corn to be seen, men broke into the houses and ransacked them."[46]

BASILICA OF ANNUNCIATION, NAZARETH

Photo courtesy of the Israeli Ministry of Tourism and is solely for this photo only at www.goisrael.com

The Basilica of the Annunciation is a Catholic Church built over the ruins of Byzantine and Crusader churches. It includes the cave where Gabriel told Mary she was to be the mother of Jesus, the Messiah:

And in the sixth month the angel Gabriel was sent from God unto a city of Galilee, named Nazareth, to a virgin espoused to a man whose name was Joseph, of the house of David; and the virgin's name was Mary. And the angel came in unto her and said, "Hail, thou that art highly favoured, the Lord is with thee: blessed art thou among women. (Luke 1:26-29)

That cave was identified in the 4th century AD. In 384 AD, an altar was mentioned, and in 570 AD, the first church was mentioned.[47]

The modern Arabic name for Nazareth is en-Nazirah. Between the Church of the Annunciation and the Church of St. Joseph (built in 1914) is a Franciscan monastery. Close by is Mary's well, which has given water to the village from the first century up until modern times. Mary's well is now located in the center of downtown Nazareth. The site today is a modern water trough built over the old one that was used for women and animals as drinking water. In late Roman times, mainly

---

46   David H. Barnhart, *Focus on Israel*. Abiding Word Ministries: The Vine and Branches, Volume 28 Midsummer 2013, Issue 4, 17.

47   www.sacred-destinations.com.

during Crusader times, tunnels were cut into the rock to take the water to houses. In the 19th century, the well house was rebuilt. In the 1960's, it was torn down and rebuilt.[48]

In 680 AD, a pilgrim, Arculf, mentioned seeing two churches in Nazareth: one at Mary's spring and the other one where the Basilica stands today. The Abbot Daniel wrote in 1106-1108 that the Byzantine Church had been destroyed and rebuilt by the Franks. The Crusader Church was larger than the Byzantine Church. There were monastery buildings on the south side, and the north side had a fancy bishop's palace. After the Battle of the Horns of Hattin in 1187, the Christian citizens of Nazareth hid in the church but the Muslims slaughtered them. The Muslims left the church standing. Saladin gave permission for some of the clergy to return and allowed Christians to visit. In 1263, the Baybars attacked Nazareth and destroyed the church.

By the 14th century, Christian pilgrims were charged money to visit the site. The site eventually was filled with garbage and used for cows. In the 14th century, the Franciscans gained control and in 1620 repaired the church. In 1730, the Franciscans built a new church in its place. In 1955, the church was torn down to build a new church over the Crusader and Byzantine foundations. In modern times, the Basilica of the Annunciation is a parish church for 7,000 catholic Christians in Nazareth and a site to visit for Protestants. The church today has an upper church decorated with mosaics of the Virgin Mary, and the lower church is centered upon the cave where Mary heard the angelic announcement.[49]

The people of Nazareth did not approve of Jesus' thinking and behavior. To them, he was just one of the sons of Joseph the carpenter. The brothers of Jesus were James, Joseph, Simeon, and Judah.

"Is not this the carpenter's son? Is not his mother called Mary? And his brethen, James and Joses and Simon, and Judas? And his sisters are they not all with us? Whence then hath this man all these things?" And they were offended in him. But Jesus said unto them, "A prophet is not without honour, save in his own country, and in his own house." And he did not many mighty works there because of their unbelief. (Matthew 13:55-58)

---

[48] www.biblewalks.com.

[49] www.sacred-destinations.com.

Nazareth was too small to be included in the list of settlements of the tribe of Zebulun (Joshua 19:10-16), which mentions twelve towns and six villages. Nazareth is not included among the forty-five cities of the Galilee that were mentioned by Josephus, and Nazareth is not mentioned in the Talmud.[50]

NAZARETH: SYNAGOGUE CHURCH (GREEK CATHOLIC)
Photo by Mordagan, courtesy of the Israeli Ministry of Tourism and is solely for this photo only at www.goisrael.com

Nazareth is located near the Plain of Esdraelon in Galilee. It is not mentioned in the Old Testament. But excavations show us that settlements were in the area dating back to the Bronze Age. Tombs date back to the Iron Age, to the Hasmonean period. Nazareth is surrounded by limestone hills. From a hilltop in Nazareth, a person can see Mt. Carmel, where Elijah had a contest with the prophets of Baal and proved that God was the true God and not Baal.

If a person looks to the south, Megiddo and the entire plain of Esdraelon can be seen. A person can also see Tabor and the hills of Gilboa, where Saul and Jonathan were killed in an ancient battle. At the foot of the hill was the Roman road, "the way of the Sea", connecting Damascus with the seaports. To the south was a road that a person could travel on to go to Egypt. Sepphoris, the capital of Herod Antipas and a strong military center, was five miles away. To see these views, a visitor needs to climb the rolling hills. Luke 4:16 tells us that Jesus preached his first recorded sermon in Nazareth.[51]

House Uncovered in Nazareth Dating to the Time of Jesus

Archaeologists in Israel discovered the remains of a house from the time of Jesus in the heart of Nazareth. The house had two rooms and a

---

50   www.inisrael.com.

51   www.bible.history.com.

courtyard where a rock-hewn cistern collected rainwater. The discovery was made during an excavation before the construction of the International Marian Center of Nazareth built to illustrate the life of Mary. The Marian Center will be next to the Church of the Annunciation. Joseph of Nazareth may have been a builder rather than a carpenter because people in a small village did not need much furniture.[52]

Focus on Israel: Ancient Roman Road Discovered

Part of an ancient 2,000-year-old Roman road was discovered in East Jerusalem by archaeologists. The road was about twenty-six feet wide and went from Jerusalem to Joppa in ancient times.

Focus on Israel: Fragment from Time of King David Found

Archaeologist Eilat Mizar discovered an ancient jar fragment dating to the time of King David in 1,000 BC, near the Temple Mount. The language on the fragment is from the Canaanite period but no one knows what it says.[53]

Focus on Israel: King David's Suburban Palace Uncovered Outside Jerusalem

Archaeologists from the Hebrew University may have uncovered one of the palaces of King David, located a short distance from Jerusalem. The remains of the large structure were found near the town of Beit Shemesh, and may be part of what is believed to be the biblical town of Sha'arayim. These remains date to the 10th century BC. In later centuries, Bedouin tribes used the site and referred to it as Khirbat Daoud, which means David's Ruins.[54]

---

[52] *House Uncovered in Nazareth Dating to the Time of Jesus.* Bible Archaeology: December 21, 2009.

[53] David H. Barnhart, *Focus on Israel.* Abiding Word Ministries: The Vine and Branches, Volume 28 Midsummer 2013, Issue 4, 20.

[54] Israel Today, July 19, 2013.

Horses as Symbols of Power

The most lethal weapon in battle in ancient times was the war horse. The weight of the mounted warrior and the war horse together was about 1,000 pounds. The war horses knocked the enemy warriors to the ground and trampled them to death with their strong hooves, so that the warrior could pin the enemy to the ground with his lance. Horses also provided escape from advancing armies. Horses had the speed of about forty miles per hour and could outrun the infantry without getting close to the range of enemy arrows. The Israelites knew from experience that horses made the difference in life and death on the battlefield. The problem was that the Israelites placed trust in the war horses instead of God. Hosea, Isaiah, Amos, and Micah, prophets of the 8th century BC, warned the people to entrust their deliverance to God and not to horses.

Psalm 20:7 says, "Some trust in chariots and some in horses, but we trust in the name of the Lord our God." Psalm 33:17 states, "A horse is a vain hope for deliverance; despite all its great strength, it cannot save." Isaiah 30:15-16 teaches, "In repentance and rest is your salvation, in quietness and trust is your strength, but you would have none of it. You said, 'No, we will flee on horses.' Therefore you will flee! You said, 'We will ride off on swift horses.' Therefore your pursuers will be swift." Hosea 14:3 tells us, "Assyria cannot save us; we will not mount war horses."

In the late 8th century BC, Israel was invaded by the Assyrian army led by Tiglath-Pileser III, Shalmaneser V, and Sargon II. Assyria had the most powerful army because of the chariots and horsemen. In the Battle of Qarqar in 853 BC, King Ahab led 2,000 chariots to fight the Assyrians. Later, King Ahab asked King Jehoshaphat of Judah to help fight the Assyrians. 1 Kings 22:4 shows Jehoshaphat's response: "My horses are as your horses." In the battle, King Ahab was killed from an arrow. King Jehoshaphat escaped in his chariot and returned to Jerusalem. Horses helped fighters to escape to safety.

The Tel Dan stele fragment (about 841 BC) proclaimed the Aramean victories against Israel and Judah and claimed that "thousands of horsemen" were involved in the battles. Israel's Queen Jezebel (ca. 841 BC) was murdered at the gates of Jezreel. She was thrown to the ground and trampled by the chariot horses of Jehu (I Kings 9:20, 32-33). In Isaiah 2:7, Isaiah described the land as "full of horses with no end to their chariots". In Isaiah 22:7, Isaiah said, "Your choicest valleys are full of chariots, and horsemen are posted at the city gates."

Archaeological excavations prove that by the late 18th century during the time of the ministry of Hosea, Israel and Judah had developed a defensive network of walled cities, with chamber gates to speed up the hitching and unhitching of chariot *horses. These six- and four-chambered gates are at Dan, Hazor, Bethsaida, Jezreel, Megiddo, Gezer, Ashdod, Lachish, and Beersheba. Armies or messengers could travel from Dan to Beersheba, the length of Israel and Judah, in one day by changing horses in the cities with the chambered gates. The largest chariot training center of the Iron Age (1200-586 BC) was at Megiddo, located on the main trade route connecting Egypt, Syria, Phoenicia, and Mesopotamia. Megiddo had seventeen permanent stables for over 450 horses. Here were two paved courtyards for training, a granary with a capacity of 12,800 bushels, and a complex water system. King Tiglath-Pileser conquered Megiddo in 732 BC and made it into the regional Assyrian army headquarters.*[55]

NAZARETH: MARY'S WELL (1)

Photo courtesy of the Israeli Ministry of Tourism and is solely for this photo only at www.goisrael.com

The Greek Orthodox Church of the Annunciation was built over Mary's well where Mary drank her water.

Mount of Beatitudes

The traditional Mount of Beatitudes is on the northwestern shore of the Sea of Galilee. It is between Capernaum and Gennesaret. The site is near Tabgha. This photo below by Itamar Grinberg shows the inside of the chapel.

---

[55] Deborah Cantrell, *Horses as Symbols of Power*. Biblical Illustrator, LifeWay: Volume 39, number 2, Winter 2012-2013, 6-10.

THE INSIDE OF THE ROMAN CATHOLIC CHAPEL ON THE MOUNT OF BEATITUDES

courtesy of the Israeli Ministry of Tourism and is solely for this photo only at www.goisrael.com

This chapel was built in 1939 by the Franciscan sisters and the Italian dictator Mussolini. The symbols on the pavement in front of the church represent justice, prudence, fortitude, charity, faith, and temperance. Inside the church hangs Pope Paul VI's cloak from his 1964 visit.[56]

Blessed are the poor in spirit; for theirs is the kingdom of heaven. Blessed are they that mourn; for they shall be comforted. Blessed are the meek; for they shall inherit the earth. Blessed are they which do hunger and thirst after righteousness; for they shall be filled. Blessed are the merciful; for they shall obtain mercy. Blessed are the pure in heart; for they shall see God. Blessed are the peacemakers; for they shall be called the children of God. Blessed are they who are persecuted for righteousness' sake; for theirs is the kingdom of heaven. Blessed are ye, when men shall revile you, and shall say all manner of evil against you falsely, for my sake. (Matthew 5:3-11)

ROMAN CATHOLIC CHAPEL ON THE MOUNT OF BEATITUDES

Photo courtesy of the Israeli Ministry of Tourism and is solely for this photo only at www.goisrael.com

There is a church as well as a monastery, hostel, gardens, and farm located on the Mount of Beatitudes. The ceiling walls of the chapel have an octagon shape with eight sides, and each side has a window with one of the eight verses of the Beatitudes. The garden area has small assembly areas where pastors and groups can read from texts,

---

[56] www.bibleplaces.com/mtbeatitudes.htm.

sing, pray, and worship. The garden has statues, benches, and signs with verses from the Bible.[57]

The Plain of Gennesaret is at the bottom of the Mount of Beatitudes. The plain is known for its fertility, and the name means "Garden of Riches." The dirt is rich, and water pours down from the surrounding hills. This plain is five miles long and two miles wide and is bordered by the city of Magdala and the old ruins of the town of Gennesaret. Some believers think Jesus was referring to the Plain of Gennesaret as the "good ground" in the Parable of the Sower. Jesus was probably speaking from a boat and looking at the Plain of Gennesaret.[58] [59]

Jesus visited Gennesaret and healed people:

And when they were gone over, they came into the land of Gennesaret. And when the men of that place had knowledge of him, they sent out into all that country roundabout, and brought unto him all that were diseased: and besought him that they might only touch the hem of his garment; and as many as touched were made perfectly whole. (Matthew 14:34-36)

The modern-day Kibbutz Ginnosar is not far from the Gennesaret in the time of Jesus. Also, the modern road near Gennesaret follows the route of the biblical Way of the Sea. [60]

Now when Jesus had heard that John was cast into prison, he departed into Galilee; and leaving Nazareth, he came and dwelt in Capernaum, which is upon the sea coast, in the borders of Zebulun and Nephthalim: that it might be fulfilled which was spoken by Esaias the prophet saying, "The land of Zebulun, and the land of Nephthalim, by the way of the sea, beyond Jordan Galilee of the Gentiles; the people which sat in darkness saw great light; and to them which sat in the region and shadow of death light is sprung up." From that time Jesus began to preach, and to say, "Repent: for the kingdom of heaven is at hand." (Matthew 4:12-17)

Horses as Symbols of Power (continued)

---

[57] www.biblewalks.com/sites/beatitudes.html.

[58] www.jesusfootsteps.com/plain_of_gennesaret.html.

[59] www.en.wikipedia/gennesaret.

[60] www.followtherabbi.com.

Isaiah warned of the dangerous enemy horses with "sharp hoofs that seem like flint" which would make Judah like "a corpse trampled underfoot." (Isaiah 5:28, Isaiah 10:6, and Isaiah 14:19.) Judah had a major horse compound at Lachish about thirty miles southwest of Jerusalem. In 700 BC Assyrian King Sennacherib conquered Lachish during King Hezekiah's reign. Isaiah warned King Hezekiah that the Egyptian chariotry should not be trusted to solve Judah's problems. "Woe to those who go down to Egypt for help, who rely on horses, who trust in the multitude of chariots and in the great strength of their horsemen, but do not look to the Holy One of Israel or seek help from the Lord" (Isaiah 31:1). Isaiah had to warn the people of Israel again in Isaiah 31:3, "The Egyptians are men and not God; their horses are flesh and not spirit." Micah 5:10 also says, "In that day," declares the Lord, "I will destroy your horses from among you and demolish your chariots."

The author, Deborah Cantrell, is a historian, lawyer, and a free-lance writer and lives in Brentwood, Tennessee. She has been a horse breeder and participated in the archaeological digs at Megiddo in 2000, 2004, 2006, and 2008.[61]

Tabgha

Tabgha is the traditional site of the miracle of the multiplication of the loaves and fishes (read Mark 6:30-46).

Tabgha means "seven springs". In 1596, Tabgha was part of the Ottoman Empire and was a village in the Nahiya subdistrict of Jira, with a population of forty-four. The village paid taxes on wheat and barley crops, goats, beehives, and orchards.

In the 1931 census, Tabgha had fifty-three occupied houses and a population of 223 Muslims, twenty-one Christians, and one Jew. Until 1948, it was an Arab village.[62]

---

[61] Deborah Cantrell, *Horses as Symbols of Power*. Biblical Illustrator, LifeWay: Volume 39, number 2, Winter 2012-2013, 6-10.

[62] www.en.wikipedia.org/wiki/tabgha.

TABGHA (MULTIPLICATION): THE BENEDICTINE CHURCH OF THE LOAVES AND FISHES

Photo courtesy of the Israeli Ministry of Tourism and is solely for this photo only at www.goisrael.com

Tabgha Excavations

Excavations in Tabgha found remains of a mosaic floor from a 5th-century church. A new church by the same name of the Church of the Multiplication of the Loaves and Fishes was built in 1982, and is styled similar to the original church. There is an altar with loaves and fishes, and beneath the altar is a stone used as a table for the blessing of loaves and fishes. Tabgha is also known as Heptapegon, el-Oreme, En Sheva et-Tabgha. Seven springs were formerly at Tabgha, but only six springs are visible there today. These springs made the water warmer than the Sea of Galilee and helped to make algae, which attracted the fish. Fishermen have fished in the Sea of Galilee for thousands of years, and Tabgha had an ancient harbor.

In 1932, German archaeologists, Mader and Schneider, discovered many Byzantine Church walls and mosaics. In modern times, the German Association of the Holy Land under the leadership of the Archbishop of Cologne oversees the restored property.[63]

The Divine Dialogue in the Book of Habakkuk

The book of Habakkuk is a dialogue between God and the prophet Habakkuk, who questioned God about the injustices he saw around him in Judah. Habakkuk was shocked at God's solution of an invasion by the Babylonians. Eventually, Habakkuk understood God's solution and rejoiced in God's plan. The book of Habakkuk plays an important role in the New Testament, when Paul uses Habakkuk 2:4 ("But the righteous will live by his faith") as a main verse in explaining justification by faith in Romans 1:17 and Galatians 3:11.

Habakkuk lived in Judah, and his dialogue with God was before one of the Babylonian invasions.(597 BC or 586 BC). The prophet Jeremiah lived at the

---

[63]   Ibid.

same time as Habakkuk. The Book of Jeremiah and II Kings 22-25 describe the conditions of Habakkuk's time. Judah had a series of weak, unfaithful kings in collusion with corrupt priests and false prophets, who had led the people of Judah away from the true God of Abraham and Moses and into idolatry.

Habakkuk's first question to God was, "Why is there so much injustice in Judah, and why don't you do something about it? How long, O Lord, must I call for help, but you do not listen? Why do you make me look at injustice? Why do you tolerate wrong?" God replied, "I am doing something. I am raising up the Babylonians to invade Judah." God told Habakkuk to "look at the nations and watch and be utterly amazed" (v. 5), for God was "raising up the Babylonians, that ruthless and impetuous people" (v. 6), "feared and dreaded" (v. 7). In verses 8-11, God describes how terrible and horrific a Babylonian invasion would be. (See Habakkuk 1:1-11.)[64]

The earliest building at Tabgha was a small chapel built in the 4th century AD. Only a part of its foundations was discovered. This may have been the shrine Egeria saw and described at the end of the 4th century. Egeria wrote: "In the same place (not far from Capernaum) facing the Sea of Galilee is a well-watered land in which lush grasses grow, with numerous trees and palms. Nearby are seven springs which provide abundant water. In this fruitful garden Jesus fed five thousand people with five loaves of bread and two fish. The stone upon which the Master placed the bread became an altar. The many pilgrims to the site broke off pieces of it as a cure for their ailments."[65]

During the 5th century, the Christians built a large monastery and a church with mosaic floor decorations. They had many courtyards and rooms used as workshops for crafts and lodging for the monks and the visiting pilgrims. The monastery and church were destroyed in the 7th century, probably during the Arab conquests. The buildings and church were buried under a thick layer of stones and silt. In the 1980's after excavations, the church was restored to its Byzantine form with portions of the original mosaics.[66]

The basilical church has two rows of columns that form a central hall and two aisles. The eastern wall is a semi-circular apse, and on

---

[64]   Daniel Hays. *The Divine Dialogue in the Book of Habakkuk*. Biblical Illustrator, LifeWay: Volume 39, number 2, Winter 2012-2013, 11-14.

[65]   www.mfa.gov.il/mfa.

[66]   Ibid.

either side of it are rooms for the clergy. There is a raised platform in front of apse that has a huge chancel screen and untrimmed stone under the altar, which is located on the traditional site of the miracle of the Loaves and the Fishes. There is a mosaic showing a basket of bread flanked by two fish, found behind the untrimmed stone added in the 6th century. In modern times, it is found in front of the altar.[67] The Church of Peter's Primacy is located about 500 yards from the Multiplication of the Loaves and Fishes Church.[68]

The Tourism Ministry built a Tabgha-Capernaum promenade as a walkway to the Tabgha cove and the Church of Peter's Primacy. This is the traditional site of John 21 after the resurrection, and describes Jesus cooking breakfast for the disciples — the miraculous catch of fish and Peter's reconciliation.[69]

MT. TABOR: CHAPEL IN CHURCH OF THE TRANSFIGURATION (FRANCISCAN)

courtesy of the Israeli Ministry of Tourism and is solely for this photo only at www.goisrael.com

Mount Tabor

Mount Tabor is in Lower Galilee at the eastern end of the Jezreel Valley, eleven miles west of the Sea of Galilee. It was the site for the Mount Tabor battle that happened during the time of the Book of Judges. This was a battle between Canaanite forces of the King of Hazor with his commander Sisera, and the Israelite army led by Barak under the leadership of the judge Deborah. The battle took place in the mid-14th century BC. Deborah ordered Barak to march on Mount Tabor with an Israelite army and promised Barak that God would deliver the Canaanites into Barak's power. The Israelites marched to Mount Tabor and their movements were reported to Sisera. However, a heavy rain soaked the ground and made the Canaanites' chariots

---

[67] Ibid.

[68] www.goisrael.com/tourism.

[69] Ibid.

useless. Sisera fell from his chariot and escaped. Later, Sisera staggered into the tent of Yael, wife of Heber the Kenite, and begged her to protect him. Yael gave him some milk to drink and later put a tent peg through his skull, killing him after he fell asleep. Deborah had predicted that Sisera would be killed at the hands of a woman.

Many Christians believe that Mount Tabor is the location of the Transfiguration of Jesus. In the Biblical accounts, Jesus and three of his apostles go to a mountain. On the mountaintop, Jesus begins to shine with rays of light. Then the prophets Moses and Elijah appear next to him and Jesus talks to them. Jesus is called "Son" by a voice in the sky, which many believe was God the Father (read Matthew 17:1-19).

Other scripture accounts are Mark 9:2-8 and Luke 9-28-36. II Peter 1:16-18 has the message that God at the Transfiguration gave Jesus special honor and glory, and it is the turning point when God exalts Jesus above all other powers in creation and makes him as ruler and judge (read 2 Peter 1:16-18).

Matthew 22:32 teaches that God is "not the God of the dead, but of the living." Although Moses had died and Elijah (2 Kings 2:11) had been taken up to heaven centuries before, they now live in the presence of the Son of God.

I am the God of Abraham, and the God of Isaac, and the God of Jacob. God is not the God of the dead, but of the living (Matthew 22:32). And it came to pass, as they still went on, and talked, that, behold, there appeared a chariot of fire, and horses of fire, which parted them both asunder; and Elijah went up by a whirlwind into heaven (2 Kings 2:11).

Origen Adamantius, a scholar, writer, and theologian, was the first to say that the appearance of Moses and Elijah represented the "Law and the Prophets." Martin Luther wrote that Moses and Elijah appearing with Jesus is a symbol of how Jesus fulfills the "Law and the Prophets." Matthew 5:17 says, "Think not that I am come to destroy the law, or the prophets: I am not come to destroy, but to fulfill." Some Christians believe in "soul sleep" until the final resurrection. Some commentators believe that Jesus used the Greek word *orama*, which can be used as a vision instead of a real physical event. Those people conclude that Elijah and Moses were not really there at the Mount of Transfiguration.[70]

Mount Tabor was an important fortress during the First and Second Temple, and during the Greek, Roman, and Crusader periods of history. Mount Tabor is nine kilometers east of Nazareth. It is 613 meters above sea level and forty-six meters above the valley. It is not an extinct volcano, although it looks similar to one.[71]

Mount Tabor is named on the border of the tribe of Issachar: "The boundary also touched Tabor, Shahazumah, and Beth-shemesh, and its boundary ends at the Jordan – sixteen cities with their villages" (Joshua 19:22, ESV). It is probably the mountain to which Zebulun and Issachar were to call the people of Israel: "They summon the people to the mountain to offer proper sacrifices there. They benefit from the riches of the sea and the hidden treasures in the sand" (Deuteronomy 33:19, NLT).

Zebulun and Issachar shared the mountain and probably went to pilgrimages on the mountain. The worshipers brought with them fish and treasures of the sand, and the authorities liked for them to come. The brothers of Gideon may have been murdered here by Zeba and Zalmunna: "Then Gideon asked Zebah and Zalmunna, 'The men you killed at Tabor – what were they like?' 'Like you,' they replied. 'They all had the look of a king's son'" (Judges 8:18, NLT).

In 218 BC, during the time of Antiochus the Great, there was a fortress at Tabor. Janneus held the fortress for the Jews in 105-70 BC. Pompey took the fortress for the Romans. In 1113 AD, the Damascus Arabs attacked the monasteries and murdered the Monks. Mount Tabor has a height of 1,843 feet above the sea. From the south it looks like the shape of a hemisphere, and from the west it looks like a sugar loaf.[72] Jeremiah mentions Tabor also: "As I live, saith the King, whose name is the Lord of hosts, surely as Tabor is among the mountains, and as Carmel by the sea, so shall he come" (Jeremiah 46:18).

Hosea also speaks of Tabor: "Hear ye this, O priests; and hearken, ye house of Israel; and give ye ear, O house of the king; for judgment is toward you, because ye have been a snare on Mizpah, and a net spread upon Tabor" (Hosea 5:1).

---

[70]   www.enwikipedia.org/wiki/mt_tabor.

[71]   www.biblewalks.com/sites/tabor.htm.

[72]   www.bibleatlas.org/mount_tabor.htm.

Cana

The first miracle of Jesus of Nazareth was turning water into fine wine at a wedding in Cana (read John 2:1-11).

Matthew Henry's Complete Commentary on the Bible gives good information on this miracle. "The miracle itself was turning water into wine; the substance of water acquiring a new form, and having all the accidents and qualities of wine. Such a transformation is a miracle; but the popish transubstantiation, the substance changed, the accidents remaining the same, is a monster. By this Christ showed himself to be the God of nature, who maketh the earth to bring forth wine. The beginning of Moses' miracles was turning water into blood, and the beginning of Christ's miracles was turning water into wine; which intimates the difference between the law of Moses and the gospel of Christ."

-Jesus had power over nature. Examples: turning water into wine, calming the tempest, and walking on the sea.

-Jesus demonstrated his power over the demon world. Examples: He cured many demon-possessed people.

-Jesus demonstrated his power over death by raising the daughter of Jairus, the widow's son, and Lazarus from being dead.[73]

Jesus uses new wine as a type of new teaching and new truth. Jesus taught, "And no man putteth new wine into old bottles: else the new wine doth burst the bottles, and the wine is spilled, and the bottles will be marred; but new wine must be put into new bottles" (Mark 2:22). The Judaism during the time of Jesus called for using old bottles. In scripture, wine is a type of blessing:

Therefore God give thee of the dew of heaven and the fatness of the earth, and plenty of corn and wine (Genesis 27:28).

And he will love thee; he will also bless the fruit of your womb, and the fruit of thy land, thine corn and thine wine, and thine oil, the increase of thine kine, and the flocks of thy sheep, in the land which he swore unto thy fathers to give thee (Deuteronomy 7:13).

---

[73] www.bibletruths.net/archives/btar186.htm.

So shall thy barns be filled with plenty, and thy presses shall burst out with new wine (Proverbs 3:10).

Thus saith the Lord, "As the new wine is found in the cluster, and one saith, 'Destroy it not; for a blessing is in it'; so will I do for my servants' sakes, that I may not destroy them all" (Isaiah 65:8).

"Behold, the days come," saith the Lord, "that the plowman shall overtake the reaper, and the treader of grapes him that soweth seed; and the mountains shall drop sweet wine, and all the hills shall melt. (Amos 9:13).

Thou hast put gladness in my heart, more than in the time that their corn and their wine increased (Psalm 4:7).

Go thy way, eat thy bread with joy, and drink thy wine with a merry heart; for God now accepteth thy works (Ecclesiastes 9:7)

And joy and gladness is taken from the plentiful field, and from the land of Moab; and I have caused wine to fail from the winepresses; none shall tread with shouting; their shouting shall be no shouting (Jeremiah 48:33).

For how great is his goodness, and how great is his beauty! Corn shall make the young men cheerful, and new wine the maids (Zechariah 9:17).

And they of Ephraim shall be like a mighty man, and their heart shall rejoice as through wine; yea, their children shall see it, and be glad; their heart shall rejoice in the Lord (Zechariah 10:7).

The water pots at the wedding in Cana represented the purification of the Jews, which is an example of a religious ceremony. But the water pots were empty, representing the empty ceremonies of man. There were six water pots representing the creation of man in the sixth day. The water pots were made of stone, which represents the stony hearts of man: "A new heart also will I give you, and a new spirit will I put within you: and I will take away the stony heart out of your flesh, and I will give you an heart of flesh" (Ezekiel 36:26).

The water pots were to be filled to the top with water: "That he might sanctify and cleanse it with the washing of water by the word" (Ephesians 5:26). The water pots also represented the Spirit of God: "He that believeth on me, as the scripture hath said, out of his belly shall flow rivers of living water. But this spake he of the Spirit, which they that believe on him should receive: for the Holy Ghost was not yet given; because that Jesus was not yet glorified" (John 7:38-39).

The water pots were filled to the top. A firkin is about nine gallons, which totals almost 120 gallons altogether in the water pots.[74] Just as the water pots were filled up to the top and emptied of everything else, we need to empty ourselves of everything else in order to fill ourselves with the Spirit.

The Divine Dialogue in the Book of Habakkuk (continued)

Habakkuk's response to God was, "But the Babylonians are worse than we are" (see Habakkuk 1:12-2:1). Habakkuk said, "My God, my Holy One, we will not die. Your eyes are too pure to look on evil. Why then do you tolerate the treacherous? Why are you silent while the wicked (Babylonians) swallow up those more righteous (the people of Judah) than themselves?" (Habakkuk 1:12-13). Next, Habakkuk poetically compared the Babylonians to fishermen, using their nets and hooks to pull in the peoples from nations like fish from the sea (Habakkuk 1:14-17).

God gave his answer in Habakkuk 2:2-20: "This coming judgment is a certainty. You are to wait in expectation for it; afterward the Babylonians will get what is coming to them. In Habakkuk 2:2, God said, "Write down the revelation and make it plain on the tablets." In Habakkuk 2:5, God gave Habakkuk an example of two people. One of these people represented the Babylonians and was arrogant and greedy, taking people into captivity. The other person, by contrast, remained faithful to God even during the Babylonian atrocities, and this righteous person of faith would live (Habakkuk 2:6).

The person representing the Babylonians would receive the appropriate judgment. God described this judgment in Habakkuk 2:6-19, using five "woe" passages to be sung over fallen Babylonians. In Habakkuk 2:14, God said that he would be glorified. "The Lord is in his holy temple; let all the earth be silent before Him" (Habakkuk 2:20).

In Habakkuk 3:1-19, Habakkuk said, "I will wait for the coming judgment and yet still rejoice in God." In Habakkuk 3:2, he pleaded with God to remember mercy during His wrath. In Habakkuk 3:3-15, he describes God as a powerful warrior judging the whole world. In Habakkuk 3:16-19, he vowed to wait patiently for the judgment on Judah and the judgment on the Babylonians. He vowed to rejoice in all things, recognizing the fact that God gave him strength to endure.

---

[74] www.learnthebible.org/miracle-of-water-into-wine.html.

Daniel Hays, author of The Divine Dialogue, *is the dean of the Pruet School of Christian Studies and professor of Biblical Studies at Ouachita Baptist University in Arkadelphia, Arkansas.*[75]

Bethsaida

Peter, Philip, and Andrew lived in Bethsaida, not far from Capernaum. Bethsaida was the birthplace of Peter: And forthwith, when they were come out of the synagogue, they entered into the house of Simon and Andrew with James and John" (Mark 1:29).[76]

BETHSAIDA: EXCAVATION OF THE ANCIENT TOWN

Photo courtesy of the Israeli Ministry of Tourism and is solely for this photo only at www.goisrael.com

Bethsaida is an ancient fishing village developed in 10th century BC. Assyrians captured and burned the gates in 732 BC. Bethsaida has been excavated since 1987. Under a 1st-century fishing village, the archaeologists discovered the remains of an Iron Age city which is also mentioned in the Bible. American Edward Robinson found a promising mound in 1938. Since 1967 after the Six Day War, archaeologists are now certain that the artifacts found in 1938 belong to Bethsaida.

In the 14th century BC, Amarna letters of correspondence between Egyptian pharaohs and rulers in Palestine talked about the area of Bethsaida. In the 10th century, Bethsaida was the capital of Geshur, a small Aramaean kingdom: "This is the land that yet remaineth all the borders of the Philistines and all Geshur" (Joshua 13:2). "Nevertheless the children of Israel expelled not the Geshurites, nor the Maachathites: but the Geshurites and the Maachathites dwell among the Israelites until this day" (Joshua 13:13).

Geshur became part of ancient Israel when it was conquered by King David. Two kings of Geshur, Ammihud and his son Talmai, are mentioned in the Bible (read 2 Samuel 3:2-3).

---

[75] Daniel Hays, *The Divine Dialogue in the Book of Habakkuk.* Biblical Illustrator, LifeWay: Volume 39, number 2, Winter 2012-2013, 11-14.

[76] www.en.wikipedia.org/wiki/bethsaida_#.

So King David did marry Maacah, the daughter of King Talmai of Geshur, later called Bethsaida. It was the custom of the day to strengthen ties between two strong nations by having a marriage between the two families. The custom was for a new queen to bring her entire court with her, including architects. Some of the artwork can be seen in Bethsaida in modern times.

Absalom murdered his half-brother Amnon (II Samuel 13), led a rebellion against his father, King David, and was killed by David's general Joab. Absalom had a daughter, Maachah, named for his mother, and she grew up to marry Rehoboam, the son of Solomon. Rehoboam later ruled Judah: "And there was war between Rehoboam and Jeroboam all the days of his life" (I Kings 15:6).

In the 9th century BC, Bethsaida was captured by Aram, a rival of Israel. And in the 8th century BC, the Assyrian empire under emperor Tiglath-Pileser III burned parts of Bethsaida in 734 BC (see II Kings 15:29-30). Tiglath-Pileser III's successor, Shalmaneser IV, conquered northern Israel and deported the residents, and some never returned again. Bethsaida was an important city during the Greek period in the 4th century BC. In 30 AD, the son of King Herod, Philip, renamed Bethsaida, calling it Julias after the mother of the Roman emperor.[77] Bethsaida is a story of two cities, an iron-age city of the land of Geshur and a Roman city known as Julias.

In Bethsaida, there is still a cobbled street from the time of Jesus. Bethsaida has natural rock seats for people to use for Bible studies.[78] Bethsaida is located in the fertile delta of the upper Jordan River, and is thirty meters higher than the valley. It is 1.5 kilometers north of the Sea of Galilee, and four kilometers northeast of Capernaum. The ruins are on about twenty acres on the hill. The land of Geshur was the border of Joshua's territory.

Josephus fought against the Romans during the revolt of 66 AD. His horse fell into a quagmire, and threw Josephus to the ground. Josephus was taken to Capernaum. The ruins of a winemaker's house were found and reconstructed. This house was two stories high with a large courtyard on the street side, residence rooms on the north side, and a wine cellar on the east side. The house is dated from the

---

[77] www.jewishmag.com/69mag/bethsaida/bethsaida.htm.

[78] www.goisrael.com/tourism_eng/tourist

Hellenistic period (2nd century BC) to the early Roman period (1st century AD). The residence rooms were found on the north side of the courtyard. Archaeologists also found a large shard incised with a cross, which was at the entrance from the courtyard to the rooms. The wine cellar was located on the external east side of the house. It was made of several long slabs of basalt stone stretched over a wall. Four huge wine jars were found in this house, and seventeen wine jugs were in a nearby house. The kitchen area was on the eastern side of the house.

The ruins of a fisherman's house were also found and reconstructed. This house was a single story with a large courtyard on the street side, residence rooms on the north side and a kitchen on the east side. Many fishing tools were found on this site, such as lead weights for the nets, iron anchors, and fishing hooks. There is a sacrificial high place on the southern side of the inner gate. Here, the pit contained bones of kosher animals. A gate altar ("bamah" in Hebrew) was discovered in front of the inner gate house. The size of the altar is 1.6 meters by 2.1 meters. It has basalt stones with two steps leading to the top.[79]

A 9th-century gatehouse was also found in Bethsaida. Radar scans have been made, and show that a 10th-century gate and bulwarks lie underneath. The early city was built in two parts: the upper city and lower city. The upper city was for public buildings and fortifications, and the lower city was for residential areas. The city wall, built on a steep ramp, is preserved to a height of 1.6 meters and is filled with field stones and outer layers of large boulders. There are two gates separated by a huge paved courtyard, and there is a tower on either side of the gates. Since there are no wheel marks, Bethsaida may not have had chariots.

The inner gatehouse has four compartments. The gatehouse was found in a huge heap of rubble and stones caused by the Assyrian destruction. The wooden beams built between the stone of the gate may have helped to preserve it. There were two rooms on either side, and the house had two or three stories. The rooms were built of large sun-dried bricks, almost three meters thick. Two of the rooms were granaries and one was full of burnt barley. One of the rooms had

---

[79] www.biblewalks.com/sites/bethsaida.html.

arrows and spear heads, from the battle against Tiglath-Pileser. A jug with an Egyptian sign of life, an *ankh*, was discovered.

On the outside on both sides of the inner gate are niches for cultic practices. There are two steps leading to a basalt stone basin with two incense burners. The archaeologists found tiny perforated cups with burn marks. Visitors may have burned incense there centuries ago. Archaeologists found scattered pieces of a basalt stele, a standing stone, which went behind the basalt basin years ago. Archaeologists studied it and saw a mean-looking bull-headed object with horns, carrying daggers. This is the only stele found in Israel, where steles are rare to find. Only three other bull steles were found in all of Mesopotamia. The figure may be the Mesopotamian moon god Sin, believed to be the creator of the universe and moon. On the left side, the niche had a shelf, maybe a biblical platform with no steps in front of it. Maybe the lack of steps had something to do with the ban on stepped altars: "Neither shalt thou go up by steps unto mine altar, that thy nakedness be not discovered thereon" (Exodus 20:26). Archaeologists think that the left niche was for Israelite visitors of the city or Israelites who had married Geshurites, and the other niche was for worshipers of the moon god.

On the inside gate was a 9th-century palace with a vestibule, a main room, a throne room, and eight other rooms. It survived the Assyrian conquest and has now been renovated. Artwork depicting the Egyptian god Pataekos was found here. Pataekos was one of the children of Ptah, the god of artists and craftsmen. It had a dwarf with a beaded necklace and two knives. Ptah probably stood on a crocodile. On Ptah's leg is a sharp cup which may be connected to a crocodile. The statuette has traces of a turquoise glaze.

The palace had a pottery inscription from the 8th century BCE, with the name "Akiba". In the rebellion against Rome in 132-135 AD, Rabbi Akiba was a famous rebel leading the way in fighting Rome. Two handles with inscriptions of the name Zechario (remembered by the Lord) were also found, which may have belonged to the son of Jeroboam II, king of Israel, before Zechariah became king in 748 BC. The second handle had the letters MKY, short for *Michyahu*, meaning "who is like the Lord."

A temple, dating to the Roman period, was dug out with a columned porch, hall, a long rectangular Holy of Holies, and a small back room. Three coins with a picture of Philip were found. It is possible that these coins were given out in the renaming ceremony of Bethsaida, when it was called Julias.[80]

Bethsaida is located north of the Sea of Gaililee. Jesus healed a blind man here, and it is the birthplace of Peter, Andrew, and Philip (read Mark 8:22-26; Luke 9:10).

Tel Hazor

Tel Hazor is also known as Hazor, Tel al-Qedah, Tel Khuralbeh, Hazzur, and Waqqas. It was known in the time of Joshua as "the head of all those kingdoms". "At that time Joshua turned back and captured Tel Hazor and put its king to the sword. Everyone in it they put to the sword. They totally destroyed them, not sparing anything that breathed, and he burned up Hazor itself" (Joshua 11:10-11). "Hazor will become a haunt of jackals, a desolate place forever. No one will live there; no man will dwell in it" (Jeremiah 49:33).

In modern times, Tel Hazor is 200 acres in size, making it the largest tell in Israel. In Israel a tell is an archaeological site. In the Canaanite period, Tel Hazor filled the entire tell. When the Israelites took over, the fortified city included only the Upper City.

Archaeologists have discovered a six-chambered gate, identified as a Solomonic gate:

"And this is the reason of the levy which King Solomon raised: for to build the house of the Lord, and his own house, and Millo, and the wall of Jerusalem, and Hazor, and Megiddo, and Gezer" (1 Kings 9:15).

One hundred years after Solomon, the Israelites built a huge shaft forty meters deep into the tell, to reach the water table. The nineteen-meter vertical shaft was about fifteen meters square and ended at a broad sloping tunnel that went twenty-five more meters. This is very similar to the one at Megiddo and Gibeon.

---

[80] www.jewishmag.com/69mag/bethsaida/bethsaida.htm

Some of the remains date to the Middle and Late Bronze Ages, during the time of the Canaanites. Many ruins in the Lower City had religious figurines or standing stones. It also has a storehouse and stable ruins. Archaeologists believe that these were used to store food and to house the royal cavalry.

A popular house plan was the "pillared house" with a variation of differing numbers of rooms; some had as many as four. The pillared house always had a row or two of pillars to separate the central court from the side room.[81]

Excavations began in 1990 with Amnon Ben-Tor of the Hebrew University of Jerusalem as the leader. Excavations run every year from the last week of June through the first week of August.

The population of the Canaanite city of Hazor was 40,000. Archaeologists have found twenty-two layers of civilization there. These layers represent 2,700 years of inhabitants. Hazor is at the foot of the eastern ridge of the Upper Galilee mountain range and is eight miles north of the Sea of Galilee. The military and commercial road in ancient times went from Egypt to Mesopotamia through Syria and the Hittite region.

Sometimes Hazor was called Hatzor, and it is the only Palestinian settlement mentioned among the 25,000 cuneiform tablets in the royal documents of Mari or Tell Hariri found in modern Syria. Most of these documents date back to the reigns of Zimri-Lin and King Hammurapi of Babylon in the 18th century BC. Seven tablets relating to Hatzor have been discovered. One of the tablets says that Hatzor was important enough for King Hammurapi to put two ambassadors there. Other tablets describe Hatzor and the trade of tin. Tin was important before the use of iron was discovered. Eighteenth-century tablets show the ambassador of the lawgiver Hammurabi as a resident in Hatzor. Hatzor was also a military target for the pharaohs of Egypt from the eighteenth dynasty until the time of Rameses II.

The Solomonic city of Hatzor was inherited by the northern kingdom of Israel. Hatzor came to a fiery end in the early 9th century BC, when Ben-Hadad I of Damascus invaded Israel at the request of King Asa of Judah. It was rebuilt later by either Omri or Ahab. They built a rectangular shaft that took the shaft and tunnel to the water

---

[81]   www.bibleplaces.com/hazor.htm.

table inside the city walls. Hatzor was destroyed by the Assyrian armies of Tiglath-Pileser during his first campaign against Israel in 733 BC.[82]

"In the days of Pekah king of Israel, Tiglath-Pileser king of Assyria came and captured Ijon and Abel-Beth-Maacah, and Janoah and Kedesh and Hazor and Gilead and Galilee, all the land of Naphtali; and he carried them captive to Assyria" (II Kings 15:29, NAS).

Earlier archaeological excavations began in 1955 when James A. de Rothschild funded the expedition. Rothschild published a five-volume set of books by the Israel Exploration Society. In 2005 Hazor was put on the World Heritage Site by UNESCO to join the Biblical Tels of Megiddo, and Beer Sheba.

Hazor is mentioned in 18th-century BC documents found in Mari on the Euphrates River. Assyrian records indicate that Joash, the King of Israel, paid tribute to Assyria, and Israel became an Assyrian vassal. This caused Israel to have a period of great prosperity during the rule of Jeroboam II.[83]

The excavation on July 25, 2012, at Tel Hazor National Park in the upper Galilee by Hebrew University of Jerusalem and the Israel Nature and Parks Authority discovered fourteen large pithoi-styled storage jugs filled with 3,300-year-old burnt wheat.[84]

BANIAS NATURE RESERVE: TRAIL ENTRANCE FOR THE BIG WATERFALL
photo courtesy of the Israeli Ministry of Tourism and is solely for this photo only at www.goisrael.com

The Banias Waterfall is the biggest waterfall in Israel. It is located in the Upper Golan area, between the fertile Hula Valley and the Mount Hermon mountain area. The falls entrance is the first one on the road heading northeast. The path to the waterfall is a short walk down to the suspended trail. The springs entrance takes you to the old temple

---

[82] www.bibarch.com/archaeologicalsites/hazor.htm.

[83] www.religion.wikia.com/wik/tel_hazor.

[84] www.travelujah.com/blogs/entry/telhazor-reveals-proof-of-the-book-of-joshua.

complex that is now ruins, which show devotion to the false gods of the Greeks and Romans. The name Banias is an Arabic word for the Greek god Pan, god of the forests and shepherds.

Banias Falls Park entrance has a large parking lot, and a place to buy ice cream, snacks, and hot Druze pitas. One ticket covers both entrances, a 45-minute walk round-trip, and the suspended trail. The waterfalls have more water in winter and spring, when the water is more plentiful on its way down to the Sea of Galilee. The waterfall is thirty-three feet high.

Banias Springs Park entrance has a smaller parking lot, with places to buy food and a gift shop. There is a wide mouth of Pan's Cave that can be seen from the road. Before the cave is Hermon Stream, which sometimes overflows onto the paved walkway. Around the temple ruins and courts, built by Agrippa II after Herod's son, Philip made the city Caesarea Philippi in the Banias. Along the trails, tourists can see the Officer's Pool, a hot spring built by the Syrians and used by officers, an old Roman bridge, an operational flour mill with olive press facilities, and a hydroelectric station. There are also gates, walls, and moats from the Crusader and Mameluke times and an old synagogue near the old city ruins.[85]

The Banias waterfall and stream provide water to the Jordan River, which it meets a few kilometers downstream. The old city that is at Banias was Dan and the Fort of Dan, and it stood on top of a cliff with a cave dedicated to Pan, the Greek god. During conquests, Dan fell to the Romans. King Herod built a temple in memory of Augustus. Phillip, Herod's son, changed Dan to Caesarea Philippi. The Banias site is where Jesus demanded from his disciples to tell who people said he was.[86]

When Jesus came into the coasts of Caesarea Philippi, he asked his disciples, saying, "Whom do men say that I the Son of man am?" And they said, "Some say that thou art John the Baptist: some, Elias; and others, Jeremias, or one of the prophets." He saith unto them, "But whom say ye that I am?" And Simon Peter answered and said, "Thou art the Christ, the Son of the living God." And Jesus answered and said unto him, "Blessed art thou, Simon Bar-jona: for flesh

---

[85] www.touristisrael.com/banias-nature-reserve/6233.

[86] www.touristisrael.com/banias-waterfall/3613.

and blood hath not revealed it unto thee, but my Father which is in heaven. And I say also unto thee, that thou art Peter, and upon this rock I will build my church; and the gates of hell shall not prevail against it. And I will give unto thee the keys of the kingdom of heaven and whatsoever thou shalt bind on earth shall be bound in heaven: and whatsoever thou shalt loose on earth shall be loosed in heaven." (Matthew 16:13-19)

Godliness: A First-Century Understanding

Pastors sometimes have difficulties in leading the church but do not know how quickly to make changes or address issues. Pastors do not want to offend anyone but they believe the issues need to be resolved.

Paul, the Apostle, first visited Ephesus on his third missionary journey where he stayed for about three years. Paul warned the church leaders that "savage wolves" would come in among them and bring "deviant doctrines" to lure them away (Acts 20:29-30). False teachers did come and taught "deviant doctrines." Because of this, Paul asked Timothy to stay in Ephesus to "instruct certain people not to teach different doctrine" (I Timothy 1:3). Paul's first instruction to Timothy was to "point out these things to the brothers" (I Timothy 4:6). "These things" refer to the false proclamations that came from "deceitful spirits and the teachings of demons" (I Timothy 4:1). The false teachers "forbid marriage and demand abstinence from food that God created to be received with gratitude" (I Timothy 4:3). Paul asked Timothy to expose the false teaching and then offer the biblical response to the heresy. Paul reminded Timothy what the Bible said about food and marriage. In I Timothy 4:4-5, Paul wrote, "Everything created by God is good, and nothing should be rejected if it is received with thanksgiving, since it is sanctified by the word of God and by prayer." Paul stressed to Timothy that marriage and food are good because God created both. Next Paul asked Timothy to train "himself in godliness" (I Timothy 4:7). Training for godliness is valuable because it "holds promise for the present life and also for the life to come" (I Timothy 4:8)

Paul used the term godliness in only three of his thirteen letters: in First and Second Timothy and Titus. People of the ancient Greek culture used the word "godliness" to describe piety, reverence, and loyalty to be used with parents or deities. The Roman culture expected people to show reverence to their parents and gods. The books of Proverbs and Isaiah use the word godliness for covenant loyalty and the appropriate response to the law. A New Testament scholar, Philip Towner, explained Paul's use of the word "godliness" to mean "comprehensively

100

the integration of the outward and inward dimensions of life, and it was to be lived actively (I Timothy 4:7-8) and intentionally" (Titus 2:12). Paul was telling Timothy that his lifestyle needed to reflect his belief in God's words.

Paul told Timothy to first teach correct doctrine. One effective way to battle false doctrine is to teach constantly the correct doctrine. One of the things in Paul's letter is teaching. Timothy learned to combat strange or unorthodox beliefs by his teaching and by modeling a godliness lifestyle. Paul's words to Timothy are relevant for us in modern times. Christians must know sound doctrine and model their lifestyle to godliness in behavior.

Shawn L. Buice is professor of New Testament and Greek and director of the Mid-Atlantic Theological Seminary, Northeast Campus, Schenectady, New York.[87]

Assyria and the Eighth-Century Hebrew Prophets

The tenth century (1000-900 BC) had events like the United Monarchy, the split of the kingdom after Solomon's death, and the early years of the Divided Monarchy. In the ninth century (900-800 BC) the northern nation of Israel dominated the Biblical story. In the eighth century (800-700 BC) it started off peacefully, but ended with the annihilation of Israel and the near destruction of Judah at the hands of the Assyrian Empire. Amos and Hosea delivered God's messages in response to this Assyrian threat.

Assyria first became an important power in northern Mesopotamia during the time of Abraham, Isaac, and Jacob, but was not as great a power as Babylon under King Hammurabi. Assyria did not become powerful for centuries until the Divided Monarchy period. The history of this era of Assyrian power was known as the New-Assyrian Empire. Cuneiform documents from sculptured panels from Assyrian royal palaces, and other archaeological evidence, prove the greatness of Assyria.[88]

Rice was the main crop during the Hellenistic period. In 636 AD, the Arabs captured the region and grew cotton and sugar cane. In the 8th century, water buffalo supplied milk and transportation. Lake Hula was called Samchuna by the Egyptians in the 14th Century BC. The

---

[87] Shawn L. Buice, *Godliness: A First Century Understanding.* Biblical Illustrator, LifeWay: Volume 39, number 2, Winter 2012-2013, 34-37.

[88] Daniel C. Browning, Jr., *Assyria and the Eighth-Century Hebrew Prophets.* Biblical Illustrator, LifeWay: Volume 39, number 2, Winter 2012-2013, 38-42.

Bible called Lake Hula by the name of Merom. It is now called Agam ha-Hula in Hebrew. On both sides of Hula Valley are steep slopes, the Golden Heights, and the Upper Galilee's Naftali Mountains.

People lived in the Lake Hula area in pre-historic times, and the first permanent settlement, Enan (Mallaha), dates back to about 9,000 years ago. The Hula Valley was a main junction on an important trade route connecting Damascus with the eastern Mediterranean coast and Egypt.[89] The Bible records Lake Merom as the site of a victory of Joshua over the Canaanites (read Joshua 11:5-7).

In the 19th century, the Hula Valley was the home of Bedouins who made handicrafts from the dry reeds. In 1882, a traveler wrote about hunting panthers, leopards, bears, wild boars, wolves, foxes, jackals, hyenas, gazelles, and otters. The first modern Jewish settlement in Hula Valley was Yesod Ha Ma'ala in 1883. In 1948, thirty-five villages were in the Hula Valley (twelve Jewish and twenty-three Arab).[90]

About two thirds of the water flowing into Lake Hula came from the Jordan River. The Dan, Hazbani, and Banias rivers begin at Mount Hermon and converge together in the flat center of the Hula River and form the Jordan River.[91]

THE SUN RISING OVER THE HULA VALLEY IN GALILEE
Photo by Itamar Grinberg, courtesy of the Israeli Ministry of Tourism and is solely for this photo only at www.goisrael.com

Assyria and the Eighth-Century Hebrew Prophets (continued)

Assyrian King Adadnirari II, who reigned from 911 BC to 891 BC, took Assyria out of the dark ages and it became a strong power in Mesopotamia. His grandson, Ashurnasirpal II, who ruled from 883-859 BC, turned Assyria into a powerful empire, using a

---

89   www.wikipedia.org/wiki/hula_valley.
90   www.wikipedia.org/wiki/hula_valley.
91   www.jewishvirtuallibrary.org/jsource/society.

method of psychological warfare involving extortion, battle tactics, expert siege warfare, and excessive cruelty and publicity.

Almost yearly, King Ashurnasirpal II took his troops out to invade smaller nations and make them give allegiance to Assyria. The king then demanded yearly payments of gold, silver, and other products of value. The Assyrians climbed the walls of cities who resisted. Rulers' heads were cut off and set on pikes. Supporters of the ruler were buried alive or impaled while prisoners were carried away as slaves. The Assyrian rulers built large palaces decorated with reliefs showing these cruel acts. The king set up puppet rulers to impose fines on the people of the conquered nation. The people paying the fines had to pass through palace rooms with pictures of what happened to people who resisted or rebelled.

Shalmaneser III, who ruled from 858 BC to 824 BC, continued to launch annual military campaigns. The Bible does not mention Shalmaneser III, but his kingdom provided the earliest certain extra-biblical mention of Hebrew kings. King Ahab was the most powerful and successful 9th-century king of Israel. Once Ahab defeated and trapped Ben-Hadad, King of Aram-Damascus or Aram or Syria (I Kings 20:26-34). The prophets of Israel condemned King Ahab because he released Ben-Hadad instead of destroying him (I Kings 20:35-43). The nations of Israel and Aram both faced problems with Assyria, and Ahab may have thought he needed Ben-Hadad later. A few years later, Jehu took over the throne and eradicated the descendants of King Ahab. In Aram, Ben-Hadad was killed by a coup.[92]

Dig Deeper into the Rich History of Israel

Northern Israel, the area along the modern-day Israel Gospel Trail, has much history in the Bible, especially the New Testament during the life of Jesus and the disciples. For more reading, below are some locations along the Jesus Trail and passages where they appear in the Bible.

Capernaum:
Matthew 9:1-9
Mark 1:21-31
Mark 2:13-17

---

[92]   Daniel C. Browning, Jr., *Assyria and the Eighth-Century Hebrew Prophets*. Biblical Illustrator, LifeWay: Volume 39, number 2, Winter 2012-2013, 38-42.

Luke 5:27-29
Luke 6:15
Luke 7:1-5

Jordan River:
Matthew 3:1-17
Luke 3:1-22

Korazim (Chorazin):
Matthew 11:20-24
Luke 8:26-39

Nazareth:
Matthew 13:53-58
Luke 1:26-29
Luke 4:16-30

Tabgha:
Mark 6:30-46
John 21:1-25
Mount Tabor:
Joshua 19:22
Judges 8:18
Matthew 17:1-9
II Peter 1:16-18

Cana:
John 2:1-11

Bethsaida:
Mark 1:29
Mark 8:22-26

Tel Hazor:
II Kings 15:29

CHAPTER 6

JERUSALEM

The Israel Museum began in 1965 as Israel's national museum. It is built on a hill near the Bible Lands Museum, the Knesset, the Israeli Supreme Court, and the Hebrew University of Jerusalem. A special building has the Shrine of the Book as well as the Dead Sea Scrolls and artifacts from Masada. The museum is known as one of the world's best museums in art and archaeology. The Israel Museum has encyclopedic collections dating from prehistoric times to modern times. This museum receives about 800,000 tourists every year. The Samuel and Saiyde Bronfman Archaeology Wing has the largest collection of Israel artifacts in the world. It has a collection of Holy Land archaeology that tells the story of the ancient Land of Israel. It is organized chronologically from prehistoric times through the Ottoman Empire. It includes Hebrew writing, glass, and coins. Interesting items from Egypt, the Near East, Greece, Italy, and the Islamic world are displayed in a nearby room.[93]

About 100,000 schoolchildren visit the youth wing of the Israel Museum each year. It has exhibition galleries, art studios, classrooms, a library of illustrated children books, and a recycling room.

Assyria and the Eighth-Century Hebrew Prophets (continued)

Jehu, who used force to take over from King Ahab, was forced to pay tribute to Assyrian King Shalmaneser III in Mt. Carmel. Jehu holds the record of being

---

[93] www.en.wikipedia.org/wiki/israel_museum.

the only Hebrew king for whom we have a likeness on a black obelisk discovered in the Assyrian capital of Calah. The image shows Jehu bowing in submission to King Shalmaneser III.

Assyria eventually left Israel and Ammon alone. Ammon became more powerful and oppressed Israel as the prophet Elisha predicted (I1 Kings 8:12). The beginning of the eighth century began peacefully and was the most prosperous time for the nation since the United Monarchy. But Israel began to show social, economic, and religious decay. When Tiglath-Pileser III became the new Assyrian king he adopted aggressive action against neighboring countries and made his military to be feared. Soon Aram (Syria) was conquered under King Rezin and Israel under King Menahem (I1 Kings 15:19-20).

In the second half of the eighth century, prophets Amos and Hosea wrote to the northern nation of Israel, and Isaiah and Micah wrote to the southern nation of Judah. The Old Testament shows how God made promises to them in covenants. God promised Abraham that his descendants would be a great nation in the Promised Land. Through Moses God promised to drive away Israel's enemies if Israel kept God's commandments. God told David that his descendants would rule forever. But the split of the kingdom brought on two centuries of Israel and Judah fighting each other and other countries. The prophets believed God's people did not keep God's commandments, so God did not want to drive their enemies out of the land. Amos announced that God had sworn, "They shall take you away with hooks, even the last of you with fishhooks" (Amos 4:2). Amos did not name Assyria as the enemy, but Assyria had the reputation of cruel treatment of prisoners. The prophet Hosea had the message that Israel's idolatry was like his wife's adultery, and both were overcome by redeeming love (Amos 1-3).

Daniel C. Browning Jr. is professor of religion and history at William Carey University in Hattiesburg, Mississippi.[94]

MODEL OF THE SECOND TEMPLE AT THE ISRAEL MUSEUM, JERUSALEM

Courtesy of the Israeli Ministry of Tourism and is solely for this photo only at www.goisrael.com

---

[94] Daniel C. Browning, Jr., *Assyria and the Eighth-Century Hebrew Prophets*. Biblical Illustrator, LifeWay: Volume 39, number 2, Winter 2012-2013, 38-42.

The Second Temple model is a replica of Herod's Temple and is now a permanent part of the museum's twenty-acre campus. It shows what Jerusalem was like before the city's destruction by the Romans. This model was first commissioned in 1966 at the Holyland Hotel in Bayit VeGan, Jerusalem, by the owner Hans Kroch to honor his son Yaakov, an IDF soldier killed in the Israeli War of Independence in 1948.[95]

The Israel Museum has a "House of David" inscription (9th century BC), a display of two shrines (8th-7th century BC), the Heliodorus Stele (178 BC), a royal Herodian bathhouse (1st century BC), a "Hadrian's Triumph" inscription from a triumphal arch (136 AD), and gold glass bases from the Roman Catacombs (4th century AD).

The Shrine of the Book, a wing of the Israel Museum, holds the Dead Sea Scrolls, the oldest biblical manuscripts in the world. The scrolls were found in 1947-1956 in eleven caves in the area of Wadi Qumran. David Samuel Gottesman, a Hungarian emigrant, bought the scrolls as a gift to Israel and paid for the construction of the building to house them. The shrine is a white dome. A rotation system is used to display some of the scrolls at the same time.

European, modern, and Israeli art is displayed. Some of the famous artists featured are Rembrandt, Marc Chagall, Camille Pissarro, Abel Pann, and Reuven Rubin. The Jack, Joseph, and Morton Mandel Wing for Jewish Art and Life has material culture of worldwide Jewish communities from the Middle Ages to the present day. Ritual ceremonies of birth, marriage, and death are included.

The Billy Rose Art Garden features modern and abstract sculptures. The garden campus was designed by Japanese-American sculptor Isamu Noguchi and is considered to be one of the best sculptures of the 20th century. The American Friends of the Israel Museum raised $270 million in cash to help fund the exhibits.[96]

---

[95]   www.en.wikipedia.org/wiki/model_of_Jerusalem_in_the_late_2nd_temple.
[96]   www.en.wikipedia.org/wiki/israel_museum.

TOWER OF DAVID: OUTSIDE VIEW

Photo courtesy of the Israeli Ministry of Tourism and is solely for this photo only at www.goisrael.com

The Tower of David is an old citadel near the Jaffa Gate entrance to the Old City of Jerusalem. The Tower of David citadel standing in modern times was built in the 2nd century BC, was later destroyed, and then rebuilt by the Christian, Muslim, Mamluk, and Ottoman conquerors of Jerusalem. It has important archaeological artifacts dating back 2,700 years. It is popular today for craft shows, concerts, and sound-and-light acts. The Byzantine Christians believed this to be the site of the palace of King David, and they named it "Tower of David."[97]

In 1989, the Jerusalem Foundation opened the Tower of David Museum of the History of Jerusalem. The museum contains a court-yard with archaeological ruins dating back 2,700 years. The exhibits use maps, videotapes, holograms, drawings, and models to tell 4,000 years of the history of Jerusalem. By 2002, over 3.5 million visitors had toured the museum.[98]

AN INSIDE VIEW FROM THE TOWER OF DAVID

Courtesy of the Israeli Ministry of Tourism and is solely for this photo only at www.goisrael.com

King David and King Solomon made the first fortifications to the Old City walls. King Hezekiah later added some fortifications. Centuries later, the Hasmonean kings made a wall and large watchtowers that historian Josephus Flavius (1st century BC) called the First Wall. Later, after the fall of the Hasmoneans, King Herod took over and added three huge towers in 37-34 BC to the fortifications at the northwest corner of the Western Hill, where the Tower of David is now. His goal was to defend Jerusalem and to protect his palace on nearby Mount Zion. King Herod named the tallest tower (145 feet tall) the Phasael in

---

97   www.en.wikipedia.org/wiki/tower_of_david.
98   www.en.wikipedia.org/wiki/tower_of_david.

memory of his brother who killed himself. Another tower was named Miriam, after his second wife whom he executed and buried in a cave to the west of the tower. King Herod named the third tower Hippicus after a friend, and this tower is the only one standing in modern era.

After the destruction of Jerusalem in 70 AD, the Romans used the tower as a barracks for the Roman troops. After the Roman Empire accepted Christianity in the 4th century, monks lived in the citadel. In 638, the Arab Muslim rulers rebuilt the citadel. The Tower of David survived the assault of the Crusaders in 1099 and surrendered only when the Muslims were guaranteed a safe trip out of Jerusalem. During the Crusader period, thousands traveled to Jerusalem by way of the port of Jaffa. To make the travelers safe from robbers, the Crusaders built a tower surrounded by a moat on top of the citadel and stationed guards to watch the road to Jaffa. In 1187, Saladin took over Jerusalem and the citadel. The Mamluks destroyed it in 1260 but built it back later. The Ottomans rebuilt it again between 1537 and 1541. For 400 years, the citadel was a garrison for Turkish troops. The Ottomans built a mosque at the citadel and added the minaret which still stands today. Minarets are described by many as a "gate from heaven and earth".

In World War I, General Edmund Allenby and the British troops captured Jerusalem. At that time, General Allenby made an announcement from a platform outside the entrance to the Tower of David.[99]

The Citadel of Jerusalem is another name for the Tower of David. The first archaeological excavations on site took place between 1934 and 1947. Other excavations took place between 1968 and 1988 to prepare for the opening of the museum. In the foundations of the citadel are the remains of Jerusalem's fortifications from the end of the monarchic period (8th to 6th centuries BC) through the early Arab period (7th to 11th centuries AD). The entrance to the citadel is from the east through an outer gate, across a bridge over the moat, and through a fortified inner gate house.

A tower in the southern part of the citadel was built in the 1st century AD and destroyed in the first Jewish Rebellion in 66-70 AD. Archaeologists uncovered a thick layer of trash, stones, plaster, and charred wooden roofing beams. Archaeologists also uncovered clay water pipe sections bearing seal impressions, "LXF" for Legio X

---

[99]   www.en.wikipedia.org/wiki/tower_of_david.

Fretensis, which was the full name of the Tenth Roman Legion stationed at the citadel. Archaeologists found fragments of fortifications, walls, cisterns, and a lintel engraved with a cross during the Byzantine period. In modern times, the citadel is not used for military activities but now functions as a museum of the history of Jerusalem.[100]

The oldest remains of a city wall date back to the time of King Hezekiah but are still buried in the bedrock of a nearby hill. King Hezekiah built a wall and towers at the end of the 8th century BC after the Assyrian invasion of Judah:

"Also he strengthened himself, and built up all the wall that was broken, and raised it up to the towers, and another wall without, and repaired Millo in the city of David, and made darts and shields in abundance" (2 Chronicles 32:5).

The wall was seven meters wide and built of large rock, and it was damaged during the Babylonian attack on Jerusalem in 587-586 BC. In future years, Jerusalem shrunk back to the city of David on the eastern hill, and therefore the western-hill wall and tower did not need to be repaired or rebuilt. King Herod built a fort at the citadel and built his wonderful palace south of the citadel. King Herod built three new towers to defend the wall, citadel, and palace. The Roman governor in 6 AD lived in Herod's palace. According to the New Testament, Jesus was judged here by Pilate (read Luke 22:54-71).

Jewish rebels were taken to the citadel before the Roman ruler, scourged, and then crucified. This cruelty was one of the causes of the First Jewish War. In 66 AD, Jewish rebels succeeded in attacking and burning the palace. They dug a mine from a great distance and made it totter, according to Josephus' *The Jewish War*. Modern archaeologists have found remains in the south of the courtyard where once one of Herod's towers may have stood. Later, the Ottoman troops were stationed inside the city walls on the south side of the fortress, which is the location of Herod's palace.

In modern times, the remains of the Turkish camp can still be seen at the base of the wall. It is recommended to tourists to first study the exhibitions and film about Jerusalem inside the towers and the former

---

[100] www.jewishvirtuallibrary.org/jsource/archaeology/citadel.html..

mosque. It is nice for tourists to climb the towers and ramps and look down at the archaeological garden below.[101]

The Bank of Israel issued a gold coin of the Tower of David in 2010. The Tower of David is the first coin in the "Jerusalem of Gold" series that will be issued annually to show a treasured historical site in Jerusalem. The coin contains one ounce of fine gold and has a face value of twenty shekels (NIS). The front of the coin has the Lion of Megiddo with the state emblem above and the word "Israel" in Hebrew, English, and Arabic below. The back side shows the Tower of David rising above the Old City of Jerusalem's walls near the Jaffa Gate. The word Jerusalem is written over the tower in Hebrew, English, and Arabic. The proof-like mintmark is a six-pointed Star of David. The catalog number is FR 118, Denomination 20 NIS, Type Gold/9999, Diameter 32 mm, weight 31.1 grams, mintage 3,600. For more information on these coins, visit www.commem.com/prod02zzzb.htm, or in the USA call toll free at 800-913-9677.

A VIEW OF JAFFA GATE (PANORAMA 3)
Photo courtesy of the Israeli Ministry of Tourism and is solely for this photo only at www.goisrael.com

Jaffa Gate

Jaffa Gate leads to the Christian, Armenian, and Jewish Quarters of the Old City. An inscription above the gate reads, "There is no God but Allah and Ibrahim is his friend." The Arabs call it the Gate of the Friend. A person can enter the Citadel of David through this gate. In 1898, Kaiser Wilhelm II of Germany influenced the Arabs to make a doorway between Jaffa Gate and David's Citadel. The Kaiser wanted to dedicate his new Lutheran Church of the Redeemer, located near the Church of the Holy Sepulchre. The Kaiser wanted to enter Jerusalem

---

[101]   www.jewishmag.com/29mag/david/david.htm.

on horseback, riding in a triumphal procession. The Arabs objected because it looked too much like a conquest. The Turks wanted to make an alliance with the Kaiser and Germany and at the same time keep peace with all the Arabs.

The compromise that they reached was not to tear down Jaffa Gate but to cut a hole big enough for the Kaiser and his horse. Everyone was happy with the arrangement: the Arabs kept their traditions, the Kaiser could ride on horseback to his new church, and the Turks achieved a new alliance with Germany. The Arabs sealed this gate in 1948 and the Israelis reopened it in 1967.

Jaffa Gate is found on the western side of the Old City, above the Hinnon Valley. Jaffa got its name because people walking from the dock at the Mediterranean port of Jaffa on Jaffa Road could reach Jaffa Gate in three days. Today, if you exit Jaffa Gate and turn left, walk across the Hinnon Valley, and walk on Hebron Road, you finally reach Hebron where Abraham is buried.[102]

Before the 19th century, Jaffa Gate was locked every night to protect the city from hyenas, jackals, and thieves. People arriving at dusk carried lanterns so they could be identified and admitted into Jerusalem. Latecomers had to sleep outside the gate until morning when the gate reopened. Today, walking through Jaffa Gate, go straight to reach the bazaar, and turn right to arrive at the Tower of David. If you keep going right on Armenian Patriarchal Road, you reach the Armenian Quarter.[103]

The beautiful view of Jaffa Gate, especially the sunset, can be enjoyed from the St. Andrews Scottish hostel, the King David Hotel balcony, the Begin Center balcony, and David Citadel Hotel. Jaffa is the only gate on the western side of the Old City, and allows for a vehicle entry point into the Old City. The Arabic name, Bab el Halil, means the Gate of the Beloved. In the Arab world it is known as the Gate of Hebron. The Beloved in this case is Abraham, the friend of God and great patriarch of the Muslim, Christian, and Jewish faiths. Inside Jaffa Gate is the Information Center which offers a free map of Jerusalem. The Tower of David is actually part of Jaffa Gate. There is also a Post Office inside Jaffa Gate.[104]

---

[102] www.itsgila.com/tipsgates.htm.
[103] Ibid.
[104] www.virtualtourist.com/travel/middle_east/israel.

Jaffa Gate is also called Chevron Gate because the gate leads to Chevron. Other names are the Gate of David's Prayer Shrine, Porta Davidi, and the Gate of David. The Crusader name was Forte David. In 1220 AD, an anonymous pilgrim wrote this while traveling through Jerusalem: "In the city of Jerusalem there are four principal gates, in the shape of a cross, one opposite the other. David's Gate faces west, and stands exactly opposite the Golden Gate, which faces east. This gate belongs to the Tower of David, and is therefore called David's Gate."

In 1917, the mayor of Jerusalem exited Jerusalem to find the British army to surrender the city to them. On December 9, 1917, Brigadier General C.F. Watson and Lt. Colonel H. Bailey entered Jerusalem near Jaffa Gate. The British General Allenby walked through Jaffa Gate and accepted the surrender of Jerusalem to the British. On May 17, 1948, Jewish legions attacked Jaffa Gate but the Jordanian and Arab armies held the gate. Bullet holes near the Jaffa Gate show the battles that were fought there. The Jordanians sealed Jaffa Gate and had control of the Old City until 1967.

David Street is inside Jaffa Gate. You can turn to the left to go to the Christian Quarter, to the right to see the Armenian Quarter, and straight ahead to the Muslim Quarter. The main road from Jaffa Gate goes between the northern hill of Acra and the southern hill named Mount Zion. It goes eastward into the city and down into the Tyropeon Valley. A square is across the street from the Tower of David. In ancient times, wheat and other items were sold in this important square. During the Crusader invasion of Jerusalem in 1099 AD, Moslem defenders and their families hid inside the Tower of David.

In the late 1800's, Jerusalem grew in tourism and population, and during this time the King David Hotel was built near Jaffa Gate. In the early 1900's, the tyrant Pasha hung people near the Jaffa Gate to coincide with the closing of Friday prayers. The location for the hangings was chosen in order for the largest number of people to view the dead bodies.

In 1907, a clock tower was built on top of Jaffa Gate to celebrate twenty-five years of the rule of the Ottoman Sultan Abdul Hammid II. The clock tower was thirteen feet tall and built of limestone. It had four clock faces, facing north, south, east, and west. The east and west had European time, and the north and south had Jerusalem time. The British destroyed the clock in 1922.[105]

Zion Gate

Zion Gate opens from the southwestern part of the wall into the Armenian and Jewish quarters of the Old City. Another name for this gate is David's Gate because it is close to the Tomb of David on Mount Zion. Heavy fighting took place here in the Israeli wars of 1948 and 1967. Deep holes from the shelling are still visible around this gate. The Jews of the Old City were forced to surrender to the Arabs in 1948 after all attempts of rescue failed. After the surrender in 1948, about 100 Israeli soldiers and 200 civilians were taken as prisoners. The other people of the Jewish Quarter were allowed to leave from Zion Gate. The Jewish Quarter was looted and burned, and Zion Gate was sealed up until 1967.

Zion is Jerusalem's earliest biblical name in Hebrew and English. The Arabic name means the Gate of the Prophet David. The Tomb of King David, which can be visited today, is located near this gate.[106]

Damascus Gate

Damascus Gate is located on the northern wall of the Old City. This gate is named after the most important city to the north, Nablus, created by the Romans 1900 years ago. The Arabic name, Bab el Amud, means the Gate of the Pillar, referring to when Damascus Gate had a tall pillar in the central plaza inside the gate. This pillar is pictured on a mosaic map of the 6th century that was found by archaeologists. The pillar itself has not been found yet. Tourists use this gate to get to the Old City Market, in order to barter and make good deals on gifts.[107]

[105] www.israel-a-history-of.com/gates-of-jerusalem.htm.
[106] www.goisrael.com/tourism_eng/articles/attractions/pages.
[107] www.itsgila.com/tipsgates.htm.

DAMASCUS GATE

Courtesy of the Israeli Ministry of Tourism and is solely for this photo only at www.goisrael.com

City Walls and Fortifications

Just before the time of the united and divided monarchies of Israel and Judah, towns had very little protection from attacking enemies, because there were no walls to protect them. Most settlements were open villages. Some towns built houses around the town, facing the village. These houses were built in such a way that they connected to form a continuous wall out of the back walls of the houses. Some towns had dry moats built around them. At the beginning of the time of the monarchs, towns began to build fortified walls around cities. From 1000 to 800 BC, most towns had walls.

The Hebrew word for walls is chomah. Archaeologists have not yet found an ancient wall at its original height. Archaeologists believe that the original walls were from thirty-two feet to forty feet. The foundations of the walls were usually made out of stone, with a depth of three to seven feet. Most of the time, the foot of the wall was sloped, which archaeologists call a "buttressed wall." People built on top of the rubble of houses and ruins that had stood at the same place. The Israelites took advantage of a hill's natural slope to prevent erosion of the mound. The gate had to be accessible and defensible. Most city gates had towers on both sides. During the United Monarchy, many gates had six chambers, three on each side. Archaeologists refer to the six chamber gates as Solomonic Gates.

Terry J. Bates is assistant professor of Old Testament Interpretation at the Southern Baptist Theological Seminary, Louisville, Kentucky.[108]

Damascus Gate was the main gateway to the Old City in ancient times. It is also known as Shechem Gate, Nablus Gate, and Column Gate. There are large steps that form what looks like an amphitheater, with the Damascus Gate as a background. Many centuries ago, there was a column with a Madaba map that dated back to Hadrian's reign. Hadrian tried to erase the memory of Jerusalem by renaming the city Aelia Capitolina and

---

[108] Terry J. Bates, *City Wall and Fortifications*. Biblical Illustrator, LifeWay: Volume 39, number 2, Winter 2012-2013, 43-46.

by preventing the Jews from entering any of the gates. Hadrian put Roman statues on the Temple Mount, and even had a Temple to Zeus.[109]

Damascus Gate faces north to Shechem and to Damascus. The Damascus Gate was built between 1537-1542 AD by the Ottoman Sultan Suleiman the Magnificent. Damascus Gate is busy on Fridays and Saturdays because of its markets. This is the largest gate in Israel. Kathleen Kenyon excavated under this gate and discovered the foundations and gate of an earlier time in history. Kathleen discovered a triple-arched gateway from 135 AD during the time of the Roman emperor Hadrian. Hadrian built this gate to honor his victory over the Bar-Kokhba revolt. The triple-arched gate was probably connected to two towers and guardrooms. In front of Hadrian's gate was a small amphitheater.[110]

Just inside the gate, Hadrian built a round plaza with a large pillar or column. On top of the column was a statue of Hadrian. The column is in the middle of the plaza that marks the spot where Rome measured the distances from Jerusalem to other cities in Canaan. An inscription describing the gate still remains. The inscription says, "To the colony of Aelia Capitolina by order of the city dignitaries."[111]

Edom: Its Land and People

Obadiah prophesied that God would make them a small nation and others would despise them (Obadiah 2). Edom originated with Esau who was the son of Isaac and Rebekah (Genesis 25:21-24). Esau and Jacob were twins but Esau was born first. Genesis 25:25 describes the birth of Esau as, "The first came out red, all his body like a hairy cloak, so they called his name Esau." Genesis 25:27 says, "As these twin boys grew up, Esau became a skilled hunter." Genesis 25:22 tells us that Jacob and Esau struggled with each other even before they were born. This struggle continued from Esau and Jacob to the two nations that would be their descendants.

The event of Esau selling his birthright to Jacob for some red stew ended with the Bible verse, "Therefore his name shall be Edom" (Genesis 25:30). Later, Jacob, with the help of his mother, received the blessing of Isaac that traditionally went to the oldest. The two events of Esau selling his birthright and Esau not getting the traditional blessing caused hostility between the two nations Israel and Edom. Esau married two Hittite women (Genesis 26:35). Later Esau married the daughter of Ishmael, a son

---

[109] www.israel-a-history-of.com/gates-of-jerusalem.html.

[110] www.virtualtourist.com/travel/middle_east/israel.

[111] www.israel-a-history-of.com/gates-of-jerusalem.html.

of Abraham. Esau settled in a rough region south of the Dead Sea (Genesis 33:16, Genesis 36:8-9, Deuteronomy 2:4-5). Moab was the northern border of Edom, and Edom was also called Seir (Genesis 32:3).

This mountainous area is forty miles wide and 100 miles long. The sides of the mountains rise steeply from the valley. The northern part of the plateau makes a good grazing ground. Mountains in the north are 1,500 feet to 2,000 feet, and some in the south reach 2,600 feet. Many areas of Edom have inaccessible peaks and gorges. In Bible times, the capital of Edom was Sela, a city cut into rock cliffs and set in a canyon with an entrance of a narrow gap. Today, Sela is known by its Greek name, Petra.

The "King's Highway" was an important caravan route linking North Africa with Europe and Asia, and it passed along the eastern plateau (Numbers 20:17). The King's Highway was the main trade route from Damascus to Arabia, passing through the Edomite heartlands on the high hills, southeast of the Dead Sea. This highway has been used for over 3,000 years. There was red limestone that gave the territory of Edom a "ruddy" appearance. Some of the land was rocky cliffs and deep gorges, and some areas had fertile soil where wheat, grapes, figs, pomegranates, and olives grew in abundance.

The descendants of Esau conquered the Horites who lived in Edom (Genesis 14:6, Deuteronomy 2:22). When Israel left Egypt, the Israelites came close to Edom. Moses sent messengers to ask the king of Edom for permission to go through Edom (Numbers 20:14-21). Moses reminded the messengers to mention that the Israelites as "your brother Israel." Moses promised that the Israelites would stay on the King's Highway and not go through the fields or vineyards. They promised not to drink any water from the wells. But the Edomites refused to let the people of Israel on their land. The king's answer was, "You shall not pass through, lest I come out with the sword against you" (Numbers 20:18). Edomites arrived with a large army to make sure the Israelites did not get on their land. The Israelites turned away. The fighting of two brothers (Jacob and Esau) spread from two family members to two nations (Israel and Edom), and was now an international incident.

While the Israelites were on the border of Edom at Mount Hor, the position of high priest passed from Aaron to his son, Eleazar. Moses took the priestly clothes from Aaron and placed them on Eleazar. Aaron died on Mount Hor. "The people wept for Aaron for thirty days" (Numbers 20:22-29).

Balaam, in his final oracle stated, "Edom shall be dispossessed; Seir also, his enemies shall be dispossessed. Israel is doing valiantly" (Numbers 11:24, 24:18). God described the land He was giving to Israel as, "Your south side shall be from the wilderness of Zion alongside Edom, and your southern border shall run from the end of the Salt Sea (Dead Sea) on the east" (Numbers 34:3). Joshua 15:2 says that this area along the border of Edom would be given to the descendants of Judah. [112]

Dung Gate

The Dung Gate is located in the south. From inside the city, a person would walk downhill to get there, and Old City residents over centuries past threw their garbage there. Today, the gate is very clean with very little trash. This gate is called Bab el Mugrabi in Arabic, which means the Gate of the North Africans. During Turkish times, a nearby neighborhood was called the Mugrabi and these residents were from North Africa.[113]

JERUSALEM: DUNG GATE, FROM WITHIN THE OLD CITY
Photo courtesy of the Israeli Ministry of Tourism and is solely for this photo only at www.goisrael.com

If you enter the Old City through the Dung Gate, you walk up through the security outpost to the Western (Wailing) Wall Plaza. If it is a weekday, the Temple Mount is open to Jews and Christians for viewing the Dome of the Rock and the Al-Aqsa Mosque from up close, and to take pictures of the Eastern Gate.[114]

Edom: Its Land and People (continued)

I Samuel 14:47 states that when Saul was king of Israel, "He fought against all his enemies on every side, against Moab, against the Ammonites, against Edom, against the kings of Zobah, and against the Philistines. Wherever he turned he routed them." King David of Israel struck down 18,000 Edomites and put garrisons of soldiers throughout Edom. The Edomites became subjects of David (II Samuel 8:13-14). King Solomon had a fleet of ships at Ezion-Geber on the Red

[112]   George H. Shaddix, *Edom: Its Land and People*. Biblical Illustrator, LifeWay: Volume 39, number 2, Winter 2012-2013, 66-69.
[113]   www.itsgila.com/tipsgates.htm.
[114]   Ibid.

Sea in the land of Edom, which was a clue that Solomon ruled Edom. These ships sailed to Ophir and brought Solomon 420 talents of gold, which is sixteen tons (1 Kings 9:26-28). Years ago, Edom would not let the Israelites pass through their land when they returned from Egypt. Now, Edom was under the rule of Israel and later Judah's kings. During the reign of Judah's King Jehoram (850-843 BC), Edom revolted and appointed an Edomite King (11 Kings 8:20).

Isaiah 34:8-9 says, "For the Lord has a day of vengeance, a year of recompense for the cause of Zion. And the streams of Edom shall be turned into pitch, and her soil into sulfur; her land shall become burning pitch." Jeremiah 49:17 says, "Edom shall become a horror. Everyone who passes by it will be horrified and will hiss because of all its diseases." Joel 3:19 says, "Egypt shall become a desolation and Edom a desolate wilderness, for the violence done to the people of Judah, because they have shed innocent blood in their land."

Obadiah's prophecy focused on Edom and prophesied that Edom would be made small among the nations and would be utterly despised (Obadiah 2). Obadiah also said, "Because of the violence done to your brother Jacob, shame shall cover you and you shall be cut off forever. There shall be no survivor for the house of Esau (Edom) for the Lord has spoken" (Obadiah 10,18). Obadiah was saying that the house of Jacob would destroy the house of Esau. The twin brothers' struggle continued for centuries, long after their deaths.

George H. Shaddix is the retired preacher of the Northwood Hills Baptist Church, Northport, Alabama.[115]

GATE OF THE FLOWERS IN JERUSALEM OLD CITY
Courtesy of the Israeli Ministry of Tourism and is solely for this photo only at www.goisrael.com

Flowers Gate

Another name for Flowers Gate is Herod's Gate. Up on the hill outside the gate is a cemetery. In Arabic, the gate is called Bab es Sahirah, which means Cemetery Gate. Arabs decided, however, to change the name to Bab el Zahirah, which means Flowers Gate. In

---

[115] George H. Shaddix, *Edom: Its Land and People*. Biblical Illustrator, LifeWay: Volume 39, number 2, Winter 2012-2013, 66-69.

Hebrew, the gate is Sha'ar Perachim, which means Flowers Gate. In Hebrew it is also called Sha'ar Hodus, which means Herod's Gate. According to Roman Catholic tradition, the home of Herod Antipas was near the Flagellation Convent, which is near the gate.[116]

This gate is next to the Muslim Quarter and close to the Damascus Gate. Flower Gate got its name from the flower design on its outer side.[117]

THE WALLS PROMENADE THAT CIRCLES THE OLD CITY
Courtesy of the Israeli Ministry of Tourism and is solely for this photo only at www.goisrael.com

Living like Pagans

In First Peter, Simon Peter talked about an age-old challenge for Christians living in a world full of sin and preventing ungodly cultures to influence their Christian life. Any believer can fall to temptation in a weak moment. Christians can also face persecution because of a commitment to live in a Christ-like, non-worldly manner (I Peter 3:14). Peter was telling people of his day not to live like the pagans of that day. Most of the people Peter addressed had been pagans before they accepted Christ. Peter wanted believers to have a passion for what is good even if it meant suffering for righteousness. Peter stressed for Christians not to go back into non-Christian behavior in order to avoid persecution. Peter encouraged Christians to live out their remaining days not "for human desires but for God's will" (I Peter 4:2). Peter thought this challenge was more urgent because he saw the end of the age as being close at hand (I Peter 4:7). Peter warned against sexual desires illicit in nature, lust, drunkenness, orgies, sins of excess, and idolatry.

Robert E. Jones is pastor of Euclid Avenue Baptist Church in Bristol, Virginia.[118]

---

[116] www.itsgila.com/tipsgates.htm.

[117] www.virtualtourist.com/travel/middle_east/israel.

[118] Robert E. Jones, *Living Like Pagans.* Biblical Illustrator, LifeWay: Volume 39, number 1, Fall 2012, 6-9.

SIGN OF THE LION'S GATE

Courtesy of the Israeli Ministry of Tourism and is solely for this photo only at www.goisrael.com

Lion's Gate

Lion's Gate is on the eastern side of the Old City. It is also known as St. Stephen's Gate. Christian tradition is that Stephen, the first Christian martyr, was stoned in the Kidron Valley below. In Arabic the gate is called Bab el Asbat, the Gate of the Tribes. Arabs believe the tribes of Israel entered the Old City through this gate. In Hebrew it is called Sha'ar Ha-Arayot, in honor of decorations above the gate. There are two stone statues of lions on either side of the outer archway. Tradition is that Suleiman the Magnificent ordered these lion sculptures in the 16th century. This was done to remind Suleiman the Magnificent of his dream to rebuild the damaged walls.

Suleiman dreamed he was being eaten by four fierce lions which jumped from the thickets of the Jordan River. He woke up from this dream in great fear. Early in the morning, he called all the wise men of his kingdom to explain what the dream meant. They could not figure out the meaning of the dream. A wise old sheikh wanted to know the last thing Suleiman was thinking about before he fell asleep. Suleiman's answer was that he was thinking about how to punish the people of Jerusalem because they had not been paying their taxes. The sheikh said, "Don't you know that our prophets David and Solomon ruled from the Holy City while lions guarded their thrones? If you treat this Holy City with goodness and mercy, you will be blessed as were David and Solomon."

Suleiman commissioned two architects who designed the route of the fortifications. It took seven years and these walls are still standing in modern times.[119]

Many Christians believe that Lion's Gate was the last entrance by Christ from the Garden of Gethsemane to his walk to the crucifixion. Many believe that this gate was the beginning of the Via Dolorosa. It is named Lion's Gate, but the figures are four panthers instead of lions.

---

[119] www.itsgila.com/tipsgates.htm.

121

This gate is the closest to the Christian sites of the Mount of Olives.[120] The Israeli Defense forces rushed through this gate to storm the Old City on June 7, 1967.

As mentioned, Lion's Gate is also called Stephen's Gate. Stephen, the first Christian martyr, may have been stoned to death outside this gate (read Acts 7:54-60).

Eastern Gate

The Eastern Gate of the Old City is nailed shut and will stay shut until the arrival of the Messiah. No one will enter the Temple Mount from the East (read Ezekiel 44:1-3).

JERUSALEM, OLD CITY: GOLDEN OR EASTERN GATE
Photo courtesy of the Israeli Ministry of Tourism and is solely for this photo only at www.goisrael.com

Another name for this gate is the Golden Gate. In the days of Peter, it was called the Beautiful Gate, and Peter healed a lame man here (read Acts 3:1-10).

It is believed that Jesus entered the temple courtyard through the Golden Gate. He drove out all people who were selling and buying, and turned over the tables of the money changers. During the time of the Second Temple, the Eastern Gate was open (read Mark 11:15-18).[121]

The Golden Gate is called the Gate of Eternal Life by the Arabs. This gate may have been built on top of the remains from the East Gate of Solomon's First Temple, from Nehemiah's rebuilt Jerusalem, and of Herodian Jerusalem during the Second Temple period. The Golden Gate has been in its present form since 630 AD, when the Byzantine Emperor Heraclius went into Jerusalem by using the Golden Gate. The Golden Gate had two doorways: the southern gate called the Gate of Mercy and the northern gate called the Gate of Repentance.

---

[120] www.virtualtourist.com/travel/middle_east/israel.
[121] www.itsgila.com/tipsgates.htm.

Muslim tradition said the pillars of the gate were given to Solomon as a gift from the Queen of Sheba. Monolithic stones in the nearby walls date back to the time of Nehemiah.

In 1969, the Muslim authorities buried a remarkable discovery that came from doing an excavation. At that time, James Fleming, an Israeli archaeologist, was simply standing in front of the Golden Gate studying. Suddenly, he fell through the ground into a sinkhole. James Fleming found five large, wedge-shaped stones of a big arch. Before Fleming could investigate, the Muslims in charge sealed the hole and poured concrete into the opening. Many scholars believe Fleming had discovered a gate dating to the time of King Solomon and the First Temple period, or from the time of Nehemiah. The ruins of the gate that Fleming found may be the East Gate mentioned in Nehemiah 3:29: "After them Zadok the son of Immer carried out repairs in front of his house. And after him Shemaia the son of Shecaniah, the keeper of the East Gate, carried out repairs."

Nehemiah's construction was in the 5th century BC, when Jews returned and rebuilt Jerusalem. Nehemiah's East Gate was called Shusha or Susa after the Persian capital. The Shushan Gate's construction was paid for by the Jewish community in Persia. The Bible also speaks of an eastern gate during the reign of Hezekiah: "And Kore the son of Imnah the Levite, the Keeper of the eastern gate" (2 Chronicles 31:14).

Many people want to be buried close to the Golden Gate, which has resulted in many cemeteries being built close to the Golden Gate. Some Jews, Christians, and Muslims are buried side by side in hopes of getting a "front row seat" to the resurrection! Cemeteries dot the adjoining Kidron Valley and the slopes of the Mount of Olives. The Jews and Christians believe this area is the site of Messiah's future appearance. The Muslims believe it is Allah's final judgment place.[122]

---

[122] www.israel-a-history-of.com/gates-of-jerusalem.htm.

THE WALL OF THE TEMPLE MOUNT, SEEN FROM THE MOUNT OF OLIVES

Courtesy of the Israeli Ministry of Tourism and is solely for this photo only at www.goisrael.com

The Temple Mount in Hebrew is known as Har haBayith and in Arabic as Haram Ash-Sharif. This is the most important religious site in the Old City of Jerusalem. At least four religions have used the Temple Mount: Judaism, Islam, Christianity, and Roman paganism. Many Bible scholars identify the Temple Mount with Mount Moriah, where Isaac was bound for sacrifice and then God provided the lamb for the substitution. Mount Zion is where the original Jebusite fortress stood. Only God knows where the exact specific location is.

Judaism believes the Temple Mount is the place where God chose the Divine Presence to rest: "Behold, I and the children whom the Lord hath given me are for signs and for wonders in Israel from the Lord of hosts, which dwelleth in Mount Zion" (Isaiah 8:18). According to the rabbinic sages who produced the Talmud, God gathered the dust from here to create the first man, Adam. The site is the location of Abraham's binding of Isaac and the location of two Jewish Temples.[123] According to the Bible, the site should one day function as the center of all national life: governmental, judicial, and religious center.

But unto the place which the Lord your God shall choose out of all your tribes to put his name there, even unto his habitation shall ye seek, and thither thou shalt come. (Deuteronomy 12:5)

And thou shalt eat before the Lord thy God, in the place which he shall choose to place his name there, the tithe of thy corn, of thy wine, and of thine oil, and the firstlings of thy herds and of thy flocks; that thou mayest learn to fear the Lord thy God always. (Deuteronomy 14:23)

And saviors shall come up on mount Zion to judge the mount of Esau; and the kingdom shall be the Lord's. (Obadiah 21)

Great is the Lord, and greatly to be praised in the city of our God, in the mountain of his holiness. Beautiful for situation the joy of the whole earth, is

---

[123] https://en.wikipedia.org/wiki/Temple_Mount.

mount Zion, on the sides of the north, the city of the great King. God is known in her palaces for a refuge. For, lo, the kings were assembled, they passed by together. They saw it, and so they marvelled; they were troubled, and hasted away. Fear took hold upon them there, and pain, as of a woman in travail. Thou breakest the ships of Tarshish with an east wind. As we have heard, so have we seen in the city of the Lord of hosts, in the city of our God; God will establish it for ever. Selah. We have thought of thy loving kindness, O God, in the midst of thy temple. According to thy name, O God, so is thy praise unto the ends of the earth: thy right hand is full of righteousness. Let mount Zion rejoice, let the daughters of Judah be glad, because of thy judgments. Walk about Zion, and go round about her: tell the towers thereof. Mark ye well her bulwarks, consider her palaces; that ye may tell it to the generation following. For this God is our God for ever; he will be our guide even unto death. (Psalm 48:1-14)

King Solomon's invitation to pray

Today, worshipers of all faiths pray near the Temple Mount. On Bar Mitzvah days, Mondays, Thursdays, and Saturdays, large crowds gather near the Temple Mount location to hear thirteen-year-olds celebrate their first public scripture reading. As 1 Kings 8:41-42 says: "Moreover concerning a stranger, that is not of thy people Israel, but cometh out of a far country for thy name's sake; for they shall hear of thy great name, and of thy strong hand, and of thy stretched out arm; when he shall come and pray toward this house."

The Temple Mount is the site of the ruins of the Jewish Holy Temple, a thirty-five-acre section of the Old City. Both Solomon's Temple and the Temple of Herod the Great were located here. The grounds where they stood are viewed as holy ground. The Ark of the Covenant may also be buried here. Many Jews believe that the Messiah will come and rebuild the Temple (Isaiah 2:2-3). Some Jews want the Temple rebuilt soon.

And it shall come to pass in the last days, that the mountain of the Lord's house shall be established in the top of the mountains, and shall be exalted above the hills; and all nations shall flow unto it. And many people shall go and say, "Come ye, and let us go up to the mountain of the Lord, to the house of the God of Jacob; and he will teach us of his ways, and we will walk in his paths": for out of Zion shall go forth the law, and the word of the Lord from Jerusalem. (Isaiah 2:2-3)

At age twelve, Jesus went to the Temple in Jerusalem for the Feast of the Passover. After three days of searching, they found him in the Temple (read Luke 4:21-52). Many years later, Jesus drove out the money changers from this area (read John 2:13-22; Matthew 21:12-13).

On Palm Sunday, Jesus rode on the back of a donkey to the Temple area. He taught in the Temple the week before his death. Many Jews will not walk on Mount Zion because they do not want to unintentionally enter the area where the Holy of Holies stood, since Rabbinical law states that some aspect of the Divine Presence is still present at the site. It was from the Holy of Holies that the High Priest communicated with God.[124]

The Wailing Wall or Western Wall is believed to be the remains of a Jewish temple or the wall surrounding the courtyard of the temple. The remaining portion of the wall extends about sixty-two feet above the ground. This wall is claimed as a sacred site by the Jews and also by the Muslims, who believe it is part of an ancient mosque or the wall to which Mohammed tied his winged horse during his night journey in the 7th century. Many Jews believe it was part of the Second Temple. The Wailing Wall is the only part still standing of this structure. After the temple was torn down, Jews visited it to weep, and non-Jews subsequently named it the Wailing Wall. Jews refer to the wall as the Western Wall or Kotel HaMaaravi in Hebrew. Muslims call the wall the Al-Buraq Wall, named for Mohammed's winged horse. Muslims believe that Jews did not visit the Wailing Wall until the 16th century. In 2002, Pope John Paul II prayed at the Wailing Wall and apologized for the way the Catholics had treated the Jews in the Crusades.[125]

---

[124] https://en.wikipedia.org/wiki/Temple_Mount.
[125] www.wisegeek.com/what-is-the-wailing.

PEOPLE PRAYING AT THE WAILING WALL

Courtesy of the Israeli Ministry of Tourism and is solely for this photo only at www.goisrael.com

Jews from all countries and also Christian tourists pray at the wall. People who cannot pray at the wall can send prayer requests to place into the cracks of the wall, and these requests are called *kvitelach*. When the prayer requests reach one million, they are taken out of the cracks and buried. Visitors to the wall are searched for security purposes, and females in particular should wear modest clothing when visiting the wall. There are separate entrances for men and women. They can join together in the plaza near the wall.[126]

The Western Wall is also known as the Kotel. This wall survived the destruction of Jerusalem in 70 AD. The Roman general (and future emperor) Titus spared this part of Jerusalem to show future generations that the wall had enormous stones, showing the greatness of Rome and its soldiers. During the Roman period, Jews were forbidden to come to Jerusalem. During the Byzantine period, Jews were allowed to come once a year on the anniversary of the destruction of the Temple, to grieve over the dispersion of their people and weep over the loss of their Temple. This section of the wall became known as the Wailing Wall due to their cries of anguish. For centuries they prayed at the wall, but from 1948-1967, Jews were not allowed near the wall because it was in a Jordanian-controlled section of Jerusalem. After the Six-Day War in 1967, in a historic and joyful moment the Jews regained control of the Western Wall area and the wall was opened to Jewish visitors once again. This year of 1967 marked the reunification of all of Jerusalem under Jewish sovereignty.

The main section of the wall where people pray is about 187 feet long and most of the stones weigh 4,000 pounds each (two tons). There are twenty-eight stone layers above the ground and seventeen layers underground. An underground tunnel runs along the length of the wall. One enormous stone, the Western Stone, weighs more than 1.1 million

---

[126]   Ibid.

pounds.[127] The Western Stone has a length of forty-five feet and a width of eleven feet. The weight of the stone is 570 short tons and 510 long tons.[128]

At the northern part of the Western Gate is an ancient water channel which once supplied water to the Temple Mount. The water channel passes through an underground pool called the Struthion Pool and dates back to the Hasmonean period. Because of this it is named the Hasmonean Channel. Benjamin Netanyahu authorized the making of an exit from it, leading to the Via Dolorosa. It is now possible for many tourists to enter the tunnel's southern entrance near the Western Wall, walk the tunnel's length with a tour guide and leave from the northern end.[129]

Non-Jews are permitted to pray at the wall, but all men have to wear hats, or Jewish *kippot* that are provided at the entrance. Scripture states, "Moreover concerning the stranger, which is not of thy people Israel, but is come from a far country for thy great name's sake, and thy mighty hand, and thy stretched out arm; if they come and pray in this house; then hear thou from the heavens, even from thy dwelling place, and do according to all that the stranger calleth to thee for; that all people of the earth may know thy name, and fear thee, as doth thy people Israel, and may know that this house which I have built is called by thy name" (2 Chronicles 6:32-33).

The Western Wall is sixty feet high and also extends seventy feet below the surface. Stones visible at ground level are from the time of Herod the Great. One of the Herodian stones discovered in the underground passage is thirty-nine feet in length, almost ten feet in height, and thirteen feet in width.

Abraham's Travels

Abraham built no cities, and left no tools, potsherd, or jewelry in garbage dumps or tombs. At least no archaeologists have discovered anything belonging to Abraham. But we cannot simply call Abraham a nomad, because scripture says he is more than a nomad. Old Testament scholar D.J. Wiseman described Abraham's lifestyle like a pastoral nomad, which is described in the mari texts and which defines it as a seasonal farmer with herds of flocks and cattle close to towns and cities. Genesis 11:31 teaches us that Abram set out from Ur of the Chaldeans

---

[127] www.wisegeek.com/what-is-the-wailing.
[128] https://en.wikipedia.org/wiki/Western_Wall_Tunnel.
[129] Ibid.

with his father, Terah, his wife, Sarai, and his nephew, Lot. They had chosen Canaan as their destination.

Genesis does not give a reason for why they stopped in Haran, how long they lived there, or why they wanted to go to Canaan. Some scholars guess about fifty years. After Terah died, God called Abram to go to the land that He would show him: their original destination of Canaan.

Abraham's journey into Canaan took them along the ridge route through the central hill country (Genesis 12:6-8). They next went through the hill country to the Negev (Genesis 12:9) and then down to Egypt when famine struck (Genesis 12:10). Then they finally settled in the central hill country close to Hebron.

Eleven years after arriving in Canaan, Hagar gave birth to Ishmael, Abram's first son (Genesis 16:3,15-16). The family remained in Hebron for the next thirteen or fourteen years before moving to the Negev where Isaac was born (Genesis 17:1, 20:1, 21:5). Scripture gives no reason for Abraham's leaving Hebron and moving to Negev. Abram was in Hebron about twenty-five years and long enough to call home. He may have moved to the Negev to look for better pasture.

Abraham's 100 years in Canaan were spent in Hebron or in the Negev in Gerar or Beersheba, and he lived in tents rather than permanent structures (Genesis 13:8 and Genesis 18:1). Archaeologists discovered sites in the Negev used as caravan stations for trade merchants traveling to and from Egypt. Much of the land in the Negev was not suitable for agriculture. Maybe Abraham participated in the trade at the caravan stations. Abraham was considered to be wealthy but scripture does not tell us how Abraham made his money.[130]

---

[130]   Alan Ray Buescher, *Abraham's Travels*. Biblical Illustrator, LifeWay: Volume 39, number 1, Fall 2012, 10-15.

THE WAILING WALL TUNNELS
Courtesy of the Israeli Ministry of Tourism and is solely for this photo only at www. goisrael.com

Charles Wilson in 1864 discovered an arch, forty-two feet wide and above the present ground level. Archaeologists believe that the arch once had a bridge that connected the Temple Mount to the city during the Second Temple period. Charles Warren in 1867-70 dug shafts through Wilson's Arch. These excavations lasted about twenty years and revealed many facts. The excavations were difficult, however, because some of the tunnels ran through residential neighborhoods built on top of very old structures.

Warren's Gate is about 150 feet into the tunnel. This area has been sealed off to form a small synagogue called the Cave by Rabbi Yehuda Getz. This is the closest that Jews can get to the site of the Holy of Holies if it was located at the traditional site under the Dome of the Rock.[131]

In 70 AD, the temple was destroyed by the army of Titus, who tried to keep all his soldiers from damaging it. But one of the soldiers threw a lighted torch through a window and set it on fire. The menorah, the seven-branched candlestick, was saved, but Titus took it back to Rome. In 636, the Moslems captured Jerusalem and Khalif Omar built a mosque in the rubble, identifying it as the place where Mohammed ascended. In 691, Abdul-Malik-Ibsen Marwan, the Omayad Khalif, replaced the tiny mosque of Omar with the present one.

---

[131] www.wisegeek.com/what-is-the-wailing.

DETAILS FROM THE YAD VASHEM HOLOCAUST HISTORY MUSEUM, JERUSALEM

Courtesy of the Israeli Ministry of Tourism and is solely for this photo only at www.goisrael.com

Israel's Holocaust Museum, Yad Vashem, was formed in 1953 when the Yad Vashem Law passed in the Knesset. Isaiah 56:5 was used to pick out the name: "And to them will I give in my house and within my walls a memorial and a name" [Yad Vashem] that shall not be cut off." The museum is in the western region of Mount Herzl, on the Mount of Remembrance in Jerusalem. It is close to the Jerusalem Forest.

The museum complex is enormous, including the Holocaust History Museum, Children's Memorial, Hall of Remembrance, Museum of Holocaust Art, sculptures, and outdoor commemorative sites such as the Valley of the Communities, a synagogue, archives, a research institute, library, publishing house, the International School for Holocaust Studies, and an educational center. It is the second most visited tourist site in Israel, surpassed only by the Western Wall. It is free to visit, and one million visitors tour it yearly. In 1993, the Yad Vashem Institute built a larger museum to replace the one built in the 1960's. The new museum is the largest Holocaust museum in the world. The museum combines stories from ninety Holocaust victims and survivors, and tells about their life situations. About 2,500 personal items are displayed. At the end of the Holocaust History Museum is the Hall of names listing the six million Jews who died. The museum also honors non-Jews who risked their own lives to save Jews during the Holocaust. The idea for a memorial to the thousands of Jews murdered in the Nazi-occupied countries was born in September 1942 at a board meeting of the Jewish National Fund.[132]

The museum complex is on a total of forty-five acres. The History Museum is actually carved into the mountain. The visitor starts in an area full of light, which catalogs the lives of European communities

---

[132] www.en.wikipedia.org/wiki/yad_vashem.

before the Holocaust. Then the tour goes through darkened areas and ends in a floor-to-ceiling view of the mountains of Jerusalem.[133]

THE CATTLE CAR MEMORIAL TO THE DEPORTEES, YAD VASHEM, JERUSALEM
Courtesy of the Israeli Ministry of Tourism and is solely for this photo only at www.goisrael.com

DAVID'S GRAVE ON MOUNT ZION
Courtesy of the Israeli Ministry of Tourism and is solely for this photo only at www.goisrael.com

Mount Zion is a hill in Jerusalem located just outside the walls of the Old City. The word "Zion" is mentioned in II Samuel 5:7: "Nevertheless David took the strong hold of Zion: the same is the city of David." After King Solomon built the temple, Mount Zion became known as the Temple Mount.

In 1948, Mount Zion was connected by a tunnel to the Yemin Moshe neigh-borhood in West Jerusalem. During World War II, the area was needed to evacuate the wounded and carry supplies to soldiers on Mount Zion. A cable car was made and secretly used at night. It was lowered into the valley in the day to keep it from being detected by the enemy. The ride from the Israeli position at St. John Eye Hospital to Mount Zion took two minutes.

Important sites on Mount Zion are Dormition Abbey, King David's Tomb, and the Room of the Last Supper. Some scholars believe the correct site is located on Mount Zion. Another name for Mount Zion is the Western Hill. It is believed by many that King David was buried here; that Mary, Mother of Jesus, died here; that this is the location of the Upper Room where Christ shared the Last Supper with his disciples; and that this is where the Holy Spirit came on the Day of Pentecost. During the 1948 War of Independence, Israel was able to

---

[133] www.jerusalem-insiders-guide.com/yad-vashem-museum.html.

keep control of Mount Zion. Other scholars believe the correct site is located near the Temple Mount.[134]

The Garden of Gethsemane is located at the bottom of the Mount of Olives in Jerusalem. It is most famous as the place where Jesus and his disciples prayed the night before the crucifixion of Jesus. The name comes from the Aramaic *Gat-Smane* which means "oil press". According to Luke 22:43-44, Jesus was in agony at the Garden of Gethsemane: "And there appeared an angel unto him from heaven, strengthening him. And being in an agony he prayed more earnestly: and his sweat was as it were great drops of blood falling down to the ground."

Eastern Orthodox Church tradition believes that the Virgin Mary was buried at Gethsemane and was taken up to heaven after her dormition on Mount Zion. Early Christians liked to visit the Garden of Gethsemane. In 333 AD, the anonymous "Pilgrim of Bordeaux", author of *Itinerarium Burdigalense*, wrote the earliest comments about the garden. In his *Eusebius of Caesarea* he wrote that Gethsemane is located at the foot of the Mount of Olives and that the faithful liked to go there and pray. Ancient olive trees located there are believed to be 900 years old or more. In 2012, the National Research Council of Italy did a study using DNA from olive trees. Carbon dating of older parts of the trunks of three trees showed dates of 1092, 1166, and 1198 AD. DNA tests showed that the three trees were from the same parent plant.[135]

OUTSIDE GETHSEMANE

Courtesy of the Israeli Ministry of Tourism and is solely for this photo only at www.goisrael.com

There are eight olive trees in this garden that are at least 2,000 to 3,000 years old. They still produce fruit and may have been young trees when Jesus came to pray and to be arrested.[136]

---

[134]   www.en.wikipedia.org/wiki/mount_zion.

[135]   www.en.wikipedia.org/wiki/gethsemane.

[136]   www.delange.org/adisrael/geth/geth.htm.

This event at Gethsemane is mentioned in Matthew 26:36: "Then cometh Jesus with them unto a place called Gethsemane, and saith unto the disciples, 'Sit ye here, while I go and pray yonder.'"

In the book of Zechariah, the Mount of Olives is the place where God will redeem the dead in the latter days. Because of what Zechariah said, Jews like to be buried on the Mount of Olives. Beginning in Biblical times to the modern era, the Mount of Olives has been used as a cemetery for Jerusalem Jews and now has about 150,000 graves. The tomb of Zechariah himself is on the Mount of Olives.

Jesus, on the night of his betrayal, left the city of Jerusalem and crossed through the Kidron Valley to get to his favorite spot, the Garden of Gethsemane. Jesus went to the garden to pray and to allow himself to be arrested (read John 18:1-19).

As a tourist going to the Mount of Olives, you exit through Stephen's Gate of the Old City, and walk down to and across the Kidron Valley. If you come by taxi, get off at the top of the Mount of Olives and walk down to Gethsemane is recommended.

In the Garden of Eden, Adam's choice to disobey God by eating the forbidden fruit brought sin and condemnation to the world. In the Garden of Gethsemane, Jesus Christ's decision to die for sins brought justification to everyone who believes: "Therefore as by the offense of one judgment came upon all men to condemnation; even so by the righteousness of one free gift came upon all men unto justification of life" (Romans 5:18). If Adam had known the consequences to himself and to all people, he may have made the decision not to disobey God by eating the forbidden fruit. All he had was God's word and its warning.

From Gethsemane, there is a view of the walls of Jerusalem. Jesus could have seen the soldiers coming to arrest him.[137] "Rise, let us be going: behold he is at hand that doth betray me" (Matthew 26:46). Although he could see those coming who would put him to death, he chose to stay in the garden and obey God the Father because of his love for the Father and for us. Because of the decision of Jesus to obey God the Father and stay in the garden, allowing himself to be arrested and crucified, we can have salvation today if we choose to accept the free gift of salvation, believe in Jesus, and follow him.

---

[137] www.waynestiles.com/eden-and-gethsemane-two-gardens-and.

A man named Mordecai Ham shared the good news of Jesus to a young boy one day and had no idea the good that would result. Through Mordecai Ham's story of Jesus, a young boy named Billy Graham believed and God converted him. And through Billy Graham millions heard the story of Jesus, believed and were converted.[138]

On the site believed to be where Jesus prayed to his Father hours before the crucifixion, three churches were built: Byzantine, Crusader, and a modern church, one by one in their respective time periods. The modern Church of All Nations has a beautiful mosaic on its building. Since the third millennium BC, the Mount of Olives has always been important to Judaism and Christianity. The Mount of Olives is 2,900 feet tall and has been one of the main burial grounds for Jerusalem. The two-mile-long ridge has three summits and each has a tower built on it.[139]

In modern times, the Garden of Gethsemane is a Franciscan monastery with a small garden of eight ancient olive trees. Gethsemane gets its name from the Hebrew word *gat* which means "a place of pressing" and *shemanim* which means "oil".[140]

On the modern site of Gethsemane, the Kidron Valley has many new roads and many buildings constructed. The property now called the Garden of Gethsemane is about 1200 square meters, in an area that is to the right of the path up the mountain, jutting out between this path and the Church of All Nations, to the Jericho Road.[141]

A SIGN IN THE GARDEN TOMB

Courtesy of the Israeli Ministry of Tourism and is solely for this photo only at www.goisrael.com

In 1863, Charles Gordon, a British general, questioned the location of the site believed for 1,600 years to be the crucifixion and burial place of Jesus: the Church of the Holy Sepulchre. Many Christians agree with Gordon. Also, Protestant or

---

138 Ibid.

139 www.bibleplaces.com/mtolives.htm.

140 www.israeljerusalem.com/garden-gethsemane-mount-olives.htm.

141 http://www.christusrex.org/www1/ofm/san/GET04gar.html.

Evangelical Christians often may not like the ritualistic atmosphere at the Church of the Holy Sepulchre. Gordon believed the correct site was another place he associated with Calvary or Golgotha, which means "Place of the Skull."

Mark 15:22 says, "And they brought him to the place called Golgotha (which means Place of a Skull)." Luke 23:33 says, "And when they came to the place that is called The Skull, there they crucified him, and the criminals, one on his right and one on his left." John 19:17 says, "So they took Jesus, and he went out, bearing his own cross, to the place called The Place of a Skull, which in Aramaic is called Golgotha."

The rocky hill believed to be Golgotha is about fifty feet high with two deep crevices that look like eye sockets, and just below the "eyes" is another formation that looks like a nose. After Gordon's view grew in popularity, excavations were done around the hill, and a garden and empty tomb was discovered. John 19:42 says, "So because of the Jewish day of Preparation, since the tomb was close at hand, they laid Jesus there."

Protestants and Evangelicals accepted the site as the burial place of Jesus and named it the Garden Tomb. A few scholars had a problem with the decision, because scripture does not say Jesus was crucified on a hill. Scripture only calls it a "place". (Examples are found in Matthew 27:33, Mark 15:22, Luke 23:33, and John 19:17.) Also, scientific studies show that the site was used as a burial site in Old Testament times. By contrast, John 19:41 says, "Now in the place where he was crucified there was a garden, and in the garden a new tomb in which no one had been laid."[142]

THE TOMB ITSELF IN THE GARDEN TOMB
Courtesy of the Israeli Ministry of Tourism and is solely for this photo only at www.goisrael.com

Some Christians think that it is not important to pinpoint the exact location of the crucifixion, burial, and resurrection of Jesus. The important thing for all of us is that Jesus died for us and rose from the dead. In the 1800's, Lord Frederic Farrar stated, "In all probability, the actual spot (where Jesus died) lies buried

---

[142] George W. Knight, *The Holy Land*, 139.

under the heaps of the ten-times-taken city. . . All we know about Golgotha is that it was without (outside) the city gate. . . The religion of Christ is spiritual; it needs no relic; it is independent of Holy Places; it says to each of its children, not 'Lo, here!' and 'Lo, there!' but "The kingdom of God is within you."[143]

Gordon's Calvary was discovered in 1885 by Charles Gordon when he was walking around the wall of the Old City. Gordon noticed a hillside which seemed to fit the Bible's description of the crucifixion and resurrection. Gordon noticed a skull-like formation on the side of the hill. Gordon used scripture from Leviticus, revisited the area now known as Gordon's Calvary, and became convinced that the Church of the Holy Sepulchre was not the correct spot.

Leviticus 1:11 states that the sacrificial offerings were to be slain on the side of the altar northward: "And he shall kill it on the side of the altar northward before the Lord: and the priests, Aaron's sons, shall sprinkle his blood round about upon the altar." Gordon knew that the Church of the Holy Sepulchre is west of the altar, and he believed that if God gave a northward direction, that it should be northward, which made Gordon's Calvary spot a fulfillment. Under his interpretation, the temple location was the altar and Gordon's Calvary spot was northward.

Gordon was so convinced of his findings that he persuaded a group from England to purchase the property. If this were the location, there also had to be a tomb nearby. Excavations later found a tomb carved out of solid rock, dating back to the 1st century. Archaeologists later found a cistern, which proved that a garden had indeed been there at one time. John 19:41-42 states, "At the place where Jesus was crucified, there was a garden, and in the garden a new tomb, in which no one had been laid. Because it was the Jewish day of Preparation and since the tomb was nearby, they laid Jesus there."[144]

Gordon later died at Khartoum in Sudan. The area he identified as the crucifixion site was once a quarry and was known for executions. Stephen, the first Christian martyr, may also have been stoned there. The gospels state that a person could look into the tomb from the entrance and see the burial chamber. Additionally, an ancient tradition

---

[143]   Frederic W. Farrar, *The Life of Christ*, http://www.cumorah.com/etexts/farrar-lifeofchrist.pdf, 502.

[144]   George W. Knight, *The Holy Land*, 139.

is that Jeremiah was imprisoned in a nearby cave when he wrote the book of Lamentations. This cave is visible from Gordon's hill of Calvary. Jeremiah asks, "Is it nothing to you who pass by?" Is it possible that God inspired Jeremiah to write this on the very location where the event would one day happen? The entire chapter of Genesis 22 may actually be referring to the land we now call Gordon's Calvary (read Genesis 22).

The chapter deals with Abraham's obedience to God's command that he sacrifice his only son on Mount Moriah. The hill on Gordon's Calvary is in the northwest corner of Mount Moriah. The temple stood at the southern end. The entire chapter of Genesis 22 portrays Isaac as a type of Christ and may prophetically look forward to the event of Christ's death. God directed Abraham and Isaac to the special place for the sacrifice which was Mount Moriah. On the opposite end of Mount Moriah was the temple where lamb sacrifices were made for sins of the people. Every animal sacrificed in the Temple pointed forward to the "Lamb of God who takes away the sin of the world" (John 1:29):

"The next day John seeth Jesus coming unto him, and saith, 'Behold the Lamb of God, which taketh away the sin of the world.'"

How prophetically it was that Abraham told Isaac that God would provide the Lamb. And God did provide a lamb instead of Isaac for the sacrifice. How fitting that on the same mountain, Jesus would offer His own body and blood as the eternal, once-for-all atonement for man's sin.

Author William McBirnie wrote *The Search for the Tomb of Jesus.* His research team flew to Rome to study Roman crucifixion methods and customs. The team also visited Egypt and Petra to study 1st-century burial customs. The team also researched archaeological libraries and other places in Jerusalem to view what has been written about the Tomb of Jesus.

Abraham's Travels (continued)

Abraham became wealthy and may have participated in trade with merchants. He had flocks, cattle, camels, flour for baking, silver, gold, and knew how to handle his finances. More than 550 years passed from Abraham's death until his descendants settled in Canaan. Jacob was fifteen years old when his grandfather Abraham died (Genesis 25:26). More than 110 years passed from Abraham's death at age 175 to Joseph's death at age 110.

The earliest extra-biblical written record for Israel's arrival into Canaan is on a stone carving called Merneptah Stele which is dated between 1213 and 1203 BC. This inscription indicates the death of Abraham in 1753 BC and the date for Abraham's first entry into Canaan as about 1853 BC, and his birth about 1928 BC. This puts Abraham in the Middle Bronze II A period.

Israeli archaeologist Amihai Mazar believes the archaeological discoveries of the Middle Bronze II period have similarities with the patriarchal record in the Bible. Customs during the Middle Bronze Ages continued for hundreds of years, making chronological dating of events that much harder.

Foreign rulers called Hyksos became powerful in Egypt. Many scholars believe these Hyksos rulers were Canaanites. This became a West-Semitic-Amorite-Canaanite culture from Egypt, northward along the coastal plain of the promised land, across the Jezreel Valley, and north along the Fertile Crescent to Babylon. This Canaanite influence could have produced one Semitic language, the common language for international trade purposes. This could explain how Abraham communicated with the Egyptians and Abimelech in the Negev.

Abraham lived in the Negev for about thirty-seven years, from the birth of Isaac to Sarah's death at age 127 in Hebron. Abraham spent the last thirty-eight years of his life in Hebron, where Ishmael and Isaac buried him with Sarah in the cave he bought from the Hittites.[145]

---

[145] Alan Ray Buescher, *Abraham's Travels*. Biblical Illustrator, LifeWay: Volume 39, number 1, Fall 2012, 10-15.

JERUSALEM: SKULL HILL, NEAR THE GARDEN TOMB (PROTESTANT) (1)

Photo courtesy of the Israeli Ministry of Tourism and is solely for this photo only at www.goisrael.com

THE VALLEY OF KIDRON

Photo courtesy of the Israeli Ministry of Tourism and is solely for this photo only at www.goisrael.com

The Valley of Kidron

The Bible calls the Kidron Valley the "Valley of Jehoshaphat". The Hebrew word is *Eek Yehoshafat,* which means "the valley where God will judge." This is referenced in Joel 3:12, which says, "Let the heathen be wakened, and come up to the valley of Jehoshaphat: for there will I sit to judge all the heathen round about." Zechariah and Mary, the mother of Jesus, are buried here. King David also fled through here during the troubled times of Absalom's rebellion. Jesus crossed this valley many times when he traveled between Jerusalem and Bethany.[146]

This valley is located between the Temple Mount and the Mount of Olives. The world's oldest Jewish cemetery is on the Mount of Olives. Some people believe that when the Messiah comes, it will bring a great resurrection of the dead to those buried here. Another name for the valley is the "Vale of the King". Once it was cultivated and the money went to the king.[147]

Absalom's Tomb has a conical-shaped roof and the Bible tells us the rebellious son of David built a monument here so he would be remembered.[148] II Samuel 15:23 says, "And all the country wept with a loud voice, and all the people passed over: the king (David) also

---

[146] www.en.wikipedia.org/wiki/kidron_valley#.

[147] www.allaboutarchaeology.org/kidron-valley.faq.htm

[148] www.goisrael.com/tourism_eng/tourist.

himself passed over the brook Kidron, and all the people passed over, toward the way of the wilderness."

The Kidron Valley is also where King Asa burned the pagan idols and Asherah poles, as written in 1 Kings 15:13: "And also Maachah his mother, even her he removed from being queen, because she had made an idol in a grove; and Asa destroyed her idol, and burnt it by the brook Kidron." The wicked Athaliah also was executed in the Kidron Valley: "And they laid hands on her; and she went by the way by the which the horses came into the king's house: and there was she slain" (I1 Kings 11:16).

The Kidron Valley became an important Jewish cemetery as far back as King Josiah: "And he brought out the grove from the house of the Lord, without Jerusalem, unto the brook Kidron, and burned it at the brook Kidron, and stamped it small to powder, and cast the powder thereof upon the graves of the children of the people" (I1 Kings 23:6).

In the New Testament, Jesus traveled from Jerusalem to Bethany through the Kidron Valley to raise Lazarus from the dead (John 11:1-46). Many Bible scholars believe Jesus Christ will return to earth on the Mount of Olives, cross over the Kidron Valley, and arrive in Jerusalem as King of Kings. Jews believe the Messiah will come from the east, and pass over the Mount of Olives and through the Kidron Valley before arriving on the Temple Mount. Muslims believe the prophet Jesus will return to Jerusalem in a similar way.[149]

The tomb of Zechariah the priest, stoned to death in the temple, is located in the Kidron Valley also. King Josiah, who ruled Judah from 640 to 609 BC, gave the Royal order (read 2 Chronicles 20-22).

The tomb of Saint James, a disciple of Jesus, is also in the Valley of Kidron. During the time of King Hezekiah (716 to 686 BC), the king's subjects threw out pagan items from the temple and piled them outside the temple courtyard. Then the Levites helped the priests by carrying the trash to the Kidron Valley: "And the priests went into the inner part of the house of the Lord, to cleanse it, and brought out all the uncleanness that they found in the temple of the Lord. And the Levites took it, to carry it out abroad into the brook Kidron" (2 Chronicles 29:16).

---

[149] www.allaboutarchaeology.org/kidron-valley.faq.htm.

This dumping of trash and pagan items used in idol worship continued until it piled up to an estimated height of fifty to 100 feet. In Bible times, a dry streambed or wadi, called Kidron Brook, flowed through the Kidron Valley. This stream is not there today because it was replaced with an underground drainage culvert underneath a modern road.[150]

King David fled across the Kidron Valley to get away from his son Absalom who was trying to take over the kingdom: "And there came a messenger to David, saying, 'The hearts of the men of Israel are after Absalom.' And David said unto all his servants that were with him at Jerusalem, 'Arise and let us flee; for we shall not else escape from Absalom; make speed to depart, lest he overtake us suddenly, and bring evil upon us, and smite the city with the edge of the sword'" (II Samuel 15:13-14).

The Valley of Hinnon

In ancient times, the Valley of Hinnon was known as Topheth and Gehenna. It extends from the base of Mount Zion to the Kidron Valley. It was the boundary between the tribes of Benjamin and Judah (Joshua 15:8, 18:16). Other scriptures in the Bible identify Hinnon as a place of wickedness. Idol worship and the sacrificing of children even by the kings took place in Hinnon (2 Chronicles 28:3, 33:6). God punished Judah for these evil practices (Jeremiah 7:30-34).

Part of the Hinnon Valley was used as a trash dump. Trash was burned there regularly and became illustrated as hell. In New Testament times, people called it the Greek word, Gehenna. Within the Valley of Hinnon but close to the Kidron Valley is the place known as the "Field of Blood", where Judas killed himself after betraying Jesus for thirty pieces of silver (Acts 1:19).[151]

The Tyropeon Valley

This valley begins at the Damascus Gate and descends to the Kidron and Hinnon Valleys just above the Pool of Siloam. It was once

---

[150]   George W. Knight, *The Holy Land*, 94-95.
[151]   David R. Barnhart, *Israel, Land of Promise and Prophecy*, 60.

a deep valley, but in modern times it is filled with debris from many centuries. In the days of Herod, this valley divided Jerusalem into two parts, called the upper and the lower. A high bridge supported by arches was in the valley and was used by residents of the upper city to go to the Temple Mount. In modern times, tourists can view two of these arches. The arch that supported the bridge is called the Wilson Arch, named for the archaeologist who discovered it. The arch that supported the steps is called the Robinson Arch, named for that archaeologist.[152]

Abraham's Travels (continued)

Abraham did not travel much because he spent twenty-five years in Hebron, thirty-seven years in the Negev, and then thirty-eight years back in Hebron. Southern Canaan was his home, yet he never possessed the land. In the Negev he "lived as a foreigner in the land of the Philistines for many days" (Genesis 21:34). Abimelech respected Abraham and they lived peacefully as neighbors except for a couple misunderstandings. In Hebron the Hittites also respected Abraham, but Abraham considered himself as "a resident alien." He owned only one piece of property, which was a burial cave.

Genesis explains that the reason Abraham went to Canaan was that he believed God and obeyed. God did not promise to give the land to Abraham only (Genesis 15:7); God promised to give it also to his descendants (Genesis 12:7, 15:18). That may be the reason that Abraham considered himself as only a sojourner. Abraham did not live long enough to see his descendants receive the land (Hebrews 11:13). Abraham had no goal to start a nation. His only goal was to live in the land. Abraham inhabited the land by faith, in spite of famine and the obstacle of Pharaoh and Abimelech wanting Sarah for themselves. Nothing stopped God's plan. Psalm 37:3 simply says that Abraham trusted God and lived accordingly.

Alan Ray Buescher is a free-lancing writer from Nashville, Tennessee.[153]

---

[152] Ibid.

[153] Alan Ray Buescher, *Abraham's Travels*. Biblical Illustrator, LifeWay: Volume 39, number 1, Fall 2012, 10-15.

THE GATE OF MERCY ON THE MOUNT OF OLIVES
Courtesy of the Israeli Ministry of Tourism and is solely for this photo only at www.goisrael.com

Breaking All the Rules: Jesus and the Samaritan Woman

Jesus constantly got in trouble with the religious rule keepers because Jesus believed people were more important than rules. The behavior of Jesus infuriated the Pharisees who thought they were keeping the Law of God and the commandments of man. John 4:27 tells us that the disciples of Jesus were shocked sometimes about His unconventional behavior. Compliance was expected while individuality was not tolerated. Jews were expected to act like Jews, men acting like men and women acting like women. If someone did not act within the norm, the people judged them.

In John 4:7, Jesus was not in the norm to ask the Samaritan woman at Jacob's well for a drink of water. He broke a rule of social behavior when he simply said, "Give me a glass of water." The rule was that Jews had no contact with Samaritans. Jesus was teaching against stereotypes that divided people then and now. Jews and Samaritans hated each other and both claimed to be the true children of Abraham. We know that the people of Judah came from the tribes of Judah and Benjamin. Some scholars think that the Samaritans came from the northern kingdom after the Assyrians conquered and colonized the Israelites (I1 Kings 17:24-41). These were the people who lived in Samaria and were called "Cutheans", named after a city just north of Babylon. The Samaritans were the result of intermarriage between Israelites and Assyrians. Their descendants may have been among those that confronted Ezra and Nehemiah (Nehemiah 4:1-4).[154]

The Mount of Olives got its name because olive trees grew there in Bible times. It is a high hill that is more than 200 feet above Jerusalem, with the Kidron Valley between it and the city walls. Visitors can look down into Jerusalem and see most of the attractions. On the opposite side of the peak, visitors can see the Judean Desert that leads to the Dead Sea about fifteen miles from Jerusalem.

---

[154] Rodney Reeves, *Breaking All the Rules: Jesus and the Samaritan Woman*. Biblical Illustrator, LifeWay: Volume 39, number 1, Fall 2012, 15-19.

William Thompson visited Jerusalem in the mid-1800's and said the following:

I was struck by the extreme contrast between the two views from the Mount of Olives. Facing eastward, my eyes fell over leagues of hopeless desert – the Wilderness of Judea ending in the Dead Sea. When I turned to the west, at my feet lay the Holy City with its sacred sites, symbolic names, and precious memories suggestive of peace with God and life eternal in the Jerusalem on high. It seemed not accidental that the Creator had placed here upon this hill one view against the other. Look to the left, and nothing appears but evil and cursing, all the way down to the bitter lake of Sodom. But on the right hand you behold with delight the symbols of life, goodness, and blessing. This was a vivid reminder of the words of Moses to the Israelites: "I have set before you life and death, blessing and cursing; therefore choose life, that both thou and thy seed may live" (Deuteronomy 30:19).[155]

In the Old Testament, King David and his aides climbed the Mount of Olives to escape the rebellion of David's son, Absalom (2 Samuel 15:30-37).

In the New Testament, the Mount of Olives is mentioned in relation to the visits of Jesus to Jerusalem:

As he sat on the Mount of Olives, the disciples came to him privately, saying, "Tell us, when will these things be, and what will be the sign of your coming and of the close of the age." (Matthew 24:3)

And when they had sung a hymn, they went out to the Mount of Olives. (Matthew 26:30) [156]

The Pater Noster church is a partially constructed Roman Catholic church located on the Mount of Olives and north of the Tombs of the Prophets in Jerusalem. It stands on the traditional site where Jesus taught the Lord's Prayer. The church is located in the At-Tur district of Jerusalem, which has a population of about 18,000 people, mainly Arabs.[157]

The Mount of Olives is one peak of a mountain ridge which goes three and a half kilometers east of Old Jerusalem, across the Kidron

---

[155] William Thompson, *The Land and the Book.*

[156] George W. Knight, *The Holy Land*, 130-131.

[157] www.en.wikipedia.org/wiki/church-of-the-pater-noster.

Valley in the area called the Valley of Jehoshaphat. The peak to the north is Mount Scopus and the peak to the south is the Mount of Corruption. The latter received its name from the idol worship begun there by King Solomon and the building of altars to the gods of his Moabite and Ammonite wives. Josiah the King of Judah finally destroyed the altars and idol worship.

Then did Solomon build an high place for Chemosh, the abomination of Moab, in the hill that is before Jerusalem, and for Molech, the abomination of the children of Ammon. And likewise did he for all his strange wives, which burnt incense and sacrificed unto their gods. (1 Kings 11: 7-8)

And the high places that were before Jerusalem, which were on the right hand of the mount of corruption, which Solomon the king of Israel had builded for Ashtoreth the abomination of the Zidonians, and for Chemosh the abomination of the Moabites, and for Milcom the abomination of the children of Ammon, did the king defile. (11 Kings 23:13)

The mountain ridge that contains the Mount of Olives is a watershed and its eastern side is the beginning of the Judean Desert. The ridge is made of oceanic sedimentary rock from the Late Cretaceous with soft chalk and a hard flint. It is easy to quarry but does not have enough strength for construction. That is why the Mount was not built with many buildings but has many burial caves. It is a burial site for the prophets Haggai, Zechariah, and Malachi.[158]

THE HURVA SYNAGOGUE FROM OUTSIDE

Courtesy of the Israeli Ministry of Tourism and is solely for this photo only at www.goisrael.com

The Hurva Synagogue is also known as Hurvat Rabbi Yehudah he-Hasid, which means "Ruin of Rabbi Judah the Pious". It is a historic synagogue found in the Jewish Quarter of the Old City of Jerusalem.

---

[158] www.en.wikipedia.org/wiki/mount_of_olives.

This synagogue was established in the early 18th century by the followers of Judah he-Hasid and was destroyed by the Muslims in 1721. The property remained only as ruins for over 140 years and was called the Ruin or Hurva. In 1864, Perushim rebuilt the synagogue and called it Hurva although it still had the name Hurvat Rabbi Yehudah he-Hasid. It was Jerusalem's Ashkenazic synagogue until the Arab Legion destroyed it during the 1948 Arab-Israeli War. The new rebuilt synagogue opened on March 15, 2010.

Rabbi Judah he-Hasid arrived from Europe in the winter of 1700 with 500 Ashkenazic believers. They wanted to settle in Jerusalem to wait for the Messianic Era and the arrival of the Messiah. A few days after their arrival, Rabbi Judah died. The followers who remained in Jerusalem managed to build forty dwellings and a small synagogue in the Ashkenazic Compound. By the late 1720's, the people were in debt and imprisoned, and the Arab lenders eventually exiled the Ashkenazic people.

When the synagogue was rebuilt, the prayer hall was reached by an entrance with three iron gates. The women's section was in the galleries, and the way to get to the galleries was through towers on the corners of the buildings. The Holy Ark could house fifty Torah scrolls and was built on two levels. The Ark came from the Nikolaijewsky Synagogue in Kherson, Russia.[159]

---

[159] www.en.wikipedia.org/wiki/the_hurva.

CHAIM STREET IN THE JEWISH QUARTER
Courtesy of the Israeli Ministry of Tourism and is solely for this photo only at www.goisrael.com

The Jewish Quarter is in the southeastern sector of the Old City of Jerusalem, and goes from Zion Gate in the south along the Armenian Quarter on the west, up to the street of the Chaim in the north and to the Western Wall and the Temple Mount in the east. About 2,000 people live in the Jewish Quarter of Jerusalem. The Hurva Synagogue is also located in the Jewish Quarter.

In Roman times, the Roman Emperor Hadrian built the city of Aelia Capitolina on the ruins of ancient Jerusalem, and the Tenth Legion had their camp on the land that is now the Jewish Quarter. The most important site in the Jewish Quarter is The Western Wall, of which a part was built by King Herod in the 1st century BC. The Temple Mount once housed the temple of Jerusalem. In modern times, the Temple Mount has the Dome of the Rock and the Al-Aqsa Mosque.[160]

Jerusalem's Cardo starts at Damascus Gate in the north and goes southward to Zion Gate. Jerusalem's Cardo is found on the Madaba Map, a highly detailed mosaic map that was the floor of a Byzantine church in the town of Madaba, which is now located in Jordan. This map is the oldest known detailed cartographic representation of Jerusalem. The northern section of the Cardo goes from Damascus Gate to David Street and dates back to the Roman period. The southern section runs to the western section of the Jewish Quarter. It was built during the Byzantine period in the 6th century AD. Excavations between Habad Street and the Street of the Jews discovered irregular sections of the Byzantine Cardo for a length of 180 meters.

The Cardo had an open main passageway for carriages and animals, and on both sides had footways for pedestrians. The street was paved with slabs of stone and was twenty-two and a half meters wide. Some sections had domed shops on the side of the passenger walk. The southern section of the Cardo excavations revealed the Byzantine

---

[160] www.en.wikipedia.org/wiki/jewish_quarter_(jerusalem).

Cardo level. In modern times, tourists can walk through the Cardo in the same way as the people did in the 6th century AD. The Crusader Bazaar was built in the 12th century on top of the Byzantine Cardo. Today it is the site of a modern commercial center.[161]

The Siebenberg House is a museum below a house on 5 Beit HaShoeva Alley in the Old City of Jerusalem. Theo and Miriam Siebenberg bought this house in 1970, and Theo was convinced he had archaeological remains around his house. He financed and directed the archaeology project. The project lasted eighteen years and discovered ancient dwellings and some rooms cut out of rock, ritual baths, aqueducts, and huge cistern and burial vaults going back 3,000 years to the days of King Solomon and the First Temple period, Second Temple period, and Byzantine period. It also shows artifacts of pottery, glass, mosaics, coins, jars, and weapons.[162]

The Roman Cardo was lined with tall columns and had the width of a modern six-lane highway. Archaeologists found a 500-foot section of a street that is about eight feet below the modern street level in the 1970's.[163]

In 1967, after reuniting Jerusalem once again under Jewish sovereignty, Israel began to rebuild the Jewish Quarter, and many discoveries from long ago were found and preserved. Visitors can see the Herodian Quarter ruins dating back to 70 AD, when Jerusalem was destroyed by the Roman Emperor Titus. There are ruins of a wall from the time of Hezekiah and a house that was destroyed by the Romans. The 1st-century house belonged to the Kathros. It is amazing that the archaeologists found items that dated the destruction of the house on the month of Elul of the eighth day in the year 70 AD. They discovered an outstretched hand of a woman and a spear nearby.

As the Old Testament says:

Hear O Israel: The Lord our God is one Lord: and thou shalt love the Lord thy God with all thy soul, and with all thy might. And these words, which I command thee this day, shall be in thine heart; and thou shalt teach them diligently unto thy children, and shalt talk of them when thou sittest in thine house, and when thou walkest by the way, and when thou liest down, and when thou risest up.

---

[161]   www.jewish-quarter.org.il/atar-kardo.asp.

[162]   www.en.wikipedia.org/wiki/siebenberg_house.

[163]   George W. Knight, *The Holy Land*, 117.

And thou shalt bind them for a sign upon thy hand, and they shall be as frontlets between thine eyes. And thou shalt write them upon the posts of thy house, and on thy gates. (Deuteronomy 6:4-9)

And it came to pass, if ye shall hearken diligently unto my commandments which I command you this day, to love the Lord your God, and to serve him with all your heart and with all your soul, that I will give you the rain of your land in his due season, the first rain and the latter rain, that thou mayest gather in thy corn, and thy wine, and thou oil. And I will send grass in thy fields for thy cattle, that thou mayest eat and be full. Take heed to yourselves that your heart be not deceived, and ye turn aside, and serve other gods, and worship them; and then the Lord's wrath be kindled against you, and he shut up the heaven, that there be no rain, and that the land yield not her fruit; and lest ye perish quickly from off the good land which the Lord giveth you. Therefore shall ye lay up these my words in your heart and in your soul, and bind them for a sign upon your hand, that they may be as frontlets between your eyes. And ye shall teach them to your children, speaking of them when thou sittest in thine house, and when thou walkest by the way, when thou liest down, and when thou risest up. And thou shalt write them upon the door posts of thine house, and upon thy gates: that your days may be multiplied, and the days of your children, in the land which the Lord sware unto your fathers to give them, as the days of heaven upon earth. (Deuteronomy 11:13-21)

These verses in Deuteronomy, beginning with "Hear, O Israel," make the Jewish prayer, known as "Shema Yisrael". In following these words from the Torah, Jewish people put a mezuzah onto the doorframe of their houses to fulfill the *mitzvah* (biblical commandment) to post the words of the Shema on the doorposts of one's house. The parchment is made by a qualified scribe who studies for years. The verses are written in black indelible ink with a special quill pen. The parchment is rolled up and placed inside the case. The case should be placed on the right side of the door or doorpost, at shoulder height.

THE ROOF OF THE CHURCH OF THE HOLY SEPULCHRE

Courtesy of the Israeli Ministry of Tourism and is solely for this photo only at www.goisrael.com

Breaking All the Rules: Jesus and the Samaritan Woman (continued)

Other scholars believe that the Samaritans are descendants of priests who defected from Jerusalem after the campaign of Ezra and Nehemiah, but before the Hasmonean dynasty that joined together the priesthood and the monarchy. These protesters withdrew to Shechem of Samaria and built a temple on Mount Gerizim, which the Samaritans claim is the original tabernacle. They preserved their own version of the Law of Moses called the Samaritan Pentateuch and claimed to be the true descendants of Abraham. In 128 BC, a Hasmonean king, John Hyrcanus, destroyed the temple of these "Shechemites" who retaliated by attacking a group of Jewish pilgrims traveling through Samaria. The Samaritans were mortal enemies of the Jewish people.

In John 4:9, the Samaritan woman was surprised when Jesus asked her for some water, due to the hatred for centuries. In the time of Jesus, men and women seldom spoke to one another in public. Even husband and wife conversed mainly in the privacy of their house. The main reason a man would talk to an unknown woman was to engage in an improper relationship. The Samaritan woman interpreted it to mean Jesus was looking for company. The fact that she was getting water out of the well by herself is something unusual because women did not draw water by themselves.

When Jesus said, "Go call your husband", the woman would have thought it was an inquiry to see if she was available. She replied, "I have no husband." That usually meant a woman was willing to get to know a man. Jesus revealed to the woman that he knew the details of her past, and she realized this was no ordinary man. The woman was puzzled as she thought, "He is a Jew, I am a Samaritan; He is a man, I am a woman; He is a prophet, and I am a sinner." In their day, a holy man would not drink from an unclean bucket. When Jesus drank from the bucket, he was signaling that she was a clean vessel, too. She asked Jesus about the location of the true temple. A Jewish man would have said, "Jerusalem." Jesus said, "Neither this mountain nor in Jerusalem will you worship the Father." Jesus made it clear to her that the time had come for all people, whether Jew or Samaritan, man or woman, clean or unclean, to worship the one, living, true God.

Rodney Reeves is dean to The Courts Redford College of Theology and Church Vocations of Southwest Baptist University in Bolivan, Missouri.[164]

The Stone of the Anointing is the place where it is believed the body of Jesus was taken, to prepare the body with spices before placing him in the tomb. This is station thirteen on the Via Dolorosa. A secret disciple of Jesus, Joseph of Arimathea, asked Pilate if he could remove the body of Jesus and prepare it for burial. Nicodemus and Joseph used seventy-five pounds of myrrh and aloe-perfumed ointment. They followed Jewish burial customs and wrapped the body of Jesus with spices and linens.[165]

Another name for the Stone of the Anointing is the Stone of Unction. The current stone was added in the 1810 reconstruction. A wall sits on top of the graves of four 12th-century kings, and the wall is no longer structurally necessary.

The twelfth station contains the Rock of Calvary that can be seen under a glass case on both sides of the altar. Beneath the altar is a hole that many believe was caused when the cross was raised.[166]

Barnabas: All We Know

Barnabas was born in Cyprus to a Levitical family and was named Joseph. The Apostles in Jerusalem named him "Barnabas" which means Son of Encouragement (Acts 4:36). The early church saw Barnabas as a "good man full of the Holy Spirit and of faith" (Acts 11:24). Barnabas sold a field and gave the profit to the church (Acts 4:36-37). Barnabas had the title of apostle (Acts 14:14). Barnabas intervened for Paul when the Jerusalem disciples and apostles were concerned about Paul's persecution of the church (Acts 9:26-27). Barnabas embraced John Mark when Paul rejected him as a partner for mission work (Acts 15:36-41). Barnabas supported Paul when the Judeans wanted to force circumcision on the Gentile believers as part of salvation (Acts 15 and Galatians 2:1-10).

---

[164]   Rodney Reeves, *Breaking All the Rules: Jesus and the Samaritan Woman.* Biblical Illustrator, LifeWay: Volume 39, number 1, Fall 2012, 15-19.

[165]   George W. Knight, *The Holy Land,* 113-114.

[166]   www.en.wikipedia.org/wiki/church_of_the_holy_sepulchre.

Barnabas was a people person and helped in the ministries with Simeon (called Niger), Lucius, Manaen, Saul who was later called Paul at Antioch (Acts 15:7), John Mark (Acts 12:25, 13:13, 15:36-41), Peter (Acts 15:7, Galatians 2:9-13), James and John (Acts 15:13, Galatians 2:9), Joseph (called Barsabbas) and Silas (Acts 15:22), and Titus (Galatians 2:1). The Jerusalem church spoke of him as "our beloved Barnabas" (Acts 15:25). Barnabas ministered with Paul for about two years, from 47 to 49 AD.

Barnabas gave the introduction of Paul when he needed an introduction to the leadership in the Jerusalem church. Barnabas shared that Paul preached the gospel while in Damascus (Acts 9:27). The issue with the Jerusalem Council was of Gentiles coming to faith in Christ. Barnabas emphasized that God saved Gentiles without them having circumcision (Acts 15).

Later, preparing for the second missionary journey, Barnabas argued with Paul that John Mark should go with Paul and himself. Paul refused because John Mark had returned early during the first missionary trip. Barnabas did not accompany Paul on this trip and took John Mark with him to Cyprus.[167]

THE TOMB OF VIRGIN MARY

Courtesy of the Israeli Ministry of Tourism and is solely for this photo only at www.goisrael.com

Mary's Tomb is in the Kidron Valley at the bottom of the Mount of Olives. The Muslims celebrate Mary as the mother of "the prophet Isa" (Jesus). The cruciform church around the tomb has a wide descending staircase to an underground rock-cut cave. On the left side of the staircase is a chapel of Saint Joseph, Mary's husband. On the right side of the staircase is a chapel of Mary's parents, Joachim and Anne.[168]

---

[167] Roy E. Lucas, *Barnabas: All We Know*. Biblical Illustrator, LifeWay: Volume 39, number 1, Fall 2012, 24-27.

[168] www.en.wikipedia.org/wiki/mary.

THE FIRST STATION OF THE VIA DOLOROSA

Courtesy of the Israeli Ministry of Tourism and is solely for this photo only at www.goisrael.com

The Via Dolorosa (with Stations of the Cross)

The Via Dolorosa, Latin for "Way of Suffering", is a street in Jerusalem believed to be the path that Jesus walked while carrying his cross on his way to his crucifixion. This current route has been used since the 18th century. The convent of the Sisters of Zion includes the Church of Ecce Homo where many archaeological remains were found.[169] The first station of the Via Dolorosa is called the Praetorium, where Pilate condemned Jesus and Jesus took up the cross.

And so Pilate, willing to content the people, released Barabbas unto them, and delivered Jesus, when he had scourged him, to be crucified. And the soldiers led him away into the hall, called Praetorium; and they called together the whole band. And they clothed him with purple, and platted a crown of thorns, and put it about his head. And began to salute him, Hail, King of the Jews! And they smote him on the head with a reed, and did spit on him. And when they had mocked him, they took off the purple from him, and put his own clothes on him, and led him out to crucify him. And they compel one Simon a Cyrenian, who passed by, coming out of the country, the father of Alexander and Rufus, to bear his cross. (Mark 15:15-21)

The first station of the Via Dolorosa is where Pontius Pilate assented to the wishes of the crowd and condemned Jesus to die although Pilate believed Jesus to be innocent.

Pilate then called together the chief priests and the rulers and the people, and said to them, "You brought me this man as one who was misleading the people. And after examining him before you, behold, I did not find this man guilty of any of your charges against him. Neither did Herod, for he sent him back to us. Look, nothing deserving death has been done by him. I will therefore punish and release

---

[169] www.en.wikipedia.org/wiki/via_dolorosa.

him." (For of necessity he must release one unto them at the feast.) But they all cried out together, "Away with this man, and release to us Barabbas", a man who had been thrown into prison for an insurrection started in the city and for murder. Pilate addressed them once more, desiring to release Jesus, but they kept shouting, "Crucify, crucify him!" A third time he said to them, "Why, what evil has he done? I have found in him no guilt deserving death. I will therefore punish and release him." But they were urgent, demanding with loud cries that he should be crucified. And their voices prevailed. So Pilate decided that their demand should be granted. He released the man who had been thrown into prison for insurrection and murder, for whom they asked, but he delivered Jesus over to them. (Luke 23:13-25)

A modern convent owned by the Sisters of Zion stands over a part of the hall where Jesus faced Pilate. In the church basement are ancient flagstones that are believed to be the Stone Pavement mentioned in scripture as the place of judgment in John 19:13: "Then Pilate sat down on the Judgment seat on the platform that is called the Stone Pavement." This convent has the base of an ancient arch called the Ecce Homo Arch that is the place where Pilate presented Jesus to his accusers with these words: "Behold the man!" (John 19:5).[170]

Beneath the pavement where the ancient flagstones were found, archaeologists found a huge water cistern built by Herod the Great. This water cistern may have been used to quench the thirst of the Roman soldiers who taunted Jesus.[171]

The Church of Condemnation contains the location where the vertical beam of the cross was placed on the shoulders of Jesus: "And he bearing his cross went forth into a place called the place of a skull, which is called in the Hebrew Golgotha" (John 19:17). On this site is also the Church of the Flagellation where the Roman soldiers beat Jesus, dressed him in purple robes, placed a mock crown on his head, and made fun of his claim to be a king. Inside the Church of Flagellation is a stained glass window that demonstrates the cruel treatment by Pilate and the Roman soldiers.[172]

The second station is near the Franciscan monastery and is across the street from the first station. The Flagellation Church has three stained-glass windows showing Pilate washing his hands from the sin,

---

[170]   George W. Knight, *The Holy Land*, 108.
[171]   www.goisrael.com/tourism_eng/tourist.
[172]   George W. Knight, *The Holy Land*, 108.

flogging Jesus, and placing a crown of thorns over his head, and shows Barabbas excited about his being chosen for release instead of Jesus.[173] "And Pilate wrote a title, and put it on the cross. And the writing was, Jesus of Nazareth the King of the Jews" (John 19:19).

The third station has a stone tablet that shows Jesus falling from the weight of the cross. There is a small Polish Catholic chapel with a painting of Jesus stumbling with the cross.[174] Around the walls of the Polish Catholic church are paintings of Jesus and the stations of the cross.

The fourth station is very close to the third station and is further south on El-Wadi (Hagai) street. Jesus met his mother, Mary, at the fourth station: "When Jesus therefore saw his mother, and the disciple standing by, whom he loved, he saith unto his mother, 'Woman, behold thy son!'" (John 19:26).

Behind the third and fourth stations is a small section of the Roman/Byzantine street. These stones may have been part of the Roman street, so Jesus may have walked on these stones.[175]

The fifth station is at the corner of the Via Dolorosa road and the El-Wadi (Hagai) street. At this corner, the road turns to the right and then starts climbing up the hill with a series of stairs. A small Franciscan church is located at the fifth station and is dedicated to Simon the Cyrenian who helped Jesus with the cross: "And as they led him away, they laid hold upon one Simon, a Cyrenian, coming out of the country, and on him they laid the cross, that he might bear it after Jesus" (Luke 23:26). Cyrenia is located in modern Libya. There is an old square stone at this station that has a cavity with the imprint of a hand. It is possible that this may belong to Jesus.[176] The Franciscan church at the fifth station was founded in 1229 AD and belongs to the Franciscans. The Bible says that Simon helped Jesus to carry the cross. Scripture does not say, however, that Jesus fell three times as the Via Dolorosa does.[177]

---

[173] www.biblewalks.com/sites/viadolorosa.html.
[174] George W. Knight, *The Holy Land*, 108.
[175] www.biblewalks.com/sites/viadolorosa.html.
[176] Ibid.
[177] George W. Knight, *The Holy Land*, 109.

Barnabas: All We Know (continued)

Barnabas was a persevering person and demonstrated this trait by supporting both Paul and John Mark. Barnabas and Paul were persecuted by devout Jewish women and men of Pisidian Antioch. Rather than abandoning preaching the gospel, they "shook the dust off their feet" and moved to Iconium (Acts 13:50-51). Barnabas remained faithful to Paul when Jews came from Antioch and Iconium to Lystra, stoned Paul, and left him for dead. Barnabas went with Paul to Derbe the next day (Acts 14:19-20). Barnabas always persevered through trouble and never ran from it.

Barnabas was a good, talented, gifted teacher and preacher. In Antioch of Syria, the church people commissioned him by the Holy Spirit to take the gospel to others (Acts 11:26 and Acts 13:1-4). Barnabas preached to Sergius Paulus, a Roman official who presided over Roman court hearings (Acts 13:7).

Roy E. Lewis is professor of Bible at Clear Creek Baptist Bible College, Pineville, Kentucky, and pastor of First Baptist Church, Loyall, Kentucky.[178]

The sixth station is further up the hill and is dedicated to the woman (Saint Veronica) who is said to have wiped the face of Jesus. Luke 23:27 says, "And there followed him a great company of people, and of women, which also bewailed and lamented him."

There is an old stone pillar between the two blue doors with the name of the station. There you can enter the right door, turn left and stand at the end of a long chamber. The interior of the Holy Face Chapel is small like a cave. Burning candles light up the darkness. You can look at a simple stone altar below. The chambers of the crypt are close by, with a stone plate commemorating the visit of Pope Paul VI in 1964.[179]

The name of the woman Veronica comes from Christian legend. According to the legend, Veronica used a silk veil to wipe the blood from the face of Jesus. The image of the face of Jesus is believed by many to have been left on the cloth and is displayed today in the Basilica of Saint Peter in Rome.[180]

---

[178] Roy E. Lucas, *Barnabas: All We Know.* Biblical Illustrator, LifeWay: Volume 39, number 1, Fall 2012, 24-27.

[179] www.biblewalks.com/sites/viadolorosa.html.

[180] George W. Knight, *The Holy Land*, 109.

The seventh station is the place where many believe that Jesus passed through the Gate of Judgment in the streets of ancient Jerusalem. This street is one of the busiest in the Old City. In ancient times, it was an intersection of the Cardo Maximus and a transverse street of the Roman Aelia Capitolina. In modern times it is a busy street intersection with the Via Dolorosa and Khan es-Zeit (the oil market).

Jesus is said to have fallen here for the second time, under the weight of the cross. Behind the doors is a small chapel with stairs leading to the second level. The Franciscans in 1875 gained control of the chapel and closed its doors to the public. A framed picture shows the second fall of Jesus with the cross. Past the Roman column is the chapel of this station. Inside, hanging on the center wall, is a golden statue of Jesus falling with the cross. The Franciscans have a procession every Friday at 3 p.m., starting at the first station of the Via Dolorosa.[181]

The eighth station is located closest to the Church of the Holy Sepulchre. This station is dedicated to the Greek Orthodox Saint Charalampos. The associated monastery is located behind the wall. This station is based on Luke 23:27: "But Jesus turning unto them said, 'Daughters of Jerusalem, weep not for me, but weep for yourselves, and for your children.'" A stone with a monogram, embedded into the wall, marks the station ("IC-XCNI-KA", which means, "Jesus Christ conquers").[182]

When Jesus spoke to the women to weep for themselves instead of him, he was talking about the future destruction of Jerusalem in 70 AD by the Romans[183]:

> *But Jesus turned and said to them, "Daughters of Jerusalem, don't weep for me, but weep for yourselves and for your children. For the days are coming when they will say, 'Fortunate indeed are the women who are childless, the wombs that have not borne a child and the breasts that have never nursed.' People will beg the mountains, 'Fall on us,' and plead with the hills, 'Bury us.' For if these things are done when the tree is green, what will happen when it is dry?" (Luke 23:28-31)*

At the ninth station, Jesus fell for the third time. The ninth station is adjacent to the Holy Sepulchre, which is the tomb of Jesus. This

---

[181] www.biblewalks.com/sites/viadolorosa.html.
[182] www.biblewalks.com/sites/viadolorosa.html.
[183] George W. Knight, *The Holy Land*, 109.

station is marked by a cross which is on a pillar on the wall of the Holy Sepulchre.

Near the ninth station is a tiny Coptic Orthodox church of Saint Helen. Inside this church is a huge water cistern that is reachable via a staircase. This was discovered in the 4th century AD by Helen, the mother of Constantine. The cistern supplies water to the Church of the Holy Sepulchre.

Interesting nearby sites are the cupola that is the top of the underground Armenian Chapel of Saint Helen, and the entrance to the Ethiopian Church of Saint Michael with an area for the Ethiopian monks. A Coptic church is located near the Ethiopian church, and a staircase entrance is in the courtyard. On the right side of this Coptic church is a painting of a Biblical scene from 1 Kings 10:1, when King Solomon received the Queen of Sheba: "And when the queen of Sheba heard of the fame of Solomon concerning the name of the Lord, she came to prove him with hard questions."[184]

Stations ten to fourteen are located inside the Church of the Holy Sepulchre. It has been debated for years whether these stations are at the correct biblical location. Traditionalists insist that this is the location because Helena, the mother of the Roman Emperor Constantine, visited the Holy Land to research the Old City. In 335 AD, she supervised the building of the first church at this location. Helena's mission was to research all areas dealing with the life and ministry of Jesus. Through the centuries, other churches were built on this site as the old churches deteriorated and had to be replaced. The Church of the Holy Sepulchre is the modern church built on the property that Helena chose as the holy site after her extensive research.

Many who question these claims believe that Jesus was crucified and buried outside the walls of Jerusalem, at a skull-shaped hill outside the Old City called Gordon's Calvary. They think that Jesus was crucified at Gordon's Calvary and was buried at what is now the location of the Garden Tomb.

---

[184] www.biblewalks.com/sites/viadolorosa.html.

THE ENTRANCE OF THE CHURCH OF THE HOLY SEPULCHRE, WITH PEOPLE
Courtesy of the Israeli Ministry of Tourism and is solely for this photo only at www.goisrael.com

The Church of the Holy Sepulchre is also known as the Church of the Resurrection. For 1,600 years, this site has been known as the site of the crucifixion, burial, and resurrection of Jesus. Mark Twain visited this church in the late 1800's. Mark Twain said, "I climbed the stairway in the church which brings one to the top of the small enclosed pinnacle of rock. Then I looked under the place where the true cross once stood. I did so with a far more absorbing interest than I had ever felt in anything earthly before. I could not believe that the three holes in the top of the rock were the actual ones the crosses stood in. But I felt satisfied that those crosses had stood so near the place now occupied by them that the few feet of possible difference were a matter of no consequence."

The Church of the Holy Sepulchre is built on an unusual floor plan of smaller chapels or little churches under one roof. The three main caretakers of the church building are the Roman Catholic, Eastern Orthodox, and Armenian Churches. The three minor caretakers are the Coptic Church (national Church of Egypt), the Syrian Orthodox Church, and the Ethiopian Orthodox Church.[185]

The entrance to the church is through a single door in the south transept. This narrow entrance can be dangerous. In 1940, there was a sudden fire, and many were trampled to death.[186]

The Catholic chapel at the tenth station is called the Chapel of the Franks. This chapel represents the place where the Roman soldiers stripped off the clothes of Jesus:[187]

Then the soldiers, when they had crucified Jesus, took his garments, and made four parts, to every soldier a part; and also his coat: now the coat was without seam, woven from the top throughout. They said therefore among themselves, Let us not rend it, but casts lots for it, whose it shall be: that the scripture might be fulfilled,

185 George W. Knight, *The Holy Land*, 113.
186 www.en.wikipedia.org/wiki/church_of_the_holy_sepulchre.
187 George W. Knight, *The Holy Land*, 109.

which saith, They parted my raiment among them, and for my vesture they did cast lots. These things therefore the soldiers did (John 19:23-24).

The church site is known as Golgotha or the Hill of Calvary, where Jesus was crucified and the place where he was buried. It was a Christian site until Emperor Hadrian covered it up with dirt. In about 135 AD, Hadrian built the temple of Aphrodite. In about 325 AD, Constantine was converted to Christianity and asked his mother to build a church on the site. In 333 AD, the Pilgrim of Bordeaux wrote about the beautiful church. During the excavation, Helena found a cross and a tomb. Eusebius believed the tomb was visible proof that it was the tomb of Jesus.

Constantine's church was built as two connecting churches, with the site of Golgotha in one corner and a rotunda which had the remains of a rock-cut room that Helena identified as the burial place. Archaeological evidence revealed that the temple of Aphrodite reached far into the rotunda area and the temple area would have gone further west.

In 614 AD, the Persians invaded Jerusalem and the building was damaged by fire. The Persians then captured the cross. In 630, Emperor Heraclius restored the cross to the rebuilt Church of the Holy Sepulchre. It remained a Christian church but was under Muslim rule, as the early Muslim rulers protected the Christian sites. On October 18, 1009, however, the new Muslim leader, Fatimid caliph Al-Hakim bi-Amr Allah, ordered the entire church to be destroyed. The foundation of the church was hacked into bedrock. The east and the west walls and the roof of the rock-cut tomb it encased were destroyed or damaged. The pillars are the only part left of the 4th-century building.

In 1027, the new caliph Ali az-Zahir reached an agreement to rebuild and redecorate the church. Many Christians who had been forced to Islam recanted and became Christians again. The rebuilt church had a courtyard with five small chapels attached to the courtyard. Many historians believe the main goal of Pope Urban II for the First Crusade on July 15, 1099, was to protect the Church of the Holy Sepulchre. Many Crusaders wanted to pray at the church. Crusader Godfrey of Bouillon was the first crusader monarch of Jerusalem and declared himself Advocate Sancti Sepulchri (Protector of the Holy

Sepulchre). During this time, people believed that the cistern under the former basilica was the location of the true cross. Modern archaeologists have dated this cistern back to the 11th century, when repairs were made, but not during the Crusades. This church was lost to the Muslim ruler Saladin in 1187.[188]

Noah: As New Testament Imagery

Noah appears in only five different episodes in the New Testament. Noah's name appears only fourteen times in the Old Testament in addition to the story of Noah in Genesis chapters 5-10. The use of Noah is an image of judgment and grace that is essential in the Bible's revelation. Each instance of Noah as imagery in the New Testament reveals prophetic urgency and fulfillment.

In Matthew 14:36-42 and Luke 17:26-36, dealing with the events of the return of Jesus and the final judgment of mankind, Jesus reveals that the judgment would come with little warning. In Noah's day, people paid little attention to what Noah said about a flood coming, and paid no attention to the ark he was building. They just kept on with their lives and probably thought Noah was crazy. In Noah's day, mankind ignored their spiritual condition. They were interested in marriages, births, economic endeavors, and social interactions. The people paid no attention to the teaching of Noah and to learning about God, and did nothing to change the sin in their lives (II Peter 2:5). Jesus said that those with little spiritual sensitivity could easily ignore the advance of God's final judgment.

An Old Testament theologian, Kenneth Matthews, teaches about the "sons of God" as the righteous lineage of Seth. Their pursuit and marriage of "whomever they chose" revealed their lack of concern about preserving the standard of righteous living (Genesis 6:2). Samson and Solomon had desires for unrighteous women that drew them into unrighteous living. Some "sons of God" had relationships with the "daughters of men." This was unacceptable to God and part of the "totality of man's sinfulness against which God's spirit wanted" (Genesis 6:3). Luke has a reference to Lot and Sodom and uses the imagery of Noah to reveal a break in the plan and purpose of God for marital relations.

Simon Peter used the imagery of Noah to emphasize the sinful times and the patience of God (I Peter 3:20). Noah contrasted the scene as God being long-suffering and delaying judgment, and man's sinfulness being a conflict. Mankind ignored the gracious call of God during the time that Noah was building the ark.

---

[188] www.en.wikipedia.org/wiki/church_of_the_holy_sepulchre.

Peter used the imagery of Noah by talking about Noah's faith that saved him and his family from destruction. Peter pointed out that the true believer does not have to fear God's judgment or the penalty of His wrath. The act of baptism is a testimony and a visual reminder of the faith of the believer, the favor of God, and the assurance of rescue (I Peter 3:20-21).[189]

Tradition holds that Jesus was nailed to the cross at the location of the eleventh station. The altar is known as the Nails of the Cross. There is a mosaic on the inside wall illustrating the crucifixion.[190]

The twelfth station is the location where it is believed that Jesus died on the cross. The Eastern Orthodox Church insists that this is the exact spot for Jesus' death, marked by a silver disk. On each side of the silver disk is a black disk that marks the spot of the two people crucified with Jesus:[191] "Then were there two thieves crucified with him, one on the right hand, and another on the left" (Matthew 27:38).

This is the place, in a hole beneath the altar, where many believe the cross was raised. The main floor has what is called the Chapel of Adam. Some people believe Jesus was crucified over the place where Adam's skull was buried.[192]

Noah: As New Testament Imagery (continued)

In II Peter, Peter used Noah and the flood as the situation in the Old Testament that made the flood of God's judgment sure for those who rejected Jesus and continued living in unrighteous unbelief. As the judgment waits for the unbeliever, so redemption awaits the believer. In II Peter 2:5 it says, "As God was able to save righteous Noah and his family, so He will forever save those who trust in Him."

The book of Hebrews urged men and women to greater trust and obedience by remembering to use the images of Noah.

"By faith Noah, being warned concerning things not yet seen, reverently prepared an ark for the salvation of his household, by which he condemned the world, and became an heir by means of righteousness of faith" (Hebrews 11:7, Translation by the author, Randall Adkisson).

---

[189] Randall L. Adkisson, *Noah: As New Testament Imagery*. Biblical Illustrator, LifeWay: Volume 39, number 1, Fall 2012, 28-31.

[190] George W. Knight, *The Holy Land*, 109.

[191] Ibid, 113.

[192] www.en.wikipedia.org/wiki/church_of_the_holy_sepulchre.

Randall L. Adkisson is senior pastor of First Baptist Church, Cookeville, Tennessee.[193]

Perfect: A Word Study

The English word "perfect" comes from the word teleios, *which in biblical times had many meanings. The word* teleios *spoke of something being* complete *in the sense that nothing that belonged to the item was missing. People spoke of* teleios *to speak of someone who had completed stages of learning and there were no more stages to complete. It referred to a doctor who had finished a course of study and lacked nothing by way of training. Translators used* teleios *to translate the Hebrew words that spoke of wholeness or reaching the purposes for which something or someone was created. This is what Jesus meant when He said in Matthew 5:48, "Be perfect, therefore as your heavenly Father is perfect." Jesus was not saying humans can be perfect. Paul the Apostle stated, "All have sinned, and fall short of the glory of God" (Romans 3:23).*

The New Testament writers used teleios *nineteen times and in a variety of ways. Paul used* teleios *to mean maturity when he said, "Brothers, don't be childish in your thinking, but be infants in regard to evil and adult in your thinking" (I Corinthians 14:20). The writer of Hebrews wrote, "But solid food is for the mature, for those whose senses have been trained to distinguish between good and evil" (Hebrews 5:14).*[194]

On the south side of the ambulatory is a stairway climbing to Calvary where many believe Jesus was crucified.[195]

The site of the anointing stone is part of the thirteenth station of the Via Dolorosa. This church is one of the oldest in the world. Catholic tradition has it that this church is built over Calvary Hill and the burial tomb of Christ. In 325 AD, Helena, the mother of Constantine, was sent to Jerusalem to find the holy sites of Jesus. Eusebius, Bishop of Caesarea, and Marcarius, Bishop of Jerusalem, searched for the sites. Constantine insisted that all the pagan buildings built by Hadrian be destroyed. When the temple of Jupiter was torn down, the excited

---

[193] Randall L. Adkisson, *Noah: As New Testament Imagery*. Biblical Illustrator, LifeWay: Volume 39, number 1, Fall 2012, 28-31.

[194] Michael Priest, *Perfect: A Word Study*. Biblical Illustrator, LifeWay: Volume 39, number 1, Fall 2012, 32-35.

[195] www.en.wikipedia.org/wiki/church_of_the_holy_sepulchre.

search team discovered the ruins of the hill of Calvary and the tomb where Jesus was buried. Some scholars think that Hadrian built on the holy sites to wipe out the spread of Christianity, having discovered the ruins of the hill of Calvary and the tomb where Jesus was buried.

The original church was dedicated in 335 AD and destroyed in 614. In 1009 it was destroyed by Khalif Hakem. This may have led to the Crusades, because Catholics did not like it being destroyed. A second building was later destroyed in 1149. The third church was damaged by fire in 1808. Some of the present building dates back to the Crusades. The church today is controlled by the Greek Orthodox, Latins, Armenians, Coptics, and Syrians. Ironically, the keys of the church are in the hands of two families of Muslims. Since the days of Saladin, it has been a tradition for Muslims to be keepers of the keys.

In the main entrance to the church is a set of stairs leading to the top of Calvary Hill. A Greek Orthodox altar is on the place where Christ was crucified. Tourists can reach through the floor and touch the hill. Catholic tradition believes Adam is buried directly under the hill of Calvary. This tradition believes that at the time of crucifixion, the earth split open and some of the blood of Jesus fell on top of Adam's remains.

JESUS IMAGE CUPOLA IN THE CHURCH OF THE HOLY SEPULCHRE
Courtesy of the Israeli Ministry of Tourism and is solely for this photo only at www. goisrael.com

PRAYING INSIDE THE CHURCH OF THE HOLY SEPULCHRE
Courtesy of the Israeli Ministry of Tourism and is solely for this photo only at www. goisrael.com

The Rotunda of the church is located in the middle of the Anastasis, beneath the church's two domes. In the center of the Rotunda is a chapel called The Edicule that holds two rooms. One room holds the Angel's Stone, a small piece of the stone believed to have sealed the tomb after the burial of Jesus. The second room is the tomb of Jesus. The Eastern Orthodox, Roman Catholic, and Armenian Apostolic churches have Holy Mass there daily. They have special masses on Holy Saturday and Holy Fire celebrations. The rest of the Rotunda is a chapel with an opening of a rock-cut chamber with several kokh-tombs. Many Christians believe that one of the graves may belong to Joseph of Arimathea.[196]

Jesus is believed to have been laid in the tomb at a spot marked by the Church of the Holy Sepulchre. On the east side opposite the Rotunda is a Crusader structure with the main altar of the Church. In the northeast side is the Prison of Christ where the Franciscans believe Jesus was held.

Sometimes there is trouble among all of the church groups who control the church. In 2002, a Coptic monk moved his chair from the agreed spot into the shade. The Ethiopians thought the monk was breaking agreement and eleven were hospitalized after the fight. In 2004 during Orthodox celebrations, the door to the Franciscan chapel was left open. A fight resulted and some were arrested.[197]

JERUSALEM: CHURCH OF THE HOLY SEPULCHRE (CRUSADER ENTRANCE)

Courtesy of the Israeli Ministry of Tourism and is solely for this photo only at www.goisrael.com

---

[196] www.en.wikipedia.org/wiki/church_of_the_holy_sepulchre.
[197] Ibid.

Scholars believe that the Church of the Holy Sepulchre is the true burial place of Jesus because the site was a disused quarry outside the city walls. Tombs dating back to the 1st century BC and AD had been cut into the vertical west wall. The topographical parts of the site of the church are similar to the Gospel descriptions, saying that Jesus was crucified on a rock that looked like a skull outside the city. John 19:17 says, "And he bearing his cross went forth into a place called the place of a skull, which is called Golgotha." John 19: 41-42 says, "Now in the place where he was crucified there was a garden; and in the garden a new sepulchre, wherein was never man yet laid. There laid they Jesus therefore because of the Jews' preparation day, for the sepulchre was right at hand."

Windblown dirt and seeds, watered by winter rains, may have created the green covering on the rock that John calls a garden. According to Eusebius and Socrates Scholasticus who wrote centuries later, the Christian community of Jerusalem held worship services at this site until 66 AD. Even when the site was brought within the city walls in 41-43 AD, the site was not built upon by the local community. In 135 AD, Emperor Hadrian built a Temple of Venus over the site, which may mean that Christians regarded it as a holy site and Hadrian wished to claim the site for the traditional Roman religion.

Constantine wanted to build his church in 326 AD, and could have chosen a site to the south, called open space for Hadrian's forum, and inexpensive. Choosing the site of the Church of the Holy Sepulchre was very expensive to have to tear down the Temple of Venus and build a large church.

Dan Bahat, former City Archaeologist of Jerusalem, said the following about this site: "We may not be absolutely certain the site of the Holy Sepulchre Church is the site of Jesus' burial, but we have no other site that can lay a claim nearly as weighty, and we really have no reason to reject the authenticity of the site."[198] In modern times, the site of the crucifixion and burial site of Jesus can be entered from the Saint Helena alley in the Christian quarter, through a gate on the right side.

There are some columns that legend says fire came out of in 1547. The Greek Orthodox Christians view this as a miracle of the Holy Fire that happened after they were not permitted to enter the Church. This

---

[198] www.sacred-destinations.com/israel.

incident helped them to reclaim the right of access. Other incidents of the Holy Fire occurred inside the church, near the tomb of Jesus. In the ceremony, the Patriarch lights up a fire which symbolizes the resurrection. Then the fire is passed to the torches held by the crowd. In 1834, the fire caused a great panic, and crowds pushed their way out and trampled other people.[199]

Perfect: A Word Study (continued)

The followers of Jesus are to express love completely on all people, not just those who are lovable or reciprocate in love. They are to love their enemies and even pray for those who persecute them. This is teleios *love. This is the kind of love God has. This is the kind of love Christians are to express because we are children of our Father in heaven.*
Michael Priest is pastor of Bartlett Baptist Church, Bartlett, Tennessee.[200]

Simon Peter: His Years of Ministry

The book of Acts describes Peter as bold, courageous, and confident. Peter addressed surprised worshipers in the temple. He spoke to crowds on the Day of Pentecost. Peter confronted Sapphira and Ananias with sharp words. Peter preached the gospel to Cornelius and witnessed the Holy Spirit empowering Gentile believers. Three times Peter was put into prison for preaching the gospel. The Lord sent angels to set Peter free for preaching the gospel two times. In Acts 5:20, the angel said, "Go and stand in the temple complex and tell the people all about this life."

Jesus gave Peter his nickname, "the Rock". Peter fell asleep in the Garden of Gethsemane when Jesus asked him to stay awake and pray. Jesus pointed out to Peter that he was sleeping and called him Simon to let him know his conduct was unacceptable for a dedicated follower. Although Peter denied Jesus three times in the Garden of Gethsemane, he later was a courageous disciple who stood before the Sanhedrin to bravely proclaim the message of Jesus.[201]

Ein Karem in Hebrew means "Spring of the Vineyard". It was an ancient village of the Jerusalem District, and in modern times is a

---

[199] www.biblewalks.com/sites/sepulcher.html.

[200] Michael Priest, *Perfect: A Word Study*. Biblical Illustrator, LifeWay: Volume 39, number 1, Fall 2012, 32-35.

[201] Mark R. Dunn, *Simon Peter: His Years of Ministry*. Biblical Illustrator, LifeWay: Volume 39, number 1, Fall 2012, 39-41.

neighborhood in southwest Jerusalem. Christians believe that John the Baptist was born here. In 2010, the neighborhood had a population of 2,000. There are about three million tourists every year from all over the world. Pottery has been discovered here, dating back to the Middle Bronze Age. During the Old Testament times the site was called Beth-Haccerem: "O ye children of Benjamin, gather yourselves to flee out of the midst of Jerusalem, and blow the trumpet in Tekoa, and set up a sign of fire in Beth-Haccerem: for evil appeareth out of the north, and great destruction" (Jeremiah 6:1). Beth-Haccerem is also mentioned in Nehemiah:

"But the dung gate repaired Malchiah the son of Rechab, the ruler of Beth-Haccerem; he built it, and set up the doors thereof, the locks thereof, and the bars thereof" (Nehemiah 3:14).

A reservoir was mentioned in the copper scroll. The reservoir was recorded during the Islamic conquest and also under the name Saint Jeehan de Bois during the Crusades. Ottoman tax registers in 1596 showed a population of twenty-nine Muslim families. A marble statue of Aphrodite (Venus) was found broken in two pieces during the Ein Karem excavations. The statue dates back to Roman times and is now at the Rockefeller Museum.

Mary's Spring is in Ein Karem and is the location where Mary and Elizabeth met. Some Christians view this spring as holy and fill up water bottles from it. This spring was repaired and renovated by Baron Edmond de Rothchild. Arab residents also built a mosque on the site. At this location, there is also a home for physically or mentally handicapped children, called Saint Vincent. It was started in 1954.[202]

Simon Peter: His Years of Ministry (continued)

Less than ninety days after the crucifixion of Jesus, Peter, led by the Holy Spirit, suggested that Judas, the disciple that betrayed Jesus, be replaced. The other disciples agreed with Peter to replace Judas. In Acts 2, the power of the Holy Spirit arrived and believers preached the word of God. Peter highlighted how the events of recent days pointed to Jesus as the Messiah that the people had crucified, who was raised from the dead and risen again. Peter proclaimed this Jesus as Lord and Messiah. Through Peter's preaching and the Holy Spirit, many of the 3,000

---

[202] www.en.wikipedia.org/wiki/ein_kerem.

believed and were baptized. Peter at this time became a dynamic speaker. One day Peter healed a lame man at the temple gate; this event gave him an opportunity to preach. Soon the religious leaders arrested Peter and John and turned them over to the Sanhedrin. Before the Sanhedrin, Peter bravely and boldly declared that he spoke in the name of Jesus, the one whom they had crucified and by whom people were being saved. The Sanhedrin let Peter and John go but prohibited them from preaching in the name of Jesus.[203]

SUN RAYS THROUGH THE WINDOW OF THE RUSSIAN ORTHODOX CHURCH EIN KAREM

Courtesy of the Israeli Ministry of Tourism and is solely for this photo only at www.goisrael.com

The Russian Orthodox Church at Ein Karem was built toward the end of the 19th century. It was nicknamed Moscovia Monastery which means Moscow in Arabic. The monastery has two churches inside a compound wall.[204]

The Russian Orthodox Church is dedicated to Zechariah, the father of John the Baptist, and a convent is dedicated to Elizabeth, the mother of John the Baptist. There is also a palace in the mountains built by a Protestant bishop in the middle of the 19th century. The walking tour starts at the well. There many artists can be found painting and displaying their paintings. There are also many fine nearby restaurants to choose from. Modern developments have not yet reached this quaint neighborhood.[205]

Another name for the Church of All Nations is the Basilica of the Agony, located at the bottom of the Mount of Olives next to the Garden of Gethsemane. This Catholic church has a section of stone believed to be where Jesus prayed on the night of his arrest:

---

[203] Mark R. Dunn, *Simon Peter: His Years of Ministry*. Biblical Illustrator, LifeWay: Volume 39, number 1, Fall 2012, 39-41.

[204] www.en.wikipedia.org/wiki/ein_kerem.

[205] www.goisrael.com/tourism_eng/articles/attractions.

Then Jesus went with his disciples to a place called Gethsemane, and he said to them, "Sit here while I go over there and pray." He took Peter and the two sons of Zebedee along with him, and he began to be sorrowful and troubled. Then he said to them, "My soul is overwhelmed with sorrow to the point of death. Stay here and watch with me." Going a little farther, he fell with his face to the ground and prayed, "My Father, if it is possible, may this cup be taken from me. Yet not as I will, but as you will." (Matthew 26:36-39)

JERUSALEM: FACADE OF THE CHURCH OF ALL NATIONS (GETHSEMANE) (1)

Photo courtesy of the Israeli Ministry of Tourism and is solely for this photo only at www.goisrael.com

The modern church at this location is built on the foundations of two ancient churches. The 4th-century Byzantine basilica was destroyed by an earthquake in 746 AD. The 12th-century Crusader chapel was abandoned in 1345. The modern church was built in 1919-1924 with funding from twelve different nations and was thus nick-named the Church of all Nations. The church has a Byzantine look, with a domed roof, pillars, and floor mosaic. Antonio Barluzzi was the architect. Twelve cupolas in the inlaid gold ceilings have symbols from the twelve countries who contributed to the building. The high altar overlooks the large slab of a rock believed to be the one Christ used when he prayed before being arrested.[206]

The Lutheran Church of the Redeemer is the only Protestant church in the Old City of Jerusalem. This church was built in the late 1800's and was dedicated by the emperor of Germany, Kaiser Wilhelm II. Redeemer Church is located next to the Church of the Holy Sepulchre. This church has the tallest bell tower in the Old City of Jerusalem. It is 177 steps to the top of the bell tower and the view is beautiful, from which the old city walls can be seen.[207]

---

[206] www.sacred-destinations.com/israel/jerusalem-church-of-all-nations.
[207] George W. Knight, *The Holy Land*, 127.

Redeemer Church was built between 1893 and 1898 by the architect Paul Ferdinand Groth. The services today are in Arabic, German, Danish, and English. This church is built on the land given to William I of Prussia in 1869 by Sultan Abdulaziz of the Ottoman Empire. In 1898, Kaiser Wilhelm II came to Jerusalem to dedicate the new church. In a special ceremony, Kaiser Wilhelm II rode on horseback through the ceremonial arches. One of the arches was a gift from the Ottoman Empire and the second arch from the local Jewish community. The church was dedicated on Reformation Day in 1898.

At the dedication, Kaiser Wilhelm II stated: "From Jerusalem came the light in splendor from which the German nation became great and glorious; and what the Germanic peoples have become, they became under the banner of the cross, the emblem of self-sacrificing charity." In the garden next to the church is a memorial marking the location of the Order of the Knights of St. John headquarters.[208]

The address of this church is 24 Muristan Road in Jerusalem. The church was built in the northeast corner of Muristan, over the Church of St. Mary of the Latins built in 1050. The old cloisters and the original plan of the church were preserved. One interesting item to see is the original scripture on the medieval northern gate of the church. This gate was the main Benedictine entrance of St. Mary of the Latins and is decorated with the signs of the Zodiac.[209]

There are about 400 members of this church. Above the entrance is a carving of the Lamb of God and the symbols of the Greek letters, Alpha and Omega, which are the first and last letters of the Greek alphabet. This is a symbol of God's eternity.[210]

The Abbey of the Dormition is a Benedictine community in Jerusalem on Mount Zion. It is near the walls of the Old City and near Zion Gate. In 1898 when Kaiser Wilhelm II visited Jerusalem for the dedication of the Lutheran Church, he bought this land on Mount Zion for 120,000 German Goldmarks from Sultan Abdul Hamid II and gave it to the German Union of the Holy Land. Local tradition believes that on this spot near the site of the Last Supper, Mary the mother of Jesus died. The church is called the Basilica of

---

[208] www.en.wikipedia.org/wiki/lutheran_church_of_the_redeemer_jerusalem.

[209] www.sacred-destinations.com/israel/jerusalem-church-of-redeemer.htm.

[210] www.holyland.pilgrimages.com/the-lutheran-church-of-the-redeemer.

the Assumption or Dormition. The basilica was dedicated on April 10, 1910, by the Latin Patriarch of Jerusalem.[211]

The church is a circular building with several altars and a choir. Two spiral staircases lead to the crypt, the site of the Dormition of the Virgin Mary, and to the organ loft and the gallery where two of the four church towers are accessible. The bell tower of the church is far away so that its shadow does not touch Nabi Da'ud that now resides in the Upper Room site. This is done to respect the Muslim Nabi Da'ud.[212]

Simon Peter: His Years of Ministry (continued)

Peter and the Apostles were put in jail. An angel freed them and ordered them to go to the temple and preach. The religious leaders went to the jail and could not find Peter or the Apostles. Someone reported to the religious leaders that they were at the temple preaching. The puzzled religious leaders asked Peter why they preached in the name of Jesus. Peter replied that they "must obey God rather than men." Gamaliel, one of the religious leaders, suggested that the apostles be released lest the Sanhedrin find themselves fighting against God (Acts 5:17-42).

Peter traveled to carry the gospel beyond Jerusalem. The Lord used Peter to heal a paralytic and to restore a woman's life (Acts 9:32-42). Peter went to the home of Cornelius and preached the gospel to him and those gathered there, and Peter witnessed the receiving of the Holy Spirit by the new believers (Acts 10).

King Herod executed James and arrested Peter because of their faith. Again the angel freed Peter and he was able to preach one more day. Paul wrote in Galatians about a dispute with Peter, about Peter's Jewish table fellowship contradicting the gospel's message of salvation by grace.

Mark R. Duncan is associate pastor of First Baptist Church in Duncanville, Texas.[213]

Abu Ghosh is a Muslim Arab village a few miles from Jerusalem. This village has been inhabited for nearly 6,000 years. In Bible times this village was called Kirjath-Jearim. For about fifty years, the Ark of the Covenant stayed at Kirjath-Jearim: "And they sent messengers to

---

[211] www.en.wikipedia.org/wiki/dormition_abbey.

[212] www.en.wikipedia.org/wiki/dormition_abbey.

[213] Mark R. Dunn, *Simon Peter: His Years of Ministry*. Biblical Illustrator, LifeWay: Volume 39, number 1, Fall 2012, 39-41.

the inhabitants of Kirjath-Jearim, saying, 'The Philistines have brought again the ark of the Lord; come ye down, and fetch it up to you'" (I Samuel 6:21).

During the time of Samuel, King Saul, and King David, the Ark of the Covenant stayed at Kirjath-Jearim. In 1050 BC, the ark was grabbed by the Philistines, who then suffered many hardships and plagues because of the ark. The Philistines finally returned the ark to Kirjath-Jearim. In 1000 BC, David took the ark to Jerusalem, his new capital.

Abu Ghosh was developed during the Ottoman Empire around the year 1000 AD by the Abu Ghosh family.[214]

ABU GHOSH: CRUSADER CHURCH IN THE HEART OF THE VILLAGE

Photo courtesy of the Israeli Ministry of Tourism and is solely for this photo only at www.goisrael.com

The Ark of the Covenant was a chest described in the book of Exodus. It contained tablets of stone with the written ten commandments and pieces of manna, the special food God rained down to the people of Israel. The ark also contained Aaron's rod. The ark was built according to the instructions God gave to Moses at Mount Sinai. The book of Exodus in the Bible describes Moses communicating with God from between the two cherubim on the cover of the ark. During the forty-year journey through the wilderness, the ark was carried by the priests about 2,000 cubits (1,000 yards) in front of the people. When the ark was carried by the priests into the water of Jordan, the river parted and made a path for the people to follow on dry land (read Joshua 3:15-17).

The city of Jericho was taken when the seven priests obeyed God and carried the ark for seven days and blew seven trumpets of rams' horns (read Joshua 6).

When the ark was carried, it was wrapped in a veil, in skins, and in a blue cloth, and was concealed even from the priests. Later, when the Philistines captured the ark, they put it in the temple of their god,

---

[214]   www.mariedenazareth.com/10468.0.

Dagon. The next morning, Dagon was found bowed down before the ark. The Philistines returned Dagon to the temple, and the next day, Dagon again was found bowing down to the ark.

King David removed the ark from Kirjath-Jearim with great rejoicing to take it to Mount Zion. Uzzah, a driver of the cart that the ark was on, put his hand on the ark to steady it and was smitten by God for touching it. King David, in fear, left the ark in the house of Obed-Edom the Gittite and left it there three months (II Samuel 6:1-11 and I Chronicles 13:1-13). When David heard that God had blessed the house of Obed-Edom, he picked up the ark once again. David asked the Levites to take the ark to Zion for him.

This time, David danced before the Lord and in the sight of all the people gathered in Jerusalem. His first wife, Michal the daughter of Saul, did not like David dancing (2 Samuel 6:12-16, 1 Chronicles16:1-3, and 2 Chronicles 1:4). The Levites were then asked to minister before the ark 1 Chronicles 16:4). David wanted to build a temple to house the Ark of the Covenant, but God stopped David's idea of building a temple himself (2 Samuel 7:1-17 and 1 Chronicles 17:1-15).

One generation later, King Solomon dismissed Abiathar from the priesthood for being a part of Adonijah's conspiracy against David. But King Solomon spared Abiathar from death because he had previously carried the ark (1 Kings 2:26). King Solomon worshipped before the ark after his dream in which God promised to give him wisdom (1 Kings 3:15). When King Solomon built the temple, he made a special inner room called *Kodesh Hakodashim* or Holy of Holies, to receive and house the ark (1 Kings 6:19). When the temple was dedicated, the ark containing the tablets with the original Ten Commandments was placed in the Holy of Holies (1 Kings 8:6-9). When the priests left the holy place, the temple was filled with a cloud, "for the glory of the Lord had filled the house of the Lord" (1 Kings 8:10-11, 2 Chronicles 5:13).

Solomon married Pharaoh's daughter and insisted that she stay in a house outside Zion because it contained the ark (2 Chronicles 8:11). King Josiah placed the ark in the temple (2 Chronicles 35:3), but one of the later kings removed the ark from the temple. During the Babylonian conquest, the Ark of the Covenant disappeared. The heavenly tabernacle and sacrifice made by Christ and how He is our High Priest is described in Hebrews 9 which you can read now.

Revelation 11:19 describes God's temple in heaven opened and the ark of His covenant was seen in his temple: "And the temple of God was opened in heaven, and there was seen in his temple the ark of his testament; and there were lightnings, and voices, and thunderings, and an earthquake, and great hail."

In Sura 2, Chapter 2, Verse 248 the Quran states: "And their Prophet says to them: 'A Sign of his authority is that there shall come to you the ark of the covenant, with an assurance therein of security (Sakina) from your Lord, and the relics left by the family of Moses and the family of Aaron, carried by angels. In this is a symbol for you if ye indeed have faith.'" Al Baidawi, an Islamic scholar, thinks the Sakina can be Tawrat, the Books of Moses. Al-Jalalan believes the relics in the ark were fragments of the two tablets, rods, robes, shoes, and the vase of manna. The Ark of the Covenant has a religious significance in Islam, and the Shia sect of Muslims believes the Ark of the Covenant will be found in Lake Tiberias by the Mahdi near the end of times.[215]

JERUSALEM (AERIAL): CHURCH OF VISITATION (FRANCISCAN) IN EIN KEREM
Photo courtesy of the Israeli Ministry of Tourism and is solely for this photo only at www.goisrael.com

The Church of Visitation is also located in the little village of Ein Kerem, the traditional place for the birthplace of John the Baptist. In a beautiful mosaic inside, this church tells about the visit of Mary, the mother of Jesus, to her cousin Elizabeth after Mary knew she was to be the mother of the Messiah. Another painting shows John the Baptist's father, Zechariah, doing his priestly duties in the temple in Jerusalem.[216] (Read Luke 1:5-25.)

Luke 1 also describes the event when Mary visits her cousin, Elizabeth:

---

215   www.en.wikipedia.org/wiki/ark_of_the_covenant.
216   George W. Knight, *The Holy Land*, 173.

In those days Mary arose and went with haste into the hill country, to a town in Judah, and she entered the house of Zacharias and greeted Elizabeth. And when Elizabeth heard the greeting of Mary, the baby leaped in her womb. And Elizabeth was filled with the Holy Spirit, and she exclaimed with a loud cry, "Blessed are you among women, and blessed is the fruit of your womb! And why is this granted to me that the mother of my Lord should come to me? For behold when the sound of your greeting came to my ears, the baby in my womb leaped for joy. And blessed is she who believed that this would be a fulfillment of what was spoken to her from the Lord." (Luke 1:39-45)

The church is built on the traditional summer home of Elizabeth and Zechariah. It was built around a large stone where Elizabeth hid John the Baptist from Herod's soldiers, because there was an order to kill all children under the age of two. Jesus, Joseph, and Mary went to Egypt. God also protected John the Baptist from the danger of Herod's order.[217]

THE ROOF OF THE ETHIOPIAN CHURCH

Courtesy of the Israeli Ministry of Tourism and is solely for this photo only at www.goisrael.com

To get to the Ethiopian Church, visitors can walk up a flight of steps behind the Church of the Holy Sepulchre, through a gateway in an old stone wall, and then arrive in a tiny African village with a group of mud huts. Here there can be heard a clutter of cooking pots. In the middle of the courtyard is a small dome. Two priests love to sit on a bench and talk. This is the roof of the Church of the Holy Sepulchre. The dome gives light to the chapel of Saint Helena below.

In the courtyard is a small chapel where the monks worship. The chapel is dedicated to the archangel Michael. It seats about seventy people in an oblong building. Below is another small chapel dedicated to the four living creatures found in the book of Ezekiel. The largest painting there is of King Solomon receiving the Queen of Sheba.

---

[217] www.goisrael.com/tourism_eng/articles/attractions.

The Ethiopians were converted to Christianity in the 4th and 5th centuries by monks from Egypt and Syria. Years ago, there were ancient Jewish communities in Ethiopia. Saturday is observed as a second favorite day after Sunday. Ethiopians like to dance and to try to copy King David's dance before the ark.

When the Queen of Sheba visited Solomon, she traveled with camels loaded with gold and special stones: "And King Solomon gave unto the queen of Sheba all her desire, whatsoever she asked, beside that which Solomon gave her of his royal bounty. So she turned and went to her own country, she and her servants" (1 Kings 10:13). Ethiopian tradition is that the Queen of Sheba returned home pregnant and that her son Menelik I, the legendary first emperor of Ethiopia, was Solomon's son.

By the end of the 4th century, Ethiopians were making trips to Jerusalem. Some Ethiopians settled in Jerusalem because of the hardship in Ethiopia when the Muslims gained power. The Ethiopian Church was led by a bishop sent from Egypt. In 1838, a plaque came to Jerusalem and killed all the Ethiopian monks. The Coptic Church of Egypt argued that the Ethiopian Church was their property. The Coptic Church burned the library that contained the documents proving Ethiopian ownership, and took over the monastery. The Anglican bishop of Jerusalem, Bishop Gobat, helped the Ethiopian Church get back their property.

There are still disagreements between the Ethiopian Church and the Coptic Church. In modern times, there is an unresolved case before the Israeli High Court. During the last 100 years, the Ethiopian Church has acquired property in Bethany, Jericho, and on the Jordan River. For more than 1,500 years, the Ethiopians have survived in Jerusalem. Most of the monks come to Jerusalem because they believe that Jerusalem is the most holy place on earth. The monks have services between 4 and 6 a.m. and between 4 and 5 p.m. The Feast of Our Lady service in August lasts from 2 to 6 a.m. The service has a lot of time of standing. Young Ethiopians attend the Anglican schools or regular Israeli schools.[218]

---

[218] www.mia.gov.il/mfa/mfaarchive/2000_2009/2003/9/africa.

OUTSIDE THE HOLY TRINITY CHURCH

Courtesy of the Israeli Ministry of Tourism and is solely for this photo only at www.goisrael.com

OUTSIDE THE MARIA MAGDALENA CHURCH

Courtesy of the Israeli Ministry of Tourism and is solely for this photo only at www.goisrael.com

The Maria Magdalena Church has seven gilded onion-shaped domes. This church honors Mary Magdalene. Jesus cast out seven demons from her and she became a good friend to Jesus and the disciples. Jesus appeared first to Mary after the resurrection, and Mary was at the crucifixion.[219] (Read Mark 16:9 and John 20:14-18.)

Trees Native to Israel

Jesus used trees and their fruits to describe people's spiritual condition (Matthew 7:16-20). We can botanically group trees of the Bible into three groups: nut and fruit trees, trees of the forest, and wilderness or desert trees.

Almond trees are members of the peach family and bloom in February. The Hebrew word for almond translates into English as "watch." In Jeremiah 1:11-13, the Lord used a play on words when He showed Jeremiah an almond branch, to signify that He was "watching" or about to act. Part of the lampstand for the wilderness tabernacle was to be shaped like almond blossoms (Exodus 25:31-36). Aaron's rod miraculously gave a sign of his God-given authority by sprouting almonds (Numbers 17:1-10).

The fig tree was used many times in illustrations in the Old and New Testaments. The figs were used as a staple in the Mediterranean diet. Fig trees reach an average height of ten to twenty feet. Fig trees produce figs in June and

---

219   George W. Knight, *The Holy Land,* 150.

August. In Matthew 7:16 and Luke 21:29-31, Jesus used fig trees to illustrate his doctrine. Sycamore trees grow up to forty-five feet tall and are a type of fig tree.

Sycamore trees like the warmer climate in Canaan. This tree has low-growing branches that are good for climbing. Luke 19:4 describes Zacchaeus climbing a sycamore tree in Jericho. [220]

JERUSALEM: EIN KEREM WITH CHURCH OF ST. JOHN THE BAPTIST (FRANCISCAN)

Photo courtesy of the Israeli Ministry of Tourism and is solely for this photo only at www.goisrael.com

The Church of St. John the Baptist was built over an early Jerusalem church; that is, seven meters below street level. The church has a bone that many believe is part of the skull of St. John the Baptist. The Byzantine empress, Eudocia, helped plan the building of this church and others in the 5th century. Eudocia's husband, Theodosius, tried to murder her for trying to influence governmental decisions. When that failed, he sent her to Jerusalem permanently.

In the 12th century, the church was renovated by the Crusaders. During the Crusaders era, the Knights Hospitaler managed a hospital next to this church. In 1187 when many Crusaders left Jerusalem, a few knights remained to protect the church.

It is a cross-shaped church with icons and themes of John the Baptist. To the right of the entrance is an icon of John the Baptist's head, with a gold and jewel-rimmed relic believed to be part of his skull. Worshipers often kiss the icon before entering the church.

Today, when you leave the modern sanctuary, turn the corner, and go down a staircase to reach the old 5th-century church. On one wall is a picture of Queen Eudocia, who is believed to have died in her sleep at age fifty-nine in the year 460 AD. You need special permission to visit the old underground church. This church is located on Christian

---

[220] B. Dale Ellenburg, *Trees Native to Israel.* Biblical Illustrator, LifeWay: Volume 39, number 1, Fall 2012, 74-77.

Quarter Road in the Old City.[221] The modern church, visible at street level, was built in the 11th century.[222]

In Ein Kerem there is also a monastery of the Sisters of Our Lady of Zion, founded by two French brothers, Theodore and Marie Alphonse Ratisbonne. These brothers were Jewish and later converted to Christianity. They started an orphanage, and Alphonse lived in the monastery and is buried in the garden of the monastery.[223]

JERUSALEM: DOME OF THE ROCK, LOOKING WEST

Photo courtesy of the Israeli Ministry of Tourism and is solely for this photo only at www.goisrael.com

The Dome of the Rock is not a mosque, but rather it is a Muslim shrine that is built over a sacred stone. Some people believe this is the location where Mohammed ascended into heaven during his night journey. Many Jews believe it is also the location where Abraham prepared to sacrifice Isaac. Muslims believe that this event happened in Mecca instead of Jerusalem. Many believe the dome is also over the site of the Holy of Holies of both Solomon's Temple and Herod's Temple.

The Dome of the Rock was built by Umayyad caliph Abd al-Malik from 688 to 691 AD. The Oxford Archaeological Guide to the Holy Land states that the real purpose of the Dome of the Rock was to show superiority of the new religion, Islam, over Judaism and Christianity. The golden dome was originally made of real gold, but was later changed to copper and then to aluminum. The dome has a full moon decoration on top.

There is an inscription on the inner side of the octagonal arcade, asking Christians to turn from the error of the Trinity and recognize the truth of Islam. The inscription says,

---

221 www.chritusrex.org/www2/baram/b-st-john.html.
222 George W. Knight, *The Holy Land*, 122.
223 www.en.wikipedia.org/wiki/ein_kerem.

O people of the book! Do not exaggerate in your religion nor utter aught concerning God save the truth. The Messiah, Jesus son of Mary, was only a Messenger of God, and his Word which he conveyed unto Mary, and a spirit from Him. So believe in God and his messengers, and say not "three". Cease! Better for you! God is only one God. Far be it removed from his transcendent majesty that He should have a son, whose disbelieveth the revelations of God. Lo! God is swift at reckoning!

Muslim tradition states that an angel will come to the sacred rock to sound the trumpet call of the Last Judgment at the end of the world. The cavity underneath the rock is known as the Well of Souls. Some believe that the voices of the dead mix with the falling waters of the lower river of paradise as they drop into eternity. Another legend is that the dead meet here twice a month to pray. Another legend is that people who prayed here after walking around the rock were given a certificate of admission to paradise that was to be buried with them.[224]

The Dome of the Rock was constructed directly above the Second Jewish Temple on the Temple Mount. A former Jewish rabbi, a convert to Islam, helped Caliph Omar ibn al Khattab find the exact location of the old Second Jewish Temple. A.C. Cresswell, in his book *Origin of the Plan of the Dome of the Rock*, states that the Muslims used the same measurements of the Church of the Holy Sepulchre.

Mark Twain wrote: "Everywhere about the Mosque of Omar are portions of pillars, curiously wrought altars, and fragments of elegantly carved marble – precious remains of Solomon's Temple. These have been dug up from all depths in the soil and rubbish of Mount Moriah, and the Muslims have always shown a disposition to preserve them with the utmost care."[225]

The Arabs call the Temple Mount the *Haram eh-Sharif* or Noble Sanctuary. The Arabs believe Mohammed ascended into Heaven from the hill while riding a winged horse, El Burak. Located on the Temple Mount are the Muslim sites of the Dome of the Rock and the Al-Aqsa Mosque. Each Friday, thousands of Muslims go there for worship and prayer.

The Al-Aqsa mosque is the third most sacred place in the Muslim religion. The Al-Aqsa Mosque was built in the 11th century. It is 262 feet in length and 180 feet in width, with room for over 5,000 Muslims

---

[224] www.sacred-destinations.com/israel/jerusalem-dome-of-the-rock.
[225] www.en.wikipedia.org/wiki/dome_of_the_rock.

every Friday. The original mosque on this property was built in the 7th century by Caliph Waleed. The Crusader Knights Templar used this mosque as a dormitory or as a palace during the Crusade years. A young Australian in 1969 set fire to this mosque and caused much damage. He even destroyed a hand-made pulpit made during the time of Saladin. In 1978, the Egyptians replaced the pulpit in honor of President Anwar Sadat's visit to Jerusalem.

In seasons of time when it is open for visiting, those who visit the Dome of the Rock must remove their shoes and pass through tight security. Photography is not allowed under any circumstance.

The inside of the Dome of the Rock is closed to Christian and Jewish visitors. The area of the Dome of the Rock takes up about one sixth of the space of the Old City.[226]

To Jews, Christians and Muslims, the area of the Temple Mount is a holy place. The Dome of the Rock is an octagonal shaped building adorned with 45,000 ornamental tiles. An aluminum-bronze alloy from Italy gives the dome its golden glow. Marble columns supporting the dome date back to the 4th century AD. These columns may have come from Hadrian's temple to Jupiter and from a Byzantine church that was located on the Mount of Olives. Sixteen stained glass windows are on the walls. The dome is 176 feet in diameter. Concerning the site, one conflict between Jews and Muslims is that Jews believe that Isaac was to be sacrificed by Abraham, whereas the Muslims believe that Ishmael was the chosen one for the sacrifice. The rock is twenty-nine feet long and thirty-nine feet wide and is surrounded by a railing. It is believed that this rock marked the spot of the Jewish animal sacrifices; there is a carved drain to carry off the blood of sacrificed animals.

The first building was built in 638 AD by Caliph Omar and was called the Mosque of Omar. Caliph Abd Al Malek's goal was to make Jerusalem a rival to Mecca and Medina. The rock was damaged by an earthquake in 1016. In 1115, the Crusaders thought the Dome of the Rock was Solomon's Temple. The Crusaders put an iron screen around the rock to keep visitors from taking some of the rock as souvenirs. The iron screen was replaced in 1959.[227]

---

[226] George W. Knight, *The Holy Land*, 125.

[227] www.geni.com/people/Agnes-de-Ferrers-de-Muscegros/6000000004 286962916.

JERUSALEM, OLD CITY: DAVIDSON VISITORS CENTER

Photo courtesy of the Israeli Ministry of Tourism and is solely for this photo only at www.goisrael.com

The Davidson Center in the Jerusalem Archaeological Park is near the Western Wall. Inside are artifacts to see, as well as a three-dimensional reconstruction of Herod's Temple. High-speed technology is used in a simulation mode that makes it seem real to watch.[228] The center was built in a basement of an 8th-century building. There is a ten-minute, high-definition digital video for visitors to view.[229]

JERUSALEM: ROCKEFELLER ARCHAEOLOGICAL MUSEUM, THE COURTYARD, AND REFLECTING POOL

Photo courtesy of the Israeli Ministry of Tourism and is solely for this photo only at www.goisrael.com

The Rockefeller Museum of Archaeology is located in East Jerusalem and has a collection of artifacts from the 1920's and 1930's. The museum was built on a hill opposite the northeastern corner of the Old City. After 1967, the museum has been managed by the Israel Museum. There are displays included from things uncovered in Jerusalem, Megiddo, Ashkelon, Lachish, Samaria, and Jericho.

A 6th-century mosaic floor from an ancient synagogue from Ein Gedi says: "Anyone who neglects his family, provokes conflict, steals property, slanders his friends, or reveals the secret of Ein Gedi's balsam industry is cursed."[230]

---

[228] George W. Knight, *The Holy Land*, 99.

[229] www.goisrael.com/tourism_eng/articles/attractions.

[230] www.en.wikipedia.org/wiki/rockefeller_museum.

The museum opened in 1938 and is one of the oldest museums in Jerusalem. The building is made of white limestone in one of the newer sections of Jerusalem.[231]

Trees Native to Israel (continued)

The olive tree produces olives that are used for food and oil. The olive tree is a slow-grower evergreen that reaches a height of forty feet. When the olive tree is about five or six years old, it flowers and produces olives that are not ready to eat. When the olive tree is ten to fifteen years old, it produces mature fruit. Olive trees can produce olives for hundreds of years. In May, olive trees produce clusters of small white flowers, and fruit appears after the flowers fall off. Green olives are harvested in September and October. Black olives are harvested in December. Exodus 27:30 tells us that fine olive oil was used in the lamp inside the tabernacle.

The date palm can reach 100 feet and produces large quantities of dates growing in clusters. The fibrous leaves were woven into mats. Date palms liked hot areas around the Dead Sea. In Judges 1:16, Jericho was known as the City of Palms. Exodus 15:27 describes the Israelites camping near the Elim Springs where 70 palms were growing during their wilderness journey. Isaiah 9:14 and Joel 1:12 tell us the date palm was used as a symbol for Israel.

Pomegranate was one of the seven foods the Old Testament used to describe the abundance of the promised land (Deuteronomy 8:8). Pomegranates grow on small trees and produce red fruit about the size of an orange. Song of Solomon 4:3 and 6:7 picture the pomegranate as a symbol of beauty in the Bible. Song of Solomon 6:11 and 7:12 symbolize in spring the awakening of love. Pomegranates were part of the decoration on the high priest's robe and on the pillars of the temple (Exodus 39:26 and 1 Kings 7:18).

The nut and fruit trees were almond, fig, sycamore, olive, date palm, and pomegranate.

The next group of Israel trees are trees of the forest. Cedar is a large and fragrant evergreen that grows mainly in the mountain regions of Israel. Cedars grow over 100 feet tall and can live for 1,000 to 2,000 years. Prophets used the cedar's height and strength to refer to the durability of nations (Amos 2:9 and Ezekiel 31:1-18). Psalm 92:12 compares the righteous to the cedars of Lebanon.

Oaks are found in Israel on high ground and often reach seventy-five feet and a crown circumference of sixty feet. Ships and buildings were made out of oak wood.

---

[231] George W. Knight, *The Holy Land*, 10.

Ancient peoples used oak to mark graves and other landmarks, as demonstrated in Genesis 35:8 and I Samuel 10:3. The oak symbolized strength and long life (Amos 2:9). The prophets condemned the idolatry and false worship under large trees like the oak.[232]

JERUSALEM: HEZEKIAH'S TUNNEL IN THE ANCIENT CITY OF DAVID

Photo courtesy of the Israeli Ministry of Tourism and is solely for this photo only at www.goisrael.com

Hezekiah's Tunnel is a tunnel that was dug underneath the City of David during the reign of Hezekiah, before 701 BC: "And the rest of the acts of Hezekiah, and all his might, and how we made a pool, and a conduit, and brought water into the city, are they not written in the book of the chronicles of the kings of Judah?" (I1 Kings 20:20). The tunnel has been dated by using the organic material in the original plaster. The tunnel leads from the Gihon Spring to the Pool of Siloam, and was built as an aqueduct to give Jerusalem water during the coming siege by the Assyrians and Sennacherib. The tunnel is 533 meters long. American Edward Robinson, a Bible scholar, discovered it in 1838. In modern times, this tunnel can be walked through from beginning to end.[233] (Read 2 Chronicles 32:2-4.)

Hezekiah's engineers and workers had to dig this tunnel more than 1,700 feet through solid rock. One group of workers started digging at the Pool of Siloam and the other group at the Gihon Springs. Months later, they met in the middle, more than 100 feet beneath Jerusalem. The modern translation of the inscription was found on Hezekiah's Tunnel in 1880:

While the tunnelers lifted the pick-axe each toward his fellow and while three cubics remained yet to be bored through, there was heard the voice of a man calling his fellow — for there was a split in the rock on the right hand. When the tunnel

---

[232] B. Dale Ellenburg, *Trees Native to Israel.* Biblical Illustrator, LifeWay: Volume 39, number 1, Fall 2012, 74-77.

[233] www.en.wikipedia.org/wiki/hezekiah.

was driven through, the tunnelers hewed the rock, each man toward his fellow, with pick-axe. And the water flowed from the spring toward the reservoir for twelve hundred cubics. The height of the rock above the head of the tunnelers was a hundred cubics.[234]

One of the healing miracles of Jesus took place in this area at the Pool of Siloam. Jesus sent a blind man there and covered his eyes with mud and his own saliva (read John 9:1-11).

So far, ruins of the palace of Solomon have not been found. More than likely, the palace was built on the north side of Jerusalem. Herod destroyed everything to make room to build his temple. Solomon had 1,000 wives.[235] (Read 1 Kings 7:1-12.)

JERUSALEM ARCHAEOLOGICAL PARK: EXCAVATIONS AND RESTORATION
Photo courtesy of the Israeli Ministry of Tourism and is solely for this photo only at www.goisrael.com

Another name for the Jerusalem Archaeological Park is the Archaeological Garden. The Jerusalem Archaeological Park researches and displays many layers of archaeological discoveries in the Old City of Jerusalem. The park has outdoor displays around the Temple Mount, in the Valley of Hinnon, and the Mount of Olives. The Davidson Center takes visitors through many different periods of history.[236]

At the Temple Mount, archaeologists discovered a 1st-century street that dates back to before 70 AD, when the Romans destroyed Jerusalem. The street is thirty-two feet (ten meters) wide and was paved with large slabs up to a foot thick. Massive stones covered the street and were pushed down by the Romans. Archaeologists found a Trumpeting Stone on the southwest corner of the mound with an inscription that read, "To the place of the trumpeting." The priest

---

[234]   George W. Knight, *The Holy Land*, 133-134.

[235]   www.bible-archaeology.info/jerusalem.htm.

[236]   www.gojerusalem.com/discover/item_113/the-jerusalem.archaeology.

blew the shofar from here to announce the start of Shabbat and festival days.

The western stairs leading to the main entrance of the Temple Mount were 200 feet wide. The eastern stairs had alternating long and short steps. Archaeologists believe the fifteen long steps may have been used for pilgrims to sing the fifteen Psalms of Ascent as they went up to worship. Archaeologists also found some public ritual bathing installations on the south side of the Temple Mount. These were used for bathing before worshipers entered holy places, and they were called *mikvah'ot.*[237]

JERUSALEM: FRANCISCAN MONASTERY OF CHURCH OF ALL NATIONS (GETHSEMANE) (1)

Photo courtesy of the Israeli Ministry of Tourism and is solely for this photo only at www.goisrael.com

Trees Native to Israel (continued)

God appeared to Abraham under the shade of the oak trees of Mamre (Genesis 18:3). Chestnut trees or plane were ornamental trees that grew along streambeds, and Jacob used branches of the chestnut to breed his flocks (Genesis 30:37). Jacob used branches of the poplar tree to help in the breeding of his flocks. The poplar tree is a fast growing tree along the streambeds. Poplar trees grow to a height of 100 feet, and their straight trunks were good for tools or roof beams. Job said the poplar trees by the stream were large enough to conceal the behemoth (Job 40:15-22). A related species, the Euphrates poplar, grows along the Jordan and the Euphrates. When the Euphrates Poplar is young, its leaves look like those of the willow tree. This may be the type of tree on which the children of Israel hung their harps during the exile (Psalm 137:2).

The willow trees grow beside fresh-water streams. The willows may have been used as branches in constructing their booths described in Nehemiah 8:15. The algum tree had rare wood and grew mainly in Lebanon (1 Kings 10:11-12). The

---

algum tree was used as part of the construction of Solomon's temple (2 Chronicles 2:8). The wood was also used for making musical instruments.

Terebinth trees were large and long-lived like the oak. In Hosea 4:13, the prophets fussed at the people for idolatrous sacrifices under the terebinth trees. Jacob buried Laban's household idols under the terebinth trees. The trees of the forest were cedar, oak, plane, poplar, willow, algum, and terebinth.[238]

JERUSALEM: THE KNESSET, ISRAEL'S PARLIAMENT, FACADE (WITH A TOUR GROUP)
Photo courtesy of the Israeli Ministry of Tourism and is solely for this photo only at www.goisrael.com

The Knesset is the legislature of Israel. The Knesset members pass all laws, elect the President and Prime Minister, approve the cabinet, and supervise the work of the government. The Knesset also has the power to remove the President and the State Comptroller from office, to remove a Prime Minister convicted of offense involving moral turpitude, and to dissolve the Knesset and call for new elections. Moral turpitude is conduct that is not considered to be standard conduct of justice, honesty, or good morals. The Knesset can pass any law by a simple majority, even a law that is in conflict with a basic law of Israel, unless the basic law includes specific modification.[239]

Trees Native to Israel (continued)

Acacia trees, also known as shittah, *grow in the wilderness or desert. The Ark of the Covenant was made of acacia wood (Exodus 25:10). Acacia is a hardwood tree that grows darker with age. In Bible times people used it for fuel, construction, and shade. Acacia trees were good for building, and insects did not like acacia wood. Some kinds of acacia trees are shrub-like and other types have a central trunk and grow to fifty feet.*

---

[238] B. Dale Ellenburg, *Trees Native to Israel.* Biblical Illustrator, LifeWay: Volume 39, number 1, Fall 2012, 74-77.

[239] www.en.wikipedia.org/wiki/knesset.

Tamarisk trees were small shrub-like desert trees. As many as twelve species of the tamarisk tree grow in modern Israel. Abraham planted a tamarisk tree in Beersheba to mark the spot he first called on the name of the Lord (Genesis 21:33). The men of Jabesh-Gilead buried the bones of Saul and his sons under a tamarisk tree (I Samuel 31:11-13). Some scholars believe the manna the Israelites ate in the wilderness may have been tamarisk resin.

B. Dale Ellenburg is pastor of First Baptist Church, Pigeon Forge, Tennessee.[240]

JERUSALEM: SUPREME COURT BUILDING

Photo courtesy of the Israeli Ministry of Tourism and is solely for this photo only at www.goisrael.com

The Supreme Court is in Jerusalem and is the head of the court system. The Supreme Court can sit as an appellate court and a court of first instance. It can even intervene in Israel Defense Forces military operations. Supreme Court justices are appointed by the Judicial Selection Committee, which has nine members. The nine members of the Judicial Selection Committee include the President of the Supreme Court and two other Supreme Court Justices, the Minister of Justice in the cabinet plus one other cabinet member, and two representatives of the Israel Bar Association. The committee is chaired by the Minister of Justice.

This building was donated by Dorothy de Rothchild and opened in 1992. The building has both open spaces and enclosed areas. There is a pyramid area that is a large space that serves as a turning point before the entrance to the courtrooms. The pyramid area acts as an inner gatehouse of the building. The idea of the pyramid was inspired by the Tomb of Zechariah and the Tomb of Absalom in the Kidron Valley in Jerusalem.

The building has three main sections: a square library wing, a rectangular administrative wing with the chambers for judges, and a wing containing the court rooms.[241]

---

[240] B. Dale Ellenburg, *Trees Native to Israel.* Biblical Illustrator, LifeWay: Volume 39, number 1, Fall 2012, 74-77.

[241] www.en.wikipedia.org/wiki/supreme_court_of_israel.

525 BIBLE LANDS MUSEUM (ARCHAEOLOGY), WEST JERUSALEM (1)

Photo courtesy of the Israeli Ministry of Tourism and is solely for this photo only at www.goisrael.com

The Bible Lands Museum is also in Jerusalem. It explores the culture of the peoples mentioned in the Bible, including ancient Egyptians, Canaanites, Philistines, Arameans, Hittites, Elamites, Phoenicians, and Persians. The goal is to put these peoples into a historical area. The museum is located on Museum Row in Givat Ram. It is in the vicinity of the Israel Museum, The National Campus for the Archaeology of Israel, and the Bloomfield Museum of Science.

The Bible Lands museum opened in 1992 to house the personal collection of Elie Borowski. He met Batya Weiss, who encouraged him to bring his collection to Israel instead of to Toronto, Canada. Batya called the Jerusalem mayor, Teddy Kollek, to start the process. Elie later married Batya. Inside the museum are displays of ancient documents, idols, coins, statues, weapons, pottery, and seals from the ancient Near East. Brief articles on the walls tell about the origins of the alphabet, embalming, and Abraham's journey. The museum uses Bible verses where applicable. For example, the exhibit has an ancient Anatolian Jug and includes the Bible verse, "Behold, Rebecca came forth with her pitcher on her shoulder, and she went down unto the fountain and drew water" (Genesis 24:25).[242]

HEBREW UNIVERSITY OF JERUSALEM, MT. SCOPUS CAMPUS (HECHT SYNAGOGUE (1)

Photo courtesy of the Israeli Ministry of Tourism and is solely for this photo only at www.goisrael.com

---

[242] https://en.wikipedia.org/wiki/Bible_Lands_Museum.

Hebrew University is Israel's second oldest university; Technion is the oldest. Hebrew University has three campuses in Jerusalem and one in Rehovot. In the last ten years, five of its graduates have received the Nobel Prize. The university opened on April 1, 1925, and offers Humanities, Social Studies, Law, the Jerusalem School of Business Administration, the Bearwald School of Social Work, the Harry S. Truman Research Institute for the Advancement of Peace, the Rothberg International School, and the Mandel Institute of Jewish Studies.[243]

JERUSALEM: TOMB OF THEODOR HERZL, FOUNDER OF THE MODERN ZIONIST MOVEMENT, AT MOUNT HERZL

Photo courtesy of the Israeli Ministry of Tourism and is solely for this photo only at www.goisrael.com

John's Vision: The River of the Water of Life

Early civilizations began near rivers such as the Tigris, Euphrates, and Nile. Rivers played a part in Israel's history. The Nile turned to blood under God's plague. The Jordan stopped its flow so the people could enter Israel, the promised land.

The Pishon, Gihon, Tigris, and Euphrates Rivers flowed from Eden and watered all the land. The tree of life was there (Genesis 2:11-14). In Genesis 3, the serpent tempted Adam and Eve, and God exiled them with a divine promise that the woman's seed would crush the serpent's head. The Bible reveals God's loving plan to fulfill his promise, rescue the fallen race, and restore all things.

The last three chapters of Revelation show that the story of Genesis 1-3 comes full circle from the time of the temptation of man and Christ crushing the serpent's head. The wicked old serpent is thrown into the fiery lake forever. The Lamb (Jesus) has conquered and the New Jerusalem descends. John describes the city of New Jerusalem as Eden regained. Revelation 22 says the tree of life is back but

---

better than Eden's. It has a crop of fruit every month, and its leaves bring good health. No one is ever denied access to the tree. There is a "river of living water that flows from God's throne" (Revelation 22:1). It is the water supply for all who live with the Lamb.

Ezekiel 40-48 gives us his vision of the restoration of Israel's temple and land. He describes a miraculous river of life (Ezekiel 47:1-12). The river began as a trickle from the temple but grew into a deep river with forest growth on both banks. All kinds of fruit trees bore fruit monthly, and the leaves had healing value. Ezekiel's river flowed eastward and ended in what used to be the Dead Sea. But in Ezekiel's vision the Dead Sea now had plenty of fish, which was another reversal of death's curse. People in John's day would have recognized that John's river of living water was parallel to and greater than the river of Ezekiel 47.[244]

THE KENNEDY MEMORIAL (1)

Photo courtesy of the Israeli Ministry of Tourism and is solely for this photo only at www.goisrael.com

Located southwest of Jerusalem, the Kennedy Memorial resembles the stump of a felled tree and is dedicated to the memory of U.S. President John F. Kennedy. It is located in the Mateh Yehuda Region near Jerusalem. The memorial is sixty feet high and is shaped like a fallen tree, symbolizing a life cut short. Inside the memorial is a bronze statue with an eternal flame burning. The statue is surrounded by fifty-one concrete columns. These represent one for each U.S. state and one for Washington D.C. The monument measures 250 feet wide, and there is space for 100 people to view it at one time. The Kennedy Memorial is built on the highest hill in Jerusalem.[245]

244 Kendell Easley, *John's Vision: The River of the Water of Life.* Biblical Illustrator, LifeWay: Volume 39, number 4, Summer 2013, 14-17.
245 www.en.wikipedia.org/wiki/yad_kennedy.

JERUSALEM, OLD CITY: POOL OF BETHESDA

Photo courtesy of the Israeli Ministry of Tourism and is solely for this photo only at www.goisrael.com

The Pool of Bethesda is a pool of water located in the Muslim Quarter of Jerusalem. It is on the path of Beth Zeta Valley. The Pool of Bethesda is close to the Sheep Gate. The Gospel of John describes this pool in New Testament times, where Jesus healed a man who had a long-standing infirmity (read John 5:2-18).

Until the 19th century, when the archaeologists found the remains of a pool, there was no evidence of the pool ever existing. The remains matched the description in John's Gospel. *Bethesda* in Hebrew means "house of mercy" or "house of grace". The pool was seen as a place of disgrace due to invalids, and a place of grace because the invalids were healed.[246] The Pool of Bethesda is also the birthplace of Anne, Mary's Mother.[247]

The first pool was built after King Solomon built the temple, to provide water for the sacrificial rites at the temple. Later, about 200 BC, the second pool was built next to the first, to increase the water supply to the temple. The area of both pools was larger than a football field, and they were hollowed out to a depth of about forty-five feet. The people believed the water had healing power and tried to go to this pool often. John's account showed that the crowd did not expect Jesus to heal them, but rather the water itself. But Jesus healed the man with words and not from the water.[248]

---

[246] www.en.wikipedia.org/wiki/pool_of_bethesda.
[247] www.goisrael.com/tourism_eng/tourist.
[248] George W. Knight, *The Holy Land*, 105-106.

EMMAUS: ANCIENT BAPTISTRY (SHEFELAH)
Photo courtesy of the Israeli Ministry of Tourism and is solely for this photo only at www.goisrael.com

Emmaus was a small village seven miles from Jerusalem. This village is where Jesus revealed himself to two of his followers after the resurrection (read Luke 24:13-32).

John's Vision: The River of the Water of Life (continued)

In John's gospel, Jesus talked to a woman of Samaria at Jacob's well: "If someone drank His water, their thirst would be eternally quenched. Further, the water I will give him will become a well of water springing up within him for eternal life" (John 4:14).

Jesus arrived in Jerusalem for the last day of the Festival of Tabernacles (John 7). This was an autumn festival recalling Israel's years of living in tents when they were in the wilderness, as described in Exodus where God provided water for them. The custom was for Jewish priests in procession to draw water into a golden pitcher from Jerusalem's water supply and pour it into the temple altar. This ceremony reminded the people that God miraculously provided water during Israel's wilderness wanderings for forty years (Exodus 17:1-7 and Numbers 20:2-13).

Imagine Jesus shouting out, maybe at the second the priest poured the ceremonial water, "If anyone is thirsty, he should come to Me and drink!" (John 7:37). The water God provided through Moses for the Israeli people during the Exodus was ordinary water and the people still died. The water Jesus gave was of eternal value. Then Jesus made a promise, "The one who believes in Me, as the Scripture has said, will have streams of living water flow from deep within him" (John 7:38). Jesus and John did not indicate the scriptures to which Jesus was referring. Remember that the best "living water" scriptures are Ezekiel 47:1-12 and Zechariah 14:8, but these do not mention Israel being a source of blessing to others. There are scriptures that tell us about God's people as a river of blessing to others, such as Proverbs 4:23 and Isaiah 58:11, but they do not contain "living water" language.

In John 7:39, John quickly interpreted that the "living water" of Jesus is His gift of the Holy Spirit to all who believe in Him. The promise is true because Spirit-filled believers are a blessing to others.

Kendell Easley is professor of Christian studies in the School of Christian Studies and also director of the Stephen Olford Center at Union University in Jackson, Tennessee.[249]

ROOM OF THE LAST SUPPER (UPPER ROOM OR CENACULUM) ON MOUNT ZION

Photo courtesy of the Israeli Ministry of Tourism and is solely for this photo only at www.goisrael.com

The Upper Room is on the second floor of a building that also houses the Tomb of David. Here Jesus had his final meal with his disciples:

And he said to them, "I have earnestly desired to eat this Passover with you before I suffer. For I tell you I will not eat it until it is fulfilled in the kingdom of God." And he took a cup, and when he had given thanks he said, "Take this, and divide it among yourselves. For I tell you that from now on I will not drink of the fruit of the vine until the Kingdom of God comes." And he took bread, and when he had given thanks, he broke it and gave it to them saying, "This is my body, which is given for you. Do this in remembrance of me." And likewise the cup after they had eaten, saying. "This cup which is poured out for you is the new covenant in my blood." (Luke 22:15-20)

The Last Supper room is known as the *Cenaculum* which means "dinner" in Latin. The room is a large rectangular room, with floor-to-ceiling arches sitting on large stone pillars. Other buildings have been built at this location since the 300's AD. There is a little shrine called the Chapel of the Holy Spirit next to the big rectangular room. A

---

[249] Kendell Easley, *John's Vision: The River of the Water of Life.* Biblical Illustrator. LifeWay, Volume 39, number 4, Summer 2013, 14-17.

Christian tradition is that the Holy Spirit descended on early believers on the day of Pentecost in this chapel.[250]

When the day of Pentecost arrived, they were all together in one place. And suddenly there came from heaven a sound like a mighty rushing wind, and it filled the entire house where they were sitting. And divided tongues as of fire appeared to them and rested on each one of them. And they were all filled with the Holy Spirit and began to speak in other tongues as the Spirit gave them utterance. Now there were dwelling in Jerusalem Jews, devout men from every nation under heaven. And at this sound the multitude came together, and they were bewildered, because each one was hearing them speak in his own language.

And they were amazed and astonished, saying, "Are not all these who are speaking Galileans? And how is it that we hear, each of us in his own native language? Parthians and Medes and Elamites, and residents of Mesopotamia, Judea and Cappadocia, Pontus and Asia, Phrygia and Pamphylia, Egypt, and the parts of Libya belonging to Cyrene, and visitors from Rome, both Jews and proselytes, Cretans and Arabians – we hear them telling in our own tongues the mighty works of God." And all were amazed and perplexed, saying to one another, "What does this mean?" (Acts 2:1-12)

The Upper Room, of course, is not the original room, but is a 14th-century structure. It is built on the foundations of a 4th-century church known as Holy Zion, which was destroyed in 614 AD. The Muslims turned the current building into a shrine in 1524, and Christians were not allowed inside until Israel opened the site to everyone in 1948.

To enter the Upper Room, a person must climb up a set of stone steps that were recently built. The old steps were worn out due to constant use over centuries. A Muslim prayer niche is still visible on a wall in the Upper Room, and a Crusader's coat of arms was recently discovered near the exit.

Jesus shared the Passover meal with his disciples the night before his crucifixion. After the meal, Jesus washed the feet of each disciple and gave them the bread and wine of the new covenant.

---

[250] George W. Knight, *The Holy Land*, 141.

Covenant as a Biblical Theme

Covenants were used in ancient times as binding agreements with defined relationships, compared to modern legal contracts and international treatments. Covenants were used throughout the Bible, from Genesis to Revelation. The Old and New Testaments contain the old covenants God made at Mount Sinai and the new covenant He made in Christ.

The word "make" is used in covenants and it means to create a covenant. The Hebrew word for covenant means "to cut" and implies the use of sacrifices in initiating covenants (Genesis 15). The second important word in Hebrew used in covenants is "establish", which means to stand up. It is about carrying out one's obligation under a covenant (Genesis 17:7).

Genesis 6:18 contains the first biblical references to covenants. Before the flood God promised Noah, "I will establish My covenant with you." After the flood God reaffirmed his covenant with Noah, saying again, "I will establish My covenant with you."[251]

JERUSALEM: ANTIQUITIES AT RAMAT RACHEL (2)
Photo courtesy of the Israeli Ministry of Tourism and is solely for this photo only at www.goisrael.com

Ramat Rachel is a kibbutz south of Jerusalem. It is an enclave within Jerusalem's city boundaries, overlooking Bethlehem and Rachel's Tomb. In 2010, the population was 400 men, women, and children. The kibbutz was founded in 1926 with trades of stonecutting, housing construction, and haulage. The kibbutz was destroyed in the riots of 1926 when hundreds of Arabs attacked the training farm and burned it down. The kibbutz economy is based in hi-tech, tourism, and agriculture. In 2002, Data Detection Technologies produced advanced counting and packaging solutions for the seed, pharmaceutical, and diamond industries.

---

[251] E. LeBron Matthews, *Covenant as a Biblical Theme*. Biblical Illustrator, LifeWay: Volume 39, number 4, Summer 2013, 26-29.

Hotel Mitzpeh Rachel is the only kibbutz hotel in Jerusalem. The hotel has a convention center, tennis courts, and a large swimming pool. The kibbutz grows cherries, oranges, nectarines, grapefruit, olives, persimmons, figs, pomelos, and tangerines. Agricultural produce was collected in ancient times to pay taxes. In July 2008, archaeologists found a 1st-century cooking pot with fifteen large coins under the floor of a columbarium.

In an archaeological expedition in 1959-1962, Yohanan Aharoni identified the city as the biblical Beit Hakerem: "O ye children of Benjamin, gather yourselves to flee out of the midst of Jerusalem, and blow the trumpet in Tekoa, and set up a sign of fire in Beth-Haccerem: for evil appeareth out of the north, and great destruction" (Jeremiah 6:1).

Archaeologist Yigael Yadin dated the palace excavated by Aharoni to the reign of Athaliah, and identified it as the House of Baal in I1 Kings 11:18: "Then all the people of the land went to the house of Baal and tore it down; his altars and his images they broke in pieces, and they killed Mattan the priest of Baal before the altars. And the priest posted watchmen over the house of the Lord."[252]

The Worship of Baal was a problem to the Israelites. Baal was associated with agriculture and was believed to be the giver of life. Baal was also called the son of Dagon who was in charge of grain. Hadad the thunder god provided rain. Israel and Judah were attracted to Ba'al worship, which in part led to their downfall (read 1 Kings 16:30-34).

The God of Israel condemned the worship of Baal, and sent his prophets to warn the people of this idolatry and of the corruption of Baal's fertility rites. During this period of the kings of Israel, Baal was prevalent. Queen Jezebel, the Phoenician wife of King Ahab, had 450 prophets of Baal who advised her. Elijah challenged them on Mount Carmel, and God proved to be the true God and Baal just an idol. Baal had many names in scripture:

-*Baal-gad* means lord of good fortune: ". . .from Mount Halak, which rises toward Seir, as far as Baal-gad in the Valley of Lebanon below Mount Hermon. And he captured all their kings and struck them and put them to death" (Joshua 11:17).

---

[252] www.en.wikipedia.org/wiki/ramat_rachel.

-*Baal-hamon* means lord of wealth: Solomon had a vineyard at Baal-hamon; he let out the vineyard to keepers; each one was to bring for its fruit a thousand pieces of silver" (Song of Solomon 8:11).

-*Baal-hazor* means Baal's village: "After two full years Absalom invited all the king's sons" (II Samuel 13:23).

-*Baal-meon* means lord of the dwelling: "Nebo, and Baal-meon and Sibmah. And they gave other names to the cities they built" (Numbers 32:38).

Baal was the god of thunder and winter storms. The peasants were concerned about rain and asked Baal for rain by rituals of magic and sexual union. The Bible mentions Baal many times:

And he put down the idolatrous priests, whom the kings of Judah had ordained to burn incense in the high places in the cities of Judah, and in the places round about Jerusalem; them also that burned incense unto Baal, to the sun, and to the moon, and to the planets, and to all the host of heaven. (I1 Kings 23:5)

For the Lord of hosts, that planted thee, hath pronounced evil against thee, for the evil of the house of Israel and of the house of Judah, which they have done against themselves to provoke me to anger in offering incense unto Baal. (Jeremiah 11:17)

And they left all the commandments of the Lord their God, and made them molten images, two calves, and made a grove, and worshipped all the host of heaven, and served Baal. (I1 Kings 17:16)

Other scripture references to Baal are as follows: I1 Kings 10:25, Jeremiah 12:16, I1 Kings 23:4, 1 Kings 18:21, 1 Kings 18:19, Jeremiah 11:13, Judges 6:31, Jeremiah 32:29, Judges 6:25, I1 Kings 21:3, Judges 6:28, I1 Kings 10:22, I1 Kings 10:18, Judges 6:30, and many more.[253]

Bethany

Bethany is a village two miles from Jerusalem. Bethany is not mentioned in the Old Testament. It was probably developed just a few

---

decades before the birth of Jesus. Bethany is only mentioned in the New Testament with visits from Jesus. He spent many happy hours visiting Lazarus and his sisters Mary and Martha, such as Matthew 21:17: "And leaving them, he went out to the city to Bethany and lodged there."

Jesus gave a gentle scolding to Martha when she complained about Mary; this took place at Bethany: "My dear Martha, you are worried and upset over all these details!" He told her, "There is only one thing worth being concerned about. Mary has discovered it, and it will not be taken away from her" (Luke 10:41-42).

It was this same Mary who anointed Jesus with expensive perfume just a few days before his crucifixion (read John 12:1-8).[254]

Before raising Lazarus from the dead, Jesus spoke these words: "I am the resurrection, and the life: he that believeth in me, though he were dead, yet shall he live: and whosoever liveth and believeth in me shall never die. Believest thou this?" (John 11:25-26).

If Christians believe these words of Jesus in John 11:25-26, we will live with the hope that we will hear Jesus call our name from the grave, and we will get up and follow him like Lazarus. The tomb of Lazarus was a cave with a stone blocking the entrance. It was a hole cut into the rock: "Jesus therefore again groaning in himself cometh to the grave. It was a cave, and a stone lay upon it" (John 11:38).

Today, twenty-two steps lead down to a dark cave that is the traditional burial place of Lazarus. The original entrance was on ground level and was sealed shut by the Muslims who built a mosque between a church and the tomb. In the 17th century, the Franciscans received permission from the Muslims to make the new entrance which still leads down to the tomb.

The Inn of the Good Samaritan is not far from Bethany on the Jericho Road. The building is from the Turkish period and was used as a police station. It is not as authentic as the inn from the time of Jesus, but it reminds visitors of the parable of Jesus (read Luke 10:29-37).

Today, Bethany is an Arab village only two miles from Jerusalem on the eastern slopes of the Mount of Olives. The name Bethany in Aramaic means "House of Poverty." The town has many tropical and subtropical fruit and vegetable stands. The weather is very pleasant

---

[254]   George W. Knight, *The Holy Land*, 158-159.

during the winter months but is very hot in summer. November 4 is a hot summer day in Jericho.

Bethlehem

Bethlehem is a city in the central West Bank (biblical Judea and Samaria) and is about five miles south of Jerusalem. About 25,000 people live in Bethlehem in modern times. Bethlehem is the capital of the Bethlehem Governorate of the Palestinian Authority. The main economy comes from tourist visitors. The Bible identifies Bethlehem as the city David was from and the place where he was crowned the king of Israel. The New Testament states that Jesus of Nazareth was also born in Bethlehem.

The Samaritans invaded Bethlehem in 529 AD and it was rebuilt by the Byzantine emperor Justinian I. Bethlehem was captured by the Arab caliph Umar ibn al-Khattab in 637 and was guaranteed protection of the religious shrines. In 1099, the Crusaders captured Bethlehem and put a Latin clergy in place of the Greek Orthodox clergy. After Bethlehem was captured by Saladin, the sultan of Egypt and Syria, the Latin clergy were sent away. In 1250 during the time of the Mamluks, the walls of the city were destroyed. The Ottoman Empire later rebuilt the city walls.

The British gained control of Bethlehem during World War I, and it was scheduled to be included in an international zone under the United Nations Partition Plan for Palestine in 1947. Jordan annexed Bethlehem in the 1948 Arab-Israeli War, and then Bethlehem was taken over by Israel in the 1967 Six-Day War. Since 1995, Bethlehem has been governed by the Palestinian Authority.

Bethlehem now has a Muslim majority and also contains a diminished minority of Palestinian Christian communities. Tourism peaks during the Christmas season when Christians tour the Church of the Nativity. This church was commissioned in 327 AD by Constantine and his mother Helena, over the site with a cave that is considered to be the birthplace of Jesus of Nazareth. The Church of the Nativity is a World Heritage Site and was the first to be listed in the Palestinian Territories. Rachel's Tomb is at the northern entrance of Bethlehem.

Bethlehem has over thirty hotels and three hundred handicraft workshops.

In 2012 during an archaeological excavation in Bethlehem, archaeologists found a bulla (seal impression of dried clay) in ancient Hebrew script that reads, "From the town of Bethlehem to the King". This indicates that a shipment of grain, wine, or other goods was sent as a tax payment in the 8th or 7th century.

Biblical scholars believe that Bethlehem, located in the hill country of Judah, may be the same place as the biblical Ephratah, which means "fertile". The Book of Micah refers to Bethlehem Ephratah. The Bible also calls it Beth-Lehem Judah and a City of David. Bethlehem is first mentioned in the Tanakh and the Bible as the place where Rachel died and was buried: "And as for me, when I came from Padan, Rachel died by me in the land of Canaan in the way, when yet there was but a little way to come unto Ephrath: and I buried her there in the way of Ephrath; the same is Beth-lehem" (Genesis 48:7).

The Book of Ruth describes the valley to the east as being where Ruth of Moab gleaned the fields and returned to Bethlehem with Naomi. Several generations later, three of David's warriors brought David water from the well at Bethlehem to his hiding place in the cave of Adullam.

Bethlehem is forty-five miles northeast of Gaza and the Mediterranean Sea; forty-seven miles west of Amman, Jordan; thirty-seven miles southeast of Tel Aviv; and about five miles south of Jerusalem. Bethlehem is 2,543 feet above sea level and ninety-eight feet higher than Jerusalem. Bethlehem is on the southern part of the Judean Mountains.

The center of Bethlehem is the old city, laid out in eight parts in a mosaic style around Manger Square. Bethlehem has a Mediterranean climate with hot and dry summers and cold winters. Winter temperatures (mid-December to mid-March) can be cold and rainy, with temperatures from 33 to 55 degrees Fahrenheit. August has the hottest temperatures, with a typical high of 81 degrees Fahrenheit. The average rainfall is twenty-eight inches per year, with most of it between November and January. Night dew can sometimes happen 180 days per year. Around midday, a Mediterranean Sea breeze arrives on most days. Khamaseen winds from the Arabian Desert blow hot, dry, sandy, and dust winds during April, May, and mid-June.

Bethlehem shops sell Palestinian handicrafts, Middle Eastern spices, jewelry, and sweets such as baklava. Tourists like to buy olive wood statues, boxes, and crosses. Bethlehem factories make paints, plastics, synthetic rubber, pharmaceuticals, construction materials, and food products. The monks in the Monastery of Cremisan sell wine. In 2008, Bethlehem hosted an enormous economic conference initiated by Palestinian Prime Minister Salam Fayyad. The United States gave 1.4 billion dollars for business investments in the Palestinian territories.

As part of life in Bethlehem, Roman Catholic and Protestant denominations celebrate Christmas on December 25. Greek, Coptic, and Syrian Orthodox Christians celebrate on January 6; and Armenian Orthodox Christians celebrate on January 19. Most Christmas processions pass through Manger Square. Roman Catholic services take place in St. Catherine's Church, and Protestants often hold services at Shepherds' Field. The Church of the Nativity is located in the center of the city and is part of Manger Square. The church is over a grotto (cave) called the Holy Crypt, where Jesus was born. The Milk Grotto is where Mary, Joseph, and Jesus are believed to have taken refuge before their flight to Egypt. Nearby is the cave where Saint Jerome spent thirty years creating the Vulgate, a Latin version of the Bible largely used until the Reformation.

Bethlehem is known for bridal clothes; it is also known for using fancy embroidery on silk and wool fabrics. The Edward Said National Conservatory of Music has about 500 students, to train teachers how to teach children music and to study Palestinian folklore music. The Crib of the Nativity Theatre and Museum has thirty-one 3-D models describing the stages of the life of Jesus. The Badd Giacaman Museum in the Old City of Bethlehem, built in the 18th century, tells the story of the production of olive oil. The Baituna al-Talhami Museum has displays of Bethlehem culture.

Bethlehem had its first city elections in 1876 to elect a local council of seven members to represent each clan. A law was made that if the winner for mayor was a Catholic, his deputy should be Greek Orthodox. In modern times, the city council has fifteen elected members, including the mayor and deputy mayor. A law requires that a majority of the council be Christians, while the remaining members are technically not restricted to any religion, though most in authority in the city are Muslim. There are currently communist, Islamist, and secular political parties. The terrorist group Hamas, running as a political party, gained the majority of the open seats in the 2005 Palestinian city elections.[255]

Tekoa: Its History and Significance

Amos claimed to be a shepherd and caretaker of sycamore trees and not to be a prophet (Amos 7:14-15). Amos called Tekoa home and it was located in Judah. The traditional site of Tekoa is called Khirbet Tequ, a site of ancient ruins near the modern Israeli village of Tekoa. These ruins are about ten miles south of Jerusalem and about six miles south of Bethlehem. Tekoa is about three miles from Herodium, the fortress of Herod the Great. Joshua 15:39 includes Tekoa as one of the towns given to Judah. Tekoa has an altitude of 2,700 feet and is on a ridge overlooking the Judean Wilderness and Dead Sea basin to the east. 2 Chronicles 20:20 describes the area east of Tekoa as the Wilderness of Tekoa. Shepherds were common in this area in the time of Amos.

Tekoa was an important place militarily to defend the southern approaches to Jerusalem. Tekoa was a north-south trade route to Jerusalem between Hebron and Bethlehem. King Rehoboam fortified Tekoa for the defense of Judah (2 Chronicles 11:5-10). King Jehoshaphat fought a battle in the Wilderness of Tekoa against Ammon, Moab, and Edom (2 Chronicles 20:20-25). The prophet Jeremiah mentioned that Tekoa was one of the fortified cities of Judah at the time of the Babylonian Invasion. Jeremiah called for a trumpet to be blown in Tekoa to warn the people in Jerusalem to flee. Blowing a trumpet was a signal to warn of danger. There is a tradition that Amos may have been buried in a tomb in Tekoa. The book of Nehemiah tells about men from Tekoa helping to rebuild the walls of Jerusalem (Nehemiah 3:5-27).

Terry W. Eddinger is the Benjamin Miller professor of Old Testament and vice president of Carolina Graduate School of Divinity in Greensboro, North Carolina.[256]

---

255 www.en.wikipedia.org/wiki/bethlehem.

256 Terry W. Eddinger, *Tekoa: Its History and Significance.* Biblical Illustrator, LifeWay: Volume 39, number 2, Winter 2012-2013, 30-32.

Covenant as a Biblical Theme (continued)

In Genesis 9:9, God specified all of Noah's descendants in the covenant. The rainbow became a symbol of the covenant and was a sign that God would never send another universal flood. God has kept his promise and this covenant remains in effect.

The next important covenant was between Abraham and God. The covenant grew out of a mandate for Abram to leave Ur and go to an unspecified location (Genesis 12:1-3). Abram obeyed and traveled to Canaan, which was about 400 miles away from Ur. Later God promised to give Canaan to the descendants of Abraham (Genesis 13:14-17). Years passed before God entered into a formal covenant with Abram.

This covenant with Abraham was the first covenant involving bloodshed. In this contract, Abram's name was changed to Abraham. Abram meant "exalted father." Abraham meant "father of a multitude." Now, Abraham's name was a reminder to God of His commitment to His promise that Abraham's descendants would be as numerous as the stars. Circumcision became the sign of the covenant with God through all generations of Abraham's descendants.

Centuries after this covenant with Abraham and his descendants, the descendants were slaves in Egypt. God sent a fugitive felon named Moses to accomplish their freedom.[257]

JERUSALEM: KNESSET PLENUM, THE SESSION HALL OF THE ISRAEL PARLIAMENT
Photo courtesy of the Israeli Ministry of Tourism and is solely for this photo only at www.goisrael.com

Israel's Parliament, the Knesset, is located in Jerusalem on a hillside overlooking the Hebrew University and the Israel Museum. The Ministry of Finance, the Ministry of Interior, the Ministry of Labor and Welfare, and the Office of the Prime Minister are located near the

---

[257] E. LeBron Matthews, *Covenant as a Biblical Theme*. Biblical Illustrator, LifeWay: Volume 39, number 4, Summer 2013, 26-29.

Parliament building. Due to high taxes, some people in Israel call the Ministry of Finance the "second Wailing Wall".

There are 120 members, men and women, who are elected to a four-year term by popular vote in Israel's Parliament. The majority party forms the administrative government led by the Prime Minister. The President's duties are ceremonial. Parliament sessions are in Hebrew and open to the public, and many are televised. Arabs living in Israel have been given full citizenship and are represented in Parliament. Visitors being admitted to Parliament go through very strict security. Artwork by Marc Chagall is displayed inside the building. The people of Great Britain presented Israel with a large menorah that is displayed in the Knesset.

EIN YAEL (LIVING MUSEUM), NEAR JERUSALEM: ANCIENT DOORWAY

Photo courtesy of the Israeli Ministry of Tourism and is solely for this photo only at www.goisrael.com

Ein Yael is a museum that takes visitors back to the life of ancient times in Israel in the 12th century BC. There are workshops on pottery, weaving, basketry, paper making, wine making, and wheat harvesting. This is an outdoor museum next to the biblical zoo, and it houses the beautiful artifacts of a Roman villa dating back to the 2nd century.[258]

Dig Deeper into the Rich History of Israel

Jerusalem is the most significant location in biblical history, and much of the Old and New Testaments speak extensively about Jerusalem and the people from the Bible who have lived in the city throughout the centuries. One of the foremost scripture passages concerning

---

[258] www.funinjerusalem.com/en/fun-list-categories/108-ein-yael.htm.

Jerusalem is Psalm 122, which speaks of the importance of praying for the peace of Jerusalem. Other key scripture passages include:

Genesis 14:18-20: Abraham's interaction with Melchizedek, the king of Salem (Jerusalem)

II Samuel 6:6-16: David possesses Jerusalem as the capital of Israel

2 Chronicles 3:1-6:2: Solomon builds and dedicates the temple in Jerusalem

2 Chronicles 36:15-21: Jerusalem falls to the Babylonians, and the people of Judah are taken into captivity

Ezra 1:1-11, Nehemiah 2:1-3:32: The Israelites return to rebuild Jerusalem

Isaiah 2:1-4, 62:1-7: Isaiah prophesies of the importance of Jerusalem in bringing salvation to all nations

Matthew 27:1-28:8, Mark 15:1-16:8, Luke 23:1-24:12, John 18:28-20:18: Jesus' trial, crucifixion, and resurrection

Acts 2:1-47: Pentecost outpouring of the Holy Spirit on the Early Church in Jerusalem

Acts 15:1-29: Jerusalem Council of the Early Church convenes

Chapter 7

Dead Sea Area

In the Dead Sea area of Israel, a remarkable region of the country, the flour caves pictured here were hollowed out of limestone, and were cut out years ago by streams of water called Nahal Perazim to form the caves. There is white dust from the limestone everywhere.

Qumran is an archaeological site in the West Bank area, located about a mile inland from the northwestern shore of the Dead Sea. It is near the kibbutz of Kalia. Some scholars believe it could have been a small fort in ancient times.[259]

QUMRAN CAVE
Courtesy of the Israeli Ministry of Tourism and is solely for this photo only at www.goisrael.com

The first Qumran cave was discovered by a Bedouin shepherd chasing a stray animal. He also at the same time discovered the Dead Sea Scrolls, inside the cave. From the eleven caves discovered in the area, every book of the Old Testament except Esther was found. Nothing was found from the New Testament.[260]

---

[259] www.en.wikipedia.org/wiki/qumran_com.
[260] www.bibleplaces.com/qumrancaves.htm.

Jum'a Muhammed and Muhammed edh-Dhib, two Bedouin cousins, threw a stone at a cave when they were looking for a stray goat. The cousins returned to the Bedouin nomad tent camp with the complete Isaiah, the Manual of Discipline and the Habakkuk Commentary. For several months, the scrolls hung from tent poles in the camp. Finally a clan member insisted that the cousins take the scrolls to Bethlehem to see if they could sell them for a few dollars.[261] Today their value is in the millions of dollars!

Shepherd Bedouins of the Syrian Desert

The word Bedouin means "those in the desert". It is derived from the Arabic words *badawi* and *badiyah*. One Bedouin expression is as follows: "I against my brother, my brothers and I against my cousins, and then my cousins and I against strangers." This type of loyalty was based on kinship that ran through their lineage and through the tribe. Up to the present time, arguments are settled under this system of order and justice.

The *bayt* is the Bedouin family unit and typically consists of a married couple, their children, and their parents. Self-responsibility and collective responsibility are emphasized in the Bedouin culture.

The *goum* is a type of family group. Several families form groups with their tents and move together as a *goum*. New tents are added when a couple marries. This is a type of interaction that might typically consist of five generations. They are typically cousins who make up the individuals in the *goum*.

The Bedouins are divided into tribes ruled by a *sheikh*. In the context of the tribe as a whole, the word *sheikh* literally means "elder". Those of this title may be descendants of one common ancestor. They help each other economically when one group has a need. The *sheikhs* are the ones from the Bedouin tribes that interact with their government. There is an honor code in these interactions. For example, the *bisha'a* is the ordeal by fire, which is often used as a method of lie detection.

Modern Bedouins call themselves Negev Arabs rather than Bedouins, because the term "bedouin" refers to a nomadic way of life that is not practiced much today. In the year 2000, the Ministry of Agriculture of Israel estimated that the Negev Arabs owned 200,000

---

[261] www.allaboutarchaeology.org/qumran.

head of sheep and 5,000 goats. In ancient times, the Bedouins practiced transporting goods and people across the desert, in the nomadic way of life.[262] Modern Bedouins also raise white doves.

The family consists of parents, children, grandparents, and friends. When they can afford it, several tents travel together as a *goum*. New wives sometimes have male friends to join the group. The tribe members claim common ancestors. The Bedouin honor codes are hospitality, courage, and bravery, which are pre-Islamic customs. In modern Bedouin tribes, *sharia* or national penal codes of justice are accepted. Conflict resolutions can be as simple as talks between families of the two tribes. Nomad Bedouins do not believe in incarceration. Petty crimes are settled by fines. If the convicted tribe member does not pay, the tribe members take up a collection to pay it, because the tribe is responsible for the fine. Serious crimes are punished by corporal punishment (beating or paddling) or capital punishment (death).

Trial by Ordeal is used by the Bedouin tribes of the Palestinian territories and the Sinai Peninsula. Trial by Ordeal is a protocol for lie detection. The accused is forced to lick a hot metal spoon and has to rinse his mouth with water. If the tongue shows signs of a burn or scar, the person is guilty of lying. Children are not disciplined until age seven. Boys and girls at age thirteen take on adult responsibilities. Between the ages of sixteen to twenty, marriage is allowed and encouraged. Parents pre-arrange marriages, which are usually enacted between first cousins. Bedouins are generally very hospitable and seldom turn away a stranger from their tent.

BEDOUIN HOSPITALITY IN TENTS
Photo courtesy of the Israeli Ministry of Tourism and is solely for this photo only at www.goisrael.com

The Negev Bedouins live in the Negev desert region in Israel. Most of these Negev Bedouins migrated from the Arabian Desert, Transjordan, Egypt, and the Sinai, from the 18th century onward. There are about 160,000 Negev Bedouins, who make up 12 percent of

---

[262] www.en.wikipedia.org/wiki/negev_bedouin.

the Arab citizens in Israel. The first Negev Bedouin town, Tel as-Sabi or Tel Sheva, was developed in 1967.

The largest Negev Bedouin urban area had a population of 28,000 by 1998, and about half of all Negev Bedouins lived in urban areas by that time. About half of all Bedouins who are citizens of Israel live in unrecognized villages. An unrecognized village is not recognized or approved by the Israeli government, and the people living there do not have electricity, running water, or trash collection. Most Bedouins live in the Negev, but some live as far north as Galilee.

Covenant as a Biblical Theme (continued)

God told Moses that He would keep His covenant obligation to give His people the land of Canaan. God told Moses to worship Him as Yahweh (Exodus 6:2-8). The name Yahweh reminded the people of Israel of their covenant with Him. God gave Moses the Law on Mount Sinai (Exodus 19:1-24:18). The Sinai covenant transferred God's covenant with Abraham to the latest generation of his descendants.

During the next 860 years, Israel showed they could not comply with the terms of the covenant. Sometimes spiritual revivals produced temporary covenant renewal. Josiah is known for leading the greatest revival in Jewish history (II Kings 23:1-25; 2 Chronicles 34:14-35:19). After Josiah's death, the people returned to their wicked ways of unfaithfulness and idolatry. Jeremiah declared that God would issue a new covenant (Jeremiah 31:31-40). In the new covenant, God would change the hearts of the people and forgive and forget their sins. This relationship with the Lord of the covenant by faith was the goal of all the earlier covenants.

In the New Testament, Hebrews 8:6-12 describes Christ as "the mediator of a better covenant". Zechariah prophesied that the birth of John the Baptist was part of God fulfilling His promise to Abraham (Luke 1:72-73). Scripture also tells us that Mary, the mother of Jesus, celebrated that the coming Savior was a fulfillment of the promise God made to Abraham (Luke 1:46-55). In Acts 3:25, early Christians associated Christ with Abraham's covenant and with Jeremiah's new covenant (Romans 11:27; II Corinthians 3:6).[263]

---

[263]   E. LeBron Matthews, *Covenant as a Biblical Theme*. Biblical Illustrator, LifeWay: Volume 39, number 4, Summer 2013, 26-29.

Starting in the late 19th century, many Bedouins under British rule began to transit to a semi-nomadic life. In the 1950's and '60's, large numbers of Bedouins throughout Midwest Asia started to leave the traditional, nomadic life to settle in the cities of the region, especially as the hot ranges have shrunk and populations have grown. There were drought conditions in 1958 through 1961, as Bedouins left herding for ordinary employment and settled in the cities in Syria. Also, in Egypt and Israel, as the oil industry intensified in the Persian Gulf, a desire to improve their living standards led Bedouins to change their ways from being national roaming herders of sheep to being regular citizens in nations of the region. They now enjoy public schools, medical care, and other modern ways of life that are provided by governments. Today, Bedouins are content to breed white doves to sell, even as many have embraced a new lifestyle in the cities.

Alexander Jannal the High Priest was the first person to build on Mount Masada, in the middle of the 2nd century BC. Herod the Great later had a fierce power struggle for Masada in 46 BC. Masada became a place of refuge for Herod's family when he was forced to run from the Parthians and make it to safety in Rome. In 30 BC, Herod built an elaborate palace on the twenty-acre summit. Herod built a large stone wall with thirty-eight points of defense.

Covenant as a Biblical Theme (continued)

During the Last Supper, Jesus took a cup and said, "This is the blood that establishes the covenant; it is shed for many for the forgiveness of sins." The words of Jeremiah's prophecy were fulfilled by Jesus. I Peter 2:9-10 shows how Jeremiah's words of a new covenant, written on people's heart and granting forgiveness, was a reality in Christ. Despite their differences, the divine covenants exhibit a structural and thematic unity. Each relates God's revelation of Himself and His desire for an intimate relationship.

The people at Sinai largely were descendants of Abraham. The majority of individuals in the new covenant do not share a common ethnic background. Each covenant relates God's revelation of Himself and His desire for an intimate relationship. Each covenant calls for godly behavior. Conduct is important in the natural outgrowth of faith in Christ.

E. LeBron Matthews is senior pastor, retired, of Eastern Heights Baptist Church, in Columbus, Georgia.[264]

QUMRAN: THE COMMUNITY BUILDINGS, WHERE THE DEAD SEA SCROLLS WERE WRITTEN (CISTERN IN THE FOREGROUND)
Photo courtesy of the Israeli Ministry of Tourism and is solely for this photo only at www.goisrael.com

More than 900 scrolls were discovered at Qumran, written on parchment and papyrus. Cisterns, Jewish ritual baths, and cemeteries have also been uncovered. Additionally, excavators found a dining or assembly room, trash from an upper story which may have been a scriptorium, pottery kilns, and a tower. Over a thousand people are buried in the cemetery.[265] The long room was used for communal meals. There were three rows of tables where the people ate in silence. In the next room, more than 1,000 cooking items were found. There were 708 cups, 210 plates, and 108 salad bowls.

The community had ritual baths twice a day. Evidence of the earthquake in 31 BC was found, and a crack shifted the left side of the *mikvah* by nearly twelve inches.[266]

Masada is an ancient fortress on top of an isolated rock plateau overlooking the Dead Sea. Herod the Great built palaces for himself and fortified the area between 37 and 31 BC. Roman Empire troops fought against Jewish rebels on Masada, and all the Jewish rebels committed suicide corporately rather than be tortured by the Romans.

Between 1963 and 1965, Israeli archeologist Yigael Yadin excavated Masada. For nearly 2,000 years, Masada had remained largely untouched by humans or nature. What remains of the Roman siege ramp still stands on the western side. Many of the old buildings have

---

[264] E. LeBron Matthews, *Covenant as a Biblical Theme*. Biblical Illustrator, LifeWay: Volume 39, number 4, Summer 2013, 26-29.

[265] www.en.wikipedia.org/wiki/qumran_com.

[266] www.bibleplaces.com/qumran.htm.

been restored from their remains and display the wall paintings of Herod's two main palaces. The synagogue, storehouses, and houses of the Jewish rebels have also been restored.[267]

TOURING ON TOP OF MASADA

Courtesy of the Israeli Ministry of Tourism and is solely for this photo only at www.goisrael.com

Inside the synagogue on top of Masada, the archaeologists found an ostracon bearing the tithe for the priest. Fragments of two scrolls, containing parts of Deuteronomy 33-34 and parts of Ezekiel 35-38, were found in pits dug under the floor of a small room in the synagogue. Excavators also found books of Genesis, Leviticus, and Psalms.

Israel's Climate

Israel is about 8,000 square miles total and slightly larger than New Jersey. Israel is divided into four regions. On the west is the coastal plain connected to the upland areas in the central and northern parts of Israel. To the east, Israel is bordered by the Great Rift Valley or Jordan Valley, and the Negev Desert to the south and the Dead Sea.

At the same time in Israel, mountains in northern Israel can be covered with snow; beautiful crops can be growing along the coastal plain; and a very dry desert can be in the south.

Israel's climate is one of extremes. Usually in Israel, winters are wet and summers are typically hot and dry.[268]

---

[267] www.en.wikipedia.org/wiki/masada.

[268] David L. Jenkins, *Israel's Climate.* Biblical Illustrator, LifeWay: Volume 39, number 4, Summer 2013, 35-38.

MASADA, DEAD SEA, AND DESERTIC PANORAMA

Courtesy of the Israeli Ministry of Tourism and is solely for this photo only at www.goisrael.com

Masada is an important mountain in Israel, but it is not mentioned in the Old or New Testaments of the Bible. Masada in Hebrew means "stronghold". The people of Israel feel patriotic toward Masada. In 73 AD, 960 brave Jewish men, women, and children made a stand at Masada against the Romans. The fact that freedom was more precious to them than life itself has become a motto for modern Israel's commitment to liberty. Masada is two and a half miles from the western shore of the Dead Sea, in the wilderness of Judea. It is a half mile long, 220 yards wide, and 2,000 feet above the Dead Sea.

Masada and donkeys were accustomed to cisterns at the top of the mountain. The path of the donkeys can still be seen in modern times. There was enough water in Herod's day to water gardens, fill up Herod's swimming pool, supply the bath houses, and provide water for personal use.

In 66 AD, Jewish zealots surprised the Romans. The zealots used the fortress at Masada for their families and as a base to attack nearby Roman garrisons. In 70 AD, the Romans destroyed Jerusalem. Some of the Jewish survivors and their families fled to Masada to join the zealots. Hundreds of people lived in the palaces built by Herod. The Jews built camp stoves on the beautiful mosaic tile floors. They also built a synagogue for worship. In 72 AD, Flavius Silva led a large force of Roman troops to attack Masada. Silva made headquarters at the base of the western side of Masada. He built eight base camps and connected them to a siege wall. The ruins of these camps made by Silva and the Romans can still be seen in modern times. Attempts to move the Jews by force failed. So Silva and his men constructed a ramp, measuring 225 yards in length and about the same in width. At the top of the assault ramp was a siege tower made of iron, which was equipped with catapults and a battering ram. It took months of hard labor to complete the project.

When it was finished, the Romans began to use the battering ram to hammer away at the outer wall of Masada. It soon became evident to both the Jews and the Romans that Silva and the Romans would have success. That night, the Jewish men of Masada chose Eleazar Ben Yair to be their leader. After much discussion about the inevitability of all the men being killed by the Romans, and wives and children being killed or made slaves or prostitutes, the decision was made for the Jews to kill each other in an orderly way. They preferred dying at their own hands than by Roman hands.

Each father would be required to kill his own family. Then ten chosen men would kill the men who were left. The ten men drew lots to see which man would be last to die. The chosen one did his work fast and killed the men. The last man took a sword through his heart and joined his friends and family in death. All the men chose to die as free Jews rather than as Roman slaves. It was Passover in 73 AD.

However, two women and five children had hidden in caves and came forward to tell their story to the Romans and to the world. The 1st-century historian Josephus wrote a detailed account of this story in his book *Jewish Wars*. Several years ago, the Israel Defense Forces used the top of Mount Masada as a location for new recruits to make their pledges to defend Israel. New recruits now use the Western Wall in Jerusalem.

Yigael Yadin was the leader of an excavation group from October 1963 to April 1965. His group unearthed buildings, beautiful mosaic floors, clothing, scrolls, fragments of parchment, weapons, and many other items. Many human skeletons were found huddled together, which agrees with the information of Josephus in his book *Jewish Wars,* written in the 1st century AD. Modern archaeology proved the story and facts of Masada from ancient times. Many scholars thought some of the things Josephus wrote to be legendary, and now archaeology has proved most of them.

Israel's Climate (continued)

God led Moses to the summit of Mount Pisgah in order for Moses to view the land. Moses was not allowed to go inside the land. From Mount Pisgah on the eastern side of the Jordan River, Moses viewed "all the land of Ephraim and Manasseh, all the land of Judah as far as the Mediterranean Sea, the Negev, and the region from the Valley of Jericho, the City of Palms, as far as Zoar" *(Deuteronomy 34:1-3). This was the land flowing with milk and honey, and the differences in weather conditions in Israel are unusual.*

Areas along the coastal plains can receive up to forty inches of rain; the inland area will receive about fifteen to twenty inches; and the desert region about two inches or less. The months of November through February usually bring many rainy days and can be extended from October through March. From the middle of June through the middle of September, the land produces very little rain. The Old Testament writers wrote about both the dry and rainy seasons and the dry summers: "My strength was dried up as by the heat of summer" (Psalm 32:4). "Lo, the winter is past, the rain is over and gone" (Song of Solomon 2:11, RSV).

Climate and rainfall influenced the resolution of the grazing land between Lot's and Abraham's herdsmen. Abraham suggested the solution of parting ways. Abraham gave Lot the first choice of land (Genesis 13:9). Lot chose the entire Jordan Valley for himself and journeyed eastward. Today, that land south of Jerusalem is a desert wilderness instead of the well-watered land Lot had chosen.[269]

A person can choose to reach the 1200-foot summit of Mount Masada by climbing the "snake path" on the eastern side, or by walking the less difficult path which goes by the old Roman ramp on the western side. Most people, however, choose the modern way, which is to ride the very safe and fast cable car. Where the cable car stops, a person has to walk on uneven ground. Visitors need to drink plenty of water, wear a covering on their heads (hat), and wear plenty of strong sun tan lotion. The sun and weather are very hot in this region.

Signs on top of the mountain point out routes to take on the tour, and they identify sites of interest. A black line painted on the ruins shows how high the rubble was before the excavations were completed. Everything below the black line is in its original condition. Everything above the line either rose above the rubble or was reconstructed by archaeologists.

The Dead Sea is a salt lake with Jordan to the east and Israel and the West Bank to the west. It is 1,388 feet below sea level. The Dead Sea is 1,237 feet deep, forty-two miles long, and eleven miles wide. The Dead Sea was both a place of refuge for King David and also a health resort for Herod the Great. The Dead Sea has been a supplier

---

[269] David L. Jenkins, *Israel's Climate*. Biblical Illustrator, LifeWay: Volume 39, number 4, Summer 2013, 35-38.

for Egyptian mummifications, and also for potash for fertilizers. The salt is also used for cosmetics and herbal sachets. The Bible calls it the Salt Sea. Rainfall is four inches per year in the northern part and two inches yearly in the southern part.[270]

The Dead Sea is also known as Bahr Lut, Eastern Sea, Lake of Asphalt, Salt Sea, Sea of Sodom and Gomorrah, Sea of the Plain, Sea of the Devil, Sea of Zoar, and Stinking Lake. Due to the heavy salt content, no animals or plants can live in the salty water. The Dead Sea is not mentioned much in the Bible. It did, however, act as a barrier, blocking traffic to Judah from the east. An army of Ammonites and Moabites crossed a shallow part of the Dead Sea on their way to attack King Jehoshaphat (2 Chronicles 20). Ezekiel prophesied that one day the Dead Sea will be fresh water and fishermen will spread their nets there and catch fish.[271]

DEAD SEA: SALT DEPOSITS ON THE ROCKS

Photo courtesy of the Israeli Ministry of Tourism and is solely for this photo only at www.goisrael.com

The Dead Sea is rich in minerals and is almost ten times as salty as the oceans in the world. The Dead Sea Works Company on the southwest side of the lake has 1600 employees around the clock to harvest the valuable minerals from the water.

The salt content of the Dead Sea can have medicinal value. Aristotle, the Queen of Sheba, King Solomon, and Cleopatra all believed in its healing properties. For patients with skin ailments, modern doctors sometimes prescribe to soak in the waters of the Dead Sea.[272]

The western shore of the Dead Sea (inside the border of Israel) has nice beaches and two specifically therapeutic beaches, Neve Zohar and Ein Bokeh. There are dozens of hotels, hostels and guest houses. There are jeep and bicycle tours, Bedouin hospitality, and camel tours. Many tourists visit Mount Sodom and the Ein Gedi Reserve. Some

---

[270] www.en.wikipedia.org/wiki/dead_sea.

[271] www.bibleplaces.com/deadsea.htm.

[272] www.bibleplaces.com/deadsea.htm.

Christians visit monasteries, such as St. George, Quruntul, Khozeba, and Mar Saba, built on the cliff walls. Some even welcome visitors. The Dead Sea also has deposits of black mud that make it easy to spread on the body, providing nourishing minerals. The bromide in the air also benefits the systems of the body.[273]

Israel's Climate (continued)

Bedouin shepherds lead their flocks in search of grass and occasional pools of water on floors of wadis. Wadis are dry river beds that flood during the spring rains. This desolate area is where John the Baptist lived. In this area south of Jerusalem, after His baptism Jesus spent forty days being tempted in the land that Lot had picked out.

God used climate for instruction. When the people took God's goodness for granted and did not take responsibility of the good care of the land God had given them, God would send drought and famine. God would send His prophets to pronounce judgment upon His disobedient people (Amos 4:7). The prophets asked the people to repent. If they did, climate was restored. If they did not, there were problems with climate and weather. During the reign of King Ahab, Elijah the prophet said to the king, "As the Lord God of Israel lives, I stand before Him, and there will be no dew or rain during these years except by my command" (1 Kings 17:1).

Koheleth, the wise teacher of Ecclesiastes, reminded his students of God's creative involvement in the forces of nature (Ecclesiastes 11:1-8). In Ecclesiastes 11:4-5 we learn, "One who watches the wind will not sow, and the one who looks at the clouds will not reap. Just as you don't know the path of the wind or how bones develop in the womb of a pregnant woman, so you don't know the work of God who makes everything." When Jesus talked to Nicodemus, He compared the divine mystery of the new birth to the wind. "The wind blows where it pleases, and you have its sound, but you don't know where it comes from or where it is going" (John 3:8). Jesus may have been thinking of Ecclesiastes 11:4-5.

In Israel sometimes there is a hot dry hamsin wind that blows in from the south. Hamsin winds blow in from the Arabian Peninsula. Israelis understand the hamsin wind. Jesus spoke of the hamsin wind when he said, "And when the south wind is blowing you say, It is going to be a scorcher! and it is" (Luke 12:55).

---

[273] www.goisrael.com/tourism_eng/tourist.

David Jenkins is a retired pastor living in Gilmer, Texas.[274]

A DATE PALM GROVE

Photo courtesy of the Israeli Ministry of Tourism and is solely for this photo only at www.goisrael.com

An extinct Judean date palm's 2,000-year-old seed was discovered by scientists, and they germinated it. They now have a healthy four-year-old seedling, which they named Methuselah after the oldest living man in the Bible. This is the oldest germinated seed. The seed itself was discovered in 1965 as archaeologists excavated Masada. They put the seed in storage for 40 years. Dr. Elaine Solowey of the Arava Institute for Environmental Studies helped to revive the dormant seeds. In 2005, the seed known as Methuselah was planted and it sprouted. After it germinated, fragments of the seed shell hung onto the roots. The seed was carbon dated, which showed the age of the date seed between 60 BC and 95 AD, which is about the age expected for a seed to survive the Masada fortress attack by the Romans in 73 AD.

According to Josephus, the nearly 1,000 Jews at Masada during the attack burned the remaining food stores except for one, to show that they were not starving to death but rather that they chose to commit suicide. Sarah Sallon, director of the Louis L. Brock Natural Medicine Research Center in Jerusalem, stated, "These people were eating these dates up on the mountain and looking down at the Roman camp, knowing that they were going to die soon, and spitting out the pits. Maybe here is one of the pits."

Sallon added in a podcast interview, "We try to reintroduce those plants back into the environment. So we're interested not only in the plants that grow in the Middle East now, but the ones that used to grow here, like the ancient date (palm), which was known in history not only as a source of delicious dates and a very important food, but also as medicine." In the meantime, Sallon must wait until Methuselah

---

[274] David L. Jenkins, *Israel's Climate.* Biblical Illustrator, LifeWay: Volume 39, number 4, Summer 2013, 35-38.

is six or seven years old to see what sex the date palm is. If it is female, it could produce fruit for replanting. If it is male, more seeds from Masada may need to be germinated.[275]

The Judean Desert in Israel is east of Jerusalem and descends to the Dead Sea and the Jordan Valley. It is sometimes called the Wilderness of Judah or Wilderness of Judea.[276] King Saul and King David hid in the Judean Desert to escape their enemies and to escape from each other. John the Baptist preached in this desert, and Jesus was tempted here. Herod the Great built two palaces and fortresses, Herodium and Masada. Nahal Darga is the largest wadi in the northern Judean Desert. The wadi is twenty-seven miles long and up to 650 feet deep. The water stays in small pools at the bottom of each fall, because the narrow shape of the canyon keeps the sunshine out. These pools are a reliable source of water north of Ein Gedi. In the Byzantine period, there were sixty-five monasteries in the Judean Desert, and they were connected by paths and were two to three miles apart. Mar Sarba Monastery survived the Muslim invasions. In 1834, an earthquake destroyed most of the monastery.

JUDEAN DESERT: DRAGOT (DARAJA) CANYON (1)
Photo courtesy of the Israeli Ministry of Tourism and is solely for this photo only at www.goisrael.com

Camel humps serve as energy reserves to be used on a long journey in the hot, dry desert.[277] Isaiah 40 talks about grass withering:

The voice said, "Cry out!" And he said, "What shall I cry?" All flesh is grass, and all its loveliness is like the flower of the field. The grass withers, the flower fades, because the breath of the Lord blows upon it; surely the people are like grass. The grass withers, the flower fades, but the word of our God stands forever." (Isaiah 40:6-8, NIV)

---

[275] www.wnd.com/2008/06/67006.

[276] www.en.wikipedia.org/wiki/judean_desert.

[277] www.bibleplaces.com/judeanwilderness.htm.

David: The King and His Kingdom

David was the youngest son of Jesse (1 Samuel16:10-11). David belonged to the tribe of Judah, the tribe God ordained to rule over Israel until the Messiah came and ruled (Genesis 49:10, Ezekiel 21:25-27). David was of the lineage of Judah through Perez, whom Judah had through his incestuous relationship with Tamar, his daughter-in-law (Genesis 38:24-30, 1 Chronicles 2:3-5, 9-15). David's ancestors included his great-great-grandmother Rahab, his great-grandfather Boaz, his great-grandmother Ruth, and his grandfather Obed (Joshua 2:1, Ruth 4:12-22, Matthew 1:5).

David described his mother's godliness by speaking of her as the Lord's "handmaid" (Psalm 116:16). David spent his boyhood in Bethlehem, his ancestral home (1 Samuel 17:58, Ruth 2:4, Luke 2:4). God wanted to replace King Saul because of his disobedience to Him (1 Samuel 13:14, 15:23). David was described as "ruddy, with bright eyes, and good-looking" (1 Samuel 16:12, NKJV). During his shepherd days, David had skill and courage when he killed a lion and a bear to protect his sheep (1 Samuel 17:36). David was skilled at playing the harp and wrote many of the Psalms. David was recommended to Saul as "skillful in playing, a mighty man of valor, a man of war, prudent in speech, and a handsome person, and the Lord is with him" (1 Samuel 16:18, NKJV). God identified David as "a man after His own heart, whom He had chosen to be Israel's king to fulfill all His will" (1 Samuel 13:14, 16:11-13; 1 Kings 8:16; Acts 13:22).

King Saul called David to his court to play the harp, to comfort him from the evil spirit that troubled him (1 Samuel 16:14,19). In the beginning, King Saul loved David and made him his armor-bearer (1 Samuel 16:21). David served as Saul's personal bodyguard and had the king's complete confidence. David became a regular member of the court of Saul. Saul's love turned to hate after David killed Goliath and had victories over Philistines, because David was popular with the people (1 Samuel 17:50, 18:6-9). King Saul tried to kill David with a javelin and then by challenging David to collect 100 Philistine foreskins as a way to marry the king's daughter, Michal (1 Samuel 18:11,25). David "behaved himself wisely in all his ways; and the Lord was with him" (1 Samuel 18:14). God gave David the love and protection of Jonathan, King Saul's son (1 Samuel 18:1-4, 19:1-7). Michal loved David *and helped him escape from her father, King Saul (1 Samuel 18:21,28; 19:12-18).*[278]

Ein Gedi

The site of Ein Gedi is associated with King David and King Saul in the Old Testament. Temperatures in this area of Israel often reach 125 degrees or higher in the summer months, and November is a summer month in Israel. Sometimes in the Judean desert, a lot of rain water from the winter rains washes out roads and causes other damages in the Ein Gedi area. It can even send cars, people, and boulders into the Dead Sea without warning. Ein Gedi is an oasis in the desert, and its name is a Hebrew word meaning "spring of the kid". David fled to Ein Gedi when King Saul was chasing him, trying to kill him:

> *And it came to pass, when Saul was returned from following the Philistines, that it was told him, saying, "Behold, David is in the wilderness of Engedi." Then Saul took three thousand chosen men out of all Israel, and went to seek David and his men upon the rocks of the wild goats. And he came to the sheepcotes by the way, where was a cave; and Saul went in to cover his feet: and David and his men remained in the sides of the cave. (1 Samuel 24:1-3)*

---

[278] John Traylor, *David: The King and His Kingdom.* Biblical Illustrator, LifeWay: Volume 39, number 4, Summer 2013, 39-42.

EIN GEDI: WATERFALL IN NAHAL DAVID (DAVID'S STREAM)

Photo courtesy of the Israeli Ministry of Tourism and is solely for this photo only at www.goisrael.com

Ein Gedi is also mentioned in Song of Solomon 1:14: "My beloved is unto me as a cluster of camphire in the vineyards of Engedi." Additionally, it appears in Ezekiel 47:10: "And it shall come to pass, that the fishers shall stand upon it from Engedi even unto Eneglaim; they shall be a place to spread forth nets; their fish shall be according to their kinds, as the fish of the great sea, exceeding many."

A large kibbutz has been built at Ein Gedi, and kibbutz members operate an inn and a restaurant. Visitors like to stop at the restaurant for a good lunch and then swim or wade in the salty waters of the Dead Sea.

Ein Gedi is an oasis located west of the Dead Sea and is near Masada and Qumran. In 2 Chronicles 20:2, it is identified with Hazazon-tamar, where the Moabites and Ammonites gathered to fight Jehoshaphat: "Some men came and told Jehoshaphat, 'A great multitude is coming against you from Edom, from beyond the sea; and behold, they are in Hazazon-tamar' (that is Ein Gedi)."

In Genesis 14:7, Hazazon-tamar is mentioned as an Amorite city: "Then they turned back and came to En-mishpat (that is Kadesh) and defeated all the country of the Amalekites, and also the Amorites who were dwelling in Hazazon-tamar." In Joshua 15:62, Ein Gedi is listed as belonging to the tribe of Judah: "Nibshan, the city of salt, and Ein Gedi: six cities with their villages."

Ein Gedi was an important source for balsam for the Greco-Roman world until the Byzantine ruler Justinian, who wanted to get rid of the Jews. In April 1848, Lieutenant William Francis Lynch led an American expedition down the Jordan River into the Dead Sea and stopped at Ein Gedi.[279] Ein Gedi is similar to a green Garden of Eden in the wilderness.[280]

David: The King and His Kingdom (continued)

God protected David during the time David hid from Saul (1 Samuel 23:14). Both Saul and his son Jonathan knew God had anointed David to reign over Israel (1 Samuel 13:13-14, 16:12-13). Jonathan accepted God's will. Saul did not accept God's will and vowed to kill David (1 Samuel 23:16-18, 20:30-31).

David remained loyal to King Saul although Saul wanted to kill him. David trusted God to put David on the throne at the right time. In the meantime, David would be loyal to Saul. David treated Saul with respect at the times God delivered the king into his hands (1 Samuel 24:1-22, 26:5-25). David refused to avenge himself against Saul and decided to leave Saul's judgment to God (1 Samuel 24:12; 26:10,23). David continued to honor Saul as God's appointed king of Israel. He refused to kill Saul if he had opportunity. David even repented for cutting off the skirt of Saul's robe when the king was in the cave (1 Samuel 24:5-8). David vowed to care for Jonathan's family and later decided to care for all of Saul's descendants (1 Samuel 20:13-17, 24:21-22).

In 1 Samuel 31:1-6, we learn that God's time for David to reign came after the Philistines killed Saul, Jonathan, and Saul's other sons. God commanded thirty-year-old David to go to Hebron to have the men of Judah anoint him king over all of Israel (2 Samuel 21:7, 5:4).[281]

---

[279] www.en.wikipedia.org/wiki/ein_gedi.

[280] www.goisrael.com/tourism_eng/tourist.

[281] John Traylor, *David: The King and His Kingdom*. Biblical Illustrator, LifeWay: Volume 39, number 4, Summer 2013, 39-42.

JERICHO: LOOKING EAST TO JORDAN

Photo courtesy of the Israeli Ministry of Tourism and is solely for this photo only at www.goisrael.com

Jericho

Only a few ruins of the Old Jericho Road from the time of Jesus remain today. The Old Jericho Road was mainly a footpath climbing up to the Mount of Olives, to Bethany, and through the barren Judean desert. Jerusalem is 2700 feet above sea level, and Jericho is 820 feet below sea level. On the old lonely Jericho Road, many walkers were robbed, maimed, killed, or victimized by savage bandits. In speaking about this road, Jesus told a parable called "The Good Samaritan" (read Luke 10:30-37).

Modern-day Jericho is a Palestinian city near the Jordan River and the West Bank. Jericho was held by Jordan from 1948 to 1967. Israel controlled it from 1967 until they gave it to the Palestinian Authority in 1994. Jericho is believed to be one of the oldest inhabited cities in the world.

The Old Testament describes Jericho as the "City of Palms." Archaeologists have uncovered the remains of more than twenty successive settlements in Jericho. Jericho was a place of worship for lunar deities by the Canaanites.[282]

Jericho is also called Tel el-Sultan, er-Riha, Eriha, and Yeriho. Scholars believe that the city Joshua and the Israelites destroyed was Tel el-Sultan. In the time of Jesus, a new town had been built on the Wadi banks by the Hasmonean rulers and Herod the Great.

In 1868, Charles Warren missed discovering the Neolithic tower by one meter. Years later, Kathleen Kenyon discovered the tower. Archaeologists Garstang and Kenyon found dozens of jars full of grain from the last Canaanite city of Jericho. Their conclusion was that these jars of grain were from the city burned by Joshua. The archaeological record fits the Biblical record precisely.[283]

---

[282] www.en.wikipedia.org/wiki/tel_el_sultan.
[283] www.bibleplaces.com/jericho.htm.

Jericho is between Mt. Nebo in the east and the Central Mountains to the west, with the Dead Sea to the left. The Jordan River goes for miles to the west. The ideal location of Jericho and her access to her neighboring city made Jericho desirable for trade routes in ancient times.

Joshua 6 describes how the Israelites took over Jericho by marching around the city wall and blowing ram's horns. Jericho was later taken over by the Babylonians. The Israelites rebuilt it when they returned from the Babylonian exile. The Romans destroyed the city in the 1st century, and it was rebuilt in its present location by the Byzantines. Caliph Hisham ibn Abd el-Malik built his winter palace here in 743 AD. An earthquake destroyed Jericho in 747. Jericho fell to the Crusaders and then was recaptured by Saladin and ignored and deserted for centuries.[284]

The main attraction of Jericho is Tel el-Sultan, with the remains of piles of rocks that were once towers, staircases, and walls. Another attraction is the Spring of Elisha where the prophet sweetened the water.

Now the men of the city said to Elisha, "Behold, the situation of this city is pleasant, as my lord sees, but the water is bad, and the land is unfruitful." He said, "Bring me a new bowl, and put salt in it." So they brought it to him. Then he went to the spring of water and threw salt in it and said, "Thus says the Lord, 'I have healed this water; from now on neither death nor miscarriage shall come from it.'" So the water has been healed to this day, according to the word that Elisha spoke. (2 Kings 2:19-22)

During the building of a new home north of the spring, builders discovered the mosaic floor of an ancient synagogue decorated with a menorah and ram's horn. They found a Hebrew inscription that read, "Peace to Israel". The name of the synagogue is Shalom Al Yisrael. An older synagogue, the Na'aran, was found after the Ottoman Turks shelled a British unit camped on the spot. This synagogue has a mosaic floor of the zodiac, the story of Daniel in the lion's den, and pictures of sacred articles from the 5th- or 6th-century temple.

There is a modern cable car that takes visitors up the Mountain of Temptation, where Satan offered Jesus the worldly kingdoms. There is a monastery that has a cave where Jesus may have stayed when he was tempted, during the forty days after his baptism. At the foot of the

[284] www.jewishvirtuallibrary.org/jsource/vie/jericho.htm.

mountain are the remains of the sugar mills built by the Crusaders in the 11th century. Less than two miles from Old Jericho are the ruins of the winter palace of Caliph Hisham, built in the 7th century. Before the Caliph had a chance to use it, an earthquake destroyed it. Four miles from Old Jericho is the Allenby Bridge to Jordan. It is named for the British general who conquered most of the Middle East during World War I.[285]

The modern town of Jericho is an Arab community in the West Bank and is now under the Palestinian Authority. At the edge of modern Jericho are some excavations of the city that are from the Jericho of the Old Testament and the Canaanites. The excavations were begun in 1907 and revealed a city had existed centuries before Joshua. Jericho may be the oldest continuing city in the world. A huge trench shows the remains of a gigantic tower, which some archaeologists date back to 7,000 BC. Results show that Jericho was built, destroyed, and rebuilt many times. From the top of ancient Jericho, the magnificent view includes the Jordan Valley and the Mount of Temptation. The Mount of Temptation may be the location of the temptation of Jesus (read Luke 4:1-13).

The Jericho that Israel destroyed was never rebuilt. Archaeologists have not found ruins of the wall that fell down from the Israelites. Scholars believe that the ruins of the wall could have been carried off to build something else. For example, King Hezekiah of Judah (716-686 BC) used debris from old houses to build up the wall of Jerusalem. That was an old custom of the ancient times. Many cities named Jericho were built nearby through the centuries.[286] After Joshua tore the wall down, he put a curse on anyone who tried to build it back: "May the curse of the Lord fall on anyone who tries to rebuild the town of Jericho" (Joshua 6:26).

Several centuries later Hiel tried to do just that: "In his days Hiel of Bethel built Jericho. He laid its foundation at the cost of Abiram his firstborn, and set up its gates at the cost of his youngest son Segub, according to the word of the Lord, which he spoke by Joshua the son of Nun" (1 Kings 16:34).

The fear of Israel's God went before them into the land of Jericho: "And as soon as we had heard these things, our hearts did melt, neither did

---

285   www.jewishvirtuallibrary.org/jsource/vie/jericho.htm.
286   George W. Knight, *The Holy Land*, 184-186.

there remain any more courage in any man, because of you: for the Lord your God, He is God in heaven above, and in earth beneath" (Joshua 2:11).

David: The King and His Kingdom (continued)

David had seven and a half years of problems with Saul before he became king over all of Israel and Judah from Dan to Beersheba (2 Samuel 2:1-7, 5:1-5). David made Jerusalem the capital and religious center of Israel (2 Samuel 5:6-7, 6:12-19). Jerusalem became known as "the City of David" (2 Samuel 5:7). David expanded his borders to be more in line with the boundaries of the promised land (Genesis 15:18, 2 Samuel 8:1-14). Although God would not let David build the temple, David designed the temple plans and gave them to his son Solomon, and provided for musical praise to God in the temple (1 Chronicles 22: 25, 28:11-12).

God made a covenant with David to fulfill His redemption plans of mankind. The covenant called for God to establish David's house, which is his kingdom, and his throne forever (2 Samuel 7:26). Although God would fulfill His covenant promises, David's successors would have to walk in God's ways as David demonstrated (1 Kings 9:4-5). Solomon worshiped other gods, and because of that God divided the kingdom in the days of Rehoboam, the son of Solomon, and left David's descendants to reign only over Judah (1 Kings 11:1-13, 12:19).

The covenant was fulfilled in the coming of Jesus Christ, the Messiah, who was and is David's son and at the same time is David's Lord (Psalm 110:1; Matthew 1:1-17, 22:41-45). The Messiah will rule over Judah and "over the house of Jacob forever; and of his kingdom there shall be no end" (Luke 1:33). In the Messiah's finished work, His kingdom will include not only Israel's redeemed but the redeemed of "every kindred, and tongue, and people, and nation" (Revelation 5:9).[287]

A day's journey of walking during Bible times is now equivalent in distance to only thirty minutes of traveling when using motorized vehicles and modern highways. Even in modern times, a person can still see shepherds leading their flocks of sheep over the Judean hills, looking for grassy areas. Tourists can see Bedouin families camped in their black goatskin tents. The Bedouins still lead a primitive lifestyle, except for modern television sets with the antenna sticking up out of the tent or shack. As travelers come closer to the Dead Sea, they

---

[287] John Traylor, *David: The King and His Kingdom.* Biblical Illustrator, LifeWay: Volume 39, number 4, Summer 2013, 39-42.

can see donkeys grazing and even camels. There are also modern-day things in view, like the Israeli military camps.

Exactly two miles from modern Jericho is the site of the New Testament Jericho. In the time of Jesus, travelers from the Galilee area walked through Jericho to Jerusalem to avoid going through Samaria. Once when Jesus was walking through Jericho on his way to Jerusalem, he met a hated tax collector, Zacchaeus, who asked Jesus into his home and his heart and became a follower of Jesus (read Luke 19:1-10).

Another time, Jesus met a blind man named Bartimaeus in Jericho. Jesus healed Bartimaeus and he could see again (read Mark 10:46-52).

The Jordan River is a stream that flows from the snow of Mount Hermon to the Dead Sea. It twists and turns for 160 miles. However, if the river went in a straight line, the distance would only be 65 miles. Its average width is 100 feet, and it is met by the Yamuk River and the Jabbok River from Gilead. The Bible mentions the plain through which the Jordan River flows as "the plain". It is also called the Plain of Jordan: "In the plain of Jordan did the king cast them, in the clay ground between Succoth and Zarthan" (1 Kings 7:46). In Biblical times, lions roamed the land around the Jordan River.[288]

SUN ON THE JORDAN RIVER

Photo courtesy of the Israeli Ministry of Tourism and is solely for this photo only at www.goisrael.com

David: The King and His Kingdom (continued)

David committed adultery with Bathsheba and murdered her husband, by sending him to the battlefield with orders for his men to pull back and leave Bathsheba's husband in danger. David did this to hide the fact that he had made Bathsheba pregnant from the adultery (2 Samuel 11:1-12:15). Nathan the prophet announced David's sin would cause the sword never to depart from David's house, his wives to be violated, and wickedness to rise against him out of his own

---

house. Since David "treated the Lord with such contempt in this matter," the child conceived by his adultery would die (2 Samuel 12:14).

David did not discipline his own children (1 Kings 1:6). As predicted, violence continued in David's household as long as he lived. When David was old, he had to stop the attempt of Adonijah, his oldest son, from taking the throne from Solomon, God's appointed king (1 Kings 1:1-38; 1 Chronicles 22:9-10, 23:1, 29:22). David's last recorded instructions to Solomon were for him to walk in God's ways. If he did so, he would always have a son on Israel's throne (1 Kings 2:1-4). David died at age seventy and was buried in Jerusalem. David had served as king of Judah and then all of Israel for a total of forty years (1 Kings 2:10-12).[289]

Naaman was an important official in the army of Syria. He went to Elisha in Israel for healing from leprosy. His reaction to Elisha's command was, "Not in that river." He did not want to take a bath in the muddy, shallow stream of the Jordan.

But the officials under Naaman probably told him, "What do you have to lose? Get in the water and see what happens!" Naaman did just that and was healed (read 2 Kings 5). By a miracle, Elisha managed to find an ax head in the Jordan (read 2 Kings 6:1-7).

The Jordan River played an important role when the Israelites, under the leadership of Joshua, crossed over the flood stage water. God stopped the water from flooding and the Israelites walked through the Jordan River on dry land (read Joshua 3:14-16).

This was a miracle of God, and was a reminder as well of the time of the Exodus with Israel crossing the Red Sea when leaving Egypt.[290]

Bethabara

The site of Bethabara is mentioned only once in the Bible, but it is important because this was located where John the Baptist was preaching, east of the Jordan River. John the Baptist preached about Jesus. "These things were done in Bethabara beyond Jordan, where John was baptizing" (John 1:28).

Jesus insisted that John baptize him. John, however, did not want to baptize a man with no sin; but Jesus insisted. The river is a holy

---

[289] John Traylor, *David: The King and His Kingdom.* Biblical Illustrator, LifeWay: Volume 39, number 4, Summer 2013, 39-42.

[290] Ibid.

place to both the Old and New Testaments. John, clothed in camel's hair and eating locusts and honey, was preaching and baptizing in the lower parts of the Jordan River. Jesus came from Galilee to be baptized by John in the Jordan (read Matthew 3).

David: The King and His Kingdom (continued)

There are four ways God uses David today to help modern people. The first way is to inspire us to have godliness by reading and re-reading the Biblical account of David. The second way is to encourage godly leadership. Leaders are to be God's representatives through whom He leads people to walk in His way. As we lead, may we do right in the sight of the Lord as David did (I1 Kings 18:3).

The third way is to show forgiveness through genuine repentance. David's sin reminds us, "All have sinned, and come short of the glory of God" (Romans 3:23). If we, like David, repent when we disobey God's will and His Word, then we too will find in God's mercy cleansing, renewal, and restoration to his favor (2 Samuel 12:13, Psalm 32, Psalm 51).

The fourth way God uses David is to call thirsty and hungry people to come to Him for life and soul satisfaction. Those who come will receive a free and everlasting covenant with God, based on "the sure mercies of David" (Isaiah 55:1-4). The One through whom God continues to make this covenant is Jesus the Messiah, who gave Himself as an offering for our sin (Jeremiah 30:9, Isaiah 52:13-53:12, Luke 23:33-46).

John Traylor is a retired pastor from First Baptist Church, Monroe, Louisiana.[291]

---

[291] John Traylor, *David: The King and His Kingdom.* Biblical Illustrator, LifeWay: Volume 39, number 4, Summer 2013, 39-42.

TEL DAN: NATURE RESERVE AND LARGEST TRIBUTARY OF THE JORDAN RIVER

Photo courtesy of the Israeli Ministry of Tourism and is solely for this photo only at www.goisrael.com

The modern site of Tel Dan is built on the ruins of the Biblical city of Dan. Tel Dan was first named Leshem, Laish, and Dan. Egyptian historical documents dating to the 19th century BC name Leshem as an important trading center. In the 11th Century BC, the Israelites conquered Leshem and changed the name of the city to Dan. The Tel Dan archaeological site gives tourists a glimpse of Biblical times in the past. The Dan River is a tributary that drains into the Jordan River. The Dan River gets melted winter snow from Mount Hermon to the Jordan River.[292]

Archaeologist Edward Robinson identified Tel Dan in 1838 as the ancient Biblical city of Dan first known as Laish (read Judges 18:27-29).

Dan had a sanctuary full of idols until the Assyrian conquest of the Kingdom of Israel. The excavations at Dan uncovered a city gate made of mud and bricks on top of megalithic basalt standing stones. It was estimated to have been built around 1750 BC, the period of the Biblical patriarchs, mentioned in Genesis 14:14: "And when he heard his brother was taken captive, he armed his trained servants, born in his own house, three hundred and eighteen, and pursued them unto Dan." The gate at Dan was restored in the late 2000s.

King Jeroboam made two golden calves as idols in Bethel and Dan: "Howbeit from the sins of Jeroboam the son of Nebat, who made Israel sin, Jehu departed not from after them, to wit, the golden calves that were in Beth-el and that were in Dan" (I1 Kings 10:29).

A stele is a rock with writing on it. Within the city wall remains at Dan, archaeologists found parts of the Tel Dan Stele. Part of the inscription says "House of David" in Hebrew. This inscription is the

---

[292] www.arzaworld.com/israel-travel-guide/israel-travel-destinations.

first time that an item inscribed with the words "House of David" has been found at an archaeological site dating before 500 BC.[293]

The phrase "from Dan to Beersheba" referred to the entire country of Israel. The people from the tribe of Dan originally settled near Joppa in central Israel. They may have moved north due to oppression from the Canaanites.

King Jeroboam I ruled from about 931 to 910 BC in the Northern Kingdom. He installed the idols after Israel split into two parts. He was afraid that the people of his kingdom would remain loyal to Judah. Excavations at Dan have uncovered a paved courtyard with a low stone platform that may be the place he put the idol calf.[294]

BANIAS (HERMON) STREAM, NATURE RESERVE AND A TRIBUTARY OF THE JORDAN RIVER (2)

Photo courtesy of the Israeli Ministry of Tourism and is solely for this photo only at www.goisrael.com

The Banias Waterfall is the largest one in Israel. Tourists enjoy walking the beautiful trails, exploring the ruins, and picnicking in the green woodlands. The Banias can be entered from the springs or the falls. The falls entrance is the first road heading northeast, for viewing the falls. The springs entrance leads to the old temple complex with Greek and Roman deities. The name Banias is an Arabic word for Paneus or the Greek god Pan, the god of the forests and shepherds.[295]

The Banias Springs start at the foot of Mount Hermon and flow through a canyon for three and a half kilometers, leading to the Banias Waterfall. Nine kilometers from Mount Hermon, the Hermon Stream meets the Dan, and together they flow to the Jordan River. A path of steps near the springs climbs to the Banias Cave. In front of the cave are remains of a temple built by Herod the Great. When Herod died,

293 www.en.wikipedia.org/wiki/tel_dan.

294 George W. Knight, *The Holy Land*, 271-272.

295 www.touristisrael.com/banias-nature-reserve/6233.

his son Philip inherited the site, and he made it his capital and called it Caesarea Philippi.

In Caesarea Philippi, Jesus asked his disciples whom people said that he was: "When Jesus came into the coasts of Caesarea Philippi, he asked his disciples, saying, 'Whom do men say that I the son of man am?'" (Matthew 16:13).

In Old Testament times, Caesarea Philippi was a place where Canaanites and Phoenicians worshiped the pagan god Baal. When the Greeks owned this area, it was devoted to the worship of the nature god Pan. During the time of Jesus, the area may have had a temple for worshiping the Roman Emperor.[296]

Peter made Jesus happy when he answered Jesus' question by saying, "You are the Messiah, the son of the Living God" (Matthew 16:16). Jesus is the living bread: "I am the living bread which came down from Heaven: if any man eat of this bread, he shall live forever: and the bread that I give is my flesh, which I will give for the life of the world" (John 6:51). Jesus is also the living water: "Jesus answered and said to her, 'If thou knewest the gift of God, and who it is that saith to thee, "Give me to drink"; thou wouldest have asked of him, and he would have given thee living water.'"

The region near Caesarea Philippi was one of the last places that Jesus and his disciples visited on earth. Soon afterward, they left for Jerusalem for Passover; and Jesus was then arrested, crucified, left for dead, and resurrected.

In the early 1900s, Henry van Dyke visited Caesarea Philippi and wrote *We Call This the Holy Land*. He wrote, "At last, Jesus turned his steps from Caesarea Philippi, this safe and lovely refuge where He might have lived in peace, or from which He might have gone out unmolested, into the wide Gentile world. He traced his steps downward to his own country, His own people, the great, turbulent, hard-hearted city of Jerusalem, and the fate that He would not turn away from because He loved sinners and came to see them. He went down into Galilee, down through Samaria, down to Jerusalem, down to Gethsemane and to Golgotha – fearless, calm, sustained, and nourished by that secret food that satisfied His heart in doing the will of God.

---

[296]   www.jewishvirtuallibrary.org/source/society_&_culture.

"In my trip to this land, I did not find this Jesus amid strange and mysterious rites or commercial travel sites, and lamp-lit shrines. The Jesus whom I discovered is the child of Nazareth playing among the flowers; the man of Galilee walking beside the lake, healing the sick, comforting the sick, comforting the sorrowful, cheering the lonely and despondent. He is the beloved Son of God transfigured in the sunset glow of snowy Mount Hermon, weeping by the tomb in Bethany, agonizing in the moonlit garden of Gethsemane. He is the Savior who gave his life for those who did not understand him, though they loved him, and for those who did not love Him because they did not understand Him.

"His teachings have not faded away nor will they ever die. His message made the country to which it came the Holy Land. And still today, receiving this message will lead any person into the kingdom of heaven. And the keeping of this faith, the following of this life, will transform any country in the world into a holy land."[297]

JORDAN VALLEY: OLD GESHER ON THE JORDAN

Photo courtesy of the Israeli Ministry of Tourism and is solely for this photo only at www.goisrael.com

The plain of the Jordan River forms two shelves, with one above the other. The southern plain was called the Plains of Moab, the location of one of Israel's battles in the book of Numbers: "And when king Arad the Canaanite, which dwelt in the south, heard tell that Israel came by the way of the spies; then he fought against Israel, and took some of them prisoners" (Numbers 21:1). The plains of Jericho are mentioned in the book of Joshua: "About forty thousand prepared for war passed over before the Lord unto battle, to the plains of Jericho" (Joshua 4:13).

---

[297]   Henry Van Dyke, *Out of Doors in the Holy Land*, cited in George W. Knight, *The Holy Land,* 274-276.

The Jordan Valley has thick vegetation and wildlife, such as wild boar and lions as mentioned in the Bible: "Behold, he shall come up like a lion from the swelling of Jordan against the habitation of the strong: but I will suddenly make him run away from her: and who is a chosen man, that I may appoint over her? For who is like me? And who will appoint me the time? And who is that shepherd that will stand before me?" (Jeremiah 49:19).

Dig Deeper into the Rich History of Israel

The Dead Sea area of Israel is part of much of biblical history and is a fascinating area unlike any other in the world. For more reading, below are some passages where this region is mentioned in the Bible.

Dead Sea (Salt Sea):
Numbers 34:1-12
Deuteronomy 3:12-17
Joshua 12:1-3
Ezekiel 47:1-10

Ein Gedi:
Joshua 15:62
1 Samuel 24:1-22
Psalm 57:1-11
Ezekiel 47:10

Jericho:
Joshua 2:1-24, 6:1-27
Mark 10:46-52
Luke 10:30-37
Luke 19:1-10

CHAPTER 8

FACTS ABOUT ISRAEL AND
EILAT REGION OF ISRAEL

Most Israelis have parents born in one of 120 countries. The parents brought with them foods, recipes, and eating traditions from six continents. Israel still has traditional food such as falafel, hummus, and tehina, with an order of couscous or gefilte. McDonald's opened in Israel in the 1990s. Israel has the world record for most sushi restaurants, led by the city of Tel Aviv. Other foods represented are Indian, Chinese, French, Belgian, Spanish, and also items from many other countries.

Many restaurants provide menus in English. Lunch is usually served from 1 p.m. to 3:00 p.m. Each day, many hotels have big breakfast buffets with vegetables, salads, cheese, eggs, smoked fish, breads, pastries, yogurts, cereals, and fruit. Israel also has more than 200 wineries. Much of the food of Israel is a blend of Middle Eastern and European dishes, with a Jewish flavor added to the entrees.

The Orthodox Jews follow strict dietary laws of cooking, which require food to be *kosher*, meaning proper and fit. Orthodox Jews do not eat pork, shellfish, or rabbit and do not serve meat with dairy products. All Orthodox Jews and all of Israel's institutions must separate all meat and dairy products using separate cooking utensils, tableware, and dishwashing methods. Many people in Israel eat fruits, vegetables, and dairy products because meat is hard to find.

When cooking Israeli food, it is important to know what each ingredient is. Falafel mix is a dry mix of chickpeas, flour, and oriental spice. Field beans are varieties of beans native to the Middle East. They are often called Egyptian field beans. Halva is a sweet candy of crushed nuts or sesame seeds in honey syrup. Matzo is crisp unleavened bread eaten mainly at Passover. Matzo meal is finely ground matzos. Pine nuts are edible seeds from pine trees. Saffron is a deep orange, aromatic spice made from the flower of the saffron plant. Tehina is a paste of ground sesame seeds. Turmeric is a yellow aromatic spice made from the root of the turmeric plant.

Most Israeli breakfast dishes, like egg and tomato scramble and Israeli salad, can be eaten at any meal. Breakfast in the country is served at daybreak. On Saturday, the Sabbath Day, breakfast consists of cold foods like olives, yogurt, breads, jams, cheeses, and smoked and pickled fish. The beverage is usually lots of hot tea or coffee. A dish of scrambled eggs and tomatoes contains three eggs, canned tomatoes, chili powder, butter, and flour. It is served hot with pita bread.

Lunch is a large meal in cities and towns. Schoolchildren eat lunch about 2 p.m. after the school day ends, and then they return home. Some office workers take a break of several hours so they can go home to eat. Most salads are prepared right at the table, but kibbutz carrot salad is prepared ahead of time and served as an appetizer. It has two cups of grated carrots, juice from three large oranges, juice from two lemons, water, four tablespoons of honey, and two sprigs of mint. It needs to be refrigerated for at least two hours to blend the flavors.

Another favorite is ground meat with sesame sauce. It has two pounds of ground lamb or beef, chopped parsley, onions, garlic, cinnamon, olive oil, pine nuts, and tehina. It is served with rice and salad. A dish of baked fish has carp, trout, or any other fresh water fish. Lemon, onions, and yogurt are added and poured over the cooked fish. Fruit soup is made from fresh fruit or dried fruit, sugar, raisins, six cups of water, and corn starch, which is then together brought to a boil, then placed over reduced heat and simmered for five minutes. The soup is cooled at room temperature, chilled, and served cold. Vegetarians like cheese blintzes, which are made with cream cheese, cottage cheese, one egg, and raisins for filling. The batter is made with two eggs, water, flour, and butter. To cook into pancakes, two tablespoons of the filling must be placed on the center of the pancake with the sides folded underneath, and then sautéed until brown. It should be served immediately with sour cream.

Falafel served in pita is Israel's national dish of filling snack foods. It has falafel mix (chickpeas, flour, and oriental spices), tomato, cucumber, green pepper that is seeded and chopped, small shredded lettuce, pita bread, and tehina (paste of ground sesame seeds). The above ingredients are made into falafel balls and put inside a pocket of pita bread. Typically, a salad mixture is added, along with a tablespoon of tehina, after which it is immediately served.

The first festival of the year in Israel begins in September or October with the Jewish New Year (Rosh Hashanah), when many people eat sweet things like apples and honey cake. Ten days later is Yom Kippur, the Day of Atonement, in which no food is eaten for twenty-four hours. This festival is followed by eight days of the harvest festival called the Feast of the Tabernacles (Sukkot), when booths are built and decorated with fruits and flowers. The Festival of Lights (around Christmas) is called Hanukkah. By tradition, the candles on a menorah are lit one by one for eight days. Treats are potato pancakes and doughnuts. In early spring is Purim, the Feast of Esther. After working hours, many people wear costumes and go to parties in the streets. People celebrate by eating cookies filled with poppy seeds or prunes. These treats of special cookies are called Haman's ears or Haman's pockets, named after the cruel enemy of the Jews from the book of Esther in the Bible.

Government

The president of Israel is symbolic and representative. The State of Israel has a legislative body known as the Knesset, an executive branch of the government that includes the prime minister, and lastly the judiciary authorities.

The Knesset chooses the president and the government, makes political decisions, and supervises the activities of the government. The Knesset has 120 members, who are elected every four years. The executive authority is responsible for administering the laws.

The prime minister's job is to be a member of the Knesset, and to form the official government coalition led by the majority party. No party in the history of the State of Israel has ever received an actual majority of votes. For this reason, Israeli governments have always been coalition governments.

The judiciary system is responsible for keeping the law. The Supreme Court hears appeals from lower courts and listens to civilian cases against the government. Israel also has a military court, the labor court, and the religious courts. The religious courts, such as Jewish, Muslim, Christian, and Druze, deal with personal matters like marriage and divorce.

The flag representing the State of Israel has two blue stripes with a white background. Between the stripes here is a blue Star of David, in the shape of a hexagram. This flag is based on the design of the tallit, the prayer shawl worn by Jewish men (and by some women in Reform and Conservative congregations) during certain services. The tallit is worn during all morning services. In addition, it is worn on the eve of Yom Kippur, the Day of Atonement. The tallit is also worn when reading the Torah during Shabbat (Sabbath) afternoon services and by the person leading evening services. Jews pray three times a day: the morning service is called *shacharit*; the afternoon service is called *minchah*; and the evening service is called *ma'ariv* or *aravit*.

There are two basic traditions regarding who wears the tallit. According to one tradition, any Jewish adult should wear the tallit at the appropriate times. A Jewish adult is one who is thirteen years of age and older (a *Bar Mitzvah*, or "son of the commandments".) According to another tradition, only married Jews wear the tallit. In addition to the exterior tallit, there is also a *tallit katan* ("small tallit"), which pious Jews wear all day under their clothes.

Because the tallit is one of the most recognizable symbols of the Jewish people, it was chosen to be the basis of the flag. (Indeed, in coming up with a design for the flag, the early Zionists came to the realization that the Jewish people had had a flag all along - the tallit - and thus there was no need to design a flag from scratch.) In the center of the flag is the *Magen David*, or "shield of [King] David", better known in English as the Star of David or Jewish Star, another recognizable Jewish symbol.

Israel has a good economy; however, Israel lacks some natural resources, has many immigrants, and has to fight against the constant threat of suicide bombers. Israel's success is in part due to direct external aid of at least $108 billion so far, as well as dedicated workers. Since the State of Israel became a country in 1948, exports of goods and services have increased from $30 million per year to $298 billion per year. In the beginning, Israel exports were citrus fruit and processed diamonds. Now, exports include electronics, software, hardware, optics, communication devices, and medical instruments.

Stores in Israel close in the middle of the day on Friday and open again on Sunday morning or Saturday evening. Stores also close in the mid-afternoon on the eve of all Jewish holidays and remain closed until the end of the holiday. Some shopping center theaters do not close on Saturdays or Jewish holidays, in order to accommodate tourist movie lovers. Muslim business owners also close on Friday for religious observances. Christian business owners close on Sundays.

Purchases made in the city of Eilat are cheaper than in other places in the country, because they are exempt from the VAT (Value-Added Tax). There are also tax-free shops in the Ben Gurion Airport near Tel Aviv. Rural cottage industries sell homemade foods, arts and crafts, and unusual items not sold in city shops.

The national anthem of the State of Israel is the *Hatikvah*, which means "the hope". The poet Naphtali Herz Imber (1856-1909) wrote the lyrics. Bedrich Smetena, a Czech composer, wrote a Romanian folk song called "My Homeland". In 1933, the Zionist Movement chose *Hatikvah* as the national anthem, and in 2004, the Knesset voted for *Hatikvah* to officially commission it to this status. The words of *Hatikvah*, translated from Hebrew into English, are as follows:

As long as the Jewish spirit is yearning
deep in the heart,
With eyes turned toward the East,
looking toward Zion,
Then our hope, the two-thousand-year-old
hope will not be lost,
To be a free people in our land,
The land of Zion and Jerusalem.

The emblem of the State of Israel is a seven-branched menorah with olive branches on both sides. The name Israel is written at the bottom of the menorah.

The main theme of the menorah is an engraving of the Arch of Titus in Rome. It represents the victory march of Titus after he destroyed the revolting Jews and destroyed the Temple in 70 AD. The source of the olive branch idea is a prophecy of Zechariah in the Old Testament. The candelabrum of the Jerusalem Temple engraved on the Arch of Titus symbolizes Israel's past, Israel's defeat, and Israel's exile. Choosing this as an emblem links the new State of Israel to its past, and the bringing of this emblem out of exile by returning it to Israel symbolizes the end of the Jewish people being scattered all over the world.

Hebrew, the original language of the majority of the Old Testament, has a strong historical connection to the land of Israel. In 200 AD, vowels and punctuation were added to the Hebrew languages. The Hebrew language, resurrected after centuries of not being spoken while the Jews were scattered around the world, experienced its revival of usage in the modern era largely due to the efforts of Eliezer Ben-Yehuda. Today it is one of the official languages of the State of Israel, along with Arabic. English is also widely spoken and can be seen on many street signs and public places.

Eilat is a busy port and resort on the northern tip of the Red Sea on the Gulf of Aqaba, situated at the southernmost point of Israel. About 46,600 people live in Eilat, which is part of the Negev Desert. Eilat is adjacent to Taba in Egypt, close to the Jordanian port city of Aqaba, and within sight of Saudi Arabia. Temperatures in the summer are often over 104 degrees. Winter temperatures are usually seventy degrees.

Eilat in Hebrew means "Pistacia tree." Archaeological excavations at the western edge of Eilat uncovered prehistoric tombs dating to the 7th millennium BC. They also found copper workings and mines in the nearby Timna Valley. In the fourth dynasty of Egypt, Eilat traded with Egypt. In Egyptian records, Eilat is mentioned as a trading partner in the twelfth dynasty. Elim and Eilat furnished frankincense and myrrh.[298]

---

[298] www.en.wikipedia.org/wiki/eilat.

JEEPS TRIP IN THE EILAT MOUNTAINS

Photo courtesy of the Israeli Ministry of Tourism and is solely for this photo only at www.goisrael.com

The Eilat Mountains are 2,927 feet above sea level. There is also a valley called the Arava and a seashore on the Gulf of Aqaba. The average rainfall is 1.1 inches. In ancient times, Eilat bordered Edom, Midian, and the tribal territory of the Rephidim who were the people of the Sinai Peninsula.

When King David conquered Edom, he took over Eilat. In Roman times, a road was built to connect Eilat to the Nabataean city of Petra (now in modern-day Jordan). Archaeologists discovered a large copper smelting and trading community in what is now Eilat's industrial zone and the nearby Kibbutz Eilat.[299]

The Red Sea is about 1,398 miles long and 220.6 miles wide at its widest point. There are also shallow shelves used for marine life and corals. It is the world's most tropical sea. The rain comes mainly in short showers and there is a low amount of annual rainfall. [300]

Pilate's Role in Jesus' Death

The emperor of Rome criticized Pilate for being incapable of providing regional stability. Now the Jewish leaders put pressure on Pilate to execute Jesus on the cross. Pilate should have upheld Roman justice and released Jesus, but he chose to give in to the Jewish leaders. In the time of Jesus, Judea was governed by Roman procurators, and Pilate was one from 26 to 30 AD. A procurator was a governor appointed by the emperor. The governor's job was to manage the military, financial, and judicial operations of sensitive regions of the Roman Empire. The procurator's residence was at the harbor city of Caesarea Maritima on the Mediterranean Sea.

Immediately after Pilate was appointed governor, Pilate's soldiers posted standards of the emperor's image within sight of the temple in Jerusalem. A standard was a plaque or flag that someone raised on a pole to rally or inspire people. The

---

[299] Ibid.
[300] www.en.wikipedia.org/wiki/red_sea.

Jews saw the standard as an idolatrous act and demanded the standards be taken away. When Pilate threatened them with execution, the Jewish protesters bared their necks in defiant willingness to die rather than back down. Pilate gave in and removed the standards to Caesarea Maritima. This information came from Josephus, the Jewish historian.

In the second incident, Pilate killed a few Galileans who were offering sacrifices. (Luke 13:1). History does not tell us what sparked the conflict but does show the difficulty Pilate had with his subjects. The third instance of trouble came when Pilate used money from the temple to build an aqueduct. The Jews objected to the sacrilege of the temple offerings and Pilate had the protesters beaten into subjection.

Josephus reported that Pilate ordered the execution of some Samaritan villagers who had followed a rebellious leader to Mount Gerizim. When Tiberius heard of this, Pilate was recalled to Rome in 36 AD, and Tiberius replaced Pilate with Marcellus. The records of three of these events showed up in the trial of Jesus.[301]

In the area of Eilat, the Red Sea is available for beach activities, the desert is nearby for desert adventures, and the mountains are available for fun mountain events. The modern city of Eilat was built in the 1950s. There is an amusement park and a new King's City, a high-tech theme park based on the Bible and Bible stories.[302]

Pilate's Role in Jesus' Death (continued)

Pilate did not seem to know how to introduce Roman rule into the politically volatile province of Judea. Brian McGing, professor of Roman and Greek history from Trinity College in Dublin, Ireland, considered Pilate "neither a monster nor a saint; merely, one suspects, a typical Roman officer of the type who displayed a general lack of sensitivity, tact, and knowledge" with the strange subjects he ruled. New Testament scholar Helen Bond surveyed the extra-biblical sources and made a similar conclusion.

Some scholars think that Pilate's trouble with the Jews was due to his character and conception of the role of a provincial prefect. He expected to be master of his own province and to honor the Emperor by bringing Judeans under control. He ignored the feelings and sensitivities of the people in the process of keeping good control.

---

[301] Thomas H. Goodman, *Pilate's Role in Jesus' Death*. Biblical Illustrator, LifeWay: Volume 39, number 4, Summer 2013, 66-69.

[302] www.goisrael.com/tourism_eng/tour.

In the trial of Jesus, Pilate wanted to maintain standards of Roman juris-prudence and could not understand why releasing an innocent man like Jesus upset Jews. The Jewish leaders were so upset that they were near rioting in Jerusalem. In Luke 23:5-15, we learn that Pilate attempted to shift the decision to Herod to satisfy the bloodlust by a flogging, and then to offer Barabbas to the people in exchange for Jesus to be freed (Luke 23:16, Matthew 27:15-21). But Pilate still faced an unruly mob. Since he was unable to uphold the Roman judicial standards, he gave in to the mob as the easiest way out of a difficulty. Pilate gave up his plan of freeing Jesus.[303]

A VIEW OF EILAT MOUNTAINS, FROM YEHORAM MOUNTAIN

Photo courtesy of the Israeli Ministry of Tourism and is solely for this photo only at www.goisrael.com

EIN AVDAT NATIONAL PARK

Photo courtesy of the Israeli Ministry of Tourism and is solely for this photo only at www.goisrael.com

Ein Avdat National Park is a canyon in the Negev Desert of Israel. It is south of Kibbutz Sde Boker. *Ein* is Hebrew for "spring" or "water source". Avdat is named for the nearby city of Avdat that was located south of the canyon. Avdat was named for the Nabatean king Obodas I who may have been buried there.[304]

The Ein Avdat Spring forms a waterfall and flows down to an eight-meter-deep pool of water. Ein Avdat was created by flowing water that eroded the rock and carved canyons out of it. The water is a little bit salty, and the trees growing in the area are Euphrates poplar trees (sometimes called a saltbush). Common animals in the area are rock pigeons, eagles, vultures, hawks, frogs, and crabs.

---

[303] Thomas H. Goodman, *Pilate's Role in Jesus' Death*. Biblical Illustrator, LifeWay: Volume 39, number 4, Summer 2013, 66-69.

[304] www.en.wikipedia.org/wiki/ein_avdat.

At the upper section of the nature reserve are caves that were used by Byzantine monks from the 6th century until the Muslim conquest. The monks made shelves, benches, stairs, and water systems from the rocks. The caves were decorated with crosses that were engraved in the rocks of the caves. The hiking paths have ladders and steps to climb. The complete hike takes one hour. There is no swimming permitted in the pools, because the pools are reserved for the animals to swim in. The old Ein Avdat is found off Route 40, just south of Kibbutz Sde Boker.[305]

Pilate's Role in Jesus' Death (continued)

Pilate posted the military rules and the votive shields to declare his intent to exert Roman rule. Then in conflict he gave in to the demands. In John 18:28-19:16, we learn that seven times Pilate "went out" to speak with the crowd and "went in" to speak to Jesus. Pilate investigated Jesus and believed that to kill Him would be an abdication of the justice he was responsible to uphold. But he knew that to release Jesus would upset the angry mob and the region could revolt. He did not know what to do.

Pilate remembered the incident with the votive shields, when the Jews complained to Tiberius and the emperor wrote to Pilate, reproaching and reviling him in the most bitter manner and commanding him to take down the shields. Pilate thought about this past event and did not want to get in trouble with the emperor again.

The Jewish leadership told Pilate, "Jesus claims to be a king, a rival to Caesar. If you let him go, Caesar will hear about it. We'll see to that. Give us what we want, Pilate. Kill Him for us. It's either His life or your career. Make your choice." (John 19:12, paraphrase by author, Thomas Goodman).

Pilate then called for a bowl of water and washed his hands while saying, "I am innocent of this man's blood" (Matthew 27:24, HCBS). Pilate ordered the execution of Jesus. After receiving many previous imperial reprimands, Pilate had no interest in defending Jesus if it meant losing the peace and his job. Mark 15:15 (HCBS) tells us the motivation behind Pilate's decision "to gratify the crowd."[306]

---

[305] www.attractions-in-israel.com/negev.

[306] Thomas H. Goodman, *Pilate's Role in Jesus' Death*. Biblical Illustrator, LifeWay: Volume 39, number 4, Summer 2013, 66-69.

CAMEL RIDING IN EILAT REGION

Photo courtesy of the Israeli Ministry of Tourism and is solely for this photo only at www.goisrael.com

Camels respond best to their regular handler. Anyone riding a camel should be sure first that the camel is domesticated. The correct way to mount a camel is to do so while he is sitting, or to mount from a scaffold. The camel's hump should be protected by a pad or saddle. In mounting the camel, the person should put one foot in the stirrup and throw the other leg over the hump of the camel. Then he or she should hold the reins confidently, due to the fact that camels can tell whether or not a person is confident and if he knows how to ride. As in mounting the camel, the dismount should take place when the camel is seated.[307]

---

[307] www.ehow.com/how_ride-camel.htm.

TIMNA: AT THE MIDIANITE SHRINE

Photo courtesy of the Israeli Ministry of Tourism and is solely for this photo only at www.goisrael.com

The Timna Valley is fifteen miles north of Eilat, which is also known by the ancient name Elath. The valley was used for copper mining during Bible times. The Valley of Timna is thirty-five square miles.[308]

The Egyptians left control of the area in the middle of the 12th century BC. After that time, the Midianites cleared out most of the Egyptian cult materials and made a bench of offerings on both sides of the entrance. Remains of woolen cloth were found on the courtyard walls, providing evidence that the Midianites turned the Egyptian temple into a tented shrine. Archaeologists also found metal jewelry and pottery that was decorated by the Midianites. They also found a copper serpent with gilded head that is similar to the brass serpent described in the book of Numbers:

And the Lord sent fiery serpents among the people; and they bit the people; and much people of Israel died. Therefore the people came to Moses, and said, "We have sinned, for we have spoken against the Lord, and against thee; pray unto the Lord, that he take away the serpents from us." And Moses prayed for the people.

And the Lord said unto Moses, "Make thee a fiery serpent, and set it upon a pole: and it shall come to pass, that every one that is bitten, when he looketh upon it shall live." And Moses made a serpent of brass, and put it upon a pole, and it came to pass, that if a serpent had bitten any man, when he beheld the serpent of brass, he lived. (Numbers 21:6-9)

The Midianite culture was very sophisticated. It is interesting to note that Moses met Jethro, the high priest of Midian, and married his daughter. Afterward, Jethro's participation assisted in the

---

[308] www.bibleplaces.com/timnavalley.htm.

organization of the children of Israel in the desert under Moses' leadership (Exodus 18).

The survey and excavations at Timna were done by B. Rotenberg, with involvement from the Arava Expedition, the Haaretz Museum of Tel Aviv, the Institute of Archaeology, and Tel Aviv University.[309]

Dig Deeper into the Rich History of Israel

The large Negev Desert region including the city of Eilat, near the Red Sea, is mentioned various times in the Bible. Read the below passages to learn more:

Negev Desert:
Genesis 12:9
Genesis 13:1-3
Genesis 20:1
Numbers 13:17-22
Joshua 13:1-4
1 Samuel 27:5-8

Red Sea:
Exodus 14:1-31
Deuteronomy 11:2-4
Joshua 24:5-7
Psalm 136:10-16
Acts 7:35-36
Hebrews 11:29

---

[309] www.mfa.gov.il/mfa/history/early.

CHAPTER 9

BE'ER SHEVA, ACRE, HAIFA

TEL BE'ER SHEVA NATIONAL PARK, NEGEV
Photo courtesy of the Israeli Ministry of Tourism and is solely for this photo only at www.goisrael.com

Modern Be'er Sheva (Beersheba) has a population of about 194,300 people. Beersheba is the largest city in the Negev Desert in southern Israel. It is the seventh largest city in all of Israel. The Russian and Ethiopian immigrants to this area made chess a major sport.

Be'er in Hebrew means "well" and *sheva* can mean "seven" or "oath". Therefore, Beersheba means "oath of the well". Tel Be'er Sheva is an archaeological site a few kilometers northeast of modern Beersheba. Tel Be'er Sheva was settled by Israel in the 10th century BC. The city has been destroyed and rebuilt many times over the centuries. The wells were dug by Abraham and Isaac. "From Dan to Beersheba" was a Biblical phrase that marked the territories of Israel. In Genesis 2623-33; 46:1-7 (read), Isaac built an altar in Beersheba:[310]

---

[310]   www.en.wikipedia.org/wiki/beersheba.

Beersheba was the territory of the tribes of Simeon and Judah: "And the second lot came forth to Simeon, even for the tribe of the children of Simeon according to their families; and their inheritance of the children of Judah. And they had in their inheritance Beersheba, or Sheba, and Moladah" (Joshua 19:1-2).

Elijah hid in Beersheba when Jezebel ordered for him to be killed: "And Ahab told Jezebel all that Elijah had done, and withal how he had slain all the prophets with the sword. Then Jezebel sent a messenger unto Elijah, saying, 'So let the gods do to me, and more also, if I make not thy life as the life of one of them by tomorrow about this time.' And when he saw that, he arose, and went for his life, and came to Beersheba, which belongeth to Judah, and left his servant there" (1 Kings 19:1-3).

Note: King Ahab and Queen Jezebel worshiped the idol Baal and sinned in God's eyes. Elijah was a prophet of God and tried to get rid of the practice of worshiping Baal.

TEL BE'ER SHEVA
NATIONAL PARK
Photo courtesy of the Israeli Ministry of Tourism and is solely for this photo only at www.goisrael.com

The sons of the prophet Samuel were judges in Beersheba: "Now the name of his firstborn was Joel; and the name of his second, Abiah: they were judges in Beersheba. And his sons walked not in his ways, but turned aside after lucre, and took bribes, and perverted judgment" (1 Samuel 8:2-3).

The prophet Amos mentions Beersheba in reference to idolatry: "They that swear by the sin of Samaria, and say, 'Thy god O Dan, liveth'; and, 'The manner of Beersheba liveth'; even they shall fall, and never rise up again" (Amos 8:14).

After the Babylonian conquest and enslavement of many Israelites, the town was abandoned. After they returned from Babylon, they resettled into Beersheba.[311]

---

[311] www.en.wikipedia.org/wiki/beersheba.

During the Roman and Byzantine times, Beersheba became a fort to fight against Nabatean attacks. The last inhabitants were the Byzantines, who abandoned Beersheba during the Arab conquest in the 7th century.

In the beginning of the 19th century, European visitors described Beersheba as a barren stretch of land with a well and a few Bedouins living in the area. The Ottomans built a police station to watch the Bedouins. They built roads and a few buildings that are still standing today. Swiss and German architects created a grid street pattern that can still be seen in modern times in Beersheba's Old City. All of the houses built at that time were one story high, and the police station was two stories. Most of the residents were Arabs from Hebron and the Gaza area. Some Jews began to resettle in Beersheba. Many Bedouins abandoned their nomadic life and settled in Beersheba.

In World War I, the Turks built a military railroad from the Hejaz line to Beersheba. The station was dedicated on October 30, 1915. The railroad was active until the British Army took over the region. On October 31, 1917, General Allenby's troops breached the Turkish troops between Gaza and Beersheba, with the help of 800 soldiers of the Australian 4th and 12th Regiments of the 4th Light Horse Brigade under Brigadier General William Grant, using only horses and bayonets. They overran the Turkish trenches and captured the wells of Beersheba. This was the last successful cavalry charge in British military history. Beersheba has a memorial park and a commonwealth cemetery in memory of and containing the graves of the fallen cavalry members.

During the time of the British Mandate for Palestine, the British built a railway between Rafah and Beersheba, in October 1917. In May 1918, it opened to serve the Negev and the settlements south of Mount Hebron. In 1928, tensions became a problem between Arabs and Jews over the control of the land. In an Arab attack, 133 Jews were killed and 339 wounded, and many Jews left Beersheba. The remaining Jews left after an Arab attack on a Jewish bus in 1936.

During the 1948 Arab-Israeli War, when Israel was attacked by neighboring countries, Prime Minister David Ben-Gurion ordered Beersheba to be captured and conquered, and the demolition of most of the town took place on October 18-19, 1948. When the fighting started, Arab residents left on foot and in buses. By 9:45, the Egyptian forces were surrounded and Beersheba was in Israel's hands. On October 25, the women, children, disabled, and elderly were driven by truck to the Gaza border. The Egyptian soldiers were put in POW camps. Around 20,000 Jewish immigrants from India settled in Beersheba after the 1948 partition. In 1970, the Ben Gurion University of the Negev was opened.[312]

A PANORAMIC VIEW OF TEL BE'ER SHEVA NATIONAL PARK, IN NEGEV REGION

075 Photo courtesy of the Israeli Ministry of Tourism and is solely for this photo only at www.goisrael.com

Pilate's Role in Jesus' Death (continued)

Simon Peter said it was "both Herod and Pontius Pilate, with the Gentiles and the people of Israel" who "assembled together" against Jesus to do what God "had predestined to take place" (Acts 4:27-28, HCBS). Mark 15:15 says, "Yet by God's plan, Pilate handed Jesus over to be crucified."

Thomas H. Goodman is pastor of Hillcrest Baptist Church, Austin, Texas.[313]

One future project for modern Beersheba is a 900-acre riverfront project with hiking trails, a 3,000-seat sports hall, a fifteen-acre boating lake filled with recycled waste water, promenades, restaurants, galleries, a 12,000-seat amphitheater, four new shopping malls, and a new central bus station.

On August 31, 2004, sixteen people were killed in a suicide bombing on buses in Beersheba, and Hamas claimed responsibility. On August 28, 2005, a suicide bomber attacked the central bus station, injuring two security guards and forty-five bystanders. In the first six months of 2008 alone, Hamas fired 2,378 rockets and mortars into Israel from

---

[312] Ibid.
[313] Thomas H. Goodman, *Pilate's Role in Jesus' Death*. Biblical Illustrator, LifeWay: Volume 39, number 4, Summer 2013, 66-69.

Gaza until the ceasefire on June 19, 2008. Israel's Iron Dome rocket defense system helps to protect Beersheba and other cities and towns.

Beersheba is seventy-one miles south of Tel Aviv and seventy-one miles southwest of Jerusalem. Beersheba is located along the main route to Eilat in the far south. The main river in Beersheba is the Nahal Beersheba, a wadi which floods in the winter. The Kovshim and Katef streams are wadis that pass through Beersheba. Beersheba had a population of 185,400 at the end of 2006.

Salaried workers in Beersheba make an average monthly wage of 5,223 NIS (about 1,085 Euro or $1,350 in the U.S.). The largest employers are the Israel Defense Forces, Ben-Gurion University, and the Soroka Medical Center. The official emblem of the municipality of Beersheba is the tamarisk tree, the tree planted by Abraham, according to Genesis. The historic mosque in Beersheba was renovated and is now used as a municipal museum of the history of Beersheba. Highway 40, the second-longest highway in Israel, connects Beersheba to Tel Aviv. Chess is taught in the city's kindergarten.

BE'ER SHEVA: THE AIR FORCE MUSEUM AT HATZEIM

Photo courtesy of the Israeli Ministry of Tourism and is solely for this photo only at www.goisrael.com

The Hatzeim Air Force Museum has real airplanes that participated in real battles. Personal stories and experiences are also shared in the museum exhibits. A movie in the museum tells about the Israeli Air Force.[314]

The museum has over 140 aircraft to view. The hot and dry desert air preserved the airplanes. The museum tells the story of the history of Israel, including planes flown by Israel, built by Israel, and captured by Israel. The museum is open daily, except for Saturday. To find the museum, visitors should go to the Hatzerim Air Force Base.[315]

---

[314] www.alljewishlinks.com/hatzeim-israel-airforce-museum.
[315] www.attractions-in-israel.com/negev/negev-museums/israel-air-force.

BE'ER SHEVA: THE ANCIENT CITY RESTORED

Photo courtesy of the Israeli Ministry of Tourism and is solely for this photo only at www.goisrael.com

Tel Be'er Sheva is an archaeological site believed to be the remains of the biblical town of Beersheba. It is east of modern Beersheba and east of the Bedouin town of Tel Sheva. Archaeologists believe by the evidence that Beersheba was inhabited from 4000 BC until the sixteenth century AD. It dates from the early Israelite period about the 10th century BC. Archaeologists discovered a unique water system and huge cistern carved out of rock under the town. They also found the ashlar blocks of a large horned heathen altar, along with small Iron Age incense altars.[316]

The horned altar had been destroyed in the late 8th century BC. It appeared that the horned altar was reconstructed at some point. This altar is now on display at the Israel Museum. The altar was made of hewn stones, and is therefore known to be heathen. Biblical law states that altars should be made of uncut stones: "And there shalt thou build an altar unto the Lord thy God of whole stones; thou shalt not lift up any iron tool upon them" (Deuteronomy 27:5).[317]

BE'ER SHEVA: AN ANCIENT WELL OUTSIDE THE CITY GATE

Photo courtesy of the Israeli Ministry of Tourism and is solely for this photo only at www.goisrael.com

Most archaeological ruins and artifacts in Beersheba are from the time of King Hezekiah. The well pictured here was dug in the 10th century BC, but the tamarisk tree planted next to it is a reminder of

---

[316] www.en.wikipedia.org/wiki/tel_beer_sheva.
[317] www.jewishmag.com/61mag/beersheva/beersheva.htm.

older times and the story of Abraham. The town is entered through the gate. There is an outer gate and an open square, and then a triple inner gate. The rooms on the sides were for the guards. In the middle of the restored town is an observation tower. Also next to the gate are three large reception rooms. Archaeologists found many pottery vessels and large jars in this location. In the walls of these buildings, archaeologists found that three of the cornerstones had a horned point, and the fourth one had a horn broken off. Another stone belonging to the altar had an engraving of a serpent.

On the left is a large governor's palace with three large reception rooms. Smaller four-room houses are scattered throughout the town and have their backsides to the wall. Next to the wall is the living room, as well as a room with an oven and with stairs leading to the roof. The two other rooms are separated by pillars and used for storage. Opposite the storehouses are the remains of the Roman fort from the 2nd and 3rd centuries AD, with smooth pavement.

Outside Tel Be'er Sheva and within the city limits of modern Beersheba, archaeologists discovered an older site that they named Nahal Be'er Sheva, with the remains of a prehistoric civilization. The people at that time lived in round or oval subterranean dwellings, which they dug into the soft soil of the riverbank. To go inside the dwellings, a person had to use the tunnels from the shallow pit. In these pits, hearths were found as well as grain silos. Archaeologists believe that these were inhabited by nomads who used them as winter homes. In the summer, they migrated with their goats and sheep.

Artifacts that were found included clay pottery and also flint tools like axes, scrapers, knives, and lances. The people also imported basalt stone from Jordan to make vessels. They used copper from Jordan to make weapons. Archaeologists found rock anvils used for the making of weapons. Beautiful ivory figurines had holes drilled in their faces and possibly real hair to make them appear more real.[318]

Precious Metals

Archaeologists discovered that ancient people in Bible times used gold, copper, and iron, and later used silver, lead, and tin. Then they learned to use alloys, which

---

[318] www.jewishmag.com/61mag/beersheva/beersheva.htm.

are a combination of metals. Electrum is a mixture of gold and silver; bronze is a mixture of copper and tin; and brass is a mixture of copper and zinc. People smelted them from ore and they searched constantly for ore. Metals were a sign of wealth, used for making tools, weapons, and utensils.

Bronze was so plentiful that archaeologists refer to the period from 3150 to 1200 BC as the Bronze Age. The Old Testament refers to bronze doors, helmets, armor, and swords (Isaiah 45:2; 2 Chronicles 33:11; 1 Samuel 17:5-6).

The New Testament writers refer to copper coins (Matthew 10:9). The Hebrew word nechosheth can mean copper or bronze. The Romans first produced brass about 20 BC, about 400 years after the last Old Testament prophet.

Gold is mentioned in the Bible more than any other metal. Goldsmiths of the Bible used gold to make jewelry and ornaments. Gold was used by craftsmen to build the tabernacle, Solomon's temple, and many of the utensils used in each (Exodus 35-39; 1 Kings 6-7). The apostle John saw a street of gold in his vision of the new Jerusalem (Revelation 21:21). Gold is used to describe anything beautiful, valuable, or pure.

The Iron Age, 1200-586 BC, was after the Bronze Age. Iron tools and weapons are more durable. God promised His children that they would find iron in the land of Canaan (Deuteronomy 8:9). The Israelites used iron to make jewelry, plows, axes, picks, swords, and spears. An army with iron weapons had a technological advantage over an enemy using bronze weapons. For a while, the Philistines had the advantage over the Israelites due to the iron weapons (1 Samuel 13:19-22, Judges 1:19). Biblical writers used iron as a symbol of judgment and hardness (Psalm 2:9, Revelation 2:27).

The Bible often mentioned gold and silver together and both became symbols of wealth (Genesis 13:2, Zephaniah 1:18, Haggai 2:8). During the time of Solomon, silver was so common that it was used as money. The Israelites did not use silver coins during the monarchy. They used weights of silver such as shekels, talents, and minas as units of exchange (Genesis 23:15-16, Exodus 21:32, Nehemiah 7:72, Isaiah 7:23).

Lead deposits in ancient times were found in Egypt and Asia Minor. Exodus 15:10, Jeremiah 6:29-30, and Ezekiel 27:12 mention lead. Sometimes silver was made from the smelting of lead (Jeremiah 6:27-30).[319]

---

[319]   J. Mark Terry, *Precious Metals.* Biblical Illustrator, LifeWay: Volume 39, number 4, Summer 2013, 74-77.

Ben Gurion University of the Negev opened in 1969. At the university, there are a total of about 20,000 students attending the many programs. Areas of study include engineering, health, natural science, humanities, social studies, and business management. The university also has advanced programs like medical school and pharmaceuticals.[320]

Acre

Acre is also known as Acco, Akko, and Acco Ptolemais. Before the Israelites arrived in Israel, Acco was an important port city. There was a river there that flowed into the Mediterranean Sea, by which ships could arrive in Acco for trading. After the conquest of Canaan when the Israelites returned from Egypt, Joshua gave Acco to the tribe of Asher. But Asher could not drive the inhabitants out of Acco: "Neither did Asher drive out the inhabitants of Accho, nor the inhabitants of Zidon, nor of Ahlab, nor of Achzib, nor of Helbah, nor of Aphik, nor of Rehob: but the Asherites dwelt among the Canaanites, the inhabitants of the land: for they did not drive them out" (Judges 1:31-32).

Acco was hard to defeat, because as archaeologists discovered, Acco was on a high cliff surrounded by the Mediterranean Sea on three sides and a marsh on the fourth side. This might explain why Asher could not drive them out and take over the settlement.

In 100 BC, King Ptolemy of Egypt captured Acco and rebuilt it. The settlement was then renamed Ptolemais after him.

In New Testament times, the Apostle Paul visited Christian believers in Ptolemais at the end of his third missionary journey, while his ship was anchored in the nearby harbor: "And when we had finished our course from Tyre, we came to Ptolemais, and saluted the brethren, and abode with them one day" (Acts 21:7).

In the Middle Ages, the name of Ptolemais was changed to Acre. The city of Acre was the last stronghold of the Christian Crusaders. A Catholic order called the Knights of the Hospital of Saint John, or the Hospitallers, built a physical structure that was a combination of a fortress, a monastery, and a hospital. The complex was called Knight's Hall and comprised about 15,000 square feet of the old city, overlooking the sea.[321]

---

[320] www.en.wikipedia.org/wiki/ben_gurion_university_of-the-negev.
[321] George W. Knight, *The Holy Land*, 273-274.

The port city of Acco was the main port of the region until the port at Caesarea was built. Herod the Great received Augustus Caesar in Acco because the port of Caesarea was not yet finished.

Vespasian docked at Ptolemais when he arrived to subdue the First Jewish Revolt. Later, the Arabs changed the name back to Acco.

The Mamluks ended the Crusader rule in 1291 AD by capturing Acco. Napoleon wanted to take over the port at Acco, but his attempt in 1799 failed.[322]

THE CRUSADER KNIGHTS HALLS AT AKKO

courtesy of the Israeli Ministry of Tourism and is solely for this photo only at www.goisrael.com

Archaeologists excavated under the citadel and prison of Acre and discovered a complex of halls built and used by the Hospitallers Knights. The complex was located in the northern wall of Acre. The archaeologists found six semi-joined halls, a dungeon, a dining room, and remains of an ancient Gothic church. Medieval European remains included the Church of Saint George, as well as remains of marketplaces run by merchants from Pisa and Amalf in Crusader and medieval Acre.[323]

Five hundred years after the time of the Crusaders, the Druze prince Fakhr ad-Din rebuilt Acco. The Muslims could not destroy the Crusaders' labyrinth, and it can still be seen today. Most of the Crusader city is still under the ground. Only the area known as the Hospitaller Quarter is open.[324]

Precious Metals (continued)

The biblical writers seldom mentioned tin, but they valued it to mix with copper to make bronze (Numbers 31:22; Ezekiel 22:18,20). Job stated that God's wisdom is more precious than gold or silver (Job 28:12-19,28). King David insisted that God's ordinances are more desirable than gold (Psalm

---

[322] www.bibleplaces.com/acco.htm.

[323] www.en.wikipedia.org/wiki/acre_israel#.

[324] www.bibleplaces.com/acco.htm.

19:10). Jesus stressed seeking spiritual treasure when He said, "Don't collect for yourselves treasures on earth, where moth and rust destroy and where thieves break in and steal. But collect for yourselves treasures in heaven" (Matthew 6:19-20). Paul warned that "the love of money is a root of all kinds of evil" (I Timothy 6:10). The idea in the Bible is that wealth is not bad, but that people are to use wealth to benefit others and expand the Lord's kingdom.

Mark Terry is adjunct professor of missions at The Southern Baptist Theological Seminary, Louisville, Kentucky.[325]

The Attraction of Idolatry

The first story of idolatry in the Bible is in Genesis 31:19, when it reports that Rachel stole and hid her family's idols. In the Old Testament period, most people recognized national, regional, and individual gods and their idol forms. Beginning with the patriarchs through the later prophets, idol worship was a big temptation. Neither warnings nor severe punishment broke them from the habit of idol worship. On Mount Sinai, Moses acquired the law from God and the main one was "You shall not make for yourself an idol" (Exodus 20:4). In the camp below, the newly freed Israelites worshiped an idol built by Aaron, the brother of Moses (Exodus 32:2-4).

Long-established gods had their place in the temples of Athens, Corinth, Ephesus, and Rome. These 1st-century people added new images of the Roman rulers and the national regions. The New Testament churches faced idol worship as a barrier to their witness and conversion of people. Paul faced wrath from craftsmen in the marketplaces when several people responded to his preaching in Ephesus. The artisans accused Paul of interfering with market sales of their idols and threatening their profits (Acts 19:23-41).

Every group of people Israel met, fought, or came into contact with believed in many gods and practiced idol worship. The idol worshipers believed every need of life was under the watch of some god. The people of Israel had interaction with the idol worshipers through intermarriage and trade. Paul wrote to the New Testament church, "Do not be deceived: bad company corrupts good morals" (I Corinthians 15:33).

One attraction to idol worship was its simplicity of form and promise of results. Idols could be seen and touched. Israel struggled to keep their worship to a

---

[325] J. Mark Terry, *Precious Metals*. Biblical Illustrator, LifeWay: Volume 39, number 4, Summer 2013, 74-77.

God whom no one could see or touch. They saw Yahweh's presence in creation, moral obligation through the law, and His personal intervention recorded in national history, but they still could not touch, handle, or see Him.[326]

ACRE/AKKO: THE OLD PISAN PORT FROM THE CRUSADER PERIOD

Photo courtesy of the Israeli Ministry of Tourism and is solely for this photo only at www.goisrael.com

Acre is a city in the Western Galilee region of northern Israel. It is located on the northern part of Haifa Bay. In 2009, the population was 46,300, with 72 percent Jewish and 28 percent Arab.[327]

The Jezzar Pasha Mosque was built in 1781. Jezzar Pasha and his successor Suleiman Pasha are buried in a small graveyard near the mosque. There is a shrine on the second level of the mosque that has one strand of hair from Muhammed's beard to be shown on special occasions.[328]

The Al-Jezzar Mosque is the third largest mosque in Israel. It was built in 1781 on the site of San Croce, the original Christian cathedral in Acco. The builders got the Roman columns inside the mosque from Caesarea.[329]

The Attraction of Idolatry (continued)

Some idols involved sex vices such as Asherah, a pole or tree representing a sex goddess in the Old Testament. Greeks and Romans worshiped Diana represented by a multi-breasted idol. Temple prostitution was practiced to ensure successful multiplication of crops, herbs, and people.

---

[326] Randall L. Adkisson, *The Attraction of Idolatry*. Biblical Illustrator, LifeWay: Volume 39, number 4, Summer 2013, 78-81.

[327] www.en.wikipedia.org/wiki/acre_israel.

[328] www.en.wikipedia.org/wiki/acre_israel#.

[329] www.bibleplaces.com/acco.htm.

The prophets' warnings sometimes included words like whoring, adultery, and chasing after the gods of the pagans. "Have you seen what faithless Israel did? She went up on every high hill and under every green tree, and she was a harlot there" (Jeremiah 3:6).

Both Israel and the early church were in danger of being seduced by the gratification and promises of gods that could be made by and in the likeness of people. Judgment for their sins was corporal punishment at time. But the worse punishment was the loss of generations who watched the idol worship of their parents and national leaders and followed them along paths of alienation from a relationship with their true God (Exodus 3:4-7).

Today in modern times, our culture is plagued by similar problems that the Israelites faced. There are many false religions and untrue doctrines. Images of gods are in Hindu closets and New Age shrines. Some Christians believe in horoscopes and good-luck charms. Modern idols keep their attractions.

Randall L. Adkisson is senior pastor of First Baptist Church, Cookeville Tennessee.[330]

Preparing for Passover

On the day before His crucifixion, Jesus asked Peter and John to go into Jerusalem and get ready for Passover (Luke 22:8). Jesus wanted them to go to a house that had an upper room for Jesus and His disciples to celebrate His last Passover. They followed His instructions and found the upper room and started preparing the meal like the Jewish people had in the 1st century. The custom was to eat the Passover meal on the fourteenth day of the first month (Leviticus 23:5). The first month is called Nisan and comes in our mid-March and April. The fourteenth day had special significance for the Jewish people, because the Lord commanded Moses to lead God's people to celebrate the first Passover meal on the fourteenth day (Exodus 12:6).

The name of the meal had a powerful connection between the people of Israel and the night when the Lord passed over His people in Egypt and spared the firstborn males in their houses (Exodus 12:20). The Lord commanded His people to observe Passover every year and to remember the night He passed over their houses with the smear of lamb's blood on the doors. The Lord also told them to

---

[330]   Randall L. Adkisson, The Attraction of Idolatry. Biblical Illustrator, LifeWay: Volume 39, number 4, Summer 2013, 78-81.

eat unleavened bread for seven days after Passover and to call it the Feast of the Unleavened Bread (Exodus 12:14-20).

During the time of the Exodus, the Jewish people celebrated Passover in their homes (Exodus 12:7). Once Solomon built the temple, Jerusalem was the main place for Passover and became a Jerusalem pilgrimage festival. During the time of the ministry of Jesus, Jewish people journeyed to Jerusalem from everywhere for the celebration of Passover and the Feast of the Unleavened Bread. Some historians have estimated that about 200,000 Israelis made it to Jerusalem for Passover every year. One ancient historian estimated about 2.7 million Jews arrived in Jerusalem for the Passover.

Imagine the difficulty in trying to find a house or a room in which to observe Passover. Extended families used every bit of space when assembling together for the Passover meal.[331]

---

[331] Argile A. Smith, *Preparing for Passover.* Biblical Illustrator, LifeWay: Volume 39, number 3, Spring 2013, 14-17.

NEAR AKKO (ACRE): BAHAI HOLY PLACE WHERE BAHA'ULLAH, ITS FOUNDING PROPHET, IS BURIED (1)
Photo courtesy of the Israeli Ministry of Tourism and is solely for this photo only at www.goisrael.com

Acre has many Bahai holy places. Baha'ullah was imprisoned in the citadel during Ottoman Rule. Baha'ullah died in Acre on May 29, 1892. The holy site contains the remains of Baha'ullah. Other Acre Baha'ullah holy sites are the House of Abbud where Baha'ullah lived with his family and the Garden of Ridvan where he spent the last days of his life. In 2008, the Bahai holy places in Acre were added to the UNESCO World Heritage List.[332]

Haifa

Haifa is the largest city in northern Israel. Haifa has a population of over 268,000. There are also another 300,000 living in nearby cities of Tirat Carmel, Daliyat al-Karmel, and Nesher. Altogether, nearly 600,000 people live in the Haifa metropolitan area. Ninety percent are Jews, mainly immigrants from the former Soviet Union, and 10 percent are Arabs. Haifa is built on the slopes of Mount Carmel and has a history of settlement for 3,000 years. The earliest known settlement was Tell Abu Hawam, a port settlement in the 14th century BC. The Haifa area was known as a dye-making center in the 3rd century AD. Haifa has been captured by the Phoenicians, Persians, Hasmoneans, Romans, Byzantines, Arabs, Crusaders, Ottomans, British, and the Israelis. Since Israel became a state in 1948, Haifa has been governed by the Haifa Municipality. The city is 24.6 square miles and is about fifty-six miles north of Tel Aviv.[333]

---

[332] www.en.wikipedia.org/wiki/acre_israel#.

[333] www.en.wikipedia.org/wiki/haifa.

The Bahai holy sites in Haifa are visited by all people of these same beliefs from all over the world. They come to show respect for the first Bahai founders. The group believes in unity across cultures and religions of the world. Haifa is the headquarters for the Bahai faith. This faith began with persecution in Persia in the mid-19th century. This group believes that Moses, Jesus, and Muhammad were sent with messages through the ages with beliefs that fit the social needs of the time. According to their beliefs, the most recent teacher of the world was Baha'ullah (1817-1892) who was imprisoned by the Turkish authority in Acre. He wrote his doctrines and died a quiet death in Bahji House. The Bab's remains remained secret for years after he was martyred in front of a firing squad in 1850. Followers secretly carried his remains to the Holy Land. Baha'ullah showed his son where Bab's remains should be put in a special tomb.[334]

The Bahai Gardens were designed by Shoghi Effendi. The gardens have hanging gardens and terraces all the way down to Ben Gurion Boulevard, as a gift to the city that helped them create something beautiful.[335] There are nineteen terraces that go all the way up the northern slopes of Mount Carmel. The gardens have graveled paths, hedges, and flower beds groomed and nurtured by dedicated gardeners.[336]

On April 27, 2008, 153 delegates from all over the world arrived in Haifa for the tenth international Bahai Convention. This convention is held every five years, from April 29 to May 2 in Haifa.[337]

In the beginning, the Bab's tomb was housed in a six-room stone building built in 1899-1909. In 1921, the Bahai leader, Abdu'l-Baha', the oldest son of Baha'ullah, was buried in the same shrine as the Bab. In 1948-1953, the architect, William Sutherland Maxwell, designed an enlargement of the shrine. In 2008, UNESCO named it a World Heritage Site. The tomb has gold ornamental flowers in almost every room. The shrine blends western and eastern styles. All the Bahai buildings face toward Acre, where Baha'ullah is buried.[338]

---

[334] www.sacred-destination.com/israel/haifa-bahai-shrine.
[335] www.sacred-destination.com/israel/haifa-bahai-shrine.
[336] Ibid., and www.ganbahai.org.il/en.
[337] www.news.bahai.org/story/624.
[338] Ibid.

The Bahai of the Bab sect separated from Iran's Shi'ite Islam in 1844. The Bahai World Center is located on the slope of Mount Carmel and contains the beautiful gardens. Beautiful "Hanging Gardens" are displayed on part of the Louis Promenade until Ha-Gefen Street. At the center is the gold-domed Shrine of the Bab and the burial place of the Bab who organized the sect.

MOUNT CARMEL: MUHRAKA (3)
Photo courtesy of the Israeli Ministry of Tourism and is solely for this photo only at www.goisrael.com

The Carmel mountain range is four to five miles wide. It slopes gradually toward the southwest and forms a steep ridge on the northeastern side, and it is 1,810 feet high. The main mountain is made of limestone and flint and has many caves. There are some volcanic rocks also at the mountain. Another name for Mount Carmel is Mount Saint Elias.[339] (Read 1 Kings 18:16-39.)

Preparing for Passover (continued)

The Upper Room gave Jesus and His disciples plenty of room to celebrate Passover. The Jews enjoyed celebrating Passover in Jerusalem, but things changed when the Romans destroyed Jerusalem and demolished the temple in 70 AD, as Jesus had foretold. Then the Jews reverted back to the tradition of celebrating in homes in many cities.

The disciples of Jesus found the Upper Room as Jesus instructed. Next they made sure the lamb had been slaughtered properly and roasted. Then they prepared the other dishes for the meal. The lamb was the centerpiece of Passover. The lamb had to be purchased by the tenth day of the first month, which was four days before Passover. The lamb had to be unblemished and not more than one year old.[340]

---

[339] www.en.wikipedia.org/wiki/mount_carmel_israel#.

[340] Argile A. Smith, *Preparing for Passover.* Biblical Illustrator, LifeWay: Volume 39, number 3, Spring 2013, 14-17.

HAIFA: STELLA MARIS MONASTERY (CARMELITE)

Courtesy of the Israeli Ministry of Tourism and is solely for this photo only at www.goisrael.com

The Carmelites are a Catholic order of monks. Their main saint is the prophet Elijah. The monastery in Haifa opened in the 17th century. It is located on the north-west corner of Mount Carmel. The monks believe that the cave inside the monastery was the cave where Elijah hid. The compound has monasteries for men and women, a church, and a hostel. The Carmelites dedicated the monastery to Mary, the mother of Jesus. Above the entrance is a symbol of a sword held by the arm of Elijah.[341]

MOUNT CARMEL: STATUE OF PROPHET ELIJAH AT MUHRAKA (CARMELITE)

courtesy of the Israeli Ministry of Tourism and is solely for this photo only at www.goisrael.com

The prophet Elijah with his upraised sword symbolizes the mass execution of the false prophets below Mount Carmel: "And Elijah said unto them, 'Take the prophets of Baal; let not one of them escape.' And they took them: and Elijah brought them down to the brook Kishon, and slew them there" (1 Kings 18:40).[342]

---

[341] www.biblewalks.com/sites/carmelitemonastery.html.

[342] George W. Knight, *The Holy Land*, 243-244.

JEZREEL VALLEY, FROM MOUNT CARMEL

courtesy of the Israeli Ministry of Tourism and is solely for this photo only at www.goisrael.com

The Jezreel Valley has the shape of a triangular wedge about fifteen by fifteen by twenty miles in size. The Jezreel Valley is the biggest section of flat land in Israel. This valley divides Samaria and Galilee. 1 Samuel 10:3 calls it the "Plain of Tabor" because Mount Tabor rises up high over all the flat land: "Then shalt thou go on forward from thence, and thou shalt come to the Plain of Tabor, and thou shall meet three men going up to God to Beth-el, one carrying three kids, and another carrying three loaves of bread, and another carrying a bottle of wine."

Zechariah the prophet called this plain the "Valley of Megiddon" because of the city of Megiddo: "In that day shall there be great mourning in Jerusalem, as the mourning of Hadadrimmon in the Valley of Megiddon" (Zechariah 12:11). The valley is also called the "Plain of Esdraelon", the Greek word for Jezreel.[343] The Bible speaks of the last battle of the world being fought in the Jezreel Valley at the place of Armageddon.[344]

The Jezreel Valley is a large fertile valley south of the Lower Galilee region in Israel and the West Bank region in the Palestinian territories. West of the Jezreel Valley is the Mount Carmel Range and to the east is the Jordan Valley. Jezreel Valley is named for the ancient town of Jezreel or the Arabic name Zir'in. Jezreel means "God sows" or "El sows." Jezreel, Megiddo, Beit She'an, Shimron, and Afula are Biblical cities in the Jezreel Valley. The book of Judges identifies the biblical city of Ophrah as the home of Gideon.[345]

---

[343] www.en.wikipedia.org/wiki/jezreel_valley.
[344] www.bibleplaces.com/jezreelvalley.htm.
[345] www.en.wikipedia.org/wiki/jezreel_valley.

Preparing for Passover (continued)

The disciples had to remove all the leaven in the room the night before Passover. Early in the morning on the day of Passover, all the leaven is taken outside and burned. At 3:00 p.m. on the day of Passover until dark, the head of the household took the lamb to the temple. The priest supervised the head of the household as he slaughtered the lamb and caught the blood in a basin. The priest threw the blood in the basin on the bottom of the altar. Then the head of the household skinned the lamb and removed the fat and kidneys to put on the altar to be burned.

The head of the household carried the lamb to the place where the meal was to be cooked. Then the lamb was roasted outside over an open fire. They prepared jars of water, bitter herbs, unleavened bread, and a fruit and raw vegetable dish dipped in tart dressing. Wine had to be available. The room had to be arranged with floor cushions in order for everyone to be able to recline at the table. The lamb and everything had to be prepared by 6:00 p.m., when the meal began. The Passover lamb reminded them of the faith of their ancestors in Egypt, who painted their doorposts with the blood of lamb sacrifices. That blood from the lamb spared them from the visit of the death angel. The bitter herbs reminded them of slavery in Egypt, and the unleavened bread reminded them of the way they hurried out of Egypt. The nuts and fruit paste reminded them to think of the clay that their ancestors used to make bricks for pharaoh. The cups of wine reminded them of God's promise in Exodus 6:6-8.

Argile A. Smith, Jr., is dean of chapel and associate dean of Christian ministry for the Caskey School of Divinity, Louisiana College, Pineville, Louisiana.[346]

---

[346] Argile A. Smith, *Preparing for Passover.* Biblical Illustrator, LifeWay: Volume 39, number 3, Spring 2013, 14-17.

The Druze are Arabic-speaking people of Israel who serve in the Israeli Defense Forces and also serve in the government of Israel. Most Druze stay away from the Arab National Movement. They combine Islam, Gnosticism, Neoplatonism, and many other philosophies. Reda Mansour, a Druze poet, said: "We are the only non-Jewish minority that is drafted into the military, and we have an even higher percentage in the combat units and as officers than the Jewish members themselves."

The Druze honor Jethro, the father-in-law of Moses. Jethro joined and assisted the Israelites in the desert after the Exodus. The tomb of Jethro is near Tiberias. In January 2004, the current spiritual leader of the Druze, Sheikh Muwaffak Tarif, asked all non-Jews to obey and observe the seven Noahide Laws in the Bible. The seven laws are prohibition of idolatry, murder, theft, sexual immorality, blasphemy, eating the flesh of an animal while it is alive, and establishment of courts of law.[347]

The pyramid in front of the Stella Maris Monastery is a memorial to the French soldiers who died here after the retreat of Napoleon. It has the inscription, "How are the mighty fallen in battle" from King David's sadness over Saul and Jonathan.[348] The statue of the Virgin Mary is made from Lebanon cedar. Across the street from the church is a cable car that is used to ride up and down Mount Carmel.[349]

The Stella Maris church contains beautiful patterns of Italian marble. The cave below the altar is believed to be a cave that Elijah frequently used. Many little votive candles burn on the altar above the Cave of Elijah. Each candle represents a Carmelite community in another country. The candle for the United States is the candle on the left.

In the rooms to the right of the entrance are a nativity scene, a museum of the artifacts from the ancient Byzantine church that used to be on the site, and a small gift shop.[350]

Brother Luigi Poggi painted colorful pictures of scenes and events from the Old Testament on the Stella Maris dome from 1924 to 1928. Included is the scene of Elijah being swept up to heaven in a chariot

---

[347] www.en.wikipedia.org/wiki/israeli_druze.

[348] www.sacred-destinations.com/israel/haifa-stella-maris-carmelite-monastery.

[349] www.goisrael.com/tourism_eng/tourist.

[350] www.sacred-destinations.com/israel/haifa-stella-maris-carmelite-monastery.

of fire. The monks are available to answer questions and describe the monastery.[351]

HAIFA: NATIONAL MARITIME MUSEUM

Photo courtesy of the Israeli Ministry of Tourism and is solely for this photo only at www.goisrael.com

Other interesting sites in Haifa are the National Maritime Museum, the National Museum of Science and Technology, the Haifa Museum of Art, the Railway Museum, the Tikotin Museum of Japanese Art, the Reuben and Edith Hecht Museum, and the Israel Oil Industry Museum.

Crowns: Their Significance and Symbolism

The Old Testament describes Israel's kings and high priests wearing crowns, some gold, and some with expensive jewelry. The Romans called crowns corona. *The person with the crown wore it around the neck or head as a decoration and as a reward.*

Emperors wore a crown called corona radiate. *These crowns were put on coins representing Nero, Caligula, and Trajan. If a military commander broke up a siege, he received from the rescued army a crown called* corona obsidionalis. *If a conquest was considered important and gratifying for the empire, the commander received the* corona triumphalis, *which was the most prestigious of all military rewards. Julius Caesar and Augustus received the* corona triumphalis *as generals and later wore it in public games when they became emperors. Even common soldiers received crowns for meritorious valor. A soldier who rescued a Roman citizen in battle received a* corona civica. *The* corona navalis *was a naval crown given to the first man to courageously board an enemy ship.[352]*

Crowns were used during religious and civic celebrations. Roman priests wore the corona sacerdotalis *to designate religious function and status. Even brides at weddings wore the* corona nuptialis *braided around her head. A couple*

---

351 Ibid.

352 M. Dean Register, *Crowns: Their Significance and Symbolism.* Biblical Illustrator, LifeWay: Volume 39, number 3, Spring 2013, 18-21.

celebrating the birth of a child put a circular wreath called a corona natalicia *on the door of their home. Crowns were given to winners of sport events and were considered as a fortune.*

Some historians believe early crowns were simple cloth turbans or headbands. Early crowns were made of leaves and flowers woven into twigs from cultivated vines. Religious celebrations used ivy crowns and wreaths of oak.[353]

HAIFA: A VIEW FROM THE KISHON STREAM

Photo courtesy of the Israeli Ministry of Tourism and is solely for this photo only at www.goisrael.com

The Kishon River flows into the Mediterranean Sea in Haifa. It is a seventy-kilometer perennial stream. Its source is the Gilboa Mountains that flow west-northwesterly through the Jezreel Valley, emptying into the Haifa Bay in the Mediterranean Sea. The Kishon has become one of the most polluted rivers in Israel.[354]

The judge Deborah and her commander Barak believed that their forces were no match for the Canaanites and their iron chariots. They knew that in the winter months the Kidron River often overflowed. Barak and Deborah kept their fighters on the higher ground near Mount Tabor and waited for the right time to strike. When the Kishon overflowed, they swooped down and surprised the Canaanites, whose chariots stuck in the mud, and the Israelites won the battle. Judges 4:4-16 describes this battle. Judges 5:20-21 then speaks of the Kishon River and the Israelites' victory there under the leadership of Deborah, as she sang: "[The stars] fought from heaven; the stars in their courses fought against Sisera. The river of Kishon swept them away, that ancient river, the river Kishon. O my soul, thou hast trodden down strength."[355]

---

[353] M. Dean Register, *Crowns: Their Significance and Symbolism.* Biblical Illustrator, LifeWay: Volume 39, number 3, Spring 2013, 18-21.

[354] www.en.wikipedia.org/wiki/kishon_river.

[355] George W. Knight, *The Holy Land*, 243-244.

Crowns: Their Significance and Symbolism (continued)

Crowns of olive leaves were popular for winners of the Olympic games. This may have been the image the Apostle Paul thought of when he wrote to Timothy explaining that the Lord had reserved for him (Paul) a "crown of righteousness" (II Timothy 4:8).

Crowns were symbols of honor for those who had distinguished themselves in military, religious, athletic, and socio-political endeavors. When Paul spoke of crowns, he emphasized that crowns for Christians were not earned by merit but were rewards based on grace. In II Timothy 4:8, the emphasis Paul made was on grace. Paul testified that the crown was a coronation of righteousness that the perfect Judge bestowed. Paul used the Greek word stephanos *to describe the Christians in Philippi as his "joy and crown" (Philippians 4:1). The Philippians were Paul's wreath of honor and his trophy for the sake of the gospel.*

We may be puzzled why crowns will be needed in heaven when the victorious and worthy One is Christ. But the New Testament does mention crowns in heaven by using the term stephanos. *James said the Lord would give a "crown of life" to "those who love Him" (James 1:12).*

Jesus echoed this same promise in His message to the church at Smyrna: "Be faithful until death, and I will give you the crown of life" (Revelation 2:10). The people of Smyrna would have understood that the image of athletic games and victors' crowns were common there. Also Peter spoke of believers receiving an "unfading crown of glory" (I Peter 5:4).[356]

While John was on Patmos, he also used stephanos *to highlight the divine glory of Christ. John described Christ as reigning with "a gold crown on His head" (Revelation 14:14). The victorious Christ is wearing a crown because He alone is the sovereign King who conquers sin and death. The book of Revelation describes the angelic twenty-four elders as wearing crowns in heaven, but even they surrender their crowns before the throne of Christ (Revelation 4:4-10). And the book of Revelation uses the Greek word* diadema *three times to describe a royal tiara. Each of these uses has to do with dominion of reign. The crowns of the dragon (Revelation 12:3) and the beast (Revelation 13:1) represent a measure of dominion, although both of them are evil. Christ displays the eternal and all-consuming dominion upon His head, where there are many crowns (Revelation 19:12). The glory of these heavenly crowns is in contrast to His experience on earth when*

---

[356] M. Dean Register, *Crowns: Their Significance and Symbolism.* Biblical Illustrator, LifeWay: Volume 39, number 3, Spring 2013, 18-21.

"[t]hey twisted together a crown (stephanos) *of thorns and put it on His head"* *(Matthew 27:29).*

M. Dean Register is pastor of Crosspoint Church, Hattiesburg, Mississippi.[357]

God's Self-Revelation at Sinai

God revealed to Moses, either on top of Mount Sinai or in the shadows of Mount Sinai, what he wanted revealed about Himself for the books of Genesis, Exodus, and Leviticus. God first appeared to Moses at Mount Sinai in the burning bush (Exodus 3). The angel of Yahweh appeared there to Moses while he looked after the flocks of sheep of his father-in-law, Jethro. God gained the attention of Moses with the burning bush, and God called him by his name. God revealed Himself as being patient, kind, and desiring a relationship with His people. God also revealed Himself as holy, and the ground in His presence as holy.

God next told Moses He was the God of Abraham, Isaac, and Jacob. God identified Himself as the God of Moses and of Israel. He revealed that He is all-knowing, recognizing Israel's sufferings and afflictions, and that He had come to deliver them from bondage. God told Moses that he was the chosen one to help deliver the people of Israel from slavery. God was more interested in using a humble shepherd than the mighty prince of Egypt that Moses once was. Moses asked God His name. God is personal and revealed His name to Moses by saying His name is "I AM", but the people were to call him "Yahweh". God is the One who self-exists and makes all things to exist. God gave the authority of His name, Yahweh, to Moses.

After they left Egypt, God led His people to Rephidim, near the base of Mount Sinai, a place with no water (Exodus 17). God tested their faithfulness and was patient with His people and ignored their failure and grumbling. God stood (in the pillar of cloud) next to Moses when Moses struck the rock to get the water.[358]

BEIT SHE'ARIM:ENTRANCE TO THE CATACOMBS

Photo courtesy of the Israeli Ministry of Tourism and is solely for this photo only at www.goisrael.com

---

[357] Ibid.

[358] Eric A. Mitchell, *God's Self-Revelation at Sinai*. Biblical Illustrator, LifeWay: Volume 39, number 3, Spring 2013, 22-25.

More Information About Other Places in the Jezreel Valley Besides Haifa

Mount Tabor looks down on the Jezreel Valley. Deborah and Barak were two judges in Israel during the period of the book of Judges, and they camped on Mount Tabor with the Israelite army before attacking and defeating Sisera's Canaanite fighters.

Mount Gilboa is on the southeastern side of the Jezreel Valley. This is the site where King Saul and his son died:

And the young man that told him said, "As I happened by chance upon Mount Gilboa, behold, Saul leaned upon his spear; and, lo, the chariots and horsemen followed hard after him. And when he looked behind him, he saw me, and called unto me. And I answered, 'Here am I.' He said unto me, 'Who art thou?' And I answered him, 'I am an Amalekite.' He said unto me again, 'Stand, I pray thee, upon me, and slay me: for anguish is come upon me, because my life is yet whole in me.'" (2 Samuel 1:6-9)

David cursed Mount Gilboa after Saul and Jonathan's death: "Ye mountains of Gilboa, let there be no dew, neither let there be rain, upon you, nor fields of offerings: for there the shield of the mighty is vilely cast away, the shield of Saul, as though he had not been anointed with oil" (2 Samuel 1:21).

Ein Harod is a spring at the foot of Mount Gilboa, where Gideon followed God's instructions and thinned out his army to 300 men[359]:

The Lord told Gideon, "There are still too many! Bring them down to the spring, and I will test them to determine who will go with you and who will not." When Gideon took his warriors down to the water, the Lord told him, "Divide the men into two groups. In one group put all those who cup water in their hands and lap it up with their tongues like dogs. In the other group put all those who kneel down and drink with their mouths in the stream." Only 300 of the men drank from their hands. All the others got down on their knees and drank with their mouths in the stream. The Lord said to Gideon, "With these 300 men I will rescue you and give you victory over the Midianites. Send all the others home."

---

[359] www.bibleplaces.com/jezreelvalley.htm.

So Gideon collected the provisions and rams' horns of the other warriors and sent them home. But he kept the 300 men with him. (Judges 7:4-8, NLT)

Negev Region

SHIVTAH NATIONAL PARK

Photo courtesy of the Israeli Ministry of Tourism and is solely for this photo only at www.goisrael.com

Archaeologists believe Shivtah was a Byzantine agricultural colony and a way station for people going to Saint Catherine Monastery in Sinai. Most of the archaeological artifacts are from the Byzantine era. Archaeologists have excavated a main church, two smaller churches, two wine presses, residential areas, and an administrative building.[360]

God's Self-Revelation at Sinai (continued)

When Israel arrived in front of Mount Sinai, God gave Moses a message that described how He had delivered them from Egypt to Himself at Sinai (Exodus 19). God offered His people a unique relationship in the form of a suzerainty covenant. God said, "Now then, if you will indeed obey My voice and keep My covenant, then you shall be My own possession among all the peoples, for all the earth is Mine; and you shall be to Me a kingdom of priests and a holy nation" (Exodus 19:5-6, NASB).

A suzerainty covenant was a covenant that a strong king (or suzerain) imposed on a weaker neighboring king or kingdom, who agreed to serve and give tribute to the suzerain. The Lord revealed Himself as Israel's Deliverer, Sustainer, Leader, Shepherd, Suzerain, Owner, and God. Now Israel had agreed to serve Him.

Next God revealed His holiness by having the people sanctify themselves for three days and by making a boundary around His holy mountain (Exodus 19:10-17). God gave Israel the threat of capital punishment to emphasize the sanctity of His holiness as something Israel could not break.

God revealed Himself as real and mighty and imminent, when He descended upon Sinai in fearsome glory in a thick cloud with thunder and lightning, fire and smoke, earthquake, and trumpet sound (Exodus 19:18-25).[361]

---

[360] www.en.wikipedia.org/wiki/shivta_national_park.
[361] Eric A. Mitchell, *God's Self-Revelation at Sinai*. Biblical Illustrator, LifeWay: Volume 39, number 3, Spring 2013, 22-25.

ARCHAEOLOGICAL RUINS AT MAMSHIT NATIONAL PARK
Photo courtesy of the Israeli Ministry of Tourism and is solely for this photo only at www.goisrael.com

The city of Mamshit covers ten acres. Mamshit has been reconstructed, although many streets were found in good condition. Originally, there were buildings with open rooms, courtyards, and terraces. Mamshit was built in the 1st century BC as a trading post on the path from Petra to Gaza. The residents raised horses and developed the breeding of Arabian horses. The Western Nile Church had a mosaic floor with birds and a fruit basket. The Eastern Church had a lectern with small marble pillars, and some of the remains can be found. Archaeologists found 10,500 silver coins and other items that appear to have been from wealthy residents.[362]

The area of Mamshit is a 350-acre national park. Mamshit was first settled 2,000 years ago and is located east of Dimona on the main Negev road to Eilat. In modern times, there is a house with a big courtyard with rooms built around it and a three-story tower that can be climbed. Archaeologists found the remains of a stable for sixteen horses. Nomadic Nabateans who founded the town made Mamshit a stop on the Incense Road. They brought frankincense and myrrh out of Arabia to sell on the settlements along the Mediterranean. Mamshit is now on the list of World Heritage Sites.[363]

MAMSHIT NATIONAL PARK, IN NEGEV REGION
Photo courtesy of the Israeli Ministry of Tourism and is solely for this photo only at www.goisrael.com

Another name for Mamshit is Mampsis. Mamshit is the only

---

[362] www.en.wikipedia.org/wiki/mamshit_national_park.
[363] www.goisrael.com/tourism_eng/articles/attractions/pages.

walled city in the Negev. Remains from the Roman period include a military cemetery, Latin inscriptions, and a bronze jug with 10,000 silver drachma and tetradrachma. Some of the buildings are more than 1,000 square meters in size. Some are two or three stories tall, and these structures show that the Nabateans were talented in masonry and stone dressing. From 1965 to 1973, Avraham Negev excavated Mamshit and saw a pile of rubble that turned out to be a second story that collapsed onto the first level. This collapse left the lower level almost all intact. The site now has been excavated.[364]

God's Self-Revelation at Sinai (continued)

God's appearing on Mount Sinai revealed God's power and majesty and instilled fear of God in the people's hearts. God had revealed to Moses that He would reveal Himself in a cloud and allow Israel to hear His voice, so that they would believe Moses forever.

While the people were slaves in Egypt, they had only heard the stories passed down for generations of the God of Abraham, Isaac, and Jacob. They had never seen or known a personal God with power to perform miracles. It was important at Sinai for God to reveal Himself as more powerful than Egypt's idols.

Exodus 24 describes a fellowship meal with the elders on Mount Sinai.

Eric A. Mitchell is assistant professor of biblical backgrounds and archaeology at Southwestern Baptist Theological Seminary, Fort Worth, Texas.[365]

MAMSHIT NATIONAL PARK, IN NEGEV REGION

Photo courtesy of the Israeli Ministry of Tourism and is solely for this photo only at www.goisrael.com

The photo included here shows the baptistery of the nearby Eastern Church in Mamshit National Park, designed in the shape of a cross.

Nilos Church is fifty-six by thirty-two feet and has a beautiful mosaic floor with the inscription *Nilos*. This church was probably built

---

[364] www.bibleplaces.com/mampsis.htm

[365] Eric A. Mitchell, *God's Self-Revelation at Sinai*. Biblical Illustrator, LifeWay: Volume 39, number 3, Spring 2013, 22-25.

in the late 4th century. There was a cistern under the courtyard of the church. This cistern received water from a channel outside the city wall, to collect runoff rain from the area's slopes.[366]

The Tradition of the Elders

"Hypocrites" referred to the profane, irreligious, and godless. In the days of Jesus, the Greek word described a play actor or pretender. In Matthew 15:7, Jesus used the forceful word, "hypocrites", to refer to the Pharisees and the scribes. The Pharisees emphasized the meticulous practice of the law. The scribes taught these laws professionally.

In Matthew 15, we learn that a group of Pharisees and scribes traveled all the way from Jerusalem to the Sea of Galilee to confront Jesus. In Matthew 15:2, the Pharisees and scribes accused the disciples of Jesus of not washing their hands before they ate. There is no law about washing hands before you eat in the Mosaic Law or in the Old Testament. The Pharisees and scribes were using a law from a document called the "Tradition of the Elders".

The "Tradition of the Elders" was developed by the religious leaders after the Babylonian Captivity, when some of the Jewish leaders were allowed to return back to Jerusalem. The religious leaders realized that God had punished them with the Babylonian Captivity. They wanted more specific instructions, like washing hands before you eat. The Mosaic Law was, "Keep the Sabbath Day holy" (Exodus 20:8). But beyond the directions not to work on the Sabbath, the Law did not give specific application for every situation relating to the Sabbath that may develop. To avoid future punishment, the people had to obey the law. So the Pharisees decided to expand and further develop things that can or cannot be done on the Sabbath. They wrote what they thought, and not by divine thoughts from God. This explanation of the Sabbath became known as the oral tradition or the "Tradition of the Elders".[367]

The remains of Avdat are on a limestone hill overlooking the desert. About the 4th century BC, Nabatean travelers led their many caravans along the Spice Trail. Another name for Avdat was Oboda, probably named for the Nabatean king, Oboda I. It was a good location, because the ancient roads went from Petra and Eilat and then

---

366 www.bibleplaces.com/mampsis.htm.

367 R. Kelvin Moore, *The Tradition of the Elders.* Biblical Illustrator, LifeWay: Volume 39, number 3, Spring 2013, 26-28.

converged into one road continuing on to the Mediterranean Sea. By the 1st century, Avdat was abandoned, possibly because of the conquest of Alexander Yannai, who interrupted the spice trade. During King Oboda III's reign, Avdat as a whole changed from trading to farming, and later the residents bred goats, sheep, and camels. King Oboda III was buried in Avdat.

The Avdat National Park has a reconstructed Roman villa and a winepress. In the Roman era, each farmer placed his grapes in baskets in the waiting room until his time to pour them into the vat. Then he would stomp on them until the desired amount of grape juice was yielded to later make into wine. The desert hot sun helped to ripen the grapes. The juice was stored in underground caves in cool temperatures. When the Muslims took over Israel, the winemaking stopped, probably because Muslims do not drink wine. The national park has an acropolis which contains a Roman fortress inside a wall, as well as an area of worship. There are also two Byzantine churches with a decorative stone, called the "preaching stone."

Stairs go down to the lower city, where there are hundreds of caves that were used for residential spaces, store rooms, and burial sites. There is also a Roman bathhouse.[368]

Ramon Crater is the largest of the three craters in the Negev.[369] It is a geological feature of the Negev Desert, located at the peak of Mount Negev. The crater is forty kilometers long, two to ten kilometers wide, and 500 meters deep; and it is shaped like an elongated heart. The Ramon Nature Reserve is the largest reserve in Israel.[370]

Snapling is a descent down a rock face using a rope. Climbers use the technique when a cliff or slope is too steep or dangerous to go down without protection. Snapling is also used for maintenance, construction, inspection, and welding. Some areas have fixed anchors for people to use. Otherwise, a person has to make his own anchor with trees or boulders and webbing. Other rope climbing equipment includes nuts, hexes, and spring-loaded camping items. It is safest to use a climbing harness around the waist. Helmets are needed to protect the head area, gloves are needed for the hands, and knee and elbow

---

[368] www.mosaic.ik.net/g-avdat.htm.

[369] www.mosaic.ik.net/g-ramon.html.

[370] www.en.wikipedia.org/wiki/makhtesh_ramon.

pads are needed for protection of the joints. Boots are safest when they have good grips for climbing.[371]

"THE PRISM": GEOLOGICAL FORMATION AT RAMON CRATER, NEGEV

Photo courtesy of the Israeli Ministry of Tourism and is solely for this photo only at www.goisrael.com

This picture shows the prismatic rocks formed by the kind of sand found on beaches. The sand heats up and turns into a liquid. When it cools, it forms rectangular and hexagonal prisms.[372]

The Tradition of the Elders (continued)

At some time between 538 BC and the time of Jesus, some people accepted the oral law (Tradition of the Elders) with the same authority as the original Law that God gave Moses. The Pharisees and the scribes used the Tradition of the Elders to criticize the disciples of Jesus for not washing hands before eating.

Jesus reacted by using the same Tradition of the Elders to point out the hypocrisy of the Pharisees. Jesus used the commandment from Moses, "Honor your mother and your father." The Mosaic Law meant not just to hold parents in high esteem but to care for them financially and in every way. In the time of Jesus, the Tradition of the Elders allowed a person to dedicate food, money, and property to the Lord for use in the temple. The owner was allowed to use this money and property during his lifetime. The Tradition of the Elders allowed the person who dedicated property to the temple to neglect parents by declaring, "Whatever benefit you might have received from me is a gift committed to the temple" (Matthew 15:5, HCSB). You can almost hear the Hebrew say, "I would care for my parents, but I have committed my money and property to the Lord and to the temple and I do not have the financial means to help my parents." Now the Tradition of the Elders gave Hebrews a religious foundation upon which to base the neglect of parents.[373]

---

[371] www.en.wikipedia.org/wiki/abselling.

[372] www.en.wikipedia.org/wiki/makhtesh_ramon.

[373] R. Kelvin Moore, *The Tradition of the Elders*. Biblical Illustrator, LifeWay: Volume 39, number 3, Spring 2013, 26-28.

NEGEV: SQUILL AT SDE TSIN

Photo courtesy of the Israeli Ministry of Tourism and is solely for this photo only at www.goisrael.com

Squill is a common name for Old World bulbous plants of the lily family. The squill is a spring-blooming low herb with deep blue, white, rose, or purple flowers and a leafless stem. This plant is tolerant of both heat and drought. The bulbs are typically collected from the Mediterranean area. The white squill is made into a diuretic and expectorant. The red squill is sold as rat poison.[374]

EIN AVDAT NATIONAL PARK, NEGEV

Photo courtesy of the Israeli Ministry of Tourism and is solely for this photo only at www.goisrael.com

Ein Avdat is at the base of a fifty-foot waterfall. The salty water of the waterfall area contains many plants that are able to survive in salty water. Scholars are puzzled about the origin of this salty water in the waterfall. The region surrounding it is a dry region, and rain does not collect in the ground.[375]

The Negev Desert spans 4,700 miles and represents at least 55 percent of Israel's land area. The Negev is a rocky desert with wadis (dry river beds that bloom briefly after a rain) and craters. Genesis 20 describes Abraham living in the Negev for awhile, near Kadesh. Later, the northern Negev was settled by the tribe of Judah. The southern Negev was inhabited by the tribe of Simeon. Later, all the Negev was part of the Kingdom of Solomon and then the Kingdom of Judah. The modern Negev has a nuclear reactor, petrochemical factories, an oil terminal, closed military

---

[374]   www.answers.com/topic/squill.

[375]   www.bibleplaces.com/nahalzin.htm.

zones, quarries, a toxic waste incinerator, cell towers, a power plant, several airports, a prison, and two rivers of open sewage.[376]

The fruit in the Negev grows in the winter months (October to March). When the prices are the highest, the fruit is shipped to Europe. The fruit includes juicy citrus, creamy avocados, tangy kiwis and litchi, aromatic guavas, succulent mangoes, sweet bananas, honey rich dates, crispy apples, tasty pears, and plump cherries. The climate allows the fruit to be picked out of season. There are special varieties of grapes available to vendors, for making prize-winning red and white wines. Some grapes are grown with saline water, a worldwide first. Farmers also export thousands of tons of oranges, pink and white grapefruits, lemons, pomelos, and tangerines.[377]

Timothy and Paul

We know information about Timothy from the two letters Paul wrote him (First and Second Timothy), plus seven other New Testament books (Acts, Romans, First and Second Corinthians, Philippians, and First and Second Thessalonians). We learn from these references that Timothy was a younger traveling companion who became an assistant in mission work and later turned into a matured co-worker.

Many scholars think that Paul met Timothy on Paul's missionary trip to Lystra (Acts 13:4-14:27). Some Bible scholars think that Paul played a part in Timothy's conversion during that ministry. Acts does not mention Paul helping to convert Timothy. The logical conclusion is that Timothy's Christian mother and grandmother helped Timothy to become a Christian (II Timothy 1:4-5).

We know that Paul and Timothy met in the events of Acts 16:1-3 in Lystra during Paul's second missionary journey. At that time, Timothy was already a Christian and a disciple of the Lord. Acts 16:2 tells us that people thought highly of Timothy. Timothy's father was Greek and his mother a believing Jewish lady. Timothy had not been circumcised as an infant. Paul wanted Timothy to join his missionary travels and insisted Timothy to be circumcised to avoid a negative reaction from Jews in other places. Paul had the missionary philosophy to be "all things to all people, so that [Paul] may by every possible means save some" (I Corinthians 9:22). Within that philosophy, Paul

---

[376] www.en.wikipedia.org/wiki/negev.
[377] www.jewishvirtuallibrary.org/jsource/agriculture/aggrowth.html.
286

included, "To the Jews, I become like a Jew to win Jews" (I Corinthians 9:20). Timothy did go with Paul on his second and third missionary journeys.[378]

MOUNT KARKOM, IN THE NEGEV DESERT

Photo courtesy of the Israeli Ministry of Tourism and is solely for this photo only at www.goisrael.com

Mount Karkom is between Petra and Kadesh Barnea. Italian Israeli archaeologist Professor Emmanuel Anati believes that the biblical Mount Sinai is in Israel and not in Egypt's Sinai Peninsula. Anati published the English edition of *The Riddle of Mount Sinai*. His theory is that Moses received the Ten Commandments from Mount Karkom from the Ramon Crater. He also changes the date to 1,000 years earlier. He deduced that if the account in the book of Exodus is historically correct, it has to be between 2200 and 2000 BC (Jewish tradition lists the year as 1313 BC).

Anati found more than 1,200 artifacts at Karkom, including sanctuaries, altars, rock paintings, and large tablets resembling the Ten Commandments. Anati believes the topography of the Mount Karkom plateau reflects that of the biblical Mount Sinai. He believes the Israelites reached the Arava, because it says in the Bible that they reached Nahal Tzin and moved on to Hebron. He believes the Israelites wandered in the Negev Desert and not the Sinai. Professor Israel Finkelstein from Tel Aviv University, however, said that he could not accept Mount Karkom as the place where Moses received the Ten Commandments. The Catholic Church is beginning to believe Anati's theory and republished his book by changing the title to *The Rediscovery of Mount Sinai*.[379]

---

[378] Jerry Batson. *Timothy and Paul.* Biblical Illustrator, LifeWay: Volume 39, number 3, Spring 2013, 29-32.

[379] www.presentthepast.com/2010/05/mount-sinai-karkom-israel.

ANCIENT ROCK DRAWINGS AT MOUNT KARKOM

Photo courtesy of the Israeli Ministry of Tourism and is solely for this photo only at www.goisrael.com

There is a rustic Mount Karkom overnight campground located on the western slopes of the mountain. Visitors must pre-arrange their overnight visit with the IDF's Southern Command, a military firing range. It is best to climb to the top of Mount Karkom in the early morning, especially at sunrise. The campground offers no water taps, toilets, showers, or electricity. The campground is free of charge and is open all year. It is only accessible to off-road cars, bicycles, or hikers. Mount Karkom is an ancient desert landscape and a sacred mountain.[380]

STRANGE STONES AT MOUNT KARKOM

Photo courtesy of the Israeli Ministry of Tourism and is solely for this photo only at www.goisrael.com

Archaeologist Emanuel Anati brought his findings on Mount Karkom as the mountain of Moses to the Vatican officials. Anati stated that it took the Vatican a few years to accept Mount Karkom as the mountain of Exodus. Anati recalled that three and a half years previously, a priest of high standing wanted to meet with him, and he arrived with a driver and asked Anati many questions. About a year later, a group of theologians from the Catholic Church appeared to Anati to investigate further. Seven theologians sat there for a whole day, and Anati spent four days with them.

Six months before the same interview, a group of theologians arrived to spend four days at Mount Karkom. Vatican publisher Edizioni Messaggero Padova asked Anati to write up his findings. Anati has spent at least forty years in this desert region, just like the Israelites with Moses did. Anati took into account the water supplies and locations of designated tribes.

Dr. Rudolph Cohen believes the Israelites and Moses were among the Middle Bronze nomadic peoples, and Mount Karkom has the greatest collection of Bronze Age artifacts. Some archaeologists date the Exodus to 2000 BC, which many believe is a millennium too early. Anati first saw Mount Karkom in 1954. In 1983, he first suggested that Mount Karkom may be the real mountain of the Exodus.[381]

TIMNA: SOLOMON'S PILLARS, NATURAL FORMATIONS

Photo courtesy of the Israeli Ministry of Tourism and is solely for this photo only at www.goisrael.com

Solomon's Pillars are natural geological formations in Timna. There were copper mines developed by the Egyptians 6,000 years ago. Erosion of sandstone caused by wind and rain make peculiar forms.[382]

Dig Deeper into the Rich History of Israel

Be'er Sheva (Beersheba), Acre, and the Haifa / Mount Carmel area all can be found in the Bible, particularly during the time of the patriarchs and the prophets. Study these scripture passages to read more about these biblical locations.

---

[381] www.moseseditor.blogspot.com/2012/03/vatican-interest-in-israels.

[382] www.sakharov.net/travel/timna.html.

Be'er Sheva (Beersheba):
Genesis 21:22-34
Genesis 26:23-33
Genesis 46:1-7
Joshua 19:1-9
1 Samuel 3:20
I1 Kings 23:1-8

Acre (Acco / Ptolemais):
Judges 1:31-32
Acts 21:6-7

Haifa / Mount Carmel:
1 Kings 18:1-46
I1 Kings 2:19-25
Amos 1:1-2

CHAPTER 10

GOLAN HEIGHTS, GEOGRAPHIC REGIONS, INTERESTING PLACES

MOUNT HERMON, FROM THE GOLAN HEIGHTS

Photo courtesy of the Israeli Ministry of Tourism and is solely for this photo only at www.goisrael.com

Mount Hermon is the highest point in Israel. On a clear day, tourists can see Mount Hermon from the Dead Sea 120 miles away. Mount Hermon is the only mountain in Israel with snow on it in winter and spring. In a few places on the mountain, the snow stays even in summer. Skiing is popular on Mount Hermon.

In Old Testament times, Mount Hermon was the northern limits of the land that God promised to the Israelites: "And we took at that time out of the hand of the two kings of the Amorites the land that was on this side Jordan, from the river of Arnon unto mount Hermon" (Deuteronomy 3:8). In modern times, Israel occupies part of the territory on the slope. The highest slopes of Mount Hermon belong to Lebanon and Syria.

During the summer months, the leftover snow on the mountain turns into water vapor and causes the heavy dew to fall on the mountain while the surrounding area is dry. The psalmist noticed this and compared the dews of Hermon to the harmony that should exist among God's people:

Behold, how good and how pleasant it is for brethren to dwell together in unity! It is like the precious ointment upon the head, that ran down upon the beard, even Aaron's beard: that went down to the skirts of his garments; as the dew of Hermon, and as the dew that descended upon the mountains of Zion: for there the Lord commanded the blessing, even life for evermore. (Psalm 133:1-3)

NIMROD'S CASTLE, ON THE SLOPES OF MOUNT HERMON, LOOKING WEST
Photo courtesy of the Israeli Ministry of Tourism and is solely for this photo only at www.goisrael.com

Nimrod means "castle of the large cliff". It is an ancient fortress on a ridge about 2,600 feet above sea level, built by the nephew of Saladin, Al-Aziz Uthman. It covered the entire ridge by 1230 AD. At the end of the 13th century, the fort began to need repairs. The Ottoman Turks captured it in 1517 and used the fortress as a luxury prison for Ottoman nobles exiled to Palestine. In the late 16th century, it was abandoned and only local shepherds and their flocks used it. In the 18th century, an earthquake damaged it. The Druze called it Nimrod. The fortress is 1350 feet long and 500 feet wide.[383]

Nimrod's Castle covers eight acres. The fortress is named after the biblical hero Nimrod, a hunter who lived on the hill where the castle was built. The castle has secret passages and exits for surprise attacks, windows that look narrow on the outside but are wide on the inside, and real dungeons.[384]

---

[383] www.en.wikipedia.org/wiki/nimrod_fortress.
[384] www.israel-travel-and-tours.com/nimrod-fortress.html.

Timothy and Paul (continued)

Once, Paul had to leave Berea quickly to avoid hostility, and left Timothy with Silas in Berea to continue the ministry. Timothy later joined Paul in Athens (Acts 17:14-15). Paul also sent Timothy to Thessalonica to strengthen and encourage the Thessalonians in their faith (I Thessalonians 3:1-6).

Paul said, "This is why I have sent Timothy to you. He will remind you about my ways in Christ Jesus, just as I teach everywhere in every church" (I Corinthians 4:17).

Another assignment for Timothy was to go with Erastus to an unidentified location in Macedonia as his assistant (Acts 19:22). In Philippians 2:19-24, Paul writes of his intention of sending Timothy to Philippi to gather news for Paul about the spiritual warfare of the believers there.

Paul sent Timothy to serve in Ephesus to "instruct certain people not to teach different doctrine or to pay attention to myths and endless genealogies" (I Timothy 1:3-4).[385]

GAMLA: THE ANCIENT TOWN (LOOKING WEST)
Photo courtesy of the Israeli Ministry of Tourism and is solely for this photo only at www.goisrael.com

The word *gamla* comes from the Arabic word for camel (*gamal*). The "camel" location is on a narrow ridge ten kilometers north of the Sea of Galilee. The ridge is surrounded on three sides by ravines and looks like the back of a camel. The eastern end of the ridge has a high hump, and Gamla was founded on the southern side that resembles a saddle. Bird lovers can watch the eagles nesting in Gamla and on the cliffs.[386]

The city of Gamla was in existence in the Early Bronze Age, about 5,000 years ago. In a fierce fight in Roman times, all 9,000 citizens were killed. Because of this event that took place, Gamla is sometimes called "the Masada of the North".

---

[385] Jerry Batson. *Timothy and Paul.* Biblical Illustrator, LifeWay: Volume 39, number 3, Spring 2013, 29-32.

[386] www.goisrael.com/tourism_eng/tourist.

Historic Gamla was first discovered after 1967, when Israel annexed the Golan region. Gamla was abandoned after 67 AD. One bowl that was discovered was made from imported copper fashioned in the typical Egyptian style. A seal is a device that makes an impression in wax, clay, or paper; its purpose is to authenticate a document. One seal found at Gamla was the earliest seal found in all of Israel.

Excavators also found 600 sickle blades used for harvesting wheat. Additionally, they found basalt mortars for grinding the wheat. In 150 BC, new settlers, probably Babylonian Jews whom the Persian emperor Cyrus allowed to return to Israel, settled in Gamla. The settlement of Gamla prospered under the rule of King Herod, due to tax cuts to the new settlers. During this time in history, olive oil production was an important industry. Gamla also sold oil to the temple in Jerusalem. Rich oil merchants also lived in Gamla in beautiful mansions. The excavation of mansions yielded jewelry, ivory, and bone dice, as well as containers for perfume and makeup and precious stones carved with images of animals or portraits of a woman. This demonstrates the importance of animals and a deity.

The houses were well built, and a recent excavation of a villa revealed a granite facade. Inside, the walls were decorated with geometrical frescoes, due to the Jewish tradition banning pictorial images and in keeping with the second commandment of the Torah. There was a 1st-century synagogue in the eastern part of the town and it has been restored in modern times. The rectangular building faces Jerusalem. The hall has three-stepped benches on the side, with stumps of columns that once supported a tin wooden roof. This was not the first synagogue in Gamla, and archaeologists are searching for an older synagogue.

Near the synagogue were the poorer people of Gamla. Their houses were very close together on terraces; the roof of the second house touched the terrace of the first. The town was protected with a six-meter wall using the foundation of the old Byzantine wall. The Romans in 66 AD wanted to destroy Gamla, because the Zealots (fighting men who wanted to destroy Rome's power) had a breeding nest for troublemakers there. The Jewish commander Josephus wrote that 4,000 citizens died by the Roman sword and 5,000 by falling from the rock.

In modern times, archaeologists discovered ballista stones, found near the wall. The Gamla defenders probably assembled the stones at night to get them ready for throwing at the Romans. Archaeologists found many arrow points, which indicate that the Romans employed many skilled archers. On top of the wall was a lance with a hook, which was probably used to climb over the wall. A rare find was a gold-plated tip of a sword sheath and a silver cheek protector of a war helmet, which may have belonged to Romans.[387]

GOLAN: GAMLA WATERFALL

Photo courtesy of the Israeli Ministry of Tourism and is solely for this photo only at www.goisrael.com

Timothy and Paul (continued)

When Paul praised Timothy for the assignment at Thessalonica, he referred to him as, "our brother and God's coworker in the gospel of Christ" (I Thessalonians 3:2). By calling him "brother", it showed the close spiritual tie that Paul shared with Timothy. By calling him "God's coworker", it witnessed to Timothy's walk with God and his work for God.

When Paul sent Timothy to the church at Corinth, Paul termed him "my dearly loved and faithful son in the Lord" (I Corinthians 4:17). This showed that Paul loved Timothy and esteemed him for his faithfulness to the Lord. Paul thought of him as a son in the ministry.

Paul wrote in his letter to the Philippians, "I have no one else like-minded who will genuinely care about your interests" (Philippians 2:20). In verse 22, Paul wrote, "You know his proven character."

Timothy stood beside Paul as the co-sender but not co-writer of five of Paul's letters to the churches. Paul corresponded with two of his ministry associates, Titus

---

[387]   www.jewishmag.com/40mag/gamla.htm.

and Timothy. In his first letter to Timothy, he addressed him as "my true son in the faith" (I Timothy 1:2). In I Timothy 6:11, Paul termed him "a man of God".

In Second Timothy, Paul wrote Timothy referring to him as "my dearly loved son". When Paul was facing the end of his life in prison, he wanted Timothy to come to see him in Rome. In II Timothy 1:4, Paul wrote, "I long to see you." Paul ended the letter with, "Come to me soon and come before winter." We do not know if Timothy was able to see Paul in time.[388]

GOLAN HEIGHTS: ANCIENT OIL PRESS AT GAMLA

Photo courtesy of the Israeli Ministry of Tourism and is solely for this photo only at www.goisrael.com

GOLAN HEIGHTS: KIBBUTZ ELROM

Photo courtesy of the Israeli Ministry of Tourism and is solely for this photo only at www.goisrael.com

Kibbutz Elrom is about two kilometers west of Mount Hermon at an elevation of 3,440 feet above sea level. Elrom has hot and dry summers and cold and humid winters. The rains begin in September and ends in May. The annual rainfall averages 940 millimeters of rain, in addition to occasional snow. In 2005, the population was 350 people. The economy is agricultural with apples, pears, strawberries, and grapes for wine. The residents also raise cows and chickens for food.[389]

Har Bental has a memorial for the fallen members of the seventy-seventh Israeli brigade. Oz 77 is the name of the memorial and it

---

[388]   Jerry Batson. *Timothy and Paul*. Biblical Illustrator, LifeWay: Volume 39, number 3, Spring 2013, 29-32.

[389]   www.en.wikipedia.org/wiki/el_rom#geography.

means "strength". The memorial has a free vocal recording of the action of the battle.[390]

Lamps: Their Development and Use

The Bible refers to lamps about sixty-five times. We know most about the size and shape of a lamp during biblical times from archaeological excavations and recovered ancient artifacts. Archaeological research teaches us how people made lamps throughout ancient history and in different cultures. Discovering a whole lamp or a piece of a lamp helps archaeologists to date a site and to determine a relative chronological picture of each level or strata excavated there.

The Bible does give a few clues about lamps and their use. People in biblical times used lamps every day as household items (11 Kings 4:10, Job 18:6, Jeremiah 25:10, Matthew 5:15, Mark 4:21, Acts 20:8). Lamps also served as religious appliances in the tabernacle and later in the temple (Exodus 27:20-21, Exodus 30:7-8, 1 Kings 7:49, 2 Chronicles 4:20-21). The lamps used in the temple and the tabernacle were pure gold (Exodus 37:23, 1 Chronicles 28:15, 2 Chronicles 4:20-21).

Household lamps burned olive oil (Matthew 25:3-4), with wicks made of flax (Isaiah 42:3). They used pure oil for tabernacle lamps (Leviticus 24:2). Lamps were put on lampstands in the tabernacle (Exodus 40:4), the temple (1 Kings 7:49), and the home (Matthew 5:15, Luke 11:33).

Lamps required trimming and may not have held enough oil to burn all night (Exodus 27:21, 1 Samuel 3:3, Matthew 25:7-8). The statement that the capable wife's lamp "never goes out at night" (Proverbs 31:18, HCBS) reflects the wife's diligence in keeping enough oil available and in refilling it in the early hours of morning when the oil began to run out.[391]

Lamps: Their Development and Use (continued)

The lamp and its light were a symbol in the Bible, especially in the Book of Proverbs. "The lamp of the righteous delivers bright light, but that of the wicked is snuffed out" (Proverbs 13:9, 20:20, 21:4, 24:20). God's lamp enables the righteous to walk through darkness (Job 29:3; Psalm 18:28, 119:105; Proverbs

390   www.israelguide.blogspot.com/2008/09/mount-bental.htm.
391   Stephen J. Andrews, *Lamps: Their Development and Use.* Biblical Illustrator, LifeWay: Volume 39, number 3, Spring 2013, 33-36.

20:27). David was called the lamp of Israel (2 Samuel 21:17), and God promised him a dynasty that would continue to shine forever (1 Kings 11:36, 11 Kings 8:19).

In the New Testament, John the Baptist was identified as a burning and shining lamp (John 5:35). Jesus declared Himself to be the light of the world (John 8:12) and said that His followers also would be (Matthew 5:14). In the end, the New Jerusalem will need neither sun nor moon. Instead, its lamp will be the Lamb (Revelation 21:23).

Archaeological investigations have discovered many details about the construction and use of early lamps. The first lamps were probably simple stone containers dating to Neolithic times (8000-4500 BC). Later, other Middle Eastern cultures used seashells, including conch shells, to make lamps in Ur found by the late archaeologist Leonard Woolley. Phoenician lamps were found that were made out of gold, silver, copper, and bronze. One unearthed bronze lamp from Ur was shaped like a crocodile.

People made lamps from clay pottery, beginning in the Early Bronze Age (3150-2200 BC). In the beginning, a small flat wheel made common household bowls and made them into a lamp. Middle Bronze Age potters pinched the bowl to form four slight spouts.

Stephen J. Andrews is professor of Old Testament, Hebrew, and archaeology and is director of the Morton-Sears Institute of Archaeology and Anthropology at Midwestern Baptist Theological Seminary, Kansas City, Missouri.[392]

Leaving Israel

Passport Control: It is very important for tourists who are going to Arab countries after touring Israel to request that an Israeli stamp does not appear on their passport. Travelers must make this request before the time of the stamping of passports. As of July 3, 2008, entry stamps on foreign passports are not required. Instead, tourists fill out form 17L, including their personal information, and that form will be stamped by passport control upon entry and exit. That form will not be collected until exiting the airport, and is necessary for collection of tax refunds and for proof of legal entry.

Flight out of Israel: Travelers should arrive to the airport three hours before the departure flight. The passengers must go through a detailed security check. The second step is to arrive at the counter of the airline flight. Passengers and luggage are inspected with modern

---

[392]   Ibid.

security equipment. Then the luggage is checked, and passengers receive a seat number and a boarding pass. At boarding, passengers must show a passport and airline ticket.

Geographic Regions of Israel and Interesting Places

Sharon Plain is part of the plain that borders the Mediterranean Sea. Sharon Plain has fertile, flat land and beautiful scenery. This plain was settled by the Philistines, who had many battles with the Israelites. King David fought the Philistine giant with a slingshot and a few stones. God made a miracle, and David, a little shepherd boy, won because of his faith in God. Joppa is one important city on the Sharon Plain, where the apostle Peter had his vision about accepting Gentiles into the Church (Acts 10:9-29).[393]

The largest city in Sharon Plain is Netanya. The Plain of Sharon is mentioned in the Bible (1 Chronicles 5:16, 27:29; Isaiah 33:9, 35:2; and Isaiah 65:10). The Rose of Sharon is mentioned in Song of Solomon 2:1.[394]

Shephelah is a strip of foothills between the Mediterranean Sea and the Dead Sea. Shephelah means "lowlands". In ancient times, the Israelites fought the Philistines in the Valley of Elah that is located in the Shephelah. David fought Goliath in the Valley of Elah (1 Samuel 17).[395]

Negev means "dry and parched". In Bible times, this desert area was dry due to lack of rainfall and had nothing but scrub bush. In modern times, Israel built irrigation systems that take water to the Negev from the Sea of Galilee. Now the Negev furnishes agricultural products for the entire nation. The patriarchs of the Bible used this area for their sheep.[396]

The **Hill Country** is also known as the Western Mountains, which run north to south across Israel all the way to the Jezreel Valley. The height of the peaks ranges from 1,500 feet to 4,000 feet. Jerusalem was built on the southern peak of these mountains, and the site was chosen

---

[393]   George W. Knight, *The Holy Land*, 11.
[394]   www.en.wikipedia.org/wiki/sharon_plain.
[395]   George W. Knight, *The Holy Land*, 11.
[396]   Ibid., 12.

as the best place to protect the people from attacks. The mother of Jesus lived north of this area in Galilee.[397]

The **Judean Desert** goes from the Negev Region, along the western side of the Dead Sea, northward to Jericho. This area is also known as the Wilderness of Judah. This area may have been where Jesus was tempted (Mark 1:12-13).[398]

The **Jezreel Valley** was important in Bible times, with economic and military roles. Megiddo is a key city in the Jezreel Valley. Armageddon means "mountain of Megiddo". Revelation describes the last battle on earth as being in the Megiddo area (Revelation 16:16, 20:1-10).[399]

Galilee: In New Testament times, the Romans divided Israel into three sections: Galilee, Judea, and Samaria. The Roman region of Galilee went from the high mountains in the northern section to sloping hills and fertile valleys in the southern part of the region.[400]

The **Dead Sea** is a mineral-filled lake that gets water from the Jordan River and other smaller streams in the Negev. It is unusual in that this lake never lets out any water to go to the ocean as a normal lake does. The hot sun evaporates the water as fast as it goes in. For centuries, this lake collected salt and minerals and turned into stagnant water, and no living things can survive in the lake. The Dead Sea is 1,300 feet below sea level and is the lowest point in the whole world.[401]

Wildernesses South of the Dead Sea

Wilderness of Paran: Hagar and Ishmael wandered around in this wilderness after they were sent away (Genesis 16:4-12).[402]

Wilderness of Zin: This wilderness is around Kadesh, southwest of the tip of the Dead Sea. Miriam, the sister of Moses, died in this wilderness (Numbers 20:1). This is where the people of Israel complained that they had no good water. God told Moses to ask a rock for water, but Moses disobeyed God and struck the rock without giving

---

[397]   Ibid., 11.
[398]   Ibid., 13.
[399]   Ibid.
[400]   Ibid.
[401]   Ibid., 14.
[402]   Ibid., 28.

credit to God. Water did gush out of the rock for the people (Numbers 20:7-12).[403]

Kadesh: Between the Wilderness of Paran and the Wilderness of Zin is where the Israelites camped during the Exodus. Excavations have been done in this area and have found fragments of pottery engraved with Hebrew writing, which links them to the Exodus period. From this area, Moses sent out scouts to check the area concerning the crops and the people who lived there. The scouts reported that the land was fertile with many crops, but the people of Canaan were in walled cites and had to be fought (Numbers 13:1-6, 13:21-29). The people lost faith in God and grumbled. God punished them by making them wander in the nearby wildernesses for forty years (Numbers 14:20, 22-23, 34-35). Kadesh is a wilderness site sixty miles southwest from the southern tip of the Dead Sea. Kadesh also is called Kadesh-Barnea.

Mount Hor is an unidentified mountain near Kadesh. Aaron, the brother of Moses and the first priest of the Israelites, died at Mount Hor (Numbers 20:28-29). The Bible implies that Mount Hor is close to Kadesh (Numbers 20:22).[404]

Sodom and Gomorrah: Sodom means "burnt" and Gomorrah means a "ruined heap." Sodom and Gomorrah were twin cities on the western shore of the Dead Sea. God destroyed Sodom and Gomorrah for their sinful ways, with fire and burning sulfur from the sky (Genesis 19:24). Enormous piles of sulfur, asphalt, and salt exist in this area in modern times. Sodom and Gomorrah were two cities of the "cities of the plain". Three other cities of the plain were Admah, Zeboiim, and Zoar (Genesis 14:2). In this area is a rock formation that is named "Lot's Wife", after Lot's wife who disobeyed God and looked back on the destroying of her town and turned into a pillar of salt (Genesis 19:26).[405]

Zoar is a village south of the tip of the Dead Sea. God spared Zoar because Lot asked if he could settle there instead of the mountains (Genesis 19:17-22). Moses led the Israelites right up to the borders of Canaan and looked out over Canaan from Mount Nebo. God would not let Moses enter the Promised Land.[406]

---

[403]   Ibid.

[404]   Ibid., 31.

[405]   Ibid., 33.

[406]   Ibid., 34.

Ezion-geber and Elath: Ezion-geber means "backbone of a man". Elath means "palm grove". These two towns are close together on the Gulf of Aqaba. In modern times, these two sites are as far south as you can go in Israel before reaching the borders of Egypt and Jordan. Ezion-geber was one of the campsites of the Israelites (Numbers 33:35-36). During Solomon's time, Ezion-geber was the center of a copper mining and smelting industry. Archaeologists found evidence of smelting furnaces dating back to Solomon. Solomon stationed a fleet of ships on the Gulf of Aqaba close to these two cities. Solomon made a trade alliance with King Hiram of Tyre to export and import goods (1 Kings 9:26-28). Today, this area of Israel has turned into the resort town of Eilat.[407]

Mount Nebo: God had promised Moses that he could view the land of Canaan but could not enter it (Numbers 20:6-12). Christians and Jews believe that Moses died on Mount Nebo. Excavations have produced evidence that a Christian church was built on this mountain in 394 AD. In modern times, there is a modern church building called the Memorial Church of Moses and an active Catholic Franciscan order. There is a platform on Mount Nebo with a modern snake-like sculpture in the form of a cross, which represents the pole Moses held up in the wilderness to cure the snake bites that God had inflicted on the Israelites for disobedience (Numbers 21:4-9). Underneath the sculpture are the words that Jesus said to Nicodemus, "As Moses lifted up the bronze snake in the wilderness, so the Son of Man must be lifted up" (John 3:14). On Mount Nebo there is a group of springs called the "Springs of Moses". J.W. McGarvey camped by the springs during a visit to Israel in the 1800's. Mr. McGarvey observed that Moses and the Israelites may have drunk water from these springs. The Bible says that Moses was as strong as ever when he died on Mount Nebo (Deuteronomy 34:1-7).[408]

West of the Dead Sea to the Mediterranean Sea: This section of land, west of the Dead Sea, played an important role in Bible times. The area closest to the Mediterranean Sea was the home of the Philistines. The Philistines defeated Saul the first king of Israel. David eventually conquered them and took over their land. Along

---

[407] Ibid., 35.
[408] Ibid., 36-37.

the lower part of the Dead Sea, David hid from King Saul who tried to harm David. Abraham wandered from place to place in this area, digging wells for his sheep and goats. God promised all of this land to Abraham and his descendants. But the only land Abraham owned was a burial plot at the cave of Machpelah near Hebron.[409]

Arnon River means "roaring stream". It is a stream originating in Jordan and running into the Dead Sea on the eastern side. The Arnon River runs through what used to be Moabite territory. Moses led the people of Israel through the Arnon River into the land of the Moabites (Numbers 21:10-13). Near this river, the soothsayer Balaam met Balak, King of Moab (Numbers 32:36). Balak hired Balaam to curse the people of Israel, but Balaam blessed the people of Israel three different times instead. The Lord prevented Balaam from cursing Israel. The modern name for the Arnon River is Wadi-el-Mujib. Minutes before emptying into the Dead Sea, it becomes a raging torrent as its waters are coerced into a narrow ravine.[410]

Herodium is named for Herod the Great and is a fortress about eight miles west of the Dead Sea. In 2007, archaeologists discovered Herod the Great's tomb. Herod ruled from 37 BC to 4 BC. Herod was the king who tried to destroy the newborn "King of the Jews" by killing all the male babies born around Bethlehem (Matthew 2:13-16). Herod was always trying to get rid of anyone who was a threat to him. He even executed one of his wives and their two sons. He built Herodium as a place for relaxing and as a place of security to run to and to hide from enemies. Herodius also strengthened the fortresses of Masada and Machaerus. Herodius built a seven-story palace in Herodium, surrounded by a big wall. Below the palace he built a Roman garden, several administrative buildings, and a lake. Herod's engineers designed an aqueduct to bring water from nearby Bethlehem. They also used cisterns for collecting rain water. Herod also had a palace in Jerusalem, but he wanted to be buried at Herodium. The historian Josephus wrote about Herod's funeral in *Antiquities of the Jews*:

After this, they betook themselves to prepare for the king's funeral and Archelaus (Herod the Great's son) omitted nothing of magnificence therein. He

---

[409] Ibid., 40-42.
[410] Ibid., 48.

brought all the royal ornaments to augment the pomp of the deceased. There was a bier all of gold embroidered with precious stones and a purple bed of various contexure with the dead body under it, covered with purple, and a diadem was put on his head and a crown of gold above it, and a scepture in his right hand. And the body was carried 200 furlongs to Herodium where he had given orders to be buried.

For 150 years, archaeologists searched for signs of the tomb of Herod. Finally in 2007, diggers found a vault fit for a king. The slab was a pink ornamented limestone burial chamber. Scholars believe this was where King Herod was buried. The ornate coffin had been shattered into many pieces, and the treasures and a few bones were not there. Scholars attribute the destruction of the site to Jewish nationalists who occupied the site seventy years after Herod's death.[411]

Machaerus is a fortress on the eastern shore of the Dead Sea. Herod rebuilt the fortress and made it stronger. In 4 BC, when Herod died, his son Herod Antipas inherited the territory east of the Jordan River in what is now Jordan. Herod Antipas ruled from 4 BC to 39 AD and is the Herod who beheaded John the Baptist. Historian Flavius Josephus believed that John the Baptist was beheaded at Machaerus (Matthew 14:3-11). The Roman army destroyed this fortress in 72 AD during a Jewish revolt, and it was never rebuilt. Excavations have found the ruins of a large courtyard, ritual bath, and the aqueduct that brought water to the fortress.[412]

Masada is a mountaintop fortress near the western shore of the Dead Sea. Masada is not mentioned in the Bible. Flavius Josephus tells us the story of Masada. Flavius Josephus was born in 37 AD and died about 100 AD. He was a Jewish writer who wrote *Antiquities of the Jews* and *The Jewish War*. He was an eyewitness to the events he wrote about, especially the Herod dynasty in Israel during his lifetime. Josephus wrote about the attack of 15,000 Roman troops marching to Masada, where they spent months building an enormous ramp with rock and dirt to walk up one side of Masada to attack it. The Jewish rebels burned their buildings and food supplies and chose suicide over being tortured by the Romans.[413]

---

[411] Ibid., 47-49.
[412] Ibid., 49-50.
[413] Ibid., 51-53.

Ein-Gedi is one of two fresh water streams that bubble up by the Dead Sea before running down the cliff to join the salt water of the Dead Sea. Once when David was hiding from King Saul in a cave, Saul accidentally went inside the same cave in a different spot. David saw King Saul, sneaked up on him and cut off a small piece of Saul's robe. King Saul left the cave, not knowing David had been in the same cave. David, from the security of a cliff above, yelled to the king and held up part of his robe to let King Saul know that David could have killed him in that cave (1 Samuel 24:1-4). Centuries later, William Tristram in the 1800's visited this area and went inside a cave. He then understood why King Saul did not see David in the same cave. The cave was very dark inside and it was not light enough for him to see David. But David had been in that cave for a long time and his eyes had adjusted to the darkness, allowing him to see the king while being undetected himself.[414]

Cave of Adullam: Sometimes David and his men hid from Saul in this cave also. The Bible mentions this cave in 1 Samuel 22:1-2, 2 Samuel 23:13, and 1 Chronicles 11:15. The location of this cave has not been identified yet. David's forces grew from only a handful to 400 men at this site.[415]

Carmel means "fruit garden". Carmel is a city about seven miles south of Hebron. Nabal, a stubborn, wealthy sheepherder, refused to provide food for David and his 400 men (1 Samuel 25:2-13). David was so angry that he took his men to fight Nabal. The wife of Nabal, Abigail, brought food for the hungry men. Abigail told David he had the wrong attitude toward her husband. Nabal then had a stroke after he heard the news that David had come close to hurting him. Nabal died ten days later. David then asked Abigail to marry him (1 Samuel 25:36-39). The site of Carmel today is known as Khirbet, meaning "ruins", or El-Kermel. Visitors can see ruins of churches and a huge castle that was built years after the time of David.[416]

The **Valley of Elah** is near the ancient city of Gath. David, the young shepherd-boy, faced Goliath with just a slingshot and a few stones. David was not afraid and trusted God to help him fight the giant. David's bravery inspired King Saul and his army, and they fought hard and defeated the Philistines. In David's time, this valley

---

[414]   Ibid., 53-54.

[415]   Ibid., 55.

[416]   Ibid., 58-59.

marked the territory between Israel and the Philistines. The two armies encamped on separate hills, with the valley between them for days until the giant challenged King Saul to send out one warrior to fight him. David accepted the challenge (1 Samuel 17:1-11, 48-50). The brook that David took the rocks from is still active with water in this valley today. The modern name of the stream is Wady es-Sunt, and it has water in the winter months and dries up in the summer. Tourists like to pick up small rocks from this stream to take home as souvenirs.[417]

Ashkelon means "migration" and is a city on the coast of the Mediterranean Sea. In the days of Saul and David, Ashkelon was in the middle of Philistine territory. The main Philistine cities were Ashkelon, Ashdod, Ekron, Gath, and Gaza (1 Samuel 6:17). Samson killed thirty Philistines at Ashkelon and took their clothes to give to thirty of his friends. Samson bet that people could not guess his riddle about a dead lion that he killed with his hands (Judges 14:8-19). Archaeologists and their excavations proved that Ashkelon was destroyed and rebuilt several times. It was inhabited by Canaanites, Philistines, Israelites, Persians, and Romans. Ashkelon was an important trade center due to the natural harbor and its location on the road from Egypt to Mesopotamia. These ruins can be visited today in Ashkelon National Park. Modern Ashkelon has a population of at least 100,000 people.[418]

Ashdod means "fortune". Modern Ashdod has more than 200,000 people living in the city and is one of the larger cities of Israel. Modern Ashdod is on the Mediterranean Sea and was a planned city in 1956. Ashdod has a large port used to import and export goods. The ruins of Ashdod are located nearby. 1 Samuel 4:10-11 describes the Philistines capturing the Ark of the Covenant and taking it to Ashkelon. It was put on display in the temple of Dagon to show that Dagon was stronger and better than the Israeli God. The next day, they were surprised to see Dagon bowing before the Ark of the Covenant (1 Samuel 5:3-8).[419]

Gath means "winepress". Gath is about twenty miles from Ashkelon. Scholars believe the descendants of the giant Anak lived here during Old Testament times. When Moses sent out scouts to check out the land, the scouts reported about the tall giants that made them feel like the size of grasshoppers (Numbers 13:32-33). About

---

[417]   Ibid., 59-60.
[418]   Ibid., 61-62.
[419]   Ibid., 63-64.

300 years later, a boy named David faced a nine-foot giant with only a sling and a few stones, not far from David's home of Bethlehem. David succeeded because he called upon the name of God, the God of the armies of Israel. Biblical Gath is identified with Tel es-Safi, where an archaeological excavation has been going on for years. Archaeologists found remains of a piece of pottery with a name similar to Goliath, and they named it the "Goliath Shard". This shard does not prove that Goliath was there, but it does prove that the people were there in David's time (1 Samuel 17:45). Gath is mentioned many times in the Bible.[420]

Gaza means "stronghold". Gaza is a city just inland from the Mediterranean Sea. Gaza is the location of the place where Samson demonstrated his great strength. One time, his enemies thought they had him trapped in the city walls, and to their surprise he ripped the gate and ran fifty miles to Hebron (Judges 16:1-3). Later, Samson's girlfriend, Delilah, betrayed him by telling his enemies that the secret to his strength was his long hair. While Samson slept, the Philistines cut his hair and took him to prison. Eventually his hair grew back, and Samson regained his strength, toppled down the Philistine temple of Dagon, and killed himself and many Philistines (Judges 16:26-30).

Modern violence has taken place between the Jews and the Palestinians at Gaza. Jesus commanded Philip to travel down the desert road from Jerusalem to Gaza (Acts 8:26). On this road, Philip met an Ethiopian man who was talking about the suffering servant from Isaiah. Philip explained to him that Jesus was the suffering servant of Isaiah. The Ethiopian man believed in Jesus and Philip baptized him in a nearby pool (Acts 8:36-37). In modern times, a nearby stream that may be the same pool Philip used is named Philip Springs in memory of Philip. The remains of a Christian church are located near the springs, which indicates that Christians believed it was a sacred place.[421]

Beth-Shemesh means "house of the sun" or "temple of the sun". This is a town twelve miles from Jerusalem. This ancient town was on the border between Israel and the Philistine region. Long ago, the ancient inhabitants worshiped the sun god. Joshua captured the town when the Israelites returned home to the Promised Land. The

---

[420] Ibid., 66-67.
[421] Ibid., 68-69.

Philistines captured the Ark of the Covenant, but quickly returned it after its people had sudden diseases and negative occurrences take place around them. To return the Ark of the Covenant to the Israelites, the Philistines loaded it on a cart pulled by cows. Amazingly, the cows took the Ark of the Covenant back to Beth-Shemesh to the Israelites (1 Samuel 5:1-12, 6:10-15).

After Israel was divided into two kingdoms, Beth-Shemesh was involved in the fight between King Amaziah of Judah and King Jehoash of Israel. King Amaziah sent King Jehoash a cryptic message which said, "Come and meet me in battle." King Amaziah's forces were defeated by King Jehoash, and Jerusalem's treasures were looted (I1 Kings 14:8-14). Excavations of Beth-Shemesh uncovered remains of the city from the time of Judges. Archaeologists found a big iron workshop that operated during the time of David. They also found an underground reservoir to provide water for the people. In 1950, the modern town of Beth-Shemesh was built. It has grown to a population of 50,000 people from immigrants from Africa, Ethiopia, Russia, and European nations.[422]

Zorah is about fifteen miles from Jerusalem. The ruins of the ancient city of Zorah is now called Tel Zora. Samson was born in Zorah (Judges 13:24, 16:31). Visitors can climb the mound that is identified as Samson's tomb. On the mound is a special rock called the Altar of Manoah. Scholars believe this is where the father of Samson offered a sacrifice to God when he was told his barren wife would have a son (Judges 13:19-24, 16:31).[423]

Timna means "allotted portion". It is an unidentified city in southern Israel. Many events happened around Timna in Samson's adventures. Samson wanted to marry a girl from the city (Judges 14:1-4). Samson killed a lion with his bare hands near Timna (Judges 14:5-7). Samson told thirty friends a riddle about a lion in this area (Judges 14:10-15). Samson killed thirty Philistines near Timna to pay his friends who guessed the riddle (Judges 14:16-19). Samson later burned the crops of the Philistines near Timna (Judges 15:3-5). Samson also killed a thousand Philistines with the jawbone of a donkey (Judges 15:14-17).[424]

---

[422] Ibid., 70-71.
[423] Ibid., 72.
[424] Ibid., 73.

Lachish: Archaeologists believe from their excavations that Lachish was inhabited at least three centuries before Joshua and the Israelites (about 1400 BC). Joshua killed all the people in Lachish (Joshua 10:31-33). Evidence indicates that Lachish remained uninhabited 400 years after the time of Joshua. Solomon's son, King Rehoboam, rebuilt Lachish and fortified it with a thick wall (2 Chronicles 11:5-12). King Jehoshaphat of Judah, in about 931-913 BC, built an enormous outer wall eighteen feet thick and fourteen feet high. Both walls had big gates.

In 701 BC, when King Sennacherib of Assyria invaded the Kingdom of Judah during King Hezekiah's reign, Lachish and other cities in southern Judah were captured by King Sennacherib. To protect Jerusalem, King Hezekiah offered to pay a lot of protection money if King Sennacherib would leave Jerusalem alone (I1 Kings 18:14-16). King Sennacherib took the money and prepared to attack Jerusalem anyway, but the Lord struck the Assyrian army with a mysterious sickness that killed thousands of their men, and King Sennacherib withdrew the Assyrian army (I1 Kings 19:35-36). King Sennacherib put the events of the attacks on Lachish on a stone slab and mounted it in his palace in the capital city, Nineveh.

In the 1800's, archaeologists unearthed this stone slab. The slab showed the siege ramps that the Assyrians used on the double walls to take over the city. The archaeologists found a note from King Sennacherib that bragged, "I besieged and conquered (forty-six walled cities of Judah) by stamping down earth ramps and then by bringing up battering rams, by the assault of foot soldiers, by breaches and tunneling. Young and old, male and female, were the spoils of war. Hezekiah, the Jew (in Jerusalem), was shut up like a caged bird within Jerusalem, his royal city." King Sennacherib had nothing to say about the mysterious disease that killed many of his men quickly. Several years after the attacks, two of his sons killed him, and a third son, Esarhaddon, became the new king (I1 Kings 19:35-37). Lachish today is thirty miles west of the Dead Sea.[425]

Gerar means "halting place" or "lodging place". It is about fifteen miles west of Beersheba. Genesis 20:1 describes Abraham entering Canaan at Gerar about 2000 BC. In modern times, archaeologists excavated a site identified as Gerar, but evidence shows that this site

---

[425]   Ibid., 74-75.

first existed about 1200 BC, about 800 years later than Abraham's time. Scholars believe that at the time of Abraham it may have been just a crossroads settlement. In Gerar, Abraham and Isaac pretended their wives were their sisters so that Abimelech would not kill them to get their wives. Beautiful Sarah and Rebekah were put into Abimelech's harem. King Abimelech discovered the truth, released Sarah and Rebekah, and scolded Abraham and Isaac for lying to him (Genesis 20:1-16, 26:1-11).

Many scholars think that the Philistines did not settle in Palestine until 800 years after Abraham's time. Other scholars say that maybe the Philistines arrived in the area in two distinctive waves: the first one before Abraham arrived and the second one about eight centuries later. One known fact is that Gerar is located in the Negev, a hot and dry area. In this area, Abraham and Isaac traveled in tents from place to place, just like some of the Bedouins do in modern times. After Abraham's death, Isaac and the Philistines argued over ownership of wells (Genesis 26:17-22).[426]

Beersheba means "well of the seven" or "well of an oath". Beersheba is located midway between the southern section of the Dead Sea and the Mediterranean Sea. Modern Beersheba has a population of about 200,000 people and is located not far from the ruins of the ancient city. Abraham, Isaac, and Jacob lived in the Negev area due to good grazing areas for the sheep and goats. There was not much surface water, but they dug wells to provide water.

When Abraham first settled there, Abimelech's men used the water too much from the new well that Abraham dug. Abimelech and Abraham pledged that both of them would live together as friends and share the water supply. The oath was sealed by Abraham giving Abimelech seven lambs from his flocks. That is where Beersheba got its name and meaning (Genesis 21:22-33). The tamarisk tree that Abraham planted by the well is similar to an oak tree. Abraham also built an altar and knelt down to worship the Lord (Genesis 21:34). Visitors can see a tamarisk tree beside a well at the site of the ruins. Ancient Beersheba is known today as Tel es-Saba. The Negev Museum

---

[426]   Ibid., 76-77.

has artifacts of this area. Bedouins have lived in this area for hundreds of years.[427]

Hebron is a city about twenty miles west of the middle section of the Dead Sea. Hebron means "alliance". Excavations show that Hebron was inhabited before the pyramids were built in Egypt. When Abraham lived there in 2000 BC, Hebron was already a thousand years old. When Sarah died, Abraham did not own any property or have a burial plot. Abraham was interested in buying a plot of land nearby that had a cave in it owned by a man named Ephron (Genesis 23:10-18). Abraham's burial plot is known as Machpelah (Genesis 25:7-10). Isaac, Rebekah, Jacob, and Leah were also buried in the plot (Genesis 49:29-33).

In modern times, an Arab town, el-Khalil, is built around the burial plot. The spot above the cave is enshrined by a mosque. The entire area is surrounded by a big wall. Herod the Great built the lower part of the wall. Visitors are allowed to tour the mosque and the tomb. Muslim tradition says that the bones of Joseph are buried in this cave. The Bible indicates that the bones of Joseph were buried in Shechem after he died in Egypt (Joshua 24:32). Hebron was David's capital the first seven and a half years of his reign (2 Samuel 2:1-4). All the tribal leaders met in Hebron and declared David to be king (2 Samuel 5:1-5). Absalom plotted against his father, King David, in Hebron. Modern Hebron has about 150,000 people, mainly Arabs and a few Jewish families.[428]

Mamre means "firmness" or "lusty". Mamre is about two miles northeast of Hebron. Mamre is now an Arab city named Ramet el-Khalil. This area is where Abraham sat at the entrance of his tent when he found out that Sarah was going to have a son. Three strangers suddenly appeared at his tent entrance. Abraham fed them a good meal (Genesis 18:11-14). When Abraham lived in Mamre, he discovered from the Lord that Sodom and Gomorrah were going to be destroyed because of their wickedness (Genesis 18:23-33). At one point in the history of Mamre, there was a pagan shrine. It was torn down to put up a church that is now in ruins.[429]

---

[427] Ibid., 78-79.
[428] Ibid., 80-81.
[429] Ibid., 76.

Arad means "fugitive". Arad is about ten miles west of the southern tip of the Dead Sea. The Israelites under the leadership of Joshua defeated the warriors of Arad (Joshua 12:7-14, 24). Before the Israelites crossed into the Holy Land, the King of Arad tried to prevent them (Numbers 21:1-3). Excavations at the site did not find any evidence of the time of Joshua. Scholars believe Arad may have been destroyed and abandoned long before the Exodus. Arad was later rebuilt as a Jewish city in David's time. Yatir Forest is near Arad. It is unusual to have a desert and a forest so close together.[430]

The **Valley of Eshcol** means "cluster" or "cluster of grapes". This valley is famous for good grapes. The scouts Joshua sent out brought Joshua a handful of grapes to show how fertile the land was. This is an unidentified valley around Hebron (Numbers 13:21-24). Sitting under a grapevine or under a fig tree was a symbol of peace and prosperity (Micah 4:4).[431]

Tekoa means "trumpet blast." Tekoa is a city ten miles south of Jerusalem. Tekoa was built close to the Judean Desert on a mountain 2,800 feet above sea level. On top of this mountain, a person can enjoy the view of the Mount of Olives. In ancient times, the people of Tekoa could warn the people of the Mount of Olives and Jerusalem that an attack force was heading towards them. In the time of the Bible, trumpets were often played loudly to warn that enemies were coming and that it was time to go to the battle stations. The playing trumpets gave them the nickname "trumpet blasting".

The Lord asked Jeremiah to blow a trumpet and tell the people, "Run for your lives, you people of Benjamin! Get out of Jerusalem! Sound the alarm in Tekoa! A powerful army is coming from the north, coming with disaster and destruction" (Jeremiah 6:1). The prophet Amos lived in Tekoa. Amos was a shepherd from the southern kingdom of Judah. God called Amos to take a special message of judgment to the people of the northern kingdom. A priest in the northern kingdom told Amos he was out of his jurisdiction and rejected his warning to the northern kingdom. A military officer of King David, Joab, called a smart lady from Tekoa to Jerusalem. The lady tried to talk King David into patching up his relationship with his

---

[430] Ibid., 83.
[431] Ibid., 84.

son Absalom (2 Samuel 14:1-24). Eventually, Absalom tried to take away the kingship from David his father (2 Samuel 15:13-14).[432]

Sites around Jerusalem

Bethphage means "house of unripe figs". Bethphage is about two miles south of Jerusalem. This town is remembered by a famous donkey, because Jesus sent two disciples to find a donkey there (Luke 19:31, 34). The actual site of Bethphage is unknown, but tradition places it on the Mount of Olives near the town of Bethany. This traditional place has a Catholic Franciscan chapel known as the Church of Bethphage. At this site is a picture of Jesus riding a donkey and the crowds placing palm leaves on the road. Near the site is a large rock that Jesus stood on to climb up on the donkey. The ride of Jesus on the back of the donkey to Jerusalem fulfilled prophecy (Zechariah 9:9, Matthew 21:5, John 12:15).[433]

Gibeah means "hill". Gibeah is a city about three miles northwest of Jerusalem. King Saul was born in Gibeah in the tribe of Benjamin (1 Samuel 10:1-26, 15:34). Most scholars believe it is the ruins of Gibeah that are known today as Tel el-Ful. Archaeologists uncovered the remains of four fortresses. Other tribes of Israel may have destroyed them during a civil war with Benjamin (Judges 20:12-48). Above these ruins was a later fortress that may have been built by King Saul to fight the Philistines. Josephus, the Jewish historian, said the Roman army camped here in 70 AD on the night before they attacked Jerusalem.[434]

Nob is an unidentified town two miles from Jerusalem. King Saul ordered the killing of eighty-five priests who lived in Nob because one of them had assisted David and his men when they ran from Saul's anger (1 Samuel 22:19). Abimelech, one of the priests, gave food to David and his men. Abimelech also gave David the sword he had previously used to kill the giant, Goliath, to use again in his defense (1 Samuel 21:6-9). Abimelech gave David the showbread from the tabernacle. About a thousand years later, Jesus cited the principle of human need versus rituals. Jesus used Abimelech as an example of acting in response to human need. The Pharisees at the time had

---

432   Ibid., 85.
433   Ibid., 160.
434   Ibid., 161.

criticized Jesus for harvesting grain on the Sabbath to feed his hungry disciples (Mark 2:27).[435]

Michmash means "a hidden place". Michmash is about seven miles northeast of Jerusalem. King Saul's son Jonathan and his armor bearer climbed up the steep cliff of Michmash and killed the Philistine sentry there. That made the entire army of Philistines to go into a panic and enabled King Saul to be victorious over them. It was a very brave action for only Jonathan and his armor bearer to accomplish so much (1 Samuel 14:1-23). Jonathan and David became friends because both were smart and depended on the Lord (1 Samuel 20:9-17). After King Saul and Jonathan were killed by the Philistines, David composed a song of sorrow named "Song of the Bow".[436]

Anathoth means "answered prayer". This town is three miles from Jerusalem. Jeremiah was born in Anathoth about 647 BC to Hilkiah, a priest (Jeremiah 1:1). God called twenty-one-year-old Jeremiah to take a message to the sinful people who had left the worship of the Lord to turn to idols. Jeremiah's message was for the people to turn back to God or face being taken over by other cities and countries. Jeremiah's message was preached for forty years. The priests did not like Jeremiah's message from God, and they criticized him and called him disloyal to Israel. Jeremiah was arrested and thrown into jail two times. Once, he was abandoned in a cistern with a layer of mud on the bottom. Luckily, one official sneaked back to Jeremiah, took him out of the cistern, and put him in a regular jail (Jeremiah 38:6-13). As the Babylonian army came closer to Jerusalem, Jeremiah preached a new message from God in 587 BC. The message was not to resist the Babylonians but to go peacefully with them into exile, and that God would return them home in seventy years after their punishment and discipline was over (Jeremiah 29:10-14). Jeremiah's cousin, Hanamel from Anathoth, wanted to see if Jeremiah really believed God would bring them back in seventy years. He asked Jeremiah to buy a plot of land from him. To show his good faith in God's promise, Jeremiah paid for the property with his own money, had witnesses record the transaction, authenticated the deed, sealed the papers in an air-tight jar, and put them in a safe place for storage to last seventy years (Jeremiah

---

[435]   Ibid., 162.
[436]   Ibid., 163.

32:8-15). There is a modern Arabic village of Anata now in this area. Scholars agree that the biblical city where Jeremiah lived is the ruins of Ras el-Kharrubeh.[437]

Emmaus means "warm wells". It is an unidentified city about seven miles from Jerusalem. This is the village where Jesus identified himself, after the resurrection, to two of his disciples who were walking from Jerusalem to their hometown of Emmaus (Luke 24:13-32). Luke did not specify what direction Emmaus was when he wrote about it.[438]

Gibeon means "hilly". Gibeon is about six miles northwest of Jerusalem. The Canaanites in Gibeon tricked Joshua and the Israelites into making a peace treaty with them (Joshua 9:3-6, 12-15). The people of Gibeon convinced Joshua that they were not Canaanites but were from a distant land. Even after the truth was discovered, Joshua had to honor the treaty that Gibeon would not be destroyed. Joshua made an agreement that the people of Gibeon had the job of cutting wood for Israel and carrying water when needed (Joshua 9:26-27). The sun and the moon stood still at Gibeon until Joshua defeated the Amorites (Joshua 10:12-14). At Gibeon, Solomon offered sacrifices and prayed for wisdom before he became king (1 Kings 3:3-15). At the end of the Babylonian exile, the people of Gibeon helped Nehemiah rebuild the walls of Jerusalem (Nehemiah 3:6-8). Archaeologists have identified this city as Tel el-Jib. The Archaeologists have found wine jugs stamped with the name of the city. They also found large underground wine cellars that could store thousands of gallons of wine. It appears that the people of Gibeon marketed wine throughout Israel at one time. They discovered the largest well ever recovered in Israel. It was thirty-seven feet around and it had a depth of eighty-two feet. A tunnel about 180 feet long was used to tap into a spring.[439]

Ramah means "height". Ramah is an unidentified city a few miles north of Jerusalem. The prophet Samuel was born and buried in Ramah (1 Samuel 1:1-2, 1:19-20, 25:1). Hannah, Samuel's mother, dedicated Samuel to God and took him to live with the priest, Eli, in Shiloh at a young age. Samuel grew up to be a priest, prophet, and judge. He lived at a time of Israel's history when they were moving away from a loose tribal confederacy to a centralized rule of a king. The elders of

---

437 Ibid., 164-165.
438 Ibid., 166.
439 Ibid., 167-168.

Israel arrived in Shiloh and demanded that Samuel appoint a king to rule Israel (1 Samuel 8:4-5). Samuel reluctantly appointed Saul as king after he warned the people of the dangers of a kingship (1 Samuel 8:10-18). Samuel traveled from Shiloh to his home in Ramah to Bethel and Gilgal (1 Samuel 7:15-17).[440]

Mizpah means "watchtower". It is about four miles from Jerusalem. Samuel gathered the people in Mizpah to give thanks for the return of the Ark of the Covenant which the Philistines captured earlier (1 Samuel 7:1-6). Near Mizpah, Samuel erected a stone to commemorate an Israelite victory over the Philistines and named it Ebenezer, which means "the stone of help" (1 Samuel 7:10-12). King Asa of Judah, who ruled about 911-869 BC, made Mizpah a defense outpost against invasion from the north (1 Kings 15:22).

Zelah means "slope". Zelah is an identified town close to Jerusalem. Zelah was given to the tribe of Benjamin (Joshua 18:25-28). King Saul and his sons were buried in Zelah in the tomb of Kish, the father of King Saul. After the Philistines killed Saul and his sons in northern Israel, they hung his body on the wall of the city of Beth-shan as an example. But a few brave men from Jabesh-gilead east of the Jordan River took their bodies and took them home to Zelah for burial (1 Samuel 31:11-12).[441]

Ein Kerem means "spring of the vineyard". It is a town about four miles from Jerusalem. John the Baptist was born there. Scriptures about John the Baptist are John 3:28-30, Luke 1:39-40, and Luke 1:57-66. The Church of Saint John the Baptist, a Catholic Franciscan order, has a tall bell tower. Underneath this church is a cave that marks the location where John was born in the home of Zechariah and Elizabeth (Luke 1:13). Inside the church is a painting of the baptism of Jesus in the Jordan River by John (Matthew 3:13-15). Other paintings are the beheading of John the Baptist and the preaching of John the Baptist in the wilderness (Mark 6:14-29, 1:1-8). There is also a Church of Visitation commemorating Mary's visit with Elizabeth. There is a special spring there, where scholars believe Mary stopped to get a drink.[442]

---

[440]   Ibid., 169.
[441]   Ibid., 171.
[442]   Ibid., 172-173.

Cities north of Jerusalem up to Shechem

Joppa means "beautiful". Joppa is a city on the coast of the Mediterranean Sea at the southern end of the Plain of Sharon. Peter believed in the crucifixion and resurrection of Jesus, but he was still a Jew with the belief of kosher and non-kosher food. God sent him a vision to cause a change in his beliefs (Acts 10:9-15). Peter was in Joppa when he had the vision. The vision was not about what food to eat; rather, it was a vision to teach Peter that Gentiles were not second-class citizens. Gentiles were people made in the image of God and were welcome in God's kingdom. A few days later, Peter met with a Gentile, Cornelius; taught him about Jesus; baptized him; and welcomed him as a member of God's kingdom (Acts 10:28, 44-48). From then on, the church was open to all people, no matter the race or national origin.

In Joppa, Peter raised Tabitha, also known as Dorcas, from the dead in the name of Jesus (Acts 9:42). The Russian Orthodox Church of Tabitha's Tomb marks the place where Tabitha was raised from the dead. There is also a Roman Catholic Church of Saint Peter. The original church by this name was built in 1654 on a medieval fortress. This building has been replaced many times, and the current church was built in 1894. Joppa was the only port in Israel in Bible times. The famous Lebanon cedar logs for Solomon's temple came this way to get to Jerusalem (2 Chronicles 2:11-12, 2 Chronicles 16). The prophet Jonah caught a ship at the port of Joppa to run away from God and from His command to go to Nineveh, Assyria. Jonah was tossed overboard into the sea, swallowed by a big fish, and then spat out on the shoreline after three days (Jonah 1:3, 1:17, 2:10). Jaffa and Tel Aviv together have a population of more than 400,000.[443]

Lydda is eleven miles from Joppa. Peter visited Lydda and met a man named Aeneas who had been bedridden for eight years. Peter told him, "Get up, and roll up your sleeping mat!" Aeneas was healed instantly (Acts 9:32). In Old Testament times, Lydda was called Lod. Jews returning from Babylonian exile repopulated it. Lod today has about 75,000 people and is called Lod instead of Lydda. The nearby airport is known as Ben Gurion International Airport. There is also a

---

[443]   Ibid., 176-178.

new museum, the Lod Mosaic Archaeological Center, which opened in 2009. Visitors view mosaic floors discovered throughout Israel. These floors date back to the Roman Period.[444]

Plain of Sharon: This area is known as the coastal plain along the Mediterranean Sea from Joppa to Mount Carmel. One of Solomon's brides compared herself to "the spring crocus blooming on the Sharon Plain" (Song of Solomon 2:1). The prophet Isaiah spoke of a time when the Lord would display His glory with the coming of the Messiah. In this time the deserts of the land of Israel would be as lovely as the Plain of Sharon (Isaiah 35:2). Beautiful wildflowers grew in the plain. Large sections of the Plain of Sharon had large sand dunes and marshland. Drainage projects have transformed it into rich farmland. The Plain of Sharon has about a million people living in the area.[445]

Aphek/Antipatris: When Joshua captured Aphek about 1300 BC, it was already a few centuries old (Joshua 12:18). Centuries later, Herod the Great rebuilt and enlarged it. He renamed it Antipatris in honor of his father, Antipater. The apostle Paul passed through this town when he was transported under Roman guard to Caesarea (Acts 23:31). The ruins of Aphek and Antipatris are off the normal path of tourists. In ancient times, they were located on the main road known as Way of the Sea that ran from Egypt to Syria. At Aphek, the Israelites carried the Ark of the Covenant into battle but the Philistines captured it (1 Samuel 4:1-11). The news was such a big shock to Eli, the priest, that he fell from his seat. Eli broke his neck and died (1 Samuel 4:13-18). The excavated ruins of the town are known as Tel Afek. On top of the ruins are the huge forts that the Ottoman Turks built. Nearby is the Yarkon Park.[446]

Gezer is about twenty-two miles from Jerusalem. It is on the main road between Jerusalem and Joppa. The Canaanites lived in the land until Joshua captured them when the Israelites returned from Egypt (Joshua 12:12). At some time, Gezer became Philistine, but David defeated the Philistines (1 Chronicles 20:4). Egypt gained control of Gezer. King Solomon married the daughter of the Egyptian Pharaoh of Egypt to seal an agreement (1 Kings 9:16). King Solomon rebuilt

---

[444] Ibid., 179.
[445] Ibid., 180.
[446] Ibid., 181-182.

Gezer and fortified the city against its enemies. Excavations began in Gezer in the early 1900's and are still active today. Archaeologists found a huge gate and parts of an ancient wall. The double wall and gate construction is the same as that of Hazor and Megiddo. The site of Gezer today is an Israeli national park.[447]

Jericho means "place of fragrance". Jericho is about twelve miles from Jerusalem. Jericho is also located about eight miles west of the Jordan River. God's plan for capturing Jericho was to march around the city for six consecutive days. On the seventh day, they were to march around the city six times. On the seventh time around the city, they were to shout and blow trumpets or ram's horns. After this loud noise, the walls of Jericho collapsed, making it easy to capture (Joshua 6:12-21). There is no evidence of the ruins of the wall that fell to Joshua. It is likely that this wall was carried off to use it to build something. After Joshua destroyed Jericho, he put a curse on it. (Joshua 6:26). Centuries later, a man named Hiel tried to rebuild Jericho. Suddenly both of his sons died (1 Kings 16:34).

A new city of Jericho was built by the Romans a few miles from Old Jericho. Herod the Great built a winter palace there. Archaeologists found gardens and sunken pools around the winter palace. This city is known as the New Testament town of Jericho. Jesus healed blind Bartimaeus and saw Zacchaeus, the tax collector, there (Mark 10:49-52, Luke 19:1-10). This Jericho was the setting for the parable of the Good Samaritan (Luke 10:30-37). In fact, along the ancient road today is the Inn of the Good Samaritan (Luke 10:34-35). The ancient inn has been turned into a museum called the Museum of the Good Samaritan. There is also a third Jericho, called Eriha, built about a mile east of the Old Testament Jericho. There is a spring called Ein es-Sultan or Elisha's Spring. This is where the prophet Elisha turned the bad water of the spring to good water for the people of this city (11 Kings 2:19-22).[448]

Ai means "the ruin". This is an unidentified town ten miles west of Jericho. The men with Joshua thought that Ai would be easy to conquer (Joshua 7:3). They were not expecting to retreat in an embarrassing run. They wondered why God was not with them in this battle. Then

---

[447] Ibid., 183-184.
[448] Ibid., 184-186.

they discovered that a man named Achan had disobeyed God and kept some of the "spoils of war" and hid them in his tent. Achan and his family were put to death for disobeying (Joshua 7:24-26). Most archaeologists identify Ai with the city of et-Tel. Evidence from these digs shows that a city existed on this site several centuries before the time of Joshua, and that another was built after his time. But the archaeologists have not discovered the city at the time of Joshua. Skeptics say that it was made up and never happened. Believers say that other difficulties of the past are eventually solved with new archaeological findings that prove and support the evidence.[449]

Gilgal means "circle of stones" or a "wheel". Gilgal is about two miles northeast of Jericho. The Israelites and Joshua encamped a few years at Gilgal in tents as they fought the Canaanites. Eventually, they settled in towns and had houses to live in. The Israelites had crossed the Jordan River on dry land. At Gilgal they set up a memorial of the crossing of the Jordan River by setting up stones (Joshua 4:19-24). At Gilgal, Joshua circumcised all male Israelites to signify their covenant with the Lord (Joshua 5:2-8). At Gilgal, they also had their first Passover celebration in the Holy Land (Joshua 5:10). King Saul's coronation was in Gilgal (1 Samuel 11:15).

Once, King Saul became impatient while waiting for Samuel to arrive at Gilgal to perform the sacrifice ceremony before the troops went to battle. So Saul performed the sacrifice himself, although only the priest was authorized to do so. Samuel rebuked King Saul and informed him that because of this action, another person had been selected to take his place (1 Samuel 13:7-14). David was then selected to replace King Saul. Later, some sad events happened here in David's personal life. When David fled from his son Absalom, the people of Gilgal welcomed him back. Absalom was then killed by David's troops when he tried to take over the throne in David's place (2 Samuel 18:31-33).[450]

Beth-Horon means "house of hollowness". These were twin towns with an upper and lower area, eight miles northwest of Jerusalem. The names of these two towns were upper Beth-Horon and lower Beth-Horon. The upper city was 800 feet above the lower city. Both

---

[449]   Ibid., 187-188.
[450]   Ibid., 188-190.

cities were on opposite sides of a deep valley, on the old road between Jerusalem and Joppa. Both towns were fortified as outposts to protect Jerusalem. Joshua had an important victory over the Amorites there (Joshua 10:9-10). In modern times, two Arab villages are on this site.[451]

Ephraim means "double fruit". It is an unidentified village somewhere north of Jerusalem. Ephraim is mentioned only one time in the Bible. After Jesus raised Lazarus from the dead, Jesus and his disciples withdrew to Ephraim while His enemies plotted His death (John 11:53-54). Jesus did not stay long in Ephraim because it was almost time for Passover (John 11:55).[452]

Timnath-Serah means "extra portion". This city is ten miles northwest of Bethel. Joshua was given this city in the mountains as a reward for his excellent leadership (Joshua 19:49-50). When Joshua died, he was buried there (Joshua 24:29-30). In modern times, Timnath-Serah is the Arab village of Kefel Hares. The Muslims say that the tombs of Joshua, Caleb, and Nun the father of Joshua are there. The Palestinian Authority controls the area and allows Jews and Christians to visit only at prescribed times and with special permission.[453]

Bethabara means "house of the ford". John the Baptist was preaching here when Jesus arrived to ask John to baptize him (John 1:28). When Jesus insisted that John baptize him, John did not think he was worthy enough (Matthew 3:13-17).[454]

Shechem means "shoulder" or "ridge". Shechem is about thirty-five miles north of Jerusalem. In Shechem, Abraham built an altar dedicated to God (Genesis 12:4-7). Shechem was probably just a camping area during the time of Abraham. But the site grew into a village, town, and eventually into a city. When Jacob built an altar there, Shechem had become a town (Genesis 33:18-20). Joshua chose to give his farewell speech to the people in Shechem (Joshua 24:1-15). Shechem was given to the Levites and made into a city of refuge for any Israelite who killed someone accidentally (Joshua 20:7). When the united kingdom of David and Solomon split into southern and northern kingdoms, King Jeroboam I ruled from 931 BC to 910 BC and made Shechem the capital of the northern kingdom (1 Kings 12:25).

---

[451]   Ibid., 190.
[452]   Ibid., 191.
[453]   Ibid., 192.
[454]   Ibid., 195-196.

During the time of Hosea the prophet, Shechem was a worship center (Hosea 6:9). The Tomb of Joseph is located there, and his bones were finally buried on the property Jacob bought before Joseph's death in Egypt (Genesis 33:18-19). Joseph asked to be buried someday back in Canaan (Genesis 50:25-26), and Moses and the Israelites took the bones of Joseph with them when they left Egypt (Exodus 13:19). Finally, the Israelites buried the bones of Joseph in Shechem on the property that his father, Jacob, had bought years ago (Joshua 24:32).

Hebrews talks about the faith that Joseph had – that the people of Israel would return to Canaan and bury his bones in Shechem (Hebrews 11:22). The Samaritans also liked to live in Shechem. The Samaritans were the children of marriages of Jews and Gentiles. Full-blooded Jews thought the Samaritans were inferior people (John 4:9). In the past, one million Samaritans lived in Shechem and the region around Mount Gerizim. Many of the Samaritans were slaughtered when they rebelled against the Romans in the 6th century AD. Samaritans have a special document called the Samaritan Pentateuch which contains Genesis, Exodus, Leviticus, Numbers, and Deuteronomy. Their version of these books differs from the Jewish and Christian books. This is the only part of the Bible that they consider to be authoritative. The ruins of ancient Shechem are a mound called Tel Balatah, not far from the modern Arab city of Nablus. Nablus is a large manufacturing and commercial center that has a population of 100,000 and is one of the largest Palestinian cities in the West Bank.[455]

Sychar is located two miles northeast of Shechem. Jesus talked to a woman by the well at Sychar about "living water" (John 4:5-14). In modern times, the 135-foot-deep well is within the compound of the Bir Yarqub Monastery owned by the Eastern Orthodox Church.[456]

Mount Gerizim and Mount Ebal: These two mountains are a half mile apart and both are 3000 feet above sea level. When Moses looked across the Jordan River from Moab, these two mountains were easy to see. Moses told the people when they entered Canaan to go to these two mountains for worship. Blessings for keeping the law were to be read from Mount Gerizim (Deuteronomy 28:7-12), and curses

---

[455]   Ibid., 197-199.
[456]   Ibid., 200-201.

for breaking the law were to be read from Mount Ebal (Deuteronomy 28:20-24, 11:29-32).

After Moses' death, Joshua took the people to these two mountains and placed half looking at Mount Gerizim and half looking at Mount Ebal (Joshua 8:33-35). Scholars believe that these two mountains formed a natural amphitheater and therefore all the people could hear Joshua reading the blessings and curses. But J.W. McGarvey in the 1880's tested this theory. He discovered that it was not a natural amphitheater and the people could not have heard Joshua speak to the people. His theory is that Joshua had the blessings and curses distributed through the crowd with many readers to read them (Deuteronomy 27:14).[457]

Mahanaim means "double camp" or "two armies". This city is east of the Jordan River, near the Jabbok River. In Genesis 32, Jacob was on the way back home to Canaan after working for Laban for twenty years. He was worried that his twin Esau was still angry over Jacob's receiving the birthright blessing and the inheritance. God sent angels to Jacob to tell him that He would be with him and protect him as he was reunited with his estranged brother (Genesis 32:2). Jacob named the place Mahanaim, which means "two camps". When Jacob saw the angels, he exclaimed, "This is God's camp!" (Genesis 32:2). One camp was for Jacob and one camp was for the angels. Esau's warm welcome assured Jacob that all was forgiven (Genesis 33:1-4). This is also the place that Ishbosheth, Saul's son, reigned for two years as king over parts of northern Israel while David ruled in the south (2 Samuel 2:8-11). Eventually, two of Ishbosheth's military commanders assassinated him and David became king of all Israel (2 Samuel 4:5-7, 5:1-4). The exact location of Mahanaim has not been identified yet.[458]

Peniel means "face of God". It is an unidentified place east of the Jordan River, also near the Jabbok River. This is the location where Jacob wrestled the angel and Jacob's hip was knocked out of joint (Genesis 32:24-25). King Jeroboam I of the northern kingdom of Israel fortified the city to protect his city from attack (1 Kings 12:25). Zerqa River is the modern name for the Jabbok River.[459]

Gilead means "mound of stone". It is a mountainous region east of the Jordan River. Although Gilead is a mountainous area, it

---

[457] Ibid., 202-203.
[458] Ibid., 204-205.
[459] Ibid., 206.

had fertile areas also. The tribes of Reuben and Gad were given this territory. Moses agreed but made them promise to help the other tribes first on the other side of the Jordan (Numbers 32:1-5, 20-27). Later, half of the tribe of Manasseh joined Reuben and Gad (Deuteronomy 3:12-13). Gilead exported spices and perfumes (Genesis 37:25). Another valuable item was ointment for the treatment of wounds (Jeremiah 8:22).[460]

Bethel means "house of God". It is located about twelve miles from Jerusalem. Jacob camped there when he left home to get away from his twin Esau who threatened to kill him (Genesis 27:1-40). Jacob had a dream there of angels going up and down a stairway. At the top of the stairway was God, who renewed the promise made to Abraham. When Jacob woke up, he marked the spot with stones. After the dream, Jacob named the place Bethel to mean "house of God", because Jacob had experienced the presence of God there. In the time of Judges, the Ark of the Covenant was kept there (Judges 20:26-28).

After Solomon's death, Israel split into two areas with a king in each area. King Jeroboam I of the northern kingdom set up a calf idol at Bethel and another calf idol in Dan. He told the people, "It is too much trouble for you to worship in Jerusalem. Look Israel, these are the gods who brought you out of Egypt" (1 Kings 12:28). Beth-el ("house of God") had degenerated into Beth-aven ("house of wickedness" – see Hosea 10:5). Bethel's original Canaanite name was Luz (Genesis 28:19). When Abraham first arrived in Canaan, he set up an altar close to Bethel (Genesis 12:8). Bethel was also part of Samuel's travel area (1 Samuel 7:15-17). The prophet Amos predicted that Bethel would be destroyed because of the calf idol (Amos 5:4-5). King Josiah of Judah later tore down the pagan calf idol and altar at Bethel (I1 Kings 23:15). Some Jews returning from the Babylonian exile made Bethel their home (Nehemiah 11:31).[461]

Kiriath-Jearim means "city of forests". It is a city about eight miles west of Jerusalem. The Ark of the Covenant spent twenty years in this city. The Philistines captured the ark but soon sent it back because they began to get sick with unusual problems (1 Samuel 6:1-12). The Israelite town of Beth-shemesh welcomed it at first. Then

---

[460] Ibid., 207.
[461] Ibid., 208-209.

the town people begged the people of Kiriath-Jearim to take it back because seventy men were killed when they looked at the ark (1 Samuel 6:13-21). The men of Kiriath-Jearim agreed to take the ark back (1 Samuel 7:1). Abinadab kept the ark in his house, and his son Eleazar was in charge of keeping the ark. King David took the ark to the tabernacle in Jerusalem.[462]

Shiloh is about twenty miles from Jerusalem. The tabernacle was set up in Shiloh after Joshua defeated the Canaanites and claimed their land (Joshua 18:1). It may have been used as a sanctuary through the time of the judges. Samuel's mother Hannah, who had been childless for a long time, traveled to Shiloh to pray to God for a son. She met the priest, Eli, and he said to her, "May the God of Israel grant the request you asked of him" (1 Samuel 1:17). Hannah had a son and named him Samuel which means "name of God". Hannah kept her promise and took Samuel to Eli, the priest (1 Samuel 1:24-28). When King David chose Jerusalem as his capital, Shiloh declined in importance. Excavations show that Shiloh was destroyed about 1050 BC.

Today at Shiloh, you can only see a pile of rocks, known as Khirbet Seilun, where Shiloh was located. The prophet Jeremiah used the destruction of Shiloh to warn people not to have idol worship. Jeremiah 7:12 states, "Go now to the place at Shiloh where I once put the tabernacle that bore my name. See what I did there because of all the wickedness of my people, the Israelites." Not far from the Old Testament Shiloh is a modern Jewish synagogue with interior furnishings that show what the biblical tabernacle looked like.[463]

Samaria

Dothan means "two wells". It is a town eleven miles north of Samaria. Some of the brothers of Joseph sold him there to a passing caravan of traders (Genesis 37:26-28). The traders then took Joseph to Egypt and sold him as a household slave. God guided Joseph through his difficult times and he eventually became a high official in the Egyptian government (Genesis 41:37-44). During the severe famine, Joseph was able to help his father and brothers by getting them to Egypt where

---

food was available (Genesis 46:28-34). Centuries later at Dothan, God helped Elisha by striking the enemy soldiers blind so that Elisha could get away to safety (I1 Kings 6:12-18). In modern times, Dothan is a large twenty-five-acre mound called Tel Dothan. Excavations have found twenty-one different levels of settlements going back several thousand years. At the base of the mound is a spring, and maybe this good water source enticed the brothers of Joseph to bring the sheep there for available water (Genesis 37:14-17).[464]

Beth-Shan means "place of security". It is located about five miles southeast of Mount Gilboa. Beth-Shan was a Canaanite city that Joshua and the Israelites could not conquer (Joshua 17:11-12). Excavations show that this city was well fortified for centuries before Joshua and the Israelites arrived. This is where the Philistines hung the dead body of King Saul on the city-wall for the humiliation of the Israelites. King Saul was killed in battle on nearby Mount Gilboa (1 Samuel 31:8-10). When David became king, he defeated the Philistines (2 Samuel 8:1). When Solomon became king, he turned Beth-Shan into one of his administrative cities responsible for collecting taxes and providing food for the royal court in Jerusalem (1 Kings 4:7-8,12). Beth-Shan later became a major Roman city called Scythopolis. Archaeologists have found the remains of this Roman city and named the remains Tel Beit Shean. There are visible remains of a Roman theater that could seat 6,000 people, a paved street, and huge stone columns along the main thoroughfare into the town.[465]

Dor means "habitation". It is eight miles north of Caesarea. Dor was a Canaanite city that Joshua captured (Joshua 12:7, 23). The tribe of Manasseh received it (Joshua 17:11). It was one of King Solomon's tax districts (1 Kings 4:7,11). It was an important port city on the Mediterranean until Herod the Great built a new port in Caesarea eight miles away. Dor is a good modern archaeological area. It may become an archaeological park in the future.[466]

Caesarea is named for the Roman emperor Caesar Augustus. Herod the Great built this port city on the site of Strato's Tower. Philip the evangelist arrived in Caesarea to preach (Acts 8:40). Paul visited Philip there at the end of his second missionary journey (Acts 21:9).

---

[464] Ibid., 216.
[465] Ibid., 217-218.
[466] Ibid., 219.

Cornelius, a Gentile military officer, had a spiritual vision and asked the apostle Peter to come and visit him (Acts 10:1-8). Peter converted Cornelius and his household in Caesarea and baptized them (Acts 10:44-48). Herod Agrippa was struck with a bad disease at Caesarea when he allowed people to worship him (Acts 12:20-23). Paul was imprisoned there for two years and made his appeal to Herod Agrippa II. (Acts 25:23-26). Herod used concrete in the building of this fort. There are also remains of a Roman theater. Archaeologists found a stone with the name of Pontius Pilate. It gives evidence of the real existence of the person who pronounced the death penalty on Jesus. An above-ground aqueduct brought water to Caesarea from Mount Carmel, thirteen miles away. This Roman city has been turned into a national park.[467]

Nazareth: Nathaniel asked Philip, "Can anything good come out of Nazareth?" (John 1:46). The Old Testament does not mention Nazareth. All important events took place in other towns instead of Nazareth. The village of Nazareth was very quiet, with only a few families living in it. Jesus tried to explain to the people of Nazareth his mission of being the Messiah (Luke 4:14-21). Jesus said that a prophet was not honored in his family or hometown (Mark 6:1-6). Jesus told them that the Gentiles were more open to God's grace than Jews. This made them angry and they tried to throw him off a cliff (Luke 4:23-30). In Nazareth, an angel told Mary that she was going to give birth to the Messiah (Luke 1:26-38). Jesus was not born in Nazareth but in Bethlehem, sixty-five miles to the south.[468]

Nain means "delightful". It is located about six miles from Nazareth. There is only one story about Nain in the Bible. During a visit there, a funeral procession passed by, and Jesus, filled with compassion, told the dead boy to get up (Luke 7:11-15). The people reacted by saying, "A mighty prophet has risen among us" (Luke 7:16). They may have been thinking of the story of Elisha, who had brought another widow's son back to life in Shunem three miles north of Nain (11 Kings 4:8-37). The people of Nain thought they had seen the hand of God (Luke 7:16).[469]

---

[467]   Ibid., 220-221.
[468]   Ibid., 222-224.
[469]   Ibid., 225-226.

Shunem is located about twelve miles southwest of the southern tip of the Sea of Galilee. In Old Testament times, a woman gave lodging and food to Elisha and his servant Gehazi. He promised her she would have a son. When the son died, she travelled all the way to Mount Carmel to get Elisha, who returned with her and brought her son back to life (I1 Kings 4:8-37).

Endor means "fountain of habitation". It is located near Mount Gilboa, where King Saul and his fighting men camped at one time. In the past, King Saul had asked Samuel for advice, but now that Samuel was dead, desperately King Saul consulted with a medium (or a witch) at the valley of Endor. King Saul wanted the witch to call up the spirit of Samuel (1 Samuel 28:3-7). King Saul had a problem because he had banned all black magic practitioners like her from Israel. King Saul was afraid that if she recognized him, she would refuse to call up Samuel. So King Saul wore clothes like a common man to trick her. King Saul was able to convince the witch to call up Samuel (1 Samuel 28:3-7). The spirit of Samuel told him the battle would go badly (1 Samuel 28:16-19).[470]

Ophrah means "fawn". Ophrah is near Mount Gilboa. There, God changed an ordinary, frightened farmer into one of the most courageous military leaders ever found. This happened during the time of the judges when the Midianites terrorized Israel. The camel-riding Midianites swept into Ophrah and grabbed livestock and destroyed crops. Gideon was threshing wheat in the bottom of a winepress to hide the wheat from detection by the Midianites. An angel appeared to him and said, "Mighty hero, the Lord is with you!" (Judges 6:12). Gideon asked the angel, "If the Lord is with us, why has all this happened to us?" (Judges 6:13). The angel showed Gideon signs that God was with him and that Gideon was the right person to fight the Midianites. Gideon collected a large army, but God thinned it down from 22,000 to 10,000 and then just to 300 warriors. With this handful of men and God's help, Gideon was victorious and drove the Midianites out of the land of Israel (Judges 6:36, 37:22). The exact location of Ophrah has not been found.

On the northwestern slope of Mount Gilboa is a spring known as Harod Spring (Judges 7:1). Scholars believe this is the spring where

---

[470] Ibid., 227-228.

the Israelite warriors quenched their thirst. God's instructions were that the men who scooped up water with their hands to drink would make the final cut of chosen men to battle the Midianites (Judges 7:4-8). These springs today are part of a national park known as Harod Springs. The spring flows from a cave named Gideon's Cave.[471]

Tirzah means "delightful". Tirzah served as capital of the northern kingdom of Israel for forty years. King Solomon declared that his bride was as beautiful as the lovely city of Tirzah (Song of Solomon 6:4). A military commander, Omri, led a rebellion against King Zimri in Tirzah. Omri captured the city. Zimri realized that assassination was next for him, so he chose to go to the citadel in his palace and burn it down over himself, and he was killed in the fire (1 Kings 16:18). King Omri ruled from Tirzah for six years before moving the capital to Samaria, just a few miles away (1 Kings 16:23-24). Excavations are called Tel el-Farah and have uncovered a layer of unfinished buildings. Scholars think that King Omri started construction, abandoned it, and then moved his capital to Samaria.[472]

Samaria means "watch station". It is a city half-way between the Jordan River and the Mediterranean Sea. Omri built Samaria to be the new capital of the northern kingdom (1 Kings 16:21-28). Samaria was named for Shemer, the person who sold Omri the property. Samaria was the capital of the northern kingdom until Assyria captured it about 150 years later. The enemy attacked the city until they ran out of food. Then the enemy army was destroyed by a mysterious disease (Il Kings 6:24). It took three years for the Assyrians to take it over (Il Kings 17:5-6). The Assyrians re-populated the city with pagans who worshiped idols (Il Kings 17:24-25). The Jews and Assyrians eventually intermarried and became known as Samaritans.

King Herod the Great renamed the city Sebaste for Caesar Augustus. Sebaste is Greek for Augustus. Archaeologists uncovered the Old Testament city and the Roman one as well. There are remains of a Roman theater and a large temple dedicated to Augustus. Ivory was found that may have been used for wall decorations or to put on furniture. King Ahab may have used it in his "ivory palace" (1 Kings 22:39, Amos 6:4). A large pool was found not far from the palace of

---

[471]   Ibid., 230-231.
[472]   Ibid., 232.

Ahab. Scholars and archaeologists speculate that this may be the pool that washed the blood from his chariot after he was killed in battle (1 Kings 22:37-38). The city of Samaria or Sebaste is now the location of the modern Arab village of Sebastiyeh.[473]

Ramoth-Gilead: King Ahab set out from Samaria on a journey to take back Ramoth-Gilead from the Assyrians, also known as Arameans. King Ahab's day ended with Ramoth-Gilead still in Assyrian control and the king mortally wounded. Some scholars believe that God was punishing King Ahab for his wickedness and idol-worship (1 Kings 16:29-33). King Ahab also sinned when he killed Naboth and confiscated his property to make a vegetable garden. The prophet Elijah told King Ahab, "Dogs will lick your blood at the very place where they licked the blood of Naboth" (1 Kings 21:19). King Ahab's son Joram became king and continued his father's goal of taking Ramoth-Gilead back. King Joram's efforts failed when he was wounded in battle and escaped to recover in the city of Jezreel (I1 Kings 8:28-29). In Jezreel, King Joram was assassinated by Jehu, a military commander. The body of Joram was dumped on the same plot of land that his father, King Ahab, had taken from Naboth (I1 Kings 9:21-26). Ramoth-Gilead is in Jordan now in modern times.[474]

Jezreel means "God scattered". Queen Jezebel, a wife of King Ahab and a wicked Queen, was thrown over the city wall of Jezreel to her death (I1 Kings 9:30-35). Then dogs made a meal of Queen Jezebel's body, just as the prophet Elijah predicted (1 Kings 21:23). Jezebel had plotted against Naboth to help her husband, King Ahab, to take his land (1 Kings 21:1-16). The Lord made it clear that the killing of Naboth would not go unpunished (1 Kings 21:17-19). God used Jehu to carry out the judgment on Jezebel and to become king (I1 Kings 9:1-23). Jehu also killed all the sons of Ahab and piled their heads outside the gates (I1 Kings 10:6-8). Jezreel was the summer palace.[475]

Cana was the location of the first miracle of Jesus when he turned water into wine (John 2:3-4, 6-10). The book of John cites the miracle at Cana as the first of seven signs. Cana is the location where Jesus

---

473 Ibid., 233-234.
474 Ibid., 234-235.
475 Ibid., 236-237.

started the process of revealing His Glory (John 2:11). Cana is now the Arab village of Kafr Kanna.[476]

Decapolis: Jesus spent most of his ministry with the Jewish people (Mark 7:27). Jesus did visit a few Gentile areas to show that he was the Savior of the entire world. He visited Decapolis at least two times. Decapolis included ten cities under the Greeks. When the Romans came into power, they continued to let them operate in the same way. In Decapolis, Jesus healed a deaf man with a speech problem by putting His fingers into the man's ear. He spit on His fingers and touched the man's tongue. The man could speak and hear and the news of the power of Jesus spread (Mark 7:31-37). The second miracle in this area was the feeding of the 4,000 (Mark 8:1-10). This made Jesus a universal Savior who did not have favorites. Christian tradition says that this miracle took place at Tel Hadar, the ruins of an Old Testament town. A monument has been erected to mark the site as the feeding of the 4,000 Gentiles.

At Decapolis, Jesus also healed a demon-possessed man living in the tombs. Jesus performed the miracle by ordering the demons to leave. The demons left and entered a group of pigs who died as they rushed down a hill to the Sea of Galilee. The Gentiles in the area became furious because their pigs had been killed, and they asked Jesus to leave (Mark 5:1-17). The man who had been demon-possessed wanted to go with Jesus, but he told him to stay there and tell people about the healing (Mark 5:20). The Gospels indicate that the miracle took place in the "region of Gadarenes" in Matthew 8:26, or the "region of Gerasenes" in Mark 5:1 and Luke 8:26. There was a city named Gadara that was one of the cities of the Decapolis. Gadara was only six miles southeast of the Sea of Galilee. There is a 1,500-year Christian tradition that it is Gergesa that is on the eastern shore of the Sea of Galilee across from Magdala. Archaeologists discovered ruins of a church and monastery there. Years ago, Christians built churches and monasteries on sites connected to Jesus. Above the monastery are ruins of a chapel that may mark the site where the pigs rushed down to the water. Only God knows the true location.[477]

---

[476]   Ibid., 260-261.
[477]   Ibid., 262-264.

In **Zarephath,** a poor woman gave the prophet Elijah bread baked from the last of her flour. Elijah then provided food for the lady and her son so that they would not go hungry. The lady also gave Elijah a place to sleep. The son died but then Elijah brought him back to life (1 Kings 17:17-24).[478]

Dig Deeper into the Rich History of Israel

The Golan Heights (region of biblical Bashan) is an area with biblical history that makes an interesting topic of study. Read these scripture passages to learn more.

Numbers 21:33-35
Deuteronomy 3:1-11
Joshua 21:27
Psalm 68:16-24
Psalm 133:1-3
Jeremiah 50:17-20

---

[478]   Ibid., 264.

Conclusion

T his concludes the first part of our Israel journey. In volume 2, we share personal photos and biblical insights into our trip. We pray you have enjoyed this rich journey to Israel and we invite you to get our second volume to enjoy some of the more personal sights and wonderful food and shops into today's Israel. We pray that you grow deeper in your relationship with Jesus Christ as you walked in His footsteps through Israel with us.

-Winkie and Harold Johnston

ISRAEL

WALKING IN HOLY FOOTSTEPS
Volume 2

Part Two:

Our Trip to Israel

Monday, January 7, 2013

We (Winkie and Harold) tearfully dropped off Joline Dog and Schnee Cat at the kennel for their vacation while we were on our trip to Israel. Joline was set to have three recess periods a day on the dog playground while Schnee would have indoor play time. The kind lady at the vet promised to let Schnee and Joline see each other to reassure each other that everything was okay.

This was the first time we had been separated from Schnee and Joline. They are both friendly, love people and animals, and adjust to new situations. It was probably harder for us to say goodbye than it was for the animals!

A good friend and his wife picked us up at home, helped us load the luggage, drove us to First Baptist Church, and stayed to hug us goodbye and wish everyone a good trip. We were happy that he solved our transportation problem and we did not have to leave our car in the way for ten days. Our friend Larry commented that Winkie's suitcase weighed more and indicated that females pack more things on trips than men do. He promised to look after our affairs while we were in Israel because we would be so far away.

VACATION FOR PETS AT THE ANIMAL KENNEL

We did not realize that we packed too many things and had too many suitcases to keep up with, because we had not flown since 1980 when people carried many things with them. We had four suitcases, two backpacks, and one red computer bag that looked like a big red pocketbook. This was to be a problem for us, although we did not yet know what was to come. We enjoyed relaxing, talking to friends, and making new friends.

We have a great time talking as we waited for the bus to arrive. We noticed we were the only ones with so much luggage and wondered why. The weather in Israel in January is similar to the weather in Augusta, so we packed the same clothes that we wear at home and had layers of clothes to wear, depending on warmness or coolness. We discussed what kinds of clothes we had packed.

Reflections on the Cross

Jesus told his disciples: "If any want to become my followers, let them deny themselves and take up their cross and follow me" (Mark 8:34). The cross symbolizes the crucifixion of Jesus and is a symbol to identify the followers of Jesus.

During the Crusades, when Europe was trying to reclaim Jerusalem from the Muslim rule, the cross became an image of political power. Even the word "crusade" comes from a French term for taking up the cross.

The cross is also a symbol for copying the way Jesus wants us to live lovingly, and for followers to practice their faith every day.[479]

---

[479] Greg DeLoach, *Reflections on the Cross.* First Baptist Church of Augusta: Spring 2013, 1.

LAST CALL FOR THE BUS: THE ISRAEL EXPRESS!

Hurrah! The bus arrived. Now the excitement was about to begin. We loaded the church bus with luggage and people, and we stood around waiting for all to come. The twenty-six brave pilgrims gathered together and talked about the anticipation of what was to happen on the trip. Many had traveled abroad before but had never been to Israel. Pastor Greg prayed for the needs of the church, for our safe and informative trip, for the sick, and for other things before we boarded the bus.

The Ankh Cross

The ancient Ankh Cross is Egyptian in origin and also has the names Ansate Cross *or* Looped Cross. *The ancient meaning of this cross was life and regeneration. "For the message about the cross is foolishness to those who are perishing, but to us who are being saved it is the power of God" (1 Corinthians 1:18).*[480]

We had mixed feelings as we waved goodbye to family and friends that we would miss, but we looked forward to a new adventure that was ahead of us. Harold wondered if the Arabs in Israel would behave. Many people had told him that the Israeli Arabs like the dollar bills that the tourists spend. He hoped that they were correct because he did not want to get into any fights or bad situations.

The Tau Cross

The Tau Cross looks like the Greek letter T *and is named for the resemblance to the letter* T. *It is a tradition that this is the form of the staff that Moses used in the wilderness (Numbers 21:4-9). Cross of the Old Testament, Prophetic Cross, and Anticipatory Cross are other names for this cross. This cross is also used in paintings for the two thieves crucified on either side of Jesus.*

---

[480] Ibid., 2.

"And just as Moses lifted up the serpent in the wilderness so must the Son of Man be lifted up, that whoever believes in him may have eternal life. For God so loved the world that He gave His only Son so that everyone who believes in Him may not perish but may have eternal life" (John 3:14-16).[481]

Chi Rho Cross

The Chi Rho Cross uses the Greek letters X or chi and P or rho. The Chi Rho Cross is a stylized monogram. This cross is an abbreviation of XPICTOC *or* Christos, *the Greek word for Christ. The shape of this cross looks like the crook of a shepherd's staff, which may represent Jesus as the Good Shepherd.*

"I am the good shepherd. I know my own and my own know me" (John 10:1-4).[482]

Halfway to Atlanta in Maddison, Georgia, we stopped at Chick-fil-A, where we had a sandwich and fresh carrot raisin salad. When we arrived at Fairfield Inn, we scrambled to claim our luggage.

Cross Crosslet

The Cross Crosslet has four Latin crosses with overlapping bases. This cross is associated with the liturgical season of Epiphany and affirms that Jesus is the Son of God; and the four crosses represent the four corners of the earth and the spreading of the Gospel to the world.

"You will be my witnesses in Jerusalem, in all Judea and Samaria, and to the ends of the earth" (Acts 1:8).[483]

Tuesday, January 8, 2013

We enjoyed a continental breakfast at Fairfield Inn. In getting ready to leave, we determined that we will pack smaller suitcases next time, because it is difficult to roll such a heavy load with so many things. We looked like a comedy team dealing with our suitcases.

Cross and Orb

[481]   Ibid., 3.
[482]   Ibid., 4.
[483]   Ibid., 5.

The orb represents the world, surrounded by the cross and representing the victory of the Savior over the sins of the world. Christian groups and mission societies adopted this cross.

It was John the Baptist who declared the truth, "Here is the Lamb of God who takes away the sin of the world" (John 1:29).[484]

Passion Cross

The Passion Cross has pointed ends on the arms and is known as the Cross of Suffering, Cross Urdee and Cross Champain. It is used as a symbol for Maundy Thursday or Good Friday. The Passion Cross is symbolic of the agony of Gethsemane.

Palm Sunday is known as Passion Sunday due to Jesus' triumphal entry into Jerusalem and the suffering he would face. It was a necessary and important journey that Jesus made alone.

"O my Father, if it be possible, let this cup pass from me; nevertheless not as I will, but as thou wilt" (Matthew 26:39).[485]

At the airport, we had to get in line and show our passports, and they were scanned. It felt to us like we had to move at the speed of lightning and we were as slow as turtles. We took off our shoes and put our belongings into a container. We then walked through metal detectors. Our bags were then x-rayed. The reason for this procedure is that some guns are made of plastic but still shoot, and they will not show up on metal detectors. We had to go through this due to safety concerns. Winkie suddenly said, "Where is my red computer bag?" She looked and saw it lying on a still conveyor belt where unclaimed items were put. Winkie had to ask someone in security to get it. Before it was handed to Winkie, the security lady looked through it quickly. Then we had to get in the ticket line to pick up our tickets.

The experience of traveling really had changed since 1980 when we flew to Hawaii. At that time years ago, we picked up our tickets, someone checked to make sure we were on the correct airplane, and they simply said, "Have a nice trip." One of our leaders guided us through the procedure because so much had changed.

---

[484] Ibid., 6.
[485] Ibid., 7.

On the airport subway, the door slid open quickly and each person had to hurry inside. Harold had to stand up and hold on tight. We passed by many airplane ticket lines and finally got to United. The last time we flew from the Atlanta airport, there was no subway to take us to our plane. This time, Winkie sat in a seat and held on tight.

Our flight was scheduled to depart from Atlanta to Newark, New Jersey, at 10:57 a.m.; and to arrive in Newark at 1:11 p.m.

At the counter, we checked in our bags and made a mistake by not checking in our two smaller bags. It was hard for us to keep up with two small bags, two backpacks, and one computer bag. Each time we changed locations, we had to move all the above items. Our Christian friends in our group helped us to carry them and to keep up with the others. The pink and black bags pictured in the photo belong to us.

Our group of friends helped us through security at Newark Airport. Not knowing the procedures, we had two huge suitcases, two small suitcase carry-ons, a computer bag, and two backpacks to keep up with all day. We learned our lesson about taking too many clothes in huge suitcases. We got in the line for Tel Aviv, along with many Jewish Americans going to Israel and a few Jewish Israelis who were visiting New York. We talked to many of them and found out many things about Israel, even some recommendations for eating in Jerusalem.

The airline was nice and prepared a Kosher supper and breakfast for the Jewish passengers, while the non-Jews received the regular menu items. We ate a delicious dinner of chicken, rice, corn, and green beans mixed together, and some kind of dish that we could not tell what it was. We also had a good tossed salad with lettuce, carrots, and raw salmon. We did not eat the raw fish because of our concern that it might hurt us. One of our tour members told us to eat it because it was beneficial. We traveled 5,600 miles and flew over Paris and other parts of Europe. The twenty-three-year-old man sitting next to me lived in the Atlanta area with his parents, due to the fact that they left Israel and moved to Georgia. He was a chemical engineer and had lived most of his life in Israel. He was going back to his house in Israel for a vacation. We talked about Israel with him.

Winkie worked on her Israel Book often, because writing a book is fun. Winkie looked up Tiberias in Part 1 of her *Walking in Holy Footsteps* e-book and read about earthquakes. Earthquakes have been in Tiberias since the beginning of time. The earthquake of 1837 shook the Sea of Galilee on January 1 with a magnitude of 6.25. Archaeologist William McClure Thomson in the 19th century documented this event and discovered that it hit in the Tiberias part of the Ottoman Empire. Winkie wondered what to do if an earthquake were to hit in January 2013, and what she would do to survive.

We left Harold's computer at home, but Winkie shared hers with her "best friend"! We had a few hours to wait before the Tel Aviv airplane arrived at the gate. Harold read on the computer that the Sea of Galilee had nine cities around it in the time of Jesus. The fish in the Sea of Galilee are carp, mullet, sardine, catfish, and combfish. In modern times, the population of Tiberias is 40,000. The old city of Tiberias was called Hamat and had hot water springs for the Roman city of Tiberias.

Cross Pattee

The Cross Pattee is used for jewelry, tattoos, and clothing industries. This was a decorative item used widely throughout Continental Europe.

"May I never boast of anything except the cross of our Lord Jesus Christ, by which the world has been crucified to me, and I to the world" (Galatians 6:14).[486]

Jerusalem Cross

The Jerusalem Cross can be found as souvenirs and at ancient churches and catacombs. This cross is a combination of four Tau Crosses, symbolic of the Old Testament, and four Greek Crosses, symbolic of the New Testament. This cross is associated with the commission of Jesus to spread the gospel all over the world. The small crosses symbolize the wounds of Christ's hands and feet. The larger cross represents the wound to his side. The four small crosses are for the four evangelists Matthew, Mark, Luke, and John.

"Pray for the peace of Jerusalem; may they prosper who love you" (Psalm 122:6).[487]

---

[486] Ibid., 8.
[487] Ibid., 9.

Winkie talked to the stranger in the next seat to pass the time. We talked about Israel and its people.

St. Andrew's Cross

The St. Andrew's Cross is shaped like an X and is often displayed on state flags, shields, and coats of arms. It is named for Andrew who introduced his brother, Simon Peter, to Jesus. Tradition is that Andrew was martyred in Greece by crucifixion on an X-shaped cross. In Christian art, Andrew is represented as holding or leaning on an X-shaped cross. Andrew is considered the first missionary because he introduced his brother Peter to Jesus.

"He (Andrew) first found his brother Simon and said to him, "We have found the Messiah" (John 1:41).[488]

Cross Triparted Fleuree

There are three horizontal and three vertical arms of this cross, which describes the name Triparted. The Fleuree describes the endings of the arms, which resemble the fleur-de-lis. It represents the Trinity because of the three vertical arms and the use of the fleur-de-lis. This cross is appropriate for the Pentecost and Trinity season.

"The grace of the Lord Jesus Christ, the love of God, and the communion of the Holy Spirit be with all of you" (II Corinthians 13:13).[489]

Latin Cross

The Latin Cross is the most common and used Christian cross. It is a simple symbol of sacrifice and death.

"May I never boast of anything except the cross of our Lord Jesus Christ" (Galatians 6:14).[490]

Cross Flamant

The Cross Flamant has the impression of its arms in flames. It can be associated with the veneration of saints and martyrs in Christian traditions.

---

[488] Ibid., 10.
[489] Ibid., 11.
[490] Ibid., 12.

"Do not lag in zeal, be ardent in spirit, serve the Lord" (Romans 12:11).[491]

OUR AIRPLANE ROUTE FROM NEWARK, NJ, TO TEL AVIV, ISRAEL

Although we were up too high to see the Atlantic Ocean and the European countries, it was fun to fly over them and make a plan to visit them one day. Harold watched many movies on the little television screen on his seat. Winkie entertained herself by looking at the flight path and following the route of our airplane. Winkie also cat-napped and ate meals and snacks when they were served.

Celtic Cross

The basic structure of the Celtic Cross is a Latin Cross with a circle surrounding the intersection. Tradition is that Saint Patrick introduced this cross to Ireland by combining the traditional cross with the sun cross, in order to convince the pagans that Christ dominates the pagan sun.

"The mighty one, God the Lord, speaks and summons the earth from the rising of the sun to the setting" (Psalm 50:1).[492]

---

[491] Ibid., 13.
[492] Ibid., 14.

OUR TOUR BUS

Wednesday, January 9, 2013

We ate an early breakfast of omelet, potato cake, fruit, rolls, coffee, and milk. Then at 9 a.m. Tel Aviv time and 1:40 a.m. Augusta time, we went through security in Israel. It was fifty-three degrees in Tel Aviv. We met our tour bus and were introduced to Mozzi the driver, who would keep us from getting lost, and to our tour guide Nader Mascobi, who promised to make the Bible come alive and influence us to read the Bible more. We had an eighty-five-mile drive to Gai Beach Hotel in Tiberias. On the way, we passed by the West Bank, which was guarded by a huge wall all around it. The Arabs build many tall minaret towers.

Nader, our guide, explained that we would visit many churches and that they charge two shekels for coffee. Tel Aviv had road closures the day before we arrived, because of heavy rain, and it also snowed in Jerusalem the day we landed. We noticed that the Arabs often build bigger houses than the Jews. We had to show our passports when we went to Bethlehem. We passed Mount Carmel and the Jezreel Valley. We also learned that Jewish citizens build cemeteries outside cities.

OUR GUIDE TELLS US EXCITING THINGS WE WILL SEE AND DO

Our bus driver was Jewish and our guide was an Arab Christian. Both were very nice and told us interesting stories. Our original plan was to tour Jaffa, but the roads were closed due to the heavy rain. Our first day was spent traveling to Tiberias, Israel. On the way, our guide told us facts about Israel. Our tour book, *A Journey to the Holy Land* by Greg DeLoach of First

Baptist Church in Augusta, Georgia, gave us many interesting facts to read. The country of Israel is over 8,000 square miles, and it is a little larger than Massachusetts and smaller than Vermont. Our state of Georgia in the USA has 58,000 square miles of land and is larger than Israel. There are three official languages in Israel – Hebrew, English, and Arabic – and we heard all three constantly. Over 75 percent of the people are Jews; 16 percent are Muslims; and 2 percent are Christians.

Tiberias is the largest city on the Sea of Galilee and is located on the western side. It is about ten miles from Capernaum. Tiberias was built in 20 AD by Herod Antipas, who named it for Emperor Tiberius. The city was built near hot springs and became famous for wine, figs, and wheat. John's gospel is the only one that mentions Tiberias as a town and as a lake. The other gospels refer to it as only the Sea of Galilee (See John 6:1, 6:23, and 21:1).

In Tiberias, we arrived at our hotel, claimed our luggage, and settled into our nice hotel room. Then we went exploring the Sea of Galilee. Although it was very cold weather, Winkie had to put one foot in the ice cold water to say that she touched the Sea of Galilee that Jesus loved and enjoyed when he was alive on earth. Her legs turned white with the cold. Winkie stayed just long enough to get the picture. She daydreamed about what it would have been like in the warm weather of summer to actually swim in the water. The bottom was muddy and her foot in the water sunk down, and that is why she did not put both feet in the water. The location of the water was in Tiberias at the Gai Beach hotel. The weather in Tiberias was rainy, and Winkie took advantage of a few minutes without the rain shower.

Our tour group wanted to take advantage of walking to nearby Tiberias sites, but the weather did not cooperate. Tiberias is the lowest city in Israel at 200 meters below sea level.

WADING IN THE SEA OF GALILEE

GAI BEACH HOTEL IN TIBERIAS

We were happy to arrive at our hotel and unpack for our three-day stay in the area. We checked into our hotel room, selected our luggage from all the other luggage pieces, and rolled it to our rooms. As the largest city on the Sea of Galilee, Tiberias is the only one big enough for thirty hotels. The Jews were against Tiberias being built over an old cemetery, but they could not change it in 20 AD when Herod Antipas built it. Herod built palaces, theaters, temples, and public baths over the hot springs.

Near Tiberias is the Hamal Tiberias National Park with seventeen hot springs. In Tiberias are excavations of ancient Tiberias. In 1998, archaeologists found large storage jars with candelabras, lampstands, scissors, bowls with old Arabic writing, and fifty-eight Byzantine coins. Archaeologists believe that these were hidden when news was heard of a crusader invasion. Lack of time kept us from seeing all of Tiberias. We had to make choices and had to accept that although the Tiberias area had much to offer, we didn't have time for it all because we wanted to explore the Sea of Galilee area.

In 70 AD, Tiberias became the seat of the religious Sanhedrin. In 1204, Tiberias had a famous doctor, Maimonides, who is known as a forerunner of modern medicine.

OUR TOUR LEADER HAS A MEETING WITH US

Greg told us the times of each meal and what time the bus left each day, to keep us all together as a group.

Jesus Christ the Victor Cross

This cross combines the Greek abbreviation for Jesus Christ (IC for Jesus and XC for Christ) and Victor of Conqueror (NIKA). This cross reminds us that the death of Jesus did not bind him. Even in death Jesus Christ has conquered, and because Christ has conquered we need not fear death.

'When this perishable body puts on imperishability, and this mortal body puts on immortality, then the saying that is written will be fulfilled: 'Death has been swallowed up in victory.' Where, O death is your victory? Where, O death, is your sting?'''

(I Corinthians 15:54-55).[493]

SALAD BAR FOR BREAKFAST AND DINNER EVERY DAY

We had a wide variety of fruits and fresh vegetables, all grown in Israel. None of us had eaten foods like this so early in the morning, but it was fun to try new things. Some of the food was hot and spicy, but most of it was not. The oranges were so sweet and good – not tart like ours back in the states. The colors of the fruits and vegetables were brighter than at home, and it made the table of food look beautiful.

Winkie's book had so many interesting sites in Tiberias to see, but time did not allow it because we wanted to see other things associated with the life of Jesus. For example, there was a tower in old Tiberias

---

[493]   Ibid., 15.

that would be fun to see. But it would take weeks to see all the sites and fun things to do. Maybe we will get to go back one day.

We ate mainly chicken, fish, and steak; and we had lamb one time. Pork was not on the menu. There were so many choices of meat, and we could choose as many as we desired.

Russian Cross

Another name for the Russian Cross is the Orthodox Cross that is found in the Eastern Orthodox Churches in Russia. The top crossbeam symbolizes the sign affixed by Pilate which read, "Jesus of Nazareth, the King of the Jews" (John 19:19). It is a cross and not a crucifix, because it has no image of the body of Christ.

"Jesus answered, 'My kingdom is not from this world'" (John 18:36).[494]

WHAT WE CHOSE FOR OUR FIRST DINNER

Our first dinner in Israel was yummy! It was delicious fish and vegetables with beautiful bright colors and part of a Mediterranean diet.

Inside View

James A. Showers, executive director of the magazine Israel My Glory, took a tour group to Jerusalem to see the Great Synagogue in March 2013. The Great Synagogue was built in 1982 and is dedicated to the memory of the six million Jewish people who died in the Holocaust, and to the people who died to establish and defend the modern state of Israel. The exterior of the synagogue looks like the ancient temple. The main sanctuary has bright stained-glass windows that tell the history, past, and future of the Jewish people.

Rabbi Zev Lanton, director general of the Great Synagogue of Jerusalem, shared the story of the synagogue. A Jewish man drapes a tallit, which is a four-cornered prayer shawl, over his shoulders and sometimes his head before praying. Today,

---

[494] Ibid., 16.

the tallit is placed over the outer garments and symbolizes the way to approach the God of the universe.

Prayer is the way we communicate with God. When Jesus was on earth, he communicated with his Father by prayer. Through prayer, Jesus asked his Father to care for his disciples.[495]

Life from the Inside Out

"But the Lord said to Samuel, 'Do not look at his appearance or at his physical stature, because I have refused him. For the Lord does not see as man sees; for man looks at the outward appearance, but the Lord looks at the heart'" (1 Samuel 16:7).

Samuel was at the home of Jesse in Bethlehem, choosing and anointing a successor to King Saul from Jesse's eight sons. When Eliab, the oldest, passed before him, Samuel thought Eliab was the person to become king. But the Lord disagreed and insisted that Samuel was about to make the same mistake the Israelites made with the choice of Saul. God pointed out to Samuel that David was the choice for king.

The Israelites had made three mistakes when they chose Saul. The first mistake was when the Israelites demanded a king because they wanted to be like the other countries around them. The second mistake was that the Israelites evaluated Saul based on outward appearance and not inward character. The third mistake was failing to judge the inward character and the ability to serve God. Samuel later described David as "a man after His (God's) own heart" (1 Samuel 13:14).[496]

Thursday, January 10, 2013

Israel Today reported that Jerusalem was covered in snow overnight, with over twelve inches in some places. Schools and public transportation were cancelled. Northern Israel experienced heavy snow, and the small town of Mitzpe Ramon in the higher peaks in the Negev Desert had enough snow to call it a winter wonderland. The rain and snow caused the Sea of Galilee to rise large amounts every hour. Many people hoped that the fresh water reservoir could refill by the end

---

[495] James A. Showers, "Inside View". *Israel My Glory*: July-August 2013, 4.

[496] Elwood McQuaid, "Life from the Inside Out". *Israel My Glory*: July-August 2013, 8-10.

of the winter season. However, some people lost their lives in flash floods. There had been flood damage from too much rain.

COURTESY OF ISRAEL NEWS, JANUARY 10, 2013

Introduction to Jeremiah

Jeremiah ministered from 627 to about 585 BC. This was more than a hundred years after Assyria's destruction of the northern kingdom of Israel in 722 BC. The southern kingdom of Judah should have learned from what happened to the northern kingdom. Maybe the Judeans thought the temple would keep them from being punished. God severely judged them for forsaking Him and sent them into captivity in Babylon, and allowed the Babylonians to tear up the temple King Solomon had built. The theme of Jeremiah is "the judgment of Jehovah".

Judah had a scare in 701 BC, when the Assyrians defeated every town in Judah except Jerusalem. God heard King Hezekiah's plea for help and God rescued Judah. Manasseh, the son of King Hezekiah, ruled for fifty-five years and even permitted child sacrifice (2 Chronicles 33:6). According to tradition, the prophet Isaiah was martyred by Manasseh. At the end of Manasseh's reign he repented and made his godly son, Josiah, king in 640 BC, who led the last revival in Judah before the Babylonian Captivity. It is believed that Jeremiah participated in this revival.

Assyria continued to dominate regional politics. Judah went to Egypt for help evaluating the role of the Babylonians. In 612 BC, the Babylonians conquered Nineveh, the capital of Assyria. The Assyrian army fled westward to Carchemish. The Egyptian Pharaoh Neco decided to keep Assyria in existence as a buffer against Babylon. Nero made it to Carchemish, about 450 miles from Jerusalem. King Josiah tried to stop Pharaoh Neco and was killed in the Valley of Armageddon. In 605 BC, General Nebuchadnezzar attacked Judah. General Nebuchadnezzar became the new Babylonian king when his father died.

The prophet Daniel and several thousand upper-class citizens were taken to the capital city of Babylon in 605 BC. The prophet Ezekiel and lower-class citizens were taken to the countryside of Babylonia about 50 miles from the attack. In 586 BC, Jerusalem was taken and the temple was destroyed.

Jeremiah was called the "weeping prophet" because of these historical events. Jeremiah 1:4-5 says, "Then the word of the Lord came to me, saying: 'Before I formed you in the womb, I knew you; before you were born I sanctified you; I ordained you a prophet to the nations.'" Other prophets during the time of Jeremiah were Nahum, Zephaniah, Habakkuk, Daniel, and Ezekiel. Daniel was the only one who referred to Jeremiah (Daniel 9), but Jeremiah did not refer to any of the other prophets. Jeremiah was from the Levi tribe and from the hometown of Anathoth. Jeremiah did not marry because he wanted to obey God. When God called Jeremiah he warned him of the Babylonian Captivity.

In Judah, Jeremiah had to put up with many wicked Kings of Israel. King Jehoiakim would not let Jeremiah enter the temple or the royal palace. He even cut up the writings of Jeremiah and threw them into a fire. This made Baruch, his secretary, to have to rewrite all the prophecies. Later, King Zedekiah arrested Jeremiah for being a traitor for predicting that Jerusalem would fall to Babylon. When the Babylonians captured Jerusalem, they freed him. Eventually some Jews kidnapped Jeremiah and fled with him to Egypt. Jeremiah probably died in Egypt.

The Babylonian Chronicles contained the Lachish Letters; a seal belonging to Gedaliah; and a seal belonging to Jeremiah's scribe, Baruch. The Babylonian Chronicles are tablets containing the history of Babylon from 2350 BC to 539 BC. The Lachish Letters are letters written by the people from a town about thirty miles from Jerusalem. The seal of Gedaliah is a signature device and may belong to the man the Babylonians made governor of Judah.

Jeremiah 44 is Jeremiah's final sermon. The theme is "the judgment of Jehovah", and Jeremiah describes Judah's refusal both to give up pagan worship and to obey the sabbatical year laws for 490 years. There is even one verse in Aramaic, the Gentile language of the region. It contains a theme verse for Gentile readers of Jeremiah. It says, "But the Lord is the true God; He is the living God and the everlasting King. At His wrath the earth will tremble, and the nations will not be able to endure His indignation" (Jeremiah 10:10).[497]

One of the items we had for breakfast was a delicious chocolate dessert. It was fun to taste each item and to know which foods to choose each day.

---

[497] Tom Davis, "Introduction to Jeremiah". *Israel My Glory*: July-August 2013, 13-15.

OLIVE CREAM CHEESE FOR BREAKFAST

There were about five varieties of cream cheese, and all of them were fabulous. Olive cream cheese was our favorite. It was so good by itself or to spread on one of the freshly baked bread choices. Since Israel is known for olive trees, it was good to eat their olives.

Salmon was offered every day for breakfast, and we had a choice of raw or cooked. Salmon was not served at lunch or dinner but for breakfast only. We never got enough courage to eat raw salmon.

YIGAL ALLON MUSEUM

We visited the Kibbutz Ginosar which has the Yigal Allon Museum, home of a 2,000-year-old fishing boat on display. This boat was discovered in the Sea of Galilee during the 1986 drought. This is an authentic boat from the time of Jesus. The kibbutz also had beautiful unusual flowers; as well as oranges; lemons; and yellow, pink, and red bananas.

This was the former home of Yigal Allon, who lived from 1918 to 1980 and was a commander of the Israeli forces during Israel's War of Independence. This museum has information on the life of Yigal Allon and the history of the Galilee region.

On the way to this site, we passed by the Horns of Hattin Battlefield where a fierce battle was fought between the Crusader Kingdom of Jerusalem and the Muslim forces of Saladin way back on July 4, 1187. This battlefield was named for an almost extinct volcano named Hattin. Winkie remembered this story from her book, *Walking in Holy Footsteps*: that Guy of Lusignan became King of Jerusalem, and that in the old days, kings went to battle and led the troops. The son of Saladin, Alafdal, wrote a first-hand story of this battle and of the capture of Guy and his troops and their executions. This battle was fought close to Tiberias and gave the Muslims control. Winkie wished we could stop and walk around and visualize this ancient battle, but there were already five or six things to see and do that day. We remembered to be thankful that we could visualize this from our bus as we drove by. Winkie really liked this story because her father's name is Guy also.

RESTORED JESUS BOAT

The Jesus Boat is 2,000 years old and was excavated from the Sea of Galilee in 1986. It was restored in order to preserve it. This boat was a 1st-century boat and was very similar to the one that Jesus and his disciples used. It was quicker to go by boat to each of the nine cities than walking the distance by land to the communities that Jesus wished to visit for his ministry.

Winkie closed her eyes and visualized what it may have been like in the time of Jesus and his followers. The Sea of Galilee was very important to them and the fish provided much food for them.

BOAT RIDE ON THE SEA OF GALILEE

It was very hard to stand up and walk around in the boat during our boat ride on the Sea of Galilee. It was very windy and the waves were rough; the sea was exactly like this during the time of Jesus. Hills can be seen around the Sea of Galilee. Jesus could cross over to the other side by boat or walk around the land to get from town to town. This is where Jesus stopped the storm and walked on the water. The boat driver stopped the boat to see if the two pastors volunteered to copy Jesus and walk on the water. Neither pastor wanted to get out of the boat and try to walk on top of the water for us, and none of us volunteered to try it, either. We could imagine what the results would be and none of us had the courage!

Brown and purple mountains wrap around all of the Sea of Galilee in God's beautiful creation. The body of fresh water is called Kinneret in Hebrew because it has the shape of a harp. It is thirteen miles long and seven miles wide. The Sea of Galilee is 687 feet below sea level and thirty-two miles in circumference. This lake separates the Golan and Decapolis regions.

The main use of the Sea of Galilee in Old Testament times was for a boundary mark. In the New Testament, Jesus used the Sea of Galilee for the main part of his ministry. Jesus liked to go there to tell to thousands his stories and parables and to use it as a quiet place to pray and meditate. On the eastern shore, Jesus healed the demoniac and caused the demons to go into a herd of pigs in Gadara.[498]

BOAT RIDE ON THE SEA OF GALILEE

We stopped the boat in the middle of the Sea of Galilee and had a worship service. One could imagine a boat with Jesus and his disciples in the same area but in a different time of history. As Jesus enjoyed the quietness centuries ago, our group enjoyed it also. We thought about Jesus quieting the storm and walking on water.

Some Biblical references for the name Chinnereth (Kinneret) are Numbers 34:11, Deuteronomy 3:17, Joshua 13:27, and Joshua 19:35. References for Galilee include Matthew 4:18, Matthew 15:29, Mark 1:16, Mark 7:31, and John 6:1.

We were happy to be on a modern boat with a good motor and gas. We could imagine the disciples with nets and Jesus telling them which side to cast their nets to catch many fish. We could visualize the disciples and Jesus building a fire on the nearby land and enjoying eating the fish together in fellowship.

---

[498] Greg DeLoach, *A Journey to the Holy Land: A Scriptural Study.* Augusta, GA: First Baptist Church, 4-5.

Russian Warship visits Haifa

World War II veterans assembled in Jerusalem to celebrate the Allied victory over Nazi Germany. A Russian warship, Azov, docked in Haifa, Israel, as the first warship ever docked in Israel in May to help celebrate the anniversary of the victory. Israeli officials said, "There are things on which we do not agree with Russia, but they share our concern over Islamic fundamentalism taking over the Middle East." The Russians loudly publicized the visit of the Azov to mark the victory celebration, and to show that Russia wanted the world to know that they had fought on the right side. The Russians' statement read, "There is something to be understood from this for the contemporary Middle East. Where we decided to make anchor is a clear statement, both to the Israelis and the entire region." Israelis are open to further cooperation with Moscow.[499]

RIDING THE BOAT ON THE SEA OF GALILEE

---

[499]   "Russian Warship visits Haifa". *Israel My Glory*: July-August 2013, 15.

Pastor Greg told us the stories of Jesus and his disciples, of their ministries, and of the life experiences they had on this same Sea of Galilee. Now we were copying Jesus and the disciples by having our own modern experiences on this same lake. This was a very spiritual time for all of us. For part of the time on our boat ride, the wind became stronger and the waves became very rough. After our worship service on the boat, one of the leaders told the waves to be still and to our astonishment they became still. We could picture what it was like when the waves became very high and the disciples were afraid of this storm, while Jesus was sleeping on the boat. They woke up Jesus to tell him of their fear and danger. Jesus told the storm to be still and it did.

Our boat driver talked to us some about his experiences on the Sea of Galilee. The man in the red jacket in the photo conducted our Bible study and worship service. This was so special, because for the first time we were on the same Sea of Galilee as Jesus had been, and we were sitting in a boat on the water like Jesus. We were looking at the beautiful mountains surrounding the Sea of Galilee.

God's Everlasting Love

The fact that the Jewish people are with us today is a testimony to God's love for them and His power to preserve them. As parents, we must discipline our children and teach them right from wrong and to obey. The same is true with God, and He disciplines His people. The Bible teaches, "Whom the Lord loves, He chastens" (Hebrews 12:6). The Jewish people have endured their share of discipline over the years. In Jeremiah 30 and 31, God explains that He still loves them, will forgive them, and will return them to their land. God mercifully left with them key men who continued to declare His Word despite the doom they faced. Jeremiah wrote: "For behold the days are coming," says the Lord, "that I will bring back from captivity My people Israel and Judah," says the Lord. "And I will cause them to return to the land that I gave to their fathers, and they shall possess it" (Jeremiah 30:1-3).

Jeremiah saw the Babylonian Captivity but also saw beyond it to the seven-year Tribulation. Jeremiah 30:7 says, "Alas! For that day is great, so that none is like it; and it is the time of Jacob's trouble, but he shall be saved out of it." "Jacob's trouble" means the nation of Israel. The time of Jacob's trouble is the future seven-year Tribulation. Jesus also echoed Jeremiah when He said, "For then there will be great tribulation, such as has not been since the beginning of the world until this time, no, nor ever shall be" (Matthew 24:21). The times of the Gentiles began with the Babylonian Captivity and will end when Jesus returns to save Israel at the end of the Tribulation and establish the Davidic, Millennial Kingdom.[500]

SEA OF GALILEE BOAT RIDE

Our boat had an upper and lower level. The upper level did not have a top, and the bottom level had a top to keep the sun out of our eyes.

God's Everlasting Love (continued)

God has always wanted the Jewish people to serve Him with willing hearts. He desires the same thing with His Church. Born-again believers have no excuses, because they have the Holy Spirit dwelling in them and possess the complete and readily available Word of God (the Bible). "To whom much is given, from him much will be required" (Luke 12:48). God is the God of redemption. He has the goal to restore people instead of to reject and abandon them. God loves Israel and will protect it and keep His promises. "Therefore do not fear, O My servant Jacob,"

---

[500] Thomas C. Simcox, "God's Everlasting Love". *Israel My Glory*: July-August 2013, 16-17.

says the Lord, "nor be dismayed, O Israel; for behold, I will save you from afar, and your seed from the land of their captivity" (Jeremiah 30:10).[501]

FRESH FRUIT AND VEGETABLES MARKET, SOLD ON STREETS

There are many fruit and vegetable stands on the streets of Israel.

Jeremiah and the New Covenant

The New Covenant was given to the Jewish people through the prophet Jeremiah. Jesus ratified it with His blood on Passover, when he journeyed to the cross. All covenants must be ratified with blood. Moses ratified the Mosaic Covenant by sprinkling blood on the people. "Moses took the blood, sprinkled it on the people, and said, 'This is the blood of the covenant which the Lord has made with you according to all these words'" (Exodus 24:8).

The New Covenant is found in Jeremiah 31 which is a chapter filled with divine assurances of God's love and redemption. God promised the Israelites a new covenant that they could not break.

Today many false teachers teach God's rejection of Israel, and also the replacement of Israel with the Church. God repeatedly declares his love for Israel, especially in the New Covenant. "Behold, the days are coming," says the Lord, "when I will make a new covenant with the house of Israel and with the house of Judah, not according to the covenant that I made with their fathers in the day that I took them by the hand to lead them out of the land of Egypt, My covenant which they broke. I will put My law in their minds, and write it on their hearts. I will forgive their iniquity, and their sin I will remember no more" (Jeremiah 31:31-34).

The first covenant revealed a need and pointed out how impossible it is to keep, because of sin. The second covenant provides "the Lamb of God who takes away the sin of the world" (John 1:29). God made one more monumental promise of declaring the permanence of Israel: "Thus says the Lord, who gives the sun for a light by day, the ordinances of the moon and the stars for a light by night, who disturbs the sea, and its waves roar (the Lord of Hosts is His name), 'If these ordinances depart from before Me,' says the Lord, 'then the

---

[501] Ibid.

seed of Israel shall also cease from being a nation before Me forever.' Thus says the Lord, 'If heaven above can be measured, and the foundations of the earth searched out beneath, I will also cast off all the seed of Israel for all that they have done,' says the Lord" (Jeremiah 31:35-37).[502]

OLIVE TREE

Olive trees provide food, and the wood is used for mangers, crosses to wear around the neck, and many other things. In the Garden of Gethsemane today are old olive trees that were young olive trees in the time of Jesus. Olive tree groves are plentiful in most areas of Israel. We were looking at olive trees and enjoying them, remembering that Jesus and his disciples spent time around them also. We have a friend attorney back home in Augusta that orders blocks of olive wood from Israel and makes beautiful shaving razors and pens to sell to the Augusta people. We bought one from him and enjoy it immensely.

CAPERNAUM

When Jesus was rejected in Nazareth, he moved his ministry headquarters to Capernaum. This region is now known as Kefar Nahum Village of Nahum the prophet. In the day of Jesus, it was a lakeside village on the northwest shore of the Sea of Galilee. It is located ten miles from Tiberias. In the days of Jesus, Capernaum was an important customs station and the home of the high Roman officer. The size of Capernaum in those days was about twenty-five acres with a population of about 1,000 inhabitants. This was the home of Peter, the beloved disciple of Jesus.

---

[502] Charles C. Ryrie, "Jeremiah and the New Covenant". *Israel My Glory*: July-August 2013, 18.

The synagogue in the time of Jesus, by definition, was a place of gathering, and secondarily was a specific building or place. The synagogue ruins we visited were from about the 5th century. There may be an older synagogue below this level, which could be where Jesus worshiped. Archaeological evidence in 1981 revealed that there may be a structure beneath the limestone synagogue of the 5th century.

A block from the synagogue, a tourist can view the remains of an octagonal church, and below the 5th-century church are the ruins of the house where Peter's mother-in-law was healed from a high fever (Mark 1:29-31). Jesus taught and performed healing miracles here, such as the healing of the centurion's servant (Luke 7:1). While Jesus was in Capernaum his fame spread (Mark 1:28, 33). Here also, Jesus listened to the dispute of the disciples over who was the greatest (Mark 9:33). In Matthew 17:24, Jesus had a conversation with Peter over the poll tax collected. The Gospel of John describes some of his followers leaving Jesus because of some of his teachings. But the twelve disciples remained (John 6:59-66). Many people in Capernaum who had witnessed miracles rejected him and did not believe. Jesus referred to the unbelieving people of Capernaum in Matthew 11:23 and Luke 10:15. There were more miracles in Capernaum, yet people did not understand. In modern times there are only ruins and no inhabitants.[503]

RUINS OF CAPERNAUM

The only modern inhabitants of Capernaum are cats who beg for attention, food, and love from tourists! It was fun to walk among these ancient ruins and imagine the people living there and their everyday activities.

Archaeological evidence shows that the town of Capernaum began in the 2nd century BC. The old city of Capernaum was abandoned about 1,000 years ago. It was rediscovered by an American archaeologist

---

[503]   Greg DeLoach, *A Journey to the Holy Land: A Scriptural Study.* Augusta, GA: First Baptist Church, 4-5.

named Edward Robinson. Reverend Eli Smith and Edward Robinson made many identifications of ancient places.

VISITING OLD CAPERNAUM

Jeremiah and the New Covenant (continued)

The apostle Paul, a Jewish rabbi, told the Gentiles in the church at Rome not to think they were better than the Jews, because God had a special plan for Israel. "The Deliverer will come out of Zion, and He will turn away ungodliness from Jacob; for this is My covenant with them, when I take away their sins" (Romans 11:26-27). Nations will come and go, but Israel will remain forever. And someday all Israel will be saved to the glory of God (Romans 11:26).[504]

ANCIENT CAPERNAUM

Synagogues in ancient Israel had a large hall used for prayer. Behind the large hall was the *D'bhir*, or Holy of Holies. All synagogues had a bema which is a special table used for the reading of the Torah. To this day, there is a desk for the prayer leader. The history of the bema goes back to the time that Ezra read the Torah on a wooden pulpit (Nehemiah 8:4-5).

---

[504]   Charles C. Ryrie, "Jeremiah and the New Covenant". *Israel My Glory*: July-August 2013, 18.

Israel's Restoration: Jeremiah 33

Jeremiah 33 is about God stressing that Judah's fight against Babylon will fail (Jeremiah 33:1-5). God will work to bring Israel back to its land, rebuild it, and forgive it (Jeremiah 33:6-8). Jerusalem, a city of desolation, will be turned into a place where the people are joyful and the people will prosper (Jeremiah 33:9-13).

Then Jeremiah informed the people about the Messiah and the Davidic Covenant. "In those days and at the time I will cause to grow up to David a Branch of righteousness; He shall execute judgment and righteousness in the earth" (Jeremiah 33:15). The branch is the Messianic King. In Jeremiah 23:5 is added, "who will rule and prosper", in reference to the Messianic King. The phrase "who will rule and prosper" in reference to the Messiah is also used in Isaiah 11:1, Zechariah 3:8, and Zechariah 6:12. The Messiah is also called "THE LORD OUR RIGHTEOUSNESS" (Jeremiah 33:16). This is talking about Jesus Christ but only at the Second Coming. The prophecy highlight is that God's ultimate plan for Israel is something greater than the return from Babylon.

"David shall never lack a man to sit on the throne of the house of Israel" (Jeremiah 33:17). Some people have a hard time with this passage because there is not an active man on the throne since Zedekiah. However, there is the multiplication of David's sons for many generations. More than likely, in modern times there are descendants of David who are males alive today. Jesus is a descendant of the line of David, is alive, and is waiting to take His place on David's throne. Therefore the Davidic line will not be broken.

Jeremiah stressed the permanence of the Davidic Covenant to assure Israel that God will never cast His people away forever. "Thus says the Lord: 'If you can break My covenant with the day and My covenant with the night, so that there will not be day and night in their season, then My covenant may also be broken with David My servant, so that he shall not have a son to reign on his throne'" (Jeremiah 33:20-21).[505]

---

[505]   Mike Stallard, "Israel's Restoration". *Israel My Glory*: July-August 2013, 23.

PRAYING AT THECAPERNAUM SYNAGOGUE RUINS

Israel's Restoration (continued)

God told the people that if they could figure out how to keep the sun and the stars from giving light by day and night, then it would be possible for the line of David to be broken. Since that was impossible for them to do, then nothing could break their covenant with Him. This was the way He acknowledged the ongoing permanent nature of the Davidic Covenant which He initiated in 2 Samuel 7.

This gave the Jewish people hope for the near future when they returned from the Babylonian Exile, and also caused their minds to glimpse the future to see the end-times glory of the Messiah reigning over Israel forever. Israel is a nation that God will never cast away for good, because it is the apple of His eye.[506]

In the 5th century, the people of Capernaum built a church and a synagogue. Christianity was legal at that time, but Galilee was predominantly Jewish. In Isaiah, the Galilee region is called "a land of Gentiles". This indicates that Gentiles lived in the region but not in the city of Capernaum.

THE ANCIENT SYNAGOGUE

Photo courtesy of the Israeli Ministry of Tourism and is solely for this photo only at www.goisrael.com

The synagogue pictured here is located very close to the Sea of Galilee. It was designed so that it faced Jerusalem. This beautiful synagogue was destroyed by the Romans in 70 AD, just as Jesus predicted when he was on earth. In 1866, Captain Charles William Wilson, an Englishman, discovered these ancient synagogue ruins. Jesus taught

---

[506]   Ibid.

often in the synagogue here, but it may have been an earlier one that may be below this level and has not been discovered yet. Jesus healed the centurion's servant by his word and the faith of the centurion.

Bulla Lessons from Jeremiah 36

The more archaeologists dig, the more Jewish history they find. There is much physical evidence found that supports the Bible. "Truth shall spring out of the earth, and righteousness shall look down from heaven" (Psalm 85:11). During the 1970s and early 1980s, many interesting archaeological finds were discovered in Jerusalem to support Jeremiah 36. Excavators found clay bullas dating back to Jeremiah 36. A bulla is a small flattened lump of hardened clay, used as a seal on official papers. It was used like a postage stamp and the sender's name or signet ring image was impressed on the clay.

The fire that destroyed Jerusalem in 586 BC hardened the clay seals and preserved them. Archaeologists found many names of people mentioned in Jeremiah 36. Baruch ben-Neriah was Jeremiah's scribe and his job was to write down all of the prophet's message. One of the bulla seals discovered and found by a prominent Israeli archaeologist belonged to Baruch. Baruch's final name was Bereklyahu, which means "the blessed of Yahweh".

"Then Jeremiah called Baruch the son of Neriah; and Baruch wrote on a scroll of a book, at the instruction of Jeremiah, all the words of the Lord which He had spoken to him. And Jeremiah commanded Baruch saying, 'I am confined, I cannot go into the house of the Lord. You go, therefore, and read from the scroll which you have written at my instruction, the words of the Lord, in the hearing of the people in the Lord's house on the day of fasting. And you shall also read them in the hearing of all of Judah who come from their cities. It may be that they will present their supplication before the Lord, and everyone will turn from their evil way. For great is the anger and the fury that the Lord has pronounced against this people'" (Jeremiah 36:4-7).[507]

---

[507] Peter Colon, "Bulla Lessons from Jeremiah 36". *Israel My Glory:* July-August 2013, 24-26.

CAPERNAUM RUINS

In Capernaum, Jesus called Levi Matthew, a tax collector, to leave tax collecting and to follow him. Jesus raised from the dead the daughter of Jairus here (Matthew 9:18-19).

Capernaum was a crossroads on a route between Damascus and Caesarea Maritima on the Mediterranean Sea, and it also was a crossroads between Tyre and Egypt. This made Capernaum an important place with plenty of trade. Customs taxes were collected from all travelers. This was where Jesus first saw Levi, who later changed his name to Matthew. Jesus looked into Levi's heart, liked what he saw, and called Levi or Matthew to follow him (Matthew 9:9 and Luke 5:27-29). Levi invited Jesus to his house for a great feast and Jesus accepted.

The ruins of Capernaum were acquired by Franciscans in 1894, and they worked hard to preserve these ancient holy places. Jesus taught here and healed the man with an unclean spirit (Mark 1:21-28). Those verses say that the people of Capernaum were astonished at his doctrine because he taught them as a person with authority and not as the scribes did. They were surprised when Jesus ordered the unclean spirit to come out of the man and the unclean spirit obeyed. The people questioned where Jesus got this authority to order unclean spirits out of a person so that the person was suddenly made normal.

Jesus named Capernaum as his own (Matthew 9:1). In the old days, caravans stopped at Capernaum to buy produce and dried fish. Archaeologists have found an old fish sales area where Peter and the other fishermen worked.

In Capernaum, the people witnessed a paralyzed man being lowered on a mat through an opening in the roof. When Jesus saw their faith, he said to the man, "Your sins are forgiven." Some of the people who heard it muttered, "He is insulting God. Only the one God can forgive sins." Jesus responded to those people by saying, "Which is easier to say to a paralyzed person: 'Your sins are forgiven', or 'Get up, take up your bed, and walk'?" Jesus wanted to show the people that the human one who is

God's servant has authority on the earth to forgive sins. Jesus raised him up and he picked up his mat and walked out (Mark 2:1-12).

CAPERNAUM RUINS

It was fantastic to see all these ruins and to walk where Jesus and the disciples walked. We pictured in our minds all the miracles that Jesus did, and we wondered if we had seen these miracles, whether we would have believed in Jesus, or instead doubted and complained about Jesus and called his works blasphemy like some of the people of Capernaum did.

BYZANTINE CHURCH OVER HOUSE OF PETER

Photo courtesy of the Israeli Ministry of Tourism and is and is solely for this photo only at www.goisrael.com

Bulla Lessons from Jeremiah 36 (continued)

This was a decisive time in Jewish history. If Judah repented and listened to Jeremiah, the Lord would forgive. If not, God was ready to punish by letting the Babylonians succeed in taking the Jewish people of Judah into captivity.

So Baruch went to the temple and read Jeremiah's prophetic messages of warning, and then he was led into a room in the palace to read to all the king's officials. "They trembled over what they heard, saying the king must also hear Jeremiah's messages" (Jeremiah 36:16).

After hearing the message of Baruch, cruel King Jehoiakim cut the scroll into tiny pieces and threw it into the fire. "Neither he nor his officials showed any godly fear over what they heard" (Jeremiah 36:21-24).

Although Baruch did not see any sign of repentance, he was faithful to his ministry and followed the instructions of Jeremiah to read God's words to the people. Baruch's testimony in the form of a small bulla is now in the Israel Museum.[508]

MODERN CHURCH OVER HOUSE OF SAINT PETER
Photo courtesy of the Israeli Ministry of Tourism and is solely for this photo only at www.goisrael.com

Under this modern church is located the ruins of the house where Peter lived. Jesus healed Peter's mother-in-law in Peter's house. Years after the resurrection of Jesus, Peter's house was used as a house church. Archaeologists discovered that the house was built at the end of the Hellenistic period, which is the 1st century AD. Many pieces of broken lamps were found in the thin layers of lime. Over 131 inscriptions written in Greek (110), Aramaic (10), Estrangelo (9), and Latin (2) were found in the thin layers of lime.

The name of Jesus appears several times, calling him Christ, the Lord, and the Most High God. There are also monograms of crosses, a boat, and a special monogram of Jesus. The name of Peter occurs at least two times. Peter's monogram is written in Latin but with Greek letters. In another one, Peter is called the helper of Rome. There are floral crosses, pomegranates, and figs. When the 5th century began, Peter's house was still standing but had been changed into a church. The walls of the house have remained the same with all the inscriptions.

The octagon-shaped church was built at the site in the 1930s by the Franciscans and has beautiful gardens.

---

[508]   Ibid.

THE SEA OF GALILEE AT TABGHA

Photo courtesy of the Israeli Ministry of Tourism and is solely for this photo only at www.goisrael.com

The building pictured here is from the 4th century AD and was the earliest structure in Tabgha. In modern times, archaeologists found only some of its foundation. The Christians built a large monastery and a church with beautiful mosaic floors. Monks and visiting Pilgrims had a place to live and stay. This monastery was destroyed in the 7th century during the Arab conquests. Sometime in the 1980s after excavations, the church was restored to its Byzantine form.

At Tabgha, Jesus fed 5,000 people with five loaves of bread and two fish, and as such it is known as the site of the multiplication of the loaves and fishes. Jesus also appeared to his disciples here after the resurrection. Tabgha is two and a half miles from Capernaum.

Bulla Lessons from Jeremiah 36 (continued)

Another artifact is a clay-disk bulla seal that reads, "belonging to Gemaryahu, son of Shaphan." Gemaryahu had a chamber in the temple, and in his room Baruch the scribe stood and read Jeremiah's prophecy before all the people (Jeremiah 36:25). Gemaryahu means "Yahweh has accomplished or perfected". He and two other officials showed moral courage and conviction when they pleaded with King Jehoiakim not to burn the scroll. One of the officials mentioned was Elnathan, who brought the prophet Urijah from Egypt to King Jehoiakim, who murdered Urijah (Jeremiah 26:20-23).

After that event, Elnathan changed his ways. Gemariah's father, Shaphan, discovered the scroll of the Law and Shaphan had the Scripture read to the people, and a great revival took place under Judean King Josiah (11 Kings 22:3-23:3).

We do not know what happened to Gemariah. He may have died during the Babylonian siege or during captivity. Gemariah was someone who honored God's

word in spite of the dangers. He lived out Psalm 31:1, which states, "In You, O Lord, I put my trust; let me never be ashamed; deliver me in Your righteousness."[509]

TOUCHING THE SEA OF GALILEE AT TABGHA

Winkie wanted to touch the water of the Sea of Galilee at Tabgha. Notice how high the wave was as it came to shore. The Sea of Galilee is known for its rough waves.

CHURCH OF THE PRIMACY OF PETER

Photo courtesy of the Israeli Ministry of Tourism and is solely for this photo only at www.goisrael.com

The Church of the Primacy of Peter is the traditional site of John 21 after the resurrection, and it describes Jesus cooking breakfast for the disciples in Tabgha.

Bulla Lessons from Jeremiah 36 (continued)

Another bulla from the archaeological Jerusalem hoard was impressed with the name of Elishama the scribe. This inscription read, "Elishama, servant of the king". When Baruch read the scroll in the temple, an official wanted him to read the scroll in the hearing of the king and all the princes (Jeremiah 36:21). Baruch left the scroll in Elishama's manuscript chamber. Later the king had someone get the scroll and read it before him. Elishama may have seen the king destroy the scroll, because he did not like the words of God. "Yet they were not afraid, nor did they tear their garments, the king nor any of his servants who heard all these words" (Jeremiah 36:24). "Elishama, servant of the king" did not beg the king to stop his sacrilege. Elishama's name in Hebrew means "God has heard".

---

[509] Ibid.

The king shredded and burned the scroll. Elishama showed neither fear nor repentance. These bullas verify the existence of the people in Jeremiah 36, whose names are full of personal meanings.

"For the word of God is living and powerful, and sharper than any two-edged sword, piercing even to the division of soul and spirit, and of joints and marrow, and is a discerner of the thoughts and intents of the heart. And there is no creature hidden from His sight, but all things are naked and open to the eyes of Him to whom we must give account" (Hebrews 4:12-13).[510]

SAINT PETER'S FISH RESTAURANT ON THE SEA OF GALILEE

We ate delicious fish from the Sea of Galilee. Jesus and his disciples caught fish in this lake, cooked them, and ate them together. Most of us ordered fish and some ordered pizza. In our experience, Israeli pizza is not tasty!

Shall Not Come to Mind Anymore

"Then it shall come to pass, when you are multiplied and increased in the land in those days," says the Lord, "that they will say no more, 'The ark of the covenant of the Lord'. It shall not come to mind, nor shall they remember it, nor shall they visit it, nor shall it be made anymore" (Jeremiah 3:16).

The Ark of the Covenant represented God's presence and His footstool (Exodus 25:22, I Chronicles 28:2, Psalm 99:5, and Psalm 132:7). The Ark of the Covenant was where the Day of Atonement (Yom Kippur) ceremony was held in ancient times. The high priest sprinkled blood on the mercy seat of the Ark to make a national covering for sins (Leviticus 16).

Jesus fulfilled the service performed on Yom Kippur with His sacrifice and shed blood to give eternal redemption. "Not with the blood of goats

---

[510]   Ibid.

and calves, but with His own blood He entered the Most Holy Place once for all, having obtained eternal redemption" (Hebrews 9:12).

Jeremiah the prophet spoke of a future time when the ceremonies of Israel at the Ark will no longer be needed or come to mind. The reason why is simple, when you look at the New Testament counterpart to Jeremiah 3:16: "For God so loved the world that He gave His only Begotten Son, that whoever believes in Him should not perish but have everlasting life. For God did not send His Son into the world to condemn the world, but that the world through Him might be saved" (John 3:16-17).[511]

FISH AND FRENCH FRIES AT PETER'S RESTAURANT

Notice that the fries are put on top of the fish and not in a stack by themselves on the plate. We were excited because we ate fish from the Sea of Galilee just as Jesus and his disciples did so long ago.

Judah's Fatal Decision

In 586 BC, the Babylonians captured Judah, destroyed Jerusalem, and took some of the Jewish people to Babylon. The Babylonians released Jeremiah and gave him the choice of staying behind in Jerusalem or migrating to Babylon. Jeremiah's choice was to remain, and the Babylonians appointed Gedaliah, an Israelite, to oversee the remnant.

Johanan, a Jewish leader of the remnant, heard rumors that King Baalis, an Ammonite, had sent Ishmael the Ammonite to kill Gedaliah. Johanan told Gedaliah about the plot against him, but he did not believe the danger and did not send anyone to kill Ishmael.

Ishmael and his men visited Gedaliah and murdered him and some of the Jewish people with him, but took some of the Jewish people captive with him. When Johanan heard the news, he chased Ishmael and his men. During the fierce battle, Ishmael and eight of his soldiers escaped, but he left behind the Jewish captives (Jeremiah 41:1-15).

---

[511] Peter Colon, "Shall Not Come to Mind Anymore". *Israel My Glory*: July-August 2013, 29.

Johanan and the Jewish captives returned to Jerusalem. Johanan was afraid that King Nebuchadnezzar would blame him for Gedaliah's murder by Ishmael, and slaughter him and the Jewish remnant (Jeremiah 41:16-18). Johanan and the remnant decided to run to Egypt but Johanan asked Jeremiah to pray and see what God's will was and for guidance on the decision (Jeremiah 42:1-3).

Jeremiah agreed to pray and said he would reveal God's entire message, whether good or bad (Jeremiah 42:4). The remnant promised to obey, whether the answer was good or bad (Jeremiah 42:6).

Ten days later, the Lord answered Jeremiah's prayer. The Judeans were told to stay in the Promised Land. If they obeyed, God promised to plant them in the land, manifest His presence and power, preserve them from Babylon's attack, and show them mercy and compassion (Jeremiah 42:7-12). God also said if they disobeyed and fled to Egypt, everyone would be destroyed by the sword, famine, and disease. The remnant did not know that soon the Babylonians would soon invade Egypt. Jeremiah emphasized that this warning was from the Lord (Jeremiah 42:13-18). Jeremiah told them their prayer request was hypocritical because they had already planned to go to Egypt. He accused them of only wanting God to approve of their plans (Jeremiah 42:19-22). They accused Jeremiah of lying and fled to Egypt anyway. They also accused Baruch of influencing Jeremiah to stop their escape and accused Baruch of working as a spy for Babylon in order to put them to death or take them captive.[512]

This location pictured has been designated the official site of the Mount of Beatitudes for 1,600 years. There is a church, monastery, hostel, gardens, and farm at the site. The ceiling walls of the chapel have an octagon shape with eight sides, and each side has a window with one of the eight verses of the Beatitudes. The garden has small areas where preachers can read from the Bible, sing, pray, and worship. The garden also has statues.

---

[512]   David M. Levy, "Judah's Fatal Decision". *Israel My Glory*: July-August 2013, 30-31.

THE VIEW OF THE SEA OF GALILEE FROM THE ROMAN CATHOLIC CHAPEL ON THE MOUNT OF BEATITUDES

Judah's Fatal Decision (Continued)

The remnant of Judah fled to Egypt with Jeremiah (Jeremiah 43:1-7). After Jeremiah arrived in Egypt, God told Jeremiah to bury large stones at the entrance of Pharaoh's house in Tahpanhes. When King Nebuchadnezzar invaded Egypt, he would capture many Egyptians, kill others, destroy and burn the houses of the Egyptians' gods, burn their golden idols, and set his throne over the stones Jeremiah buried (Jeremiah 43:8-13).

We can learn many lessons from Jeremiah chapters 42-43. First lesson: the Judean remnant was wise in seeking divine guidance about going to Egypt. Second lesson: the Judean remnant waited patiently for ten days to wait for an answer. Third lesson: It was wrong for the remnant to use double talk, promising to obey when they knew they had decided to go to Egypt.[513]

VIEWING THE SEA OF GALILEE FROM MOUNT OF BEATITUDES

The Consequences of Defying God

Jeremiah's last recorded message was for the remnant in Jerusalem to remain in Jerusalem and God would protect them. Instead, the remnant disobeyed God and fled to Egypt because of fear that the Babylonians would come back. They took Jeremiah with them to Egypt. In Chapter 43, Jeremiah denounced those who fled Judah to escape the prophesied Babylonian Captivity and their practice of worshiping other Gods, especially the Queen of Heaven. The Egyptian god was known as Isis (Jeremiah 44:21). "I have sent to you My servants, the prophets, rising early and sending them, saying, 'Oh, do not do this abominable thing that I

---

[513]   Ibid.

hate!' But they did not listen or incline their ear to turn from their wickedness, to burn incense to other gods. So My anger was poured out and kindled in the cities of Judah and in the streets of Jerusalem" (Jeremiah 43:4-6).

The people insisted on attributing their past prosperity to the Queen of Heaven. "We will not listen to you! But we will burn incense to the Queen of Heaven. For then we had plenty of food, were well-off, and saw no trouble. But since we stopped burning incense to the Queen of Heaven and pouring out drink offerings to her, we have lacked everything and have been consumed by the sword and by famine (Jeremiah 43:16-18).

Twisting the Law of Moses, they told Jeremiah that they had their husbands' consent and that Jeremiah had no right to interfere.

"And all the remnant of Judah, who have gone to the land of Egypt to dwell there, shall know whose words will stand, mine or theirs. And this shall be a sign to you," says the Lord, "that I will punish you in this place, that you may know that My words will surely stand against you for adversity" (Jeremiah 44:28-29).

"For thus says the Lord of hosts, the God of Israel: As My anger and My fury have been poured out on the inhabitants of Jerusalem, so will My fury be poured out on you when you enter Egypt" (Jeremiah 42:18).

God also gave a sign: "Behold, I will give Pharaoh Hophra king of Egypt into the hand of those who seek his life" (Jeremiah 44:30). Records show that Hophra lost his throne in 570 BC. Jeremiah used four metaphors to describe the Egyptian army's vulnerabilities. First metaphor: Egypt was described as "a very pretty heifer" about to be destroyed (Jeremiah 46:20). Second metaphor: Egyptian armies were characterized as "fat bulls awaiting slaughter" (Jeremiah 46:21). Third metaphor: Egypt's bragging was pictured as the hissing of a snake that slithers away in the face of real danger (Jeremiah 46:22). Fourth metaphor: The Babylonian army was pictured as covering Egypt like a cloud of grasshoppers, devastating the forest with axes (Jeremiah 46:23). The Babylonians conquered Egypt in 568-567 BC, fulfilling the prophecy of Jeremiah.[514]

OUR ROOM IN GAI BEACH RESORT HOTEL

Winkie noticed the mezuzah on the side of every door to the hotel rooms. The mezuzah comes from the scripture in Deuteronomy 6:9 which says to the people of Israel to write God's commands on the doorposts of

---

[514]   Charles E. McCracken, "Consequences of Defying God". *Israel My Glory*: July-August 2013, 32-33.

their homes. The Hebrew letter *shin* (the first letter in the Name of God, *Shaddai*) commonly appears on the outside of the mezuzah.

MEZUZAH ON EVERY DOOR

The menorah (candelabrum) could be found in the temple of the Jews and was the everlasting light. It represented the fact that the light or spirit of God never dies. It is the symbol of Israel in modern times. Full size menorahs have nine candles.

Incidents at Temple Mount

In May 2013, the Israeli police arrested the Grand Mufti for throwing chairs at Jewish people on the Temple Mount. Jordan's parliament demanded that Jordan expel Daniel Nevo, the Israeli Ambassador and recall the Jordanian ambassador in Israel.

After Israel liberated the Temple Mount during the 1967 Six-Day War, it put the Waqf in charge of the compound. The Waqf has removed every sign of ancient Jewish connections to the Temple Mount and destroyed Jewish antiquities on the Temple Mount in violation of the ruling by the Israeli Supreme Court.[515]

Jews arrested for Praying: Jerusalem's Mufti, Sheikh Muhammad Hussein, arrested five Jewish men for praying quietly on top of the Temple Mount. Police reported that a mob of Muslims gathered around the Jews and shouted insults and almost caused a fight. Islamic officials stepped in to restore calm with the condition that the Jewish worshipers be arrested. Jews and Christians are not allowed to pray on top of the Temple Mount, for fear of upsetting the Muslims who control the Temple Mount. The Mufti was arrested due to suspicion of inciting a mob, and one young Muslim boy yelled insults at Jewish visitors for simply being Jews. The mob attacked and killed two police officers who tried to quiet the screaming young Muslim boy.[516] (Israel Today).

Why Two Kingdoms?

[515] *Arutz-7* IsraelNationalNews.com, May 9, 2013, www.israelnationalnews.com/News/News.aspx/167866#.Vh8VtflViko.

[516] "Incidents at Temple Mount". *Israel My Glory*: July-August 2013, 34.

The United Kingdom was called Israel and there was only one kingdom during the time of Saul, David, and Solomon. Solomon had a lot of wisdom in most things, but he was foolish to forsake God and worship pagan gods. God used the foolishness of Solomon's son, King Rehoboam, to divide the kingdom around 922 BC (1 Kings 11:9-13). The ten northern tribes of Reuben, Simeon, Dan, Naphtali, Gad, Asher, Ephraim, Manasseh, Issachar, and Zebulun became the northern kingdom, using the name Israel. David's tribe of Judah and the small tribe of Benjamin became the southern kingdom, which was called Judah. In the beginning, the Levites were spread throughout both kingdoms, but eventually most Levites ended up in Judah where the temple was.

Judah was the Davidic kingdom and all its kings were the descendants of David. Israel had many murderers as kings, including Ahab, and none of these kings were descendants of David. Eight of Judah's kings were righteous and none of Israel's kings were righteous.

Jerusalem, the old capital of David (around 1000 BC) continued as the capital of Judah until it was captured by Babylon in 586 BC. Samaria was the capital of the northern kingdom. By the time of Jeremiah the prophet, the northern kingdom had already been captured by Assyria. Twenty-two years after Jeremiah began prophesying, the Babylonians captured Judah and began deporting Judah's best and brightest to Babylon.

By the time Babylon burned Jerusalem and the temple in 586 BC, it was a world power. So all the Israelites captured by Assyria came under Babylonian dominion. Later, Babylon fell to the Medo-Persian empire in 539 BC. All the Jews captured returned home to their land when King Cyrus of Persia released them from captivity in 538 BC.[517]

GAI BEACH HOTEL IN TIBERIAS

Fellowship with God

The apostle John's epistle gives a lesson on fellowship with God the Father and God the Son. Believers must walk in the light revealed by God's word to have this special fellowship with God. A person will not engage in habitual sin if he walks in God's light. John teaches that if a person confesses his sin, there is

---

[517] "Why Two Kingdoms?" *Israel My Glory*: July-August 2013, 35.

cleansing, forgiveness, and renewed fellowship with God. "This is the message which we have heard from Him and declare to you, that God is light and in Him is no darkness at all, not one single bit of darkness" (1 John 1:5).

1 John 1:5 implies more than the absence of darkness. It does not tell us that God has light or created light, but that He is uncreated light, which states the nature of God. Scriptures say that God was covered with light (Psalm 104:2) and dwelt in unapproachable light (I Timothy 6:16) before He created anything. Throughout Scripture, light symbolizes God's purity, holiness, virtue, morality, truth, character, and glory. Light describes God's true nature.

John added, "and in Him is no darkness at all" (1 John 1:5, James 1:17). John said darkness is used in Scripture to talk of evil, wickedness, and deception, and it leads to death.

God's nature became visible in Jesus Christ at His Incarnation. Jesus said, "I am the light of the world. He who follows Me shall not walk in darkness, but have the light of life" (John 8:12). Just as light is necessary for physical life on Earth, so spiritual light is necessary for one to have spiritual life. Christ is the true light of the world (John 1:9).

In 1 John 1:6 and through the end of the chapter, John used five clauses that some professing believers were leading double lives before God, when they claimed to walk intimately with Him but were walking in the darkness of sin. "If we say that we have fellowship with Him, and walk in darkness, we lie and do not practice the truth" (1 John 1:6). "But if we walk in the light as He is in the light, we have fellowship with one another, and the blood of Jesus Christ His Son cleanses us from all sin" (1 John 1:7).[518]

Friday, January 11, 2013

Fellowship with God (continued)

"If we say that we have fellowship with Him, and walk in darkness, we lie and do not practice truth" (1 John 1:6). "Walk in darkness" refers to wicked thoughts and deeds. "But if we walk in the light as He is in the light, we have fellowship with one another, and the blood of Jesus Christ His Son cleanses us from all sin" (1 John 1:7). True believers have thoughts and conduct that revolve around

---

[518]   David M. Levy, "Fellowship with God". *Israel My Glory*: July-August 2013, 36-37.

God's light that they have received from God. Others see this in them and they have true unbroken fellowship with God.[519]

CANA AND
THE FIRST MIRACLE

Jesus' first miracle was to turn water into fine wine at a wedding (John 2). Mary was happy when Jesus made the water into wine, when the wedding celebration with friends gave out of wine and Jesus miraculously made it possible for the guests to be served.

Israel in the News

Israel Launches News Network: *Communication mavens believe that Israel needs to get its message out to the world. French businessman Patrick Drahi, owner of the controlling interest in Hot cable television, is one of the financiers of i24 News. i24 News was started by Frank Malloui, who will act as its CEO. It will have 24/7 coverage and a website that will discuss politics, international affairs, culture, and sports. It will broadcast from Jaffa Port and will be started this summer. (The Jerusalem Post)*

Poverty Rating High in Israel: *Israel struggles with high poverty levels. Israel has the highest poverty rate of all developed nations. Nearly 21 percent of all Israelis live below the poverty line. Israel has a poverty rate higher than Mexico. Middle-class Israelis live from paycheck to paycheck. (Israel Today)*

Mega Drought: *Israel has just recovered from a seven-year drought. Experts with the Water Authority's Hydrological Service predict the next drought in 2015 to be worse than the last one. Israel reclaims wastewater for agriculture and has a desalination program that covers water needs. (Israel Today)*

PA Arabs Gifted Israeli Citizenship: *Several thousand Palestinian Authority Arabs who live in certain neighborhoods on the Israeli side of the security fence and work in Israel were granted Israeli citizenship, to be eligible to vote and to receive National Insurance. (Israel Today)*

Google Officially OK's Palestine: *Google made a decision to recognize Palestine as an independent state. Israel expressed its displeasure with Google's*

---

[519]   Ibid.

decision. Google based its decision on the recent UN decision to award non-member state status to Palestine. UNESCO approved Palestine's status as a sovereign Palestine state. Israel stated to Google, "This is intervention by an international company in politics, and does not serve interests of either party in the long-term." (Israel Today)

IDF gets Riot Suits: *The Israel Defense Forces (IDF) has received new riot dispersal equipment such as protective suits for soldiers and an advanced GPS system. These will be helpful in handling violent riots in Judea and Samaria. The suits are designed to absorb shocks, stones and clubs. (Israel National News)*[520]

CANA WINE CONTAINER

Cana is a small village called Kefar Cana. The word *Cana* means "reed" in Hebrew. The first miracle of Jesus was turning water into the best wine that people had ever tasted. Jesus was at the wedding celebration with Mary when the hosts ran out of wine. Mary asked Jesus to do something about the problem. Jesus replied, "My time has not yet come." Jesus decided to please Mary and turned the water into wine. Notice how big the container is in the photo. Cana is only mentioned in the book of John.

Jesus was visiting Cana when a royal official of Capernaum approached him with news that his son was very ill. The official believed him, and his son was healed. Nathanael, a disciple of Jesus, was from Cana.

This place (pictured) is the traditional site of Cana in the days of Jesus. There are two other probable locations of biblical Cana. This Cana has been the traditional site since the 4th century.

---

[520] "Israel in the News". *Israel My Glory*: July-August 2013, 40.

REFLECTIONS IN THE CHURCH AT CANA

Scripture references to Cana are John 2:1, John 2:11, John 4:46, and John 21:2.

Inside the church, we reflected on how the first miracle of Jesus was turning water into wine. In those days for a wedding celebration, the entire town was invited and there was a big celebration. It was important to provide wine for the guests, and it is nice that Mary was concerned about it. Jesus wanted to make Mary happy and he did not see anything wrong with a happy celebration.

CHRISTMAS TREE IN CANA

Christmas in Israel is celebrated through January 14, so we enjoyed Christmas in many places.

SYNAGOGUE IN NAZARETH

Nazareth is eighteen miles from Tiberias. Nazareth is the boyhood home of Jesus. The word *Nazareth* means "branch" or "shoot". Isaiah 11:1 says, "A branch shall grow out of his (Jesse's) roots." God probably chose Nazareth because of the meaning of the word and because Jesus was a branch from the line of Jesse and David. Nazareth is north of the Valley of Jezreel. The gospels of Matthew and Luke identify the village of Nazareth as the home of Mary and Joseph. Luke 4:16 describes Jesus as an adult, speaking to the people at the synagogue in Nazareth, and they did not believe him.

In the 1st century AD, the population of Nazareth was about 480 people, with a total area of about sixty acres. Nazareth began about the 3rd century AD as an agricultural area, according to archaeological excavations.[521]

NAZARETH SYNAGOGUE: THE SYNAGOGUE WHERE JESUS TAUGHT WAS LOCATED ON THIS SPOT

We sat in an old synagogue in Nazareth and had a worship service with the singing of hymns, with prayer, and with reading of scripture. This was not the synagogue from the time of Jesus, but it was a very old one. We felt close to Jesus, Mary, and Joseph, as we worshiped with prayer, scripture, and songs; and we imagined what it was like when Jesus and the family worshiped in the synagogue.

NAZARETH: SYNAGOGUE CHURCH (GREEK CATHOLIC)

Saint Peter's Cross

This Petrine cross is inverted and is the symbol for the cross of Peter. Tradition is that Peter was crucified upside down. Recently this symbol has become a satanic symbol.

"But when you grow old, you will stretch out your hands, and someone else will fasten a belt around you and take you where you do not wish to go" (John 21:18).[522]

---

[521] Greg DeLoach, *A Journey to the Holy Land: A Scriptural Study.* Augusta, GA: First Baptist Church, 10.

[522] Greg DeLoach, *Reflections on the Cross.* First Baptist Church of Augusta: Spring 2013, 17.

Archaeologists discovered artifacts that show that Nazareth was a small agricultural village with a population of only about a dozen or so during Old Testament times. The artifacts show that the settlement was used from 900-600 BC. Most of the artifacts are caves, cisterns, and grain storage bins.

Anchor Cross

The Anchor Cross looks like an anchor. It is also called the Cross of Saint Clement, because Saint Clement was martyred with an anchor tied to his neck and thrown into the sea. This cross is connected with hope.

"We have hope, a sure and steadfast anchor of the soul" (Hebrews 6:19).[523]

Coptic Cross

The Coptic Cross may have been an adaptation from the Ankh Cross. This cross was adopted early by the Christian Gnostics from North Africa, where Coptic Christianity began. It is a tradition that Christianity was begun in Egypt by Mark. In art, the halo of Christ is often depicted as cross, a custom based mainly in Eastern Orthodox traditions.

"They compelled a passerby, who was coming in from the country, to carry his cross; it was Simon of Cyrene, the father of Alexander and Rufus" (Mark 15:21).[524]

WALKING IN THE STREETS OF NAZARETH

---

[523] Ibid., 19.
[524] Ibid., 19.

We enjoyed listening to a nice man in the wheelchair play songs for tourists. We tipped him for bringing music to our ears as we walked down the street. In Nazareth, the sidewalks were nice and we could walk on them, instead of narrow streets like we saw in the Old City of Jerusalem.

Nazareth is located near the Plain of Esdraelon in Galilee. Nazareth is not mentioned in the Old Testament. But excavations prove that settlements were there during the Bronze Age. Tombs have been found that date back to the Iron Age and to the Hasmonean period.

From a hilltop in Nazareth, tourists can see Mount Carmel. On this same hilltop, tourists can look south and see Megiddo and the entire Plain of Esdraelon. Tourists can also view Tabor and the hills of Gilboa, where Saul and Jonathan were killed in an ancient battle.

BASILICA OF THE ANNUNCIATION IN NAZARETH

The Basilica of the Annunciation is a Catholic Church built over the ruins of a Byzantine and Crusader Church, which includes the cave where Gabriel told Mary she was to be the mother of the Messiah (Luke 1:26-29). This cave was identified in the 4th century AD.

This church was dedicated by Pope Paul VI in 1964 and was completed in 1969. The lower level has the remains of Mary's house, and the upper level is the church with murals of Mary. One mural shows a picture of Jesus with Peter on Mount Zion, and another shows Mary sitting and praying for her husband.

In modern times, the Basilica of the Annunciation is a parish church for 7,000 Catholics in Nazareth and is a Christian site for Protestants.

We enjoyed looking at all the beautiful murals of Mary and scenes dealing with Mary's life. These murals made us think of the life of Jesus on earth and his activities with Mary, his mother. We were happy that taking pictures was allowed.

Centuries ago in 680 AD, a pilgrim named Arculf wrote about seeing two churches in Nazareth: one at Mary's Spring and one where the Basilica stands today.

After the Battle of the Horns of Hattin in 1187 in the Tiberias area, the Christians of Nazareth hid in the church. The Muslims discovered them and slaughtered them all, but left the church standing. Salah Al-Din gave permission for some of the clergy to return and allowed Christians to visit. The Muslims finally decided to fill the church with garbage and use it for cows. But luckily, in the 14th century the Franciscans gained control, and repaired the church in 1620. By 1730, the Franciscans built a new church. In 1955, this church was torn down to build a new church over the Crusader and Byzantine foundations.

Modern Coptic Cross

The Modern Coptic Cross is used by the Coptic Church around the world, especially in Ethiopia. The cross has bold, intersecting lines and has three points at the end of each arm, which symbolizes the Trinity. There is a total of twelve points, which symbolize the Apostles and their mission to the world. Some Coptics have this cross tattooed on their arms and wear it with pride and dignity.

"Set me as a seal upon your arm, for love is strong as death, passion as fierce as the grave" (Song of Solomon 8:6).[525]

We ate lunch at the gas station shown in this photo. Gas sells for about eight shekels a liter. We noticed that a large majority of cars all over Israel are small.

LUNCH INSIDE THE GAS STATION IN NAZARETH: A GOOD PLACE KNOWN FOR ITS GOOD FOOD

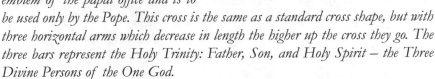

The Papal Cross

The Papal Cross is the official emblem of the papal office and is to be used only by the Pope. This cross is the same as a standard cross shape, but with three horizontal arms which decrease in length the higher up the cross they go. The three bars represent the Holy Trinity: Father, Son, and Holy Spirit – the Three Divine Persons of the One God.

"Whoever wishes to become great among you must be your servant, and whoever wishes to be first among you must be slave of all" (Mark 10:43-44).[526]

---

[525] Ibid., 20.
[526] Ibid., 21.

The Baptismal Cross

In Egypt, the eight spokes of the Baptismal Cross symbolized the eight ema-nations of creation. In Christianity, the number eight came to symbolize the seven days of creation, with the eighth day representing resurrection. Baptismal fonts and ancient churches were marked with eight sides as a reminder of the resurrection.

"Therefore we have been buried with him by baptism into death, so that, just as Christ was raised from the dead by the glory of the Father, so we too might walk in the newness of life" (Romans 6:4).[527]

EATING FALAFEL FOR LUNCH IN NAZARETH

Most of us chose falafel to eat in Nazareth. This is a popular sand-wich made out of pita bread and fried chick pea patties, along with many raw vegetables.

Cross of Calvary

The Cross of Calvary is a Latin Cross on three steps. It is used today for altar arrangements and on top of communion tables. The Cross of Calvary is also called the Stepped Cross or Graded Cross. This cross reminds people of ascending to or climbing towards Calvary, which is Latin for Golgotha, the Place of a Skull.

"Then he handed him over to them to be crucified. So they took Jesus; and carrying the cross by himself, he went out to what is called The Place of the Skull, which in Hebrew is called Golgotha" (John 19:16-17).[528]

The Greek Cross

The Greek Cross is believed to be one of the earliest and most common symbols of Christianity. It is found in the old catacombs of Rome. There are four simple and equal lines on this simple cross.

---

[527] Ibid., 22.
[528] Ibid., 23.

"For God so loved the world that he gave his only begotten Son, so that everyone who believes in him may not perish but may have eternal life" (John 3:16).[529]

NAZARETH MANGER SCENE IN JANUARY

The Grapevine Cross

The Grapevine Cross has drooping arms and is also known as the Georgian Cross or the Cross of Saint Nino. Saint Nino was the Cappadocian woman who preached Christianity in the 4th century in what is now the Republic of Georgia. Legend has it that Mary, the mother of Jesus, gave her the cross of grapevines. Today this cross is kept in Sioni Cathedral in Tbilisi, Georgia, and is the symbol of the Georgian Orthodox Church.

"Meanwhile, standing near the cross of Jesus was his mother" (John 19:25).[530]

"WC" MEANS RESTROOM IN ISRAEL ("WATER CLOSET")

Some restrooms in Israel are free of charge, and others cost one U.S. dollar or three shekels. Some restrooms provide toilet paper, and some require you to use one of your Kleenex that you carry in your pocket in case you need it. Some restrooms are for men, and separate ones are for ladies. Some restrooms have many stalls with doors that are used for both men and women.

---

[529]   Ibid., 24.
[530]   Ibid., 25.

The Staurogram Cross

The Staurogram Cross means "cross monogram". This cross is also called the Tau-Rho Cross because it is shaped like the Greek letters tau, symbolizing the cross, and rho, recalling Jesus as Messiah. It also symbolizes "Jesus saves", and by the 5th and 6th centuries, the symbol was found all over Western Europe.

"But we proclaim Christ crucified, a stumbling block to Jews and foolishness to Gentiles, but to those who are the called, both Jews and Greeks, Christ the power of God and the wisdom of God" (1 Corinthians 1:23-24).[531]

NAZARETH

In modern times, archaeologists uncovered the remains of a house dating to the time of Jesus. The house had two rooms, as well as a courtyard where a cistern collected rain water.

Budded Cross

The Budded Cross is also called the Apostles Cross, the Treflee, or the Cathedral Cross. It has three circles at the end of each arm, representing the Trinity. Legend says that it came from Celtic Druidry, where the circles symbolized the dominions of earth, sky, and sea.

"What sort of man is this, that even the winds and the sea obey him?" (Matthew 8:27).[532]

---

[531] Ibid., 26.
[532] Ibid., 27.

MODERN NAZARETH STORE WELCOMES US

The store owner in the photo showed us ancient antiques and how they were used in the past in Israel. The owner served us good, hot tea and made us feel welcome. There were many interesting items in the store, but they all were expensive.

Maltese Cross

The Maltese Cross is also known as the Amalfi cross and is associated with the people of Malta. It is also a modern symbol of Amalfi, a small Italian republic of the 11th century. The Maltese Cross represents political causes or domains and is not from religious origins.

"For I am not ashamed of the gospel; it is the power of God for salvation to everyone who has faith" (Romans 1:16).[533]

Huguenot Cross

The Huguenot Cross is used often on jewelry, but in the beginning it was a Christian religious symbol originating in France. This cross first appeared during the Huguenot wars of 1562-1598. The eight points on this cross symbolize the eight Beatitudes in Matthew. Descending from the cross is the dove, a symbol of the Holy Spirit. Today this cross is used by the descendants of the Huguenots.

"Blessed are the peacemakers, for they will be called children of God" (Matthew 5:9).[534]

The Salem Cross

The Salem Cross is connected to freemasonry and the Knights Templar. The three bars suggest head, crossbeam, and footrest. The three can refer to the Trinity or to the three crosses on Calvary.

"Blessed are the merciful, for they will receive mercy" (Matthew 5:7).[535]

---

[533] Ibid., 28.

[534] Ibid., 29.

[535] Ibid., 30.

SHOPPING IN NAZARETH:SHOPKEEPER SHOWS US ANTIQUES

Patriarchal Cross

The Patriarchal Cross is a variation of the Russian Cross and the Papal Cross. This cross was used by many in the Byzantine Empire by the 10th century. Many believe it was given to Saint Stephen by the pope as a symbol of the apostolic kingdom in Hungary. Since 1190, it has been one of the main elements in the coats of arms of the Kingdom of Hungary.

"But strive first for the kingdom of God and his righteousness, and all these things will be given to you as well" (Matthew 6:33).[536]

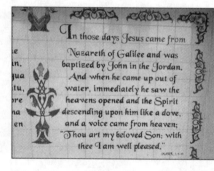

JORDAN RIVER: BAPTISM OF JESUS BY JOHN THE BAPTIST

Macedonian Cross

This cross is also known as the Veljusa Cross because it was first presented and displayed in the Veljusa monastery near Strumica about 1085. The Macedonian Cross is associated with Christianity in Macedonia. It is also a symbol of the Macedonian Orthodox Church and is found on the coat of arms. The arms of the cross interlock and represent the everlasting love of God. The center square represents the four corners of the world.

---

[536] Ibid., 31.

"I have loved you with an everlasting love; therefore I have continued my faithfulness to you" (Jeremiah 31:3).[537]

Cross Potent

The Cross Potent is pre-Christian and has been found in Neolithic petroglyphs going back to 2500 BC. Other names for this cross are the Crutch Cross and the Teutonic Cross. The name "potent" comes from the French word potentcee, meaning "strong". In modern times, this cross is used for logos and insignia by Christians and secular organizations. The Cross Potent was used as a national symbol of the Austrian First Republic and minted on the backside of Groschen coins. Bolivia uses this cross in the coats of arms at the Santa Cruz Department. Germany, Austria, and Estonia use it for the Wingolf Christian student fraternities.

"Be strong in the Lord and in the strength of his power" (Ephesians 6:10).[538]

Trinity Cross

The Trinity Cross is a simple version of the Latin Cross. It is an equilateral triangle that symbolizes the Holy Trinity. The spiritual meaning of this cross is that salvation is the work and gift of Jesus Christ. It is prompted by the love of the Father and received by men and women with the help of the Holy Spirit. The term "trinity" is not found in the Bible. Trinity is a theological affirmation embraced as orthodox by the fourth century.

"I give them eternal life, and they will never perish. No one will snatch them out of my hand. What my Father has given me is greater than all else, and no one can snatch it out of the Father's hand. The Father and I are one" (John 10:28-30).[539]

---

[537] Ibid., 32.
[538] Ibid., 33.
[539] Ibid., 36.

JORDAN RIVER

Serbian Cross

The Serbian Cross is a national symbol of Serbia, part of the Coat of Arms of Serbia, and part of the flag of Serbia. It is a cross symbol with four stylized letters, "beta" (B), o   n each ofits corners. The origin of the beta (B) symbol goes back to the Byzantine Empire and the motto of the Palaiologoi Dynasty which said: "King of Kings, Ruling Over Kings".

"For he is Lord of lords and King of kings, and those with him are called and chosen and faithful." (Revelation 17:14).[540]

VIDEO BY THE JORDAN RIVER OFFICIALS

Jordan River officials video each group and sell the copies for $15. One or two people in our group bought it. Winkie fell backward when she tried to touch the water. She hit the ground on her seat instead of falling face forward into the water. The officials did not include that in the video. Winkie would have bought it if it had shown her falling backward and the two gentlemen friends trying to get her up.

Consecration Cross

The Consecration Cross has prehistoric origins used as veneration of the sun. It is even known as the Sun Cross. Astronomers used this symbol as the planetary system of earth. In Christian iconography, the sun and the cross appear in the Celtic Cross, the Glory Cross, in halos, and in communion wafers.

---

[540]   Ibid., 37.

"It is I, Jesus, who sent my angel to you with this testimony for the churches. I am the root and the descendant of David, the bright morning star" (Revelation 22:16).[541]

Cross Fitchy

This design may have been used by traveling Crusaders, who would drive Cross Fitchy into the ground. The shape of the cross looks like a sword, which was a symbol of the Crusaders. The name "fitchy" comes from the French word for "fixed", which refers to the pointed lower part.

"Then Jesus said to him, 'Put your sword back into its place; for all who take the sword will perish by the sword'" (Matthew 26:52).[542]

Arrow Cross

The Arrow Cross is also called Cross Barbee in heraldry. Christians think the ends of the cross look like the barbs of fish hooks. This suggests the "fishers of people" theme found in the Gospel. Some people think that the arrows represent a call to spread the Gospel all over the world. In Europe and the United States, this cross is associated with extremist groups.

"Follow me, and I will make you fish for people" (Matthew 4:19).[543]

JEWISH SINGERS CELEBRATING THE SABBATH

We were eating in the same room as a large group of Jews celebrating the Sabbath (*Shabbat*). These two little boys sang solos and duets in joyful voices. We talked to this family and asked if we could take their pictures, and the father said, "Put it on Facebook if you desire." These two little Jewish boys gave us a good example of singing joyously before God and honoring God. They were good models from which we could learn.

---

[541]   Ibid., 38.

[542]   Ibid., 39.

[543]   Ibid., 40.

Cross of Glory

The Cross of Glory is popular during Easter season. It is a simple Latin Cross with a rising sun behind it. In some traditions, as the sun rises, people sing Gloria, an old Latin doxology. Singing as the sun rises is a reminder of the resurrection of Christ and looking for the return of Jesus Christ.

"The one who testifies to these things says, 'Surely I am coming soon.' Amen. Come, Lord Jesus! The grace of the Lord Jesus be with all the saints. Amen." (Revelation 22:20-21).[544]

Saturday, January 12, 2013

On this day of our trip, we traveled south through the Jordan River Valley to Bethlehem. Bethlehem is only about five miles south of Jerusalem, thirty-seven miles from Tel Aviv, and forty-five miles northeast of Gaza and the Mediterranean Sea. Bethlehem is 2,543 feet above sea level and ninety-eight feet higher than Jerusalem. Bethlehem is on the southern part of the Judean Mountains. Modern Bethlehem has a population of about 25,000 people and is the capital of the Bethlehem Governorate of the Palestinian National Authority. The main economy is the tourism income from visitors.

---

[544] Ibid., 41.

BETHLEHEM SQUARE

The majority of the people in Bethlehem are Muslim, but the city has a number of surviving Palestinian Christian communities. The people were very friendly and made us feel welcome and safe.

Rachel's Tomb is at the northern entrance of Bethlehem. Rachel was a wife of Jacob and the mother of Joseph and Benjamin. The book of Ruth describes the valley to the east of Bethlehem as the place where Ruth of Moab gleaned the fields of Boaz, after she went to Bethlehem with her mother-in-law Ruth. Ruth later married Boaz, and one of their descendants was King David. Three of David's warriors brought David water from the well at Bethlehem to him at his hiding place in the cave of Adullam.

The Bible identifies Bethlehem as the city that David was from and the place where he was crowned the King of Israel. The New Testament states that Jesus of Nazareth was born in Bethlehem.

In 2012, Archaeologists found a bulla (a seal impression of dried clay) in ancient Hebrew script that reads, "From the town of Bethlehem to the King". That may have meant that a shipment of grain, wine, or other goods was sent as a tax payment in the 8th or 7th century BC.

Biblical scholars believe that the hill country of Judah may be the same place as the biblical Ephratah, which means "fertile". The book of Micah refers to Bethlehem Ephratah. The Bible also calls it "Judah" and "a City of David". Bethlehem is first mentioned in the Bible in Genesis 48:7 as the place where Rachel died and was buried.

Bethlehem enjoys a Mediterranean climate with hot and dry summers and cold winters. Winter temperatures are cold and rainy, at 33 to 55 degrees Fahrenheit. August is the hottest month, with a high of 81 degrees. Rainfall averages twenty-eight inches per year, with most of it taking place between November and January. On most days, a Mediterranean Sea breeze blows around noon. Between April, May, and mid-June, Khamaseen winds from the Arabian Desert blow hot, dry, sandy, and dusty winds.

Bethlehem factories make paints, plastics, synthetic rubber, pharmaceuticals, construction materials, and food products. The monks in the Monastery of Cremisan sell wine.

In 2008, the Palestinian prime minister hosted a huge economic conference. The United States donated 1.4 billion dollars for business investments in Palestinian areas.

OUR GUIDE

Roman Catholics and Protestants celebrate Christmas on December 25. Greek, Coptic, and Syrian Orthodox Christians celebrate Christmas on January 6. Our guide was a Syrian Orthodox Christian who lives in nearby Jerusalem. Armenian Orthodox

Christians celebrate Christmas on January 19. So we were able to celebrate Christmas in January in Bethlehem, where the First Christmas was when Jesus was born in Bethlehem. Most Christmas processions pass through Manger Square. Christmas Roman Catholic services take place at Saint Catherine's Church. Protestants mainly hold Christmas services at Shepherd's Field.

The Church of the Nativity is located in the center of Bethlehem and is part of Manger Square. The church is built over a cave called the Holy Crypt, where Jesus was born. Nearby is the Milk Grotto where Mary, Joseph, and Jesus hid before their flight to Egypt.

Tensions flare over Women's Prayers at Western Wall

On April 4, 2013, the ultra-Orthodox rabbi in charge of the Western Wall assured a government emissary that Jewish women will not be arrested if they try to recite the mourner's prayer, although they received a warning from the Israeli police. Traditional Jews and reform-minded women disagree over the type of prayers. The Western Wall contains the remains of the temple destroyed by the Romans thousands of years ago.

Prime Minister Benjamin Netanyahu picked Natan Sharansky, chairman of the Jewish agency, to settle the prayer conflict and ensure that every Jew in the world can pray like they are accustomed to at this most religious site. Prime Minister Netanyahu and Sharansky had a meeting three weeks after the Israeli police told the women that if they recited the Kaddish mourner's prayer at the Western Wall again they would be arrested.

The ultra-Orthodox Jews believe that women should not sing or pray aloud in public because their voices are provocative to men. Tradition is that the Kaddish mourner's prayer is only recited when at least ten men are present. They argue that it is offensive to traditionalists for the women to recite the prayer.

Members of Women of the Wall, a group of Reform, Conservative and modern-Orthodox women have been praying together at the Western Wall for more than twenty years. During that time, the ultra-Orthodox Jews have tried to put restrictions on the women.

Recently, several Women of the Wall have been detained for wearing prayer shawls and bringing in a Torah scroll to the women's section, which was banned by a 2005 High Court ruling that mandated the status quo at this famous holy site.

The women's group holds monthly prayer services at the holy site. In March, three female Israeli parliamentarians dressed in prayer shawls joined the 300 worshipers. No one was arrested.[545]

BETHLEHEM: CHURCH OF THE NATIVITY

Giving and Getting

In 1 Kings 17:1-7 is Elijah's first appearance in scripture. Elijah walked up to King Ahab and said that the rains and the morning dew would cease until Elijah gave the word for it to return raining. Elijah's name means, "My God is Yahweh." King Ahab was a wicked king who married Jezebel, the daughter of the King of Sidon. King Ahab followed his wife into the worship of Baal. After Elijah gave the king the message, the word of the Lord sent Elijah into hiding at the brook called Cherith, a tributary of the Jordan. Yahweh sent ravens to take food to Elijah. Finally, when the water ran out, Elijah needed to find a new hiding place.

Elijah traveled north and west to a city called Zarephath, near the coastal city of Sidon, not far from the hometown of Jezebel and within the kingdom of the father of Jezebel. Ahab and Jezebel searched for Elijah but could not find him (1 Kings 17:8-16).

Elijah was staying in the home of a poor Phoenician widow. Elijah appeared suddenly and requested food and water. The woman did not have much food or water, but finally agreed to share what she had with Elijah. She was gathering firewood to prepare her final cake before the last of the flour and oil was gone. Elijah promised the woman that her food supply would last as long as the drought if she shared with him. A woman close to Sidon would not be expected to worship Yahweh or look after Yahweh's prophet. When the woman accepted the offer to provide food for Elijah, the prediction of Elijah came true and the food lasted as long as Elijah remained.

The widow's son became very sick and died. She became very upset and said to Elijah, "What have you against me, O man of God? You have come to me to bring my sin to remembrance, and to cause the death of my son!" (1 Kings 17:18). In verse 19, Elijah responded by taking the boy upstairs where the prophet could talk to God better. In verse 20, Elijah cried out to God with words very similar

[545] Michele Chabin, "Tensions Flare Over Women's Prayers at Western Wall". *Baptists Today News Journal*: May 2013, 11.

to those of the widow. Elijah may have thought God was responsible and did not understand why God responded to the widow's hospitality so cruelly. Elijah prayed, "Yahweh, my God, please let the life of this boy return within him" (1 Kings 17:22). As Elijah carried the widow's son downstairs to his mother, the son came back to life (1 Kings 17:22).[546]

BETHLEHEM: CHURCH OF THE NATIVITY

I Want It

In 1 Kings 21:1-29 is the story of Jezebel, who was married to King Ahab and used to getting everything she wanted. King Ahab wanted some land next to his palace in Jezreel. He offered Naboth, the land owner, more than the land was worth. Naboth believed that God did not want him to sell his ancestral inheritance, and refused to sell. Jezebel forged a letter from her husband, accusing Naboth of cursing God and King Ahab and to be killed for his betrayal. Jezebel's plan worked and Naboth was falsely murdered.

Elijah heard about what happened and confronted King Ahab. When Elijah told King Ahab how he had been tricked, he was upset, and he followed the Jewish custom of ripping off his clothes and walking around in sackcloth. God accepted the remorse of King Ahab and delayed his punishment for another generation.[547]

BETHLEHEM

Listen to the Silence

In 1 Kings 19:1-18, Elijah received a death threat from Jezebel. Elijah traveled to Beersheba to hide with his servant. He left the servant in Beersheba and hurried to the wilderness, where he rested under a broom tree. Elijah went to sleep, and an angel came twice to tell him

---

[546] Tony W. Cartledge, "Giving and Getting". *Baptists Today News Journal*: May 2013, 20-21.

[547] David Cassady, "I Want It", Youth Lessons. *Baptists Today News Journal*: May 2013, 22-23.

to get up and eat and drink. Elijah ate a couple of meals and traveled forty days to Mount Horeb, the mount of God.

At Horeb, the word of the LORD came to him and told him to go stand on the mountain, because God would pass by. Elijah obeyed and he endured a wind strong enough to break rocks, an earthquake, and a fire – and then silence. Elijah heard the voice of the LORD in the silence, and the voice told him to return to Damascus and anoint Hazael as king.[548]

Wear It

Elijah followed God's instruction in 1 Kings 19:15-21 and was on the way to Damascus. On the trip to Damascus he was to anoint Hazael as king over Aram, Jehu over Israel, and Elisha as a prophet. He anointed Elisha first by simply tossing his mantle over Elisha.

Elisha asked to leave to tell his parents before he began working with Elijah. When Elisha returned, he killed his oxen and gave the meat away to the people. Then he was ready to begin working with Elijah.[549]

BETHLEHEM: BEAUTIFUL CEILING MOSAICS ILLUSTRATING THE LIFE OF JESUS

Bible Study with Tony W. Cartledge: 1 Kings 21:1-20 (Elijah)

King Ahab and Jezebel learned that what they wanted and what they needed they did not always get, and that God has a "say-so" in the issue. King Ahab wanted to buy the vineyard belonging to Naboth and use it for his vegetable garden. King Ahab offered to pay a good sum in cash for the property or to exchange it for a better property. Naboth's answer was no. Naboth believed that God had entrusted the land to Israel and that the land had been divided by the tribes when they entered Canaan (Joshua 13:22). And Naboth's family had received this piece of land for an inheritance.

---

[548] David Cassady, "Listen to the Silence", Youth Lessons. *Baptists Today News Journal*: May 2013, 22-23.

[549] David Cassady, "Wear It", Youth Lessons. *Baptists Today News Journal*: May 2013, 22-23.

Leviticus 25:23-28 states that the land could not be bought or sold like other commodities. If someone was poverty-stricken, the land could be sold temporarily. Hopefully a kinsman would redeem the land to keep it in the family. It was supposed to revert back to the ancestral house during the next Jubilee year.

King Ahab did not try to convince Naboth any further, but was resentful over the refusal to buy this prized property. King Ahab even refused to eat. Queen Jezebel ignored the traditions of Israel and believed that the king had complete power to get what he wanted. Jezebel talked her husband into telling her the details of why he was so unhappy. Jezebel scolded the king and told him to act as a king. Jezebel secretly wrote letters in Ahab's name and sealed them with the king's seal. She also instructed the citizens of Jezreel to have a fast, and to call everyone to a special assembly. She also provided Naboth a good seat and appointed two people to bring against Naboth accusations of cursing both the king and God. Both crimes were punishable by death. Jezebel commanded them to take Naboth outside and stone him. Deuteronomy 17:6 required two witnesses, but Jezebel twisted it by providing the two witnesses, who broke the commandment of not bearing false witness. Jezebel sent King Ahab out immediately to claim the land.

Elijah showed up and told Ahab that he would soon get more than the land: he would get the punishment he needed. Because Ahab had done evil in God's sight, God would bring evil on him (1 Kings 21:20-21).[550]

LUNCH IN BETHLEHEM

---

[550] Tony W. Cartledge, "Bible Study with Tony W. Cartledge: I Kings 21:1-20". *Baptists Today News Journal* May 2013, 24-25.

Bible Study with Tony W. Cartledge: 1 Kings 21:1-20 (continued)

"Deuteronomistic History" is a narrative from Joshua through 11 Kings (with the exception of Ruth), which illustrates the belief that obedience to God results in blessing, and rebellion results in curses. In Deuteronomy 28, good is repaid with blessings, and evil is repaid with evil. Prophets warned Jeroboam, Baasha, and Ahab that their dynasties would not last and that their bodies would become food for dogs or birds. And all had sons who died after becoming kings for only two years.

Elijah said to King Ahab, *"Because you have provoked me to anger and have caused Israel to sin"* (1 Kings 21:22). King Ahab had also built a temple to Baal for Jezebel, and he allowed her to oppress the prophets of Yahweh and promote Baal worship among the Israelites.

King Ahab was so touched by the words of Elijah that he repented. God responded by telling Elijah that He would delay the predicted disasters until the reign of Ahab's son.[551]

Bible Study with Tony W. Cartledge: 1 Kings 19:1-18

Jezebel was angry with Elijah for challenging 400 prophets of Baal to a *"dueling prophets"* match, and Jezebel was furious that the prophets of Baal had lost. Jezebel wanted to get Elijah out of the country, so she sent Elijah a warning: *"So may the gods do to me, and more also, if I do not make your life like the life of one of them (the dead priests of Baal) by this time tomorrow."*

---

[551]   Ibid.

Elijah fled for his life, running all the way from the northern kingdom of Israel to Beersheba, near the southern border of Judah. Elijah became afraid and left his servant in Beersheba, and he traveled south into the desert and hid in the wilderness of the Negev.

Elijah collapsed under a tree and prayed for himself to die. "It is enough; now, O Lord, take away my life, for I am no better than my ancestors" (1 Kings 19:4). God knew that Elijah needed rest and food. When he woke up, he felt the touch of an angel, who said, "Get up and eat, or else the journey will be too great for you."

Elijah found a steaming cake of bread and a jug of water close to him. He ate and drank and rested for a long time. Elijah left and walked for forty days to Mount Horeb, which some people call Sinai. Although Elijah was exhausted, he climbed until he came to a cave, maybe the same one Moses used. There Elijah spent the night (1 Kings 19:5-9).

Then the word of the Lord came to him, saying, "What are you doing here, Elijah?" (1 Kings 19:9). Elijah insisted that the people of Israel had left Yahweh and that he was the only prophet left. He did not mention the faithful Obadiah and the 100 prophets he had kept safe, and the repentance after the miracle on Mount Carmel (1 Kings 18:39-40). God called Elijah to come out of his cave and stand on the mountain before God.[552]

Bible Study with Tony W. Cartledge: 1 Kings 19:1-18 (continued)

Elijah responded to God's question of why he was here, by complaining about Jezebel and all his problems. God invited Elijah to come out of the cave and stand on the mountain before God. Elijah stayed in the cave when a howling wind blew past him so fast that it was splitting part of the mountain and breaking rocks in pieces. Elijah said, "Lord," but the Lord was not in the wind. God sent an earthquake after the wind, but God was not in the earthquake. Elijah felt the heat of a roaring of a wildfire, but God was not in the fire (1 Kings 19:11-12).

After the wind, earthquake, and fire, there was "a sound of thin silence." And in the silence, Elijah found the voice of God. Elijah learned that God was not part of Elijah's unhappiness. God may have been teaching Elijah that during the storms of life God is still there with us.

---

[552] Tony W. Cartledge, "Bible Study with Tony W. Cartledge: I Kings 19:1-18". *Baptists Today News Journal*: May 2013, 26-27.

In verse 13, God asks again, "What are you doing here, Elijah?" Again Elijah complained about all his problems. God responded by giving Elijah specific assignments.

The "broom tree" Elijah slept under in verse 4 is a juniper bush. It can live in the hot desert and even in modern times continues to grow.

God sometimes speaks in the silence if we are willing to listen. Sometimes silence can be frightening because it strips away our excuses. We need to let our hearts and minds listen to God, who sends us thought waves and ideas to try.[553]

Bible Study with Tony W. Cartledge: 1 Kings 19:15-21

Elijah had the problem of being self-absorbed in his personal problems. God asked Elijah what he was doing there when he should have been at work in Israel. Elijah acted like he was afraid of his opponents. God gave him orders to go to the enemy of Israel to Damascus, the capital of Aram, and anoint Hazael to replace Ben-hadad as king. Then Elijah was ordered to go to Israel and anoint Jehu to become king of Israel; and this was a political problem, because by openly endorsing Jehu, it could cause Elijah to become a target. And lastly, he was to go to Abel-meholah to find a man named Elisha and anoint him to become a prophet. In verse 18, God tells Elijah that there were at least 7,000 other prophets to stand with him.

Elijah chose to do the last assignment first instead of following God's orders precisely. In verse 19, Elijah was still cranky by the time he met Elisha, who was plowing with twelve men and twelve oxen. Instead of talking to Elisha, Elijah chose to throw him the mantle as Elisha passed by him. This action suggests that Elijah was reluctant to work with Elisha and share his role of prophet with him. Elisha had to run to catch up with Elijah to find out what the mantle meant. Elisha asked to be able to go and tell his family. In verse 20, Elijah responded by saying, "Go back again; for what have I done to you?"

Elisha killed his oxen and burned his farming equipment, and he gave himself a goodbye ceremony and something good to celebrate. On several occasions, Elijah tried to leave Elisha, but Elisha always chased Elijah to keep up with him. In 2 Kings 2:1-14, it is described how Elijah's mantle fell to the ground when he was taken to heaven by a whirlwind, and Elisha claimed it for him.[554]

---

[553] Ibid.

[554] Tony W. Cartledge, "Bible Study with Tony W. Cartledge: I Kings 19:15-21". *Baptists Today News Journal*: May 2013, 28-29.

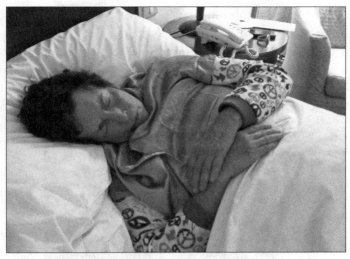

A good night's sleep

Bible Study with Tony W. Cartledge Luke 13: 1-9

In verses 1-3 we hear of Roman soldiers killed some men from Galilee who were worshiping in the Temple. Josephus, a Jewish historian of this time period, writes about the atrocities of the Romans and writes that Herod Antipas was removed from office for the massacre of Samaritan worshipers on Mt. Gerizim.

Jesus was asked if this incidence in the Temple by the Romans and the deaths of these worshipers were caused by a big sin in their lives. In verse 2 Jesus replied, "Do you think that these Galileans suffered in this way they were worse sinners than all other Galileans?" Most people of that day believed if a person has much sin, tragedy could occur to kill them because of that sin. In verse 3 Jesus replied, "No, I tell you; but unless you repent, you will all perish as they did." Jesus denied the deaths were caused by great sin. But he did say that everyone is a sinner and needs to repent to avoid the great judgment day.

Jesus used the illustration of the tragic accident when a stone tower near the pool of Siloam collapsed and killed eighteen people. The point Jesus makes is who knows whether these people were big sinners or not. Jesus indicated that these people who died under the tower were no worse than the people of Jerusalem. All people are sinful. Jesus stressed the point that God does not cause bad things to happen to individuals.

Jesus told the parable of the fig tree which teaches us about fruitless faith in Luke 13: 6-9. The parables of Jesus had one point and that was we all have a choice of repentance that leads to life or rebellion that leads to death. Although God is patient, judgment is coming.[555]

Eating dinner in the King David hotel in Jerusalem

The Greg DeLoach Menu

The menu had Greg DeLoach written over the menu. Greg pretended he was famous and autographed our menus.

---

[555] Ibid., 18-19.

Bible Study with Tony W. Cartledge (Luke 13: 1-9 continued)

In the parable of the fig tree, Jesus may be pointing to a debate in God's mind whether to give us what we deserve (cut it down or to offer what we do not deserve (give it more time. When the gardener asked to give the tree another year uses the same Greek word *aphes* translated *forgive*. The gardener was asking forgiveness for the tree. People are unfruitful like the fig tree. God gives people a choice to repent and be forgiven or to be rebellious and not forgiven. Some of the fruits to produce are the fruit of obedience, the fruit of goodness, and the fruit of new believers coming to Christ because of your witness.

During his earthly ministry Jesus called people to bear fruit by repenting and believing in Him. Some of these same people chose to nail Him to the cross and went back to their normal lives. Jesus said on the cross, "forgive them, for they don't know what they're doing" (Luke 23: 34).[556]

Sunday- January 13, 2013

We began our day with scripture and prayer on the bus. We parked the bus on top of the Mount of Olives and walked down the traditional "Palm Sunday Walk" where Jesus walked for his triumphal entry into Jerusalem.

Old Olive Trees in Jerusalem

---

[556]   Tony W. Cartledge. Bible Study with Tony W. Cartledge. Luke 13: 1-9. Baptists Today News Journal, February 2013. 18-19.

Some of these trees were little baby olive trees when Jesus was in Jerusalem. It is amazing that we saw these same trees in Jerusalem as old trees and Jesus saw them as little baby trees. The Garden of Gethsemane is beautiful and these olive trees add to the beauty.

Bible Study with Tony W. Cartledge (Luke 15: 1-3; 11;32)

The background for the parable of the prodigal son is a party where Jesus was eating with sinners and tax collectors. The Pharisees complained about Jesus welcoming sinners and eating with them. Verses 1-2. Jesus gave this parable to teach the Pharisees about going out of their way to find what was lost. The parable of the prodigal son is the story of one son asking for his inheritance early, leaving home, spending all of his inheritance, returning home, father welcoming back with big feast and the younger brother resenting the attention his brother is getting. Carob pods containing bitter beans and gelatinous goo that poor people eat was his menu. Finally, he decided to go home because the servants at his father's house ate better than he was eating now. He even ate out of the pig trough when he was starving.

So the son headed for home to confess his failure and ask for a job as a hired hand. When he returned home to a loving father who loved him and the son repented of his failure to succeed, the prodigal son became a model for others who needed to repent.[557]

Mount of Olives

---

[557] Ibid., 20-21

We walked down this road from the top of the Mount of Olives and thought about Jesus being in this same area when he was on earth. We stopped at the Garden of Gethsemane and saw the Church of All Nations. We went to the City of David, a narrow hill near the Western Wall where Jerusalem began. We saw walls, towers and fortifications used to protect the area. We saw ancient water systems and the Gihon Spring.

Jerusalem: Facade of the Church of All Nations

This church is located next to the Garden of Gethsemane. This Catholic Church has a piece of stone that marks the spot believed to be where Jesus prayed on the night of his arrest.

Bible Study with Tony W. Cartledge (Luke 15:1-3; 11:3 continued)

The father welcomed his lost son home, forgave him, prepared a feast for him and celebrated the return of the son he loved. The older brother had a normal reaction and resented all the attention his younger brother received. The older brother by his attitude was in danger of rejecting his father for being nice to his son. The elder brother was acting like a prodigal son also by his bad attitude but he was blinded by his self-righteous attitude and contempt for his brother.

The father tried to convince his oldest son to come to the feast. There was plenty of room for both sons and they needed to become friends again. The father had given his son the acceptance he needed instead of the hired hand job he requested.[558]

Meditation and a Rest at the Church of All Nations in Jerusalem

Bible Study with Tony W. Cartledge (John 12:1-8)

Mary, Martha and Lazarus were very good friends of Jesus and lived in the near-by village of Bethany near Jerusalem. Jesus enjoyed having fun and talking to friends although He concentrated on His ministry. Sometimes the scribes and Pharisees criticized Jesus for relaxing and enjoying His friends. In John 12: 1-8 Martha is busy serving food while Mary knelt at the feet of Jesus with her ointment and "nard" expensive imported perfume. If the estimate of Judas is correct of a 300 denarii, the perfume may have been worth as much as a common laborer's annual income. Mary probably worked for that money and saved it over a lifetime and loved Jesus so much she wanted to display her love for Him. Mary sacrificed her money and dignity for Jesus. In first century times it would have been shocking for Mary to pour expensive perfume on the feet of Jesus. Mary even wiped the feet of Jesus with her own unbraided hair considered the most glorious part of the body. According to 1 Corinthians 11:15, it was an unusual act for her to do in her cultural setting but she loved Jesus and wanted to show it.

---

[558] Tony W. Cartledge. Bible Study with Tony W. Cartledge. Luke 15: 1-3, 11-32. Baptists Today News Journal, February 2013. 20-21.

Judas did not like the waste of the perfume by Martha or Jesus allowing it. Judas wanted the perfume to be sold and the money given to the poor. Jesus responded to Judas by saying, "Leave her alone. She has kept it for the day of my burial. For you will always have the poor with you, but you will not always have me" (John 12:7-8).[559]

Room of the Last Supper on Mount Zion

A Night to Remember

Jesus and His disciples went to an upper room to celebrate Passover. They reclined around a low, three sided table (Luke 22:15). "With fervent desire I have desired to eat this Passover with you before I suffer." This night would be different from all of the other nights the disciples experienced. In the first Passover in the days of Moses, only three things were on the table; roasted lamb, unleavened bread, and bitter herbs (Exodus 12:8). The lamb stood for a submissive Messiah. In the First Passover the Israelites were instructed to pick out one male lamb per household, bring it home, kill it after four days, and put the blood on the outer doorposts and upper posts of their homes. When God saw the blood of the lamb on the doorposts He passed over those homes. And the tenth plaque of death of first born did not strike that house (Exodus 12).

At the Last Supper, Jesus the Messiah would be the submissive lamb even when led to be slaughtered. The prophet Isaiah foretold

---

[559]   Ibid., 24-25.

of Jesus. "He was oppressed and He was afflicted, yet He opened not His mouth; He was led as a lamb to the slaughter, and as a sheep before its shearers is silent, so He opened not his mouth" (Isaiah 53:7). Jesus suffered silently before the religious and civil authorities as they interrogated Him (See Matthew 26:62-63; Matthew 27:12-14; Mark 14:60-61; Mark 15:3-5; Luke 23:8-9 and John 1:29.)

The unleavened bread represented a Sinless Messiah. In the first Passover during the time of Moses, the people of God were asked to eat unleavened bread that represented a sinless Messiah to be a perfect sacrifice. Isaiah prophesied "Yet it pleased the Lord to bruise Him; He has put him to grief. When You make His soul an offering for sin. He shall see His seed, He shall prolong His days, and the pleasure of the Lord shall prosper in His hand" (Isaiah 53:10). Sin offerings had to be perfect (Leviticus 1-5). The lamb could have no blemishes. And the Passover Lamb had to be without blemish. The religious authorities challenged Jesus with questions trying to entrap him and find fault with Him but they could not succeed. The Pharisees and Herodians tried to trick Jesus about paying taxes. Jesus said "Render therefore to Caesar the things that are Caesar's and to God the things that are God's" (Matthew 22:21). The Sadducees did not believe in the concept of resurrection. The Sadducees asked a question about a widow marrying seven brothers and wanted to know whose wife she would be at the resurrection. Jesus said that people will not be married after they are resurrected (Matthew 22:29-30).

The bitter herbs stood for a suffering Messiah. Seven hundred years before Jesus was born, the prophet Isaiah explained why the Messiah would suffer. "Surely He has borne our griefs and carried our sorrows; yet we esteemed Him stricken, smitten by God, and afflicted. But He was wounded for our transgressions, He was bruised for our iniquities; the chastisement for our peace was upon Him, and by His stripes we are healed. All we like sheep have gone astray; we have turned, every one, to his own way; and the Lord has laid on Him the iniquity of us all (Isaiah 53:4-6).

After the Passover with his disciples, Jesus went to an olive grove in Jerusalem called Gethsemane. He was soon facing dread and crushed with sorrow (Matthew 14:34). He was then arrested and deserted by His disciples (Matthew 14:46-50). Jesus was accused of blasphemy, spit on, blindfolded, and hit many times in the face (Matthew 14:63-65). Pontius Pilate charged him with treason and had Jesus flogged with a lead-tipped whip. The Romans put a crown of thorns on Him and then beat Him with a staff driving sharp points into His skull and spitting on Him (Matthew 27:29-30 and Mark 15:19). Jesus then carried His cross most of the way to Golgotha and was crucified (John 19:17-18).

The Bible teaches that everyone born of humans is under a sentence of spiritual death (Romans 3: 23; Romans 5;12; and John 3:3). The good news of Passover is that Jesus, the submissive, sinless, and suffering Lamb of God, suffered, died, and rose again so that in Him we have redemption through His blood, the forgiveness of sins, according to the riches of His grace (Ephesians 1:7). Jesus was willing to become our substitute and through faith in Him, we have everlasting life. The Apostle Paul wrote "For indeed Christ, our Passover, was sacrificed for us" (1 Corinthians 5:7). Our life is in the blood of the Lamb.[560]

The Last Supper made out of Olive Wood

We admired the Last Supper carved out of Olive Wood and wanted to own it. But the cost was one thousand dollars and we quickly walked away from temptation. It was for sale in the antique store in Bethlehem.

---

[560] Peter Colon. A Night to Remember. Israel My Glory, March- April, 2013. 24-26.

The Seder Plate

The Betzah is a boiled egg that represents winter yielding to spring and life. In Jewish tradition eggs are eaten when mourning the death of a loved one. The Jewish people mourn the destruction of their Temple, where Passover lambs were sacrificed. The Jewish people dip the egg in salt water and eat it. The Zerah is a shank bone of a lamb. Some people use a chicken bone instead of a lamb bone. The Zerah symbolizes the Passover lambs sacrificed at the Temple and the lambs slain in Egypt to protect the Israelites from the tenth plague of death of the firstborn. The maror is bitter herbs mainly horseradish. The maror reminds the Jewish people of their bitter bondage in Egypt. The maror has to be strong enough to bring tears to the eyes. Karpas is a green vegetable usually parsley. This symbolizes the hyssop used to apply the lamb's blood on the doorposts in Egypt. Charoset is a mixture of honey, apples and nuts.[561]

The Mystery Kingdom

God's solution to sin was for Jesus to be crucified as a sacrifice and resurrected as the Lamb of God. During his earthly ministry Jesus told Israel, "Repent for the kingdom is at hand." Everyone at that time understood it meant the Davidic Kingdom. The problem was that the people of Israel was unwilling to follow Him and accept Him as Messiah. In Matthew 12 the religious leaders accused Jesus of casting out demons by Beelzebub (Satan) the ruler of demons (Matthew 12:24). Jesus answered, "A house divided against itself will not stand. If Satan casts out Satan, he is divided against himself. How then will his kingdom stand?" (Matthew 12:25-26). Jesus then told them they had blasphemed the Spirit of God by giving Satan credit for a miracle He had performed in the Spirit's power. "Whoever speaks against the Holy Spirit it will not be forgiven him, either in this age or in the age to come" (Matthew 12:32). It is sad that the religious leaders of the time of Jesus cut themselves from God's Kingdom forever.

Jesus spoke many things in parables (Matthew 13:1-3). Jesus told His disciples "It has been given to you to know the mysteries of the

---

[561]   The Seder Plate. *Israel My Glory*, March- April, 2013. 30.

kingdom of heaven" (Matthew 13:11). Jesus hinted about a new phase in God's agenda, the mystery kingdom, the church.

On the day of Pentecost which is also the Jewish holiday of Shavuot, God instituted the church. The Spirit of God fell on about 120 men gathered in an upper room. This event became known as the "baptism of the Spirit" (Acts 2). This event took place fifty days after the resurrection of Jesus and ten days after His ascension.

Many years later, the Apostle Paul explained this special baptism. "For by one Spirit we were all baptized into one body whether Jews or Greeks, whether slave or free and have all been made to drink into one Spirit" (1 Corinthians 12:13). With the baptism of the Spirit the church began. When the rejection of the Jewish leaders took place, God revealed His plan to reach out to the Gentiles and make them fellow-heirs and members of the body of Christ along with believing Jews.

Paul explained this concept to the Ephesians. "When you read, you may understand my knowledge in the mystery of Christ, which in other ages was not made known to the sons of men, as it has now been revealed by the Spirit to His holy apostles and prophets; that the Gentiles should be fellow heirs, of the same body, and partakers of His promise in Christ through the gospel" (Ephesians 3:4-6).

This plan had been a "mystery" from the beginning and hidden in God who created all things through Jesus Christ (Ephesians 3:9-10).

The church has Spirit-baptized believers from Pentecost to the Rapture. There was no spirit baptism in the Old Testament. Jesus told his disciples, "You shall be baptized with the Holy Spirit" (Acts 1:5). This ministry is in the Church Age only.

There is a bond between Jewish Christians and Gentile Christians. God had given all of the covenants to Israel. Unless Gentiles came to God through Israel, they were lost. Paul said, "You were without Christ being aliens from the commonwealth of Israel and strangers from the covenants of promise, having no hope and without God in the world. But now in Christ Jesus you who once were far off have been brought near by the blood of Christ. For He Himself is our peace, who has made both one, and has broken down the middle wall of separation, that is the law of commandments (the ten commandments and Old Testament Law) so as to create in Himself one new man from the two, thus making peace" (Ephesians 2:12-15).

In modern times, Jewish people who accept Jesus as Savior belong to the church with Gentiles who become Christians and are graphed into God's program for Israel.

"For if you were cut out of the olive tree which is wild by nature, and were grafted contrary to nature into a cultivated olive tree (Israel) how much more will these, who are natural branches, (Jewish people) be grafted into their own olive tree. For I do not desire, brethren, that you should be ignorant of this mystery, lest you should be wise in your own opinion, that blindness in part has happened to Israel until the fullness of the Gentiles has come in" (Romans 11:24-25).

Everyone in the world falls into one of two categories. There are Jews and Gentiles who reject Jesus as the Messiah. There are Jews and Gentiles who are part of the body of Christ and believe Jesus is the Messiah.

Under the law, the believer's stewardship was to glorify God by obeying the Law. Under the church the stewardship is to glorify God by walking under the Spirit's control and growing to maturity. "If you are a believer, God has given you all the help you need to walk in the Spirit and glorify Him, which is Christ in you, the hope of glory." Richard D Emmons said, "If you have placed your faith in Christ alone (not in good works), you have Christ in you and therefore are part of the church."

At the end of the church age is the Rapture. Paul said, "The Lord Himself will descend from heaven with a shout, with the voice of an archangel, and with the trumpet of God. And the dead in Christ shall rise first. Then we that are alive and remain shall be caught up together with them in the clouds to meet the Lord in the air. And thus we shall always be with the Lord" (1 Thessalonians 4:16-17). The church program of God ends with the Rapture. The life of the believers will continue in heaven but Jesus will no longer be building His church. All Church Age believers will then appear before the judgment seat of Christ to receive what God wants to give them for the degree of faithfulness they had on Earth (2 Corinthians 5:10). Then the Marriage of the Lamb to the church takes place (Revelation 19:7). God turned Israel's rejection of Christ into a blessing for the Gentiles. For 2,000 years God has brought Gentiles from every nation, tribe, and tongue into His Kingdom. One day, God will bring the Jewish people back into the fold (Romans 11:26-27).[562]

---

[562]   Emmons, Richard D., Key 6: The Church. *Israel My Glory*, March- April, 2013. 32.

Wooden Communion Cups

We used these wooden communion cups for our communion in the Garden Tomb. In the middle of our service, we heard the loud cry of coming to pray of the Muslims. In the Garden Tomb with birds singing, the service was very meaningful and we felt close to Christ and what He did for our sins so that we could be joint heirs with Him.

The Grace of God

There are many examples of God's grace in the Old Testament. The cry for God's grace by the godly people of the southern kingdom of Judah when the Assyrians attacked. "O Lord, be gracious to us; we have waited for You. Be their arm every morning, our salvation also in the time of trouble" (Isaiah 33:2).

God's grace for all the people of Israel threatened by Assyria. King Hezekiah of Judah sent a message to everyone in the norther kingdom of Israel, southern kingdom of Judah, and the tribes of Ephraim and Manasseh. "Children of Israel, return to the Lord God of Abraham, Isaac, and Israel; then He will return to the remnant of you who have escaped from the hand of the kings of Assyria. And do not be like your fathers and your brethren, who trespassed against the Lord God of their fathers, so that He gave them up in desolation, as you see. Now do not be stiff-necked, as your fathers were, but yield yourselves to the Lord; and enter His sanctuary, which He has sanctified forever, and serve the Lord your God, that the fierceness of His wrath may turn away from you. For if you return to the Lord, your brethren and your children will be treated with compassion by those who lead them captive, so that they may come back to this land; for the Lord your God is gracious and merciful, and will not turn His face from you if you return to Him" (2 Chronicles 30:6-9). [563]

Jerusalem Sightseeing

The Grace of God (continued)

God's grace for the Israelites who were not killed by the Assyrians and Babylonians but were scattered from their homeland: "Thus says the Lord: "The people who survived the sword found grace in the wilderness-Israel when I went to give him rest" (Jeremiah 31:2).

God's grace for the Israelites who returned to their homeland from their captivity in Babylon: Ezra, a priest and scribe of the Law of Moses, went home to Israel after the Babylonian captivity ended. He said, "And now for a little while grace has been shown from the Lord our God, to leave us a remnant to escape, and to give us a peg in His holy place, that our God may enlighten our eyes and give us a measure of revival in our bondage" (Ezra 9:8).

God's grace for the fathers and people of Israel: Levites who returned to Israel after the Babylonian captivity remembered God's

---

[563] Showers, Renald. *The Grace of God. Israel My Glory*, March-April, 2013. 38.

422

gracious response to their ancestors' rebellion against Him after He brought them out of Egypt: "Our fathers acted proudly, hardened their necks, and did not heed Your commandments. They refused to obey, and they were not mindful of Your wonders that You did among them. But they hardened their necks, and in their rebellion they appointed a leader to return to their bondage. But You are God, ready to pardon, gracious and merciful, slow to anger, abundant in kindness and did not forsake them" (Nehemiah 9:16-17).[564]

Old City of David

The Hebrew word for grace in the Old Testament is hanan which means "be gracious" or "show favor". It can mean "seek favor" which is favor of God and of mankind. To be gracious means to aid the poor, feed the hungry, and to deliver from defeat and death. Hanan is a verb and shows action such as someone helping a person. A person cannot be angry and show favor to someone. Favor cannot coexist with judgment.

The noun form of hanan is hen and it appears 67 times in the Old Testament and has two basic meanings, favor and grace. Some examples are Esther 2:15, Malachi 1:9, and Psalm 25:16-17.

Both Hebrew nouns, *hen* and *hesed*, can be translated lovingkindness or mercy. *Hesed* refers to a covenant relationship between people and hen does not. *Hesed* has established rights and obligations and requires

---

[564]   Ibid.

a favorable attitude by both parties and is long term arrangement. *Hen* relationship is given to one person from another person and is short term. *Hen* can be withdrawn without consequences.

As the two angels helped Lot and his family leave Sodom, Lot said to them, "Indeed now, your servant has found favor (hen) in your sight, and you have increased your mercy which you have shown me by saving my life" (Genesis 19:19).

Another example of hen is Ruth 2:1-3 that states, "Ruth asked Naomi for permission to go to the field and glean heads of grain after him in whose sight I may find favor (*hen*). Naomi said to her, Go my daughter. So Ruth began to glean after the reapers."[565]

Old City of David

Israel is known for its diamonds. The Gemological Institute of America has opened a new laboratory in Ramat Gan, Israel. Israel is a global center for world diamond trading.

Israeli scientist-professor Irun Cohen has met its first and secondary goals in a Phase III clinical trial. The drug, DiaPep277 was tested on 457 diabetic patients aged 16 to 45 in 40 medical centers in Europe, Israel, and South Africa. When perfected the drug will face no competition as the first drug to combat Juvenile diabetes.[566]

---

[565] "The Foundations of Faith: the Grace of God", *Israel My Glory*, November-December 2012, page 38-39.

[566] Israel in the News. *Israel My Glory*, November- December 2012, page 40-41.

Old City of Jerusalem

Elijah was important in the Old and New Testaments. This material is based on 1 Kings 17 and 18. The name, Elijah, means Eliyahu in Hebrew which is translated, "My God is Yahweh (Jehovah)." Elijah was like Enoch and both were taken up to heaven without dying. (See 2 Kings 2.) Elijah was a prophet from the 9th century but his influence and significance was so important that he is mentioned in the New Testament.

When the disciples questioned Jesus about Elijah, his reply was, "Truly I say to you, among those born of women there has not arisen anyone greater than John the Baptist. And if you are willing to accept it, John himself is Elijah who was to come" (Matthew 11:11-14). Jesus was not referring to reincarnation but the fulfillment of an Old Testament prophecy and the words spoken by the angel Gabriel to Zacharias in the temple. Gabriel brought the message that Elizabeth would have a baby in her old age and to name him John. "He will go as a forerunner before Him (Jesus) in the spirit and power of Elijah" (Luke 1:1-7).

According to 2 Kings 1:8 and Matthew 3:4, the type of clothing Elijah and John wore was very much alike. Both had ministries that took place in the wilderness and both confronted kings from northern Israel. Elijah confronted King Ahab and John confronted King Herod Antipas.[567]

---

[567] Barnhart, David R., A look at Eliyahu. The Vine and the Branches. Mid-Winter, 2012. p. 3.

Old City of Jerusalem

Peter, James, and John were with Jesus during His Transfiguration on the mountain (Matthew 17). They witnessed Moses (representing the Law), and Elijah (representing the Prophets) appearing with and talking to Jesus. The Transfiguration shows that God has one plan of salvation for the ages which is the life, death, burial, resurrection and coming again of Jesus Christ. "Jesus said to Peter, James, and John, 'Elijah is coming and will restore all things: but I say to you that Elijah already came, and they did not recognize him, but did to him whatever they wished. So also the Son of Man is going to suffer at their hands.' Then the disciples understood that He was talking about John the Baptist" (Matthew 17:10-13).

Elijah had the power of prayer. He prayed that it would not rain and it did not rain for three years and six months. Then he prayed for rain and the rains came and the soil produced much fruit (James 5:16-18).

The prophet Malachi proclaimed, "Behold I am going to send you Elijah the prophet before the coming of the great and terrible day of the Lord. He will restore the hearts of the children to their fathers, so that I will not come and smite the land with a curse" (Malachi 4:5-6).

Most scholars of prophecy believe the two witnesses of Revelation 11 are Moses and Elijah based on the powers the two witnesses have which are the power to shut up the sky so rain will not fall during their days of prophesying, the power to turn the water into blood and to strike the earth with plaques (Revelation 11:6).[568]

The Grace of God

The Levites reminded God of His gracious response to the rebellion of the Israelites who lived in the Promised Land for centuries. "Yet for many years You had patience with them, and testified against them by Your Spirit in Your prophets. Yet they would not listen; therefore You gave them into the hand of the peoples of the lands. Nevertheless in Your great mercy You did not utterly consume them nor forsake them; for You are God, gracious and merciful" (Nehemiah 9:30-31).

God's grace for the people of Nineveh: Because God forgave the people of Nineveh when they repented of their evil, Jonah was displeased and angry, so he prayed. "Ah, Lord was not this what I said when I was still in my country? Therefore I fled previously to Tarshish; for I know that You are a gracious, and merciful God, slow to anger and abundant in lovingkindness, One who relents from doing harm" (Jonah 4:1-2).

God's grace for David: King David wrote, "The Lord is merciful and gracious, slow to anger, and abounding in mercy" (Psalm 103:8). When proud people rose against David and a mob of violent men tried to kill him, David placed his trust in God who is "full of compassion, and gracious" (Psalm 86:14-15).

God's grace for people of Israel willing to repent of their rebellion against God. God said the following when He was threatening to bring a massive devastating army against the people of Israel because of their rebellion against Him: "'Now therefore,' says the Lord, 'turn to Me with all your heart, with fasting, with weeping, and with mourning." So rend your heart, and not your garments; return to the Lord your God, for He is gracious and merciful, slow to anger, and of great kindness; and He relents from doing harm. Joel 2:12-13.[569]

---

[568] Barnhart, David R., A look at Eliyahu: The Vine and the Branches. Mid-Winter, 2012. p. 3-4.

[569] Showers, Renald. The Grace of God. *Israel My Glory*, March- April, 2013. 38.-39

Old City of Jerusalem

We walked up and down many steps as we walked our four to five miles a day. But the sites were breath taking and our experiences exciting, informative, and interesting. The sites of the Bible made the Bible come alive and to be more interesting when we read the Bible with our new depth of understanding the land, history, and people of Israel.

Paul and the Apostles

On the day of his resurrection, Jesus appeared to Mary Magdalene, then in Emmaus to two disciples, then to Peter and then to the eleven disciples in the Upper Room where they had eaten the last supper. Saul from Tarsus went to Jerusalem to study under the Pharisees. Saul stormed into Jewish homes and seized the followers of Jesus and put some in jail and some slaughtered. The High Priest, impressed with Saul gave him permission to go to Damascus to arrest followers of Jesus. As Saul came near Damascus he was blinded by a great light. A voice said, "Saul, why persecutest me? I am Jesus, whom thou persecutest. Arise and go into the city, and it shall be told to thee what thou must do." Saul was baptized and for the cause of Jesus. Saul's name was changed to Paul and he became the "Apostle to the Gentiles" with the "Gospel of Grace."[570]

---

[570] Robert Sullivan, editor. *Life:Places of the Bible*. Time Inc. July, 2013. 112-123.

Old City of Jerusalem

James used Elijah's prayer life to encourage believers. He gave the example of Elijah praying for no rain for three years and six months (James 5:16-18). We need to use the power of prayer to get the United States out of debt and a stronger prosperous economy.

The reason Elijah prayed earnestly for no rain was the people of Israel worshiped Baal and the goddess of fertility, Asherah. Asherah was responsible for bringing rain, wind, lightening and clouds. The sins of Israel at this time included homosexual acts and the sacrifice of infants by fire. This form of idolatry may have been the reason God decided to hold the rain from Israel for three years and six months. It was probably why God called Elijah to have a contest on Mount Carmel to determine which God could answer by fire. Archaeologists discovered a stone showing Baal standing with a bolt of lightning in his hand. The day of the contest, there were two altars with sacrifices on them (1 Kings 18:24). Baal ignored the cries of his prophets. God sent down fire. We have silly non-existent gods of our time in our sin-laden cultures. The false teachers attack the true God and promotes their own false and empty religions.

Modern cultures all over the world are as bad as Israel was in sacrificing babies. Modern cultures do it by calling it abortion. They call it a medical procedure, but it is the murder of innocent babies who do feel pain inside the womb. Over 54 million babies have been aborted since the Roe vs Wade decision in 1973.[571]

---

[571] Barnhart, David R., *A look at Eliyahu: The Vine and the Branches*. Mid-winter, 2012. p. 4-5.

A Narrow Street in Jerusalem

At the time of Elijah, King Ahab ruled the northern kingdom of Israel. The Bible says that King Ahab did more evil in Israel than all the others. 1 Kings 16:30. His wife, Jezebel, was the daughter of Ethbaal, the grand master of Baal worship in the region. Jezebel attempted to kill all of the prophets of God.[572]

Passover is as important to Christians as to Jews because it is a wonderful picture of God's plan of redemption for all mankind. Seder is a Hebrew word meaning "order" and refers to the service at the dinner table. All participants follow along in a Haggadah, a booklet containing the service. It tells the story of the first Passover under Moses, and includes Exodus 12, and includes songs and prayers. It also has a requirement to drink four cups of wine or grape juice. The four cups relate to the four "I Wills" God promised the Jewish people in Exodus 12. The first cup relates to, "I will bring you out from under the burdens of the Egyptians" (v. 6). The second cup relates to, "I will rescue you from their bondage" (v. 6). The third cup relates to, "I will redeem you with an out-stretched arm and with great judgments" (v. 6). The fourth cup relates to "I will take you as My people, and I will be your God" (v. 7). The four cups recognize that God delivered His people from slavery in Egypt.[573]

---

[572] Ibid., 4-5.

[573] Robert J. Stahler. "The Four Cups." *Israel My Glory*. March/April 2013, p 14-16.

Viewing Ruins of Jerusalem

The first cup of Passover is the Cup of Sanctification and means "set apart." The Jewish people acknowledge that God selected them to receive the Ten Commandments. There is a prayer of praise before the cup is drunk. Sanctification means "kiddush" in Hebrew and the cup has become known as the Kiddush Cup. This cup is used every Sabbath and every Passover.

The second cup is the Cup of Praise. The Exodus story is told about the liberation from slavery. God is praised for delivery from Egypt, Babylon, Medo-Persia, Greece, Assyria, Rome, and all other foreign countries from Abraham to today.

The third cup is the Cup of Redemption. It is drunk after the meal and after the *afikomen* is found. This cup is important to Christians because this is the cup Jesus used when he said, "This cup is the new covenant in My blood, which is shed for you" (Luke 22:20). The Cup of Redemption symbolizes what Jesus did for us by shedding his blood to redeem us from slavery to sin. The apostle Paul wrote in 1 Corinthians 5:7, "For indeed Christ, our Passover, was sacrificed for us."[574]

---

[574] Ibid., 14-16

A Good View of Jerusalem

The fourth cup is for everyone near the end of dinner. It is called the Cup of Acceptance or the Cup of Anticipation and celebrates the relationship God wants with his chosen people. This is the cup Jesus used to symbolize the ratification of the New Covenant and to institute communion. Jesus did not drink it Himself but stated He will drink it when the Messianic Kingdom is established. Matthew 26:27-29 says, "Then He took the cup and gave thanks, and gave it to them, saying, 'Drink from it, all of you. For this is My blood of the new covenant, which is shed for many for the remission of sins. But I say to you, I will not drink of this fruit of the vine from now on until that day when I drink it new with you in My Father's kingdom.'"[575]

---

[575] Robert J. Stahler. "The Four Cups" Israel My Glory. March/April 2013, p 14-16.

432

Archaeology Workers on a Site Working

The Jewish Passover lasts for eight days with a seder on the first and second nights. It is a celebration of God's deliverance of His people from the Egyptians more than 3,400 years ago. Jewish families get rid of all yeast in their homes. No yeast products are to be eaten during the Passover week. Jewish children eat peanut butter and jelly sandwiches on matzoh instead of bread this week. The youngest child asks the famous four questions to the seder leader. The first question is, Why is this night different from all other nights? The answer is, "All other nights, we eat leavened bread or matzoh. The second question is, Why do we eat bitter herbs on this night? On other nights we eat vegetables. Question 3 is Why on this night do we dip twice? On other nights we never dip once. Question 4 is Why on this night do we recline? On other nights we sit up straight at the table. The seder leader answers these questions and tells the story of Exodus. Sometimes finger puppets and props are used for all ten plagues. Parsley dipped in salt water symbolizes the tears shed as slaves. More horseradish is available to try with the matzoh. The horseradish is a reminder of the bitterness the Israelites endured. They eat charoset, a mixture of apples and honey as a treat and as a reminder of the sweetness of freedom when Pharoh let the people go. The dinner is a treat with real food such as chicken, potatoes, and green beans.[576]

---

[576] Ibid.

Charoset is a mixture of apples, nuts, honey, and cinnamon. This dish symbolizes the mortar the Israelites used to build bricks when they were slaves in Egypt. This dish is very important in the seder celebrations during Passover. Each participant makes a small matzoh sandwich of bitter herbs (horseradish) and chamset. This custom began with Rabbi Hillel who lived in 110 BC and 10 AD. Rabbi Hillel liked bitter herbs, unleavened bread and lamb. After the Temple was destroyed in 70 AD and the sacrificing of lambs, the sandwich became charoset and bitter herbs. Put apples and nuts in a blender or food processor and chop until finely diced. Sprinkle lemon juice on the mixture to keep the apples from turning brown. Some people even mix grape juice or wine to give flavor.[577]

Why Unleavened Bread for Passover

Another name for unleavened bread is matzoh. God commanded the Jewish people to eat the Passover lamb with unleavened bread (Exodus 12:8). "On the first day you shall remove leaven from your houses. For whoever eats leavened bread from the first day until the seventh day, that person shall be cut off from Israel (Exodus 12:15).

Modern day Jews remove all leavened bread from their homes. They even sell their baked goods to a Gentile friend and buy it back after Passover.

The Jewish people came out of Egypt in a big hurry and had no time to wait for the bread to rise. Another reason is that God sometimes associates it with sin. Jesus told his disciples, "Take heed and beware of the leaven of the Pharisees and the Sadducees" (Matthew 16:6). The disciples did not understand immediately that Jesus thought the Pharisees and the Sadducees were characterized by sin and hypocrisy. Jesus later told the Pharisees, "For you travel land and sea to win one proselyte, and when he is won, you make him twice as much a son of hell as yourselves (Matthew 23:15).[578]

---

[577] *Israel My Glory*. March/April 2013, p 20.

[578] Thomas C. Simcox. "Why Unleavened Bread" *Israel My Glory* March/April 2013, 21.

Entering the Old City of Jerusalem

We had to go through security to enter the Old City. The soldiers were friendly. Once inside we walked down old ancient streets. The area where Jesus walked is down below in ruins. The level we are on was made to look like it did in the time of Jesus. We walk pass fruit markets and merchandise markets where the people like to barter over the price. The Church of the Holy Sepulcher is built all around the sites where Jesus experienced the steps of being crucified. Helena the mother of Constantine was commissioned to study and locate the sites of the Crucifixion after Constantine became a follower of Jesus and a Christian.

God's Grace (continued)

God's grace for the people of the northern kingdom of Israel willing to repent: "Seek good and not evil, that you may live; so the Lord God of hosts will be with you, as you have spoken, Hate evil, love good; establish justice in the gate. It may be that the Lord God of hosts will be gracious to the remnant of Joseph" (Amos 5:14-15).[579]

---

[579]   Showers, Renald. The Grace of God. *Israel My Glory*, March April, 2013. 39.

Lamb hanging up in the Market Place

Jesus wanted his followers to be unique. His goal was to make them holy. Later in the New Testament, the apostle Paul wrote to the church at Corinth: "Do you not know that a little leaven leavens the whole lump?" (1 Corinthians 5:6). A tiny package of yeast can make two large loaves of bread. Leaven permeates the other ingredients, begins to ferment and expands. Sin is like that because it begins small, and then grows bigger.

God required His people to eat unleavened bread for eight days to teach them that they were to be a separate people from the world and that God had redeemed them from slavery in Egypt by the ten plagues. Then God told Israel, "You shall be holy for I the Lord your God am holy" (Leviticus 19:2). God also told the people of Israel, "I am the Lord, I do not change" (Malachi 3:6). God also said, "I am the same yesterday, today and forever" (Hebrews 13:8). [580]

---

[580] Thomas C. Simcox. "Why Unleavened Bread." *Israel My Glory*. March/April 2013, 21.

Merchandise on sale at Market Place Stores in Old Jerusalem

God's Grace

God's grace for the people of Israel at the end of the seven-year Tribulation, when they turn to their Messiah and are reconciled to Him: The armed forces of all the nations of the world will come against Israel near the end of the Tribulation (Zechariah 12:1-8; Revelations 16:12-16). At that time, two thirds of the people of Israel living in their homeland will perish (Zechariah 13:8). The remaining third will be surrounded and attacked in Jerusalem (Zechariah 14:2). With their backs to the wall and every nation trying to eliminate them, the Jewish people will realize their only hope of survival is God. They will plead with Him to send their Messiah (Matthew 23:37-39). Then God will go to war against the nations and fight for His beloved Israel (Zechariah 12:8-9; 14:3.) To rescue them, He will send the resurrected Messiah with the wounds of His crucifixion still in His body. "And I will pour on the house of David and on the inhabitants of Jerusalem the Spirit of grace and supplication; then they will look on Me whom they pierced. Yes, they will mourn for Him as one mourns for his only son, and grieve for Him as one grieves for a firstborn. In that day there shall be a great mourning in Jerusalem, and the land shall mourn, every family by itself (Zechariah 12:10-12).

Then a fountain shall be opened for the house of David and for the inhabitants of Jerusalem, for sin and for uncleanness" (Zechariah 13:1).

And God "will say this is My people; and each one will say, "The Lord is my God" (Zechariah 13:9). Christ will descend to the Mount of Olives in His Second Coming (Zechariah 14:3-4). And a plaque will strike "all the people who fought against Jerusalem" (Zechariah 14:12 and Revelations 19:11-21). Then He shall restore God's theocratic Kingdom and reign as God's appointed King over the earth for the last 1,000 years of its existence (Zechariah 14:9, 16-21 and Revelations 20:1-6).[581]

Pomegranate Juice Break in the Old City of Jerusalem

This juice is known in clinical studies to prevent heart disease. In one eight-ounce glass there is about 40 percent US Recommended Daily Allowance of Vitamin C. It also contains vitamins A,E, and folic acid. It has about three times more antioxidants than red wine or green tea. Some research shows that Pomegranate Juice may be a good blood thinner and may reduce plaque in arteries, and raise the good levels of cholesterol. It may even help lower risk of stokes, heart attacks, and heart disease. Pomegranate Juice may help fight specific forms of cancer such as breast and skin cancer.[582]

The Pomegranate Juice we tried was okay but needed some sweet and low, equal, or Splenda to make it sweeter. This was the first Pomegranate Juice we had ever tasted. It was fun to watch the man cut and squeeze out the juice.

---

[581] Showers, Renald. The Grace of God. Israel My Glory, March April, 2013. 39.

[582] www.wisegeek.org/what-are-the-benefits-of-pomegranate-juice!

An Underground Site in the Via Dolorosa

Next year in Jerusalem was said over and over for the 2,000 years of dispersion. The Jewish people never lost hope of returning to the promised land. Their national anthem, Hatikvah offered them a living hope.

> "So long our hopes are not yet lost
> Two thousand years we cherished them
> To live in freedom in the land
> of Zion and Jerusalem."

Israel My Glory magazines explains how God looks after them. "God articulates, history confirms. Israel has been delivered from every conceivable attempt to destroy it and thus disrupt God's plan. In biblical revelation from Moses to Malachi, God empowered extraordinary people, often in spite of themselves, to rescue the nation. Neither Israel nor Jewry will be destroyed or diminished because the Jews are a people destined to complete a divine mission possessing spectacular elements yet to be seen."[583]

"To the fallen humanity, the church is an inconvenient contradiction to every godless thing it desires. Thus from the beginning, hostile forces have tried to annihilate Christians their God-loving culture, and their faith. Over 2,000 years, the conflict accelerated in stages until

---

[583] *Israel My Glory*, November-December, 2012, 11.

we now find ourselves in what has all the markings of a final push to finish the crusade to wipe out the faith-the same faith that has brought stability, truth, justice, social order, morality, and a sanctity of life previously unknown in history. Our confidence is in Jehovah, who steps in to take control. God has not left the arena. The last page of earth's history has yet to be turned, and we rest in the competence of a God who will perform what he has promised. God articulate, history confirms. Our Lord speaks, and debate ceases. His Word is immutable fact, and history is the record of how He executed His Word."[584]

You can go to http://tinyurl.com/q3hpuhj on the web and see images and a map of the Via Dolorosa in Jerusalem.

Church of the Holy Sepulcher

God's Grace

God offered grace to the people of Israel who lived in their homeland during the first century after their captivity in Babylon

---

[584] *Israel My Glory*, November-December, 2012, 11.

and completion of the second Temple. The priests and the people questioned God's love and His covenant promises. The people and the priest ignored the Mosaic Law, resented God, and offered sacrifices to idols. God used the prophet Malachi to send the people a message. "But now entreat God's favor, that He may be gracious to us. While this is being done by your hands, will He accept you favorably" says the Lord of Hosts (Malachi 1:9).[585]

God's Grace

Random expressions of God's grace: "The Lord will give grace and glory; no good thing will He withhold from those who walk uprightly" (Psalm 84:11). "The Lord is gracious and full of compassion" (Psalm 111:4). "Gracious is the Lord, and righteous; yes, our God is merciful" (Psalm 116:5). Psalm 77 talks about the turmoil of a person who is convinced he cannot be helped in a serious problem and he asks, "Has God forgotten to be gracious? Has He in anger shut up His tender mercies?" (Psalm 77:9). A father tells his son God, "gives grace to the humble" (Proverbs 3:34).[586]

Church of the Holy Sepulcher

---

[585]   Showers, Renald. The Grace of God. *Israel My Glory*, March-April, 2013. 39.
[586]   Showers, Renald. The Grace of God. *Israel My Glory*, March-April, 2013. 39.

Seven Keys to History: Key 2: Corruption

God created the world in six days and rested on the seventh day. God saw all He had made and declared it to be good. God created Adam and Eve and placed them in the perfect environment of the Garden of Eden. God told them what He expects of all mankind to glorify Him by governing the earth in worshipful submission. Adam was to be fruitful and multiply, cultivate the garden, subdue the earth and rule over it, and refrain from eating from the tree of the knowledge of good and evil. God said, "In the day that you eat of it you shall surely die" (Genesis 2:17). Man was in a perfect relationship with God and He even came everyday to walk with them in the garden and Adam glorified God. God is not interested in just beautiful words that a person does not mean, He is interested in your heart and genuine praise and love of Him. Scripture even says that some people praise Him with their lips but ignore Him in their hearts.

Adam did not know about a rebellion in heaven that happened before the creation of the universe. Lucifer, an angel, rebelled against God's holiness. Lucifer said, "I will be like the Most High" (Isaiah 14:14). Lucifer became known as Satan and believed he was equal to God. The Bible said at least a third of the angels agreed with Lucifer or Satan. There are a minimum of 400 million good angels (Revelation 5:11). At least 200 million angels rebelled and became demons. God could have destroyed Satan and the demons but that would not have been being holy and God is holy. Having developed His relationship with Adam, God set the stage for the test to see if Adam and Eve could obey and not eat the fruit from the forbidden tree. Satan entered the garden as a snake and used the lie to trick Eve into eating the forbidden fruit. The lie was if you eat this fruit you will be like God. Eve decided she wanted to be like God instead of obeying God. Eve was deceived and gave Adam the fruit. Eve was deceived but Adam was not (Timothy 2:14). Sin entered the perfect earth.[587]

---

[587] Richard D. Emmons. The Seven Keys to History Key 2 Corruption. *Israel My Glory*, July-August 2012, 28-29.

Corruption

When Adam and Eve sinned, death came into the world. Fossils do not predate Adam. In Genesis 3, death came into the world. The moment Adam and Eve sinned they died spiritually. Spiritual death is a separation of the soul and spirit from God. Physical death is a separation of the soul and spirit from the body. When God reentered the garden, Adam and Eve hid from Him for the first time and their relationship with Him was broken. As descendants of Adam and Eve, we are all born spiritually dead and alienated from God (Ephesians 2:1-3). God cursed Satan for tricking Eve and God promised to bring a Redeemer, the Messiah, into the world from the Seed of the woman. Satan would bruise the Redeemer's heel and the Redeemer one day will bruise Satan's head, destroying him (Genesis 3:15).[588]

Talking to Friendly Israeli Soldiers

The Final Warning to Jewish Believers in Christ: Hebrews 12:18-29

The book of Hebrews compares the experience of God's people at Mount Sinai as they received the Mosaic Covenant to the blessedness of being associated with Mount Zion under the New Covenant. Both Mountains represent defining moments as God

---

[588] Richard D. Emmons. The Seven Keys to History Key 2 Corruption. *Israel My Glory*, July-August 2012. 28-29.

spoke to His people. For Israel, Mount Sinai was a place of terror and judgment if the nation disobeyed God's Law. Mount Zion is a place of grace, joy, and eternal redemption for all believers in Christ. Hebrews 12:18-29 emphasizes that what Christians possess in Christ, their great High Priest puts them in a better position than under the Mosaic Covenant. Mount Sinai had restrictions. "The mountain was off limits to both people and animals. Anyone touching even its base was to be stoned or shot with an arrow" (Hebrews 12:20). At Mount Sinai when the people heard God speak, they were terrified. "You speak with us and we will hear, but let not God speak with us, less we die" (Exodus 20:19). Hebrews 12:19-20 explains the people were convinced if God continued to speak His Law, they would perish because of their sin. Mount Sinai represented the Old Covenant with its Mosaic system of laws that required people to keep all its commandments which no human could keep. God originated the sacrificial system to provide atonement for sin so that sinful people could approach a holy God. Mount Zion is free from bondage (Galatians 4:26). Mount Zion is described in the book of Revelation (Revelations 21:2; 22:5. Israelites at Mount Sinai could not approach God's presence, they would have died. But at the crucifixion of Christ, the veil into the Temple's Holy of Holies was torn from top to bottom giving all believers access to God's presence, where they can receive mercy and grace (Matthew 27:51. Hebrews 4:16). People have a choice of being under the Old Covenant of Law or the New Covenant of light, grace, peace, rest, forgiveness of sin, joy, access to God and eternal life. Believers must choose Mount Zion.[589]

We also visited Mount Zion and the traditional Room of the Last Supper. And then we went to Gordon's Calvary and the Garden Tomb.

---

[589] David M. Levy. The Final Warning. Israel My Glory, July-August 2012. p. 36-37.

The Garden Tomb

In 1863, General Charles Gordon questioned the location site of the crucifixion and burial place of Jesus in the Church of the Holy Sepulcher. For 1,600 years that location had never been questioned. Many Christians agreed with Gordon because they did not like the ritualistic atmosphere at the Church of the Holy Sepulcher.

In 1885, Gordon was walking around the walls of the Old City. Gordon noticed a hillside which seemed to fit the Bible's description of the crucifixion and resurrection. Gordon used scripture from Leviticus 1:11 which states, "The victims are to be slain on the side of the altar northward. And he shall kill it on the side of the altar northward before the Lord; and the priests, Aaron's sons, shall sprinkle his blood round about upon the altar."

Gordon knew that the Church of the Holy Sepulcher is west of the altar. Gordon believed if God gave a northward direction that it should be northward which made Gordon's Calvary a fulfillment. Gordon convinced a group from England to purchase the property. Excavations later found a tomb carved out of solid rock dating back to the first century. Archaeologist found a cistern that proved that a garden had been there at one time. The area was once a quarry and known for executions. Stephen might have been stoned there. After Gordon's popularity, excavations were done around the hill, and a garden and empty tomb was discovered. John 19:42 says, "So because of the Jewish day of Preparation, since the tomb was close at hand, they laid Jesus there."

Protestants and evangelicals accepted it as the burial place of Jesus and named it "Garden Tomb." Some scholars had a problem accepting it because scripture does not say Jesus was crucified on a hill. Scripture calls it a place. Scientific studies show that it was used as a burial place in Old Testament times. John 19:17 says, "Now in the place where he was crucified there was a garden, and in the garden a new tomb in which no one had been laid."

Gordon's Calvary

We celebrated the resurrection of Jesus with a communion service in the garden. In the middle of our communion service we heard the Muslim cry for prayer that can be heard all over Jerusalem. The Muslims have the call to prayer five times a day. We could also hear the birds chirping for us. This was the most meaningful communion because we were in Jerusalem.

Gordon's Calvary

The Love and Mercy of God Part 6

Jesus showed mercy for the unsaved. Jesus and His disciples went to a house and ate a meal with publicans and sinners that the Pharisees considered evil and defiling in God's sight. They asked the disciples, Why does your Teacher eat with tax collectors and sinners?" (Matthew 9:11, Mark 2:16, Luke 5:30). When Jesus heard their question, He said, "Those who are well have no need of a physician, but those who are sick. But go and learn what this means: "I desire mercy and not sacrifice. For I did not come to call the righteous, but sinners, to repentance" (Matthew 9:12-13).

Jesus showed mercy for the guiltless. One time Jesus and His disciples walked through grain fields on the Sabbath. His hungry disciples picked and ate heads of grain. When the Pharisees saw it, they said to Jesus, "Your disciples are doing what is not lawful to do on the Sabbath!" (Matthew 12:2, Mark 2:23-24, Luke 6:1-2). Jesus asked the Pharisees if they had read about King David and his men eating the showbread which was lawful for only priests to eat. Then He said, "In this place there is One greater than the temple. But if you had known what this means, 'I desire mercy and not sacrifice,' you would not have condemned the guiltless. For the Son of Man is Lord even of the Sabbath" (Matthew 12:6-8). He indicated that it was He who determined what may or may not be done on the Sabbath.[590]

---

[590] Renald E. Showers. The Love and Mercy of God, Part 6. *Israel My Glory*, July-August 2012. 38.

Skull Hill at Gordon's Calvary

The rocky hill is about fifty feet high with two deep crevices that look like eye sockets and just below the eye is a formation that looks like a nose.

Gordon believed this site was Calvary which means "Place of the Skull". Mark 15: 22 says, "And they brought him to the place called Golgotha (which means Place of a Skull). Luke 23:33 says, "And when they came to the place that is called, The Skull, there they crucified him, and the criminals, one on his right and one on his left." John 19:17 says, "So they took Jesus, and he went out, bearing his own cross, to the place called The Place of a Skull which in Aramaic is called Golgotha."

Whispers

The Love and Mercy of God Part 6.

Jesus showed mercy for healing. "Then Jesus went about all the cities and villages, teaching in their synagogues, preaching the gospel of the kingdom, and healing every sickness and every disease among the people" (Matthew 9:35). "And when Jesus went out and saw a great multitude; and He was moved with compassion for them, and healed their sick" (Matthew 14:14). Two blind men followed Jesus, begging for His mercy, and came to Him while he was in a house. Jesus said to them, "Do you believe that I am able to do this?" They said to Him "Yes, Lord." Then He touched their eyes, saying, "According to thou faith, let it be to you." And their eyes were opened. And Jesus sternly warned them saying, "See that no one knows it" (Matthew 9:28-30). When Jesus left Jericho, two blind men sitting by the road heard He was passing by. They cried out, "Have mercy on us, O Lord, Son of David!" (Matthew 20:30). When Jesus asked them what they wanted Him to do, they asked for healing. Jesus touched their eyes and they could see again immediately and they followed him (Matthew 20:34; Luke 18:35-43).

Jesus also healed the demon-possessed. A man brought his demon-possessed son that the demon threw the boy to the ground and he foamed at the mouth and became stiff. The man told Jesus that His disciples were not able to heal his son. Jesus asked the man to bring the boy to him. The man told Jesus that the demon often threw his son into fire and water trying to kill him (Matthew 9:21). The man asked Jesus to help him if He could. Jesus answered, "If you can believe, all things are possible to him who believes." Mark 9:23. The father cried out in tears, "Lord, I believe; help my unbelief" (Mark 9: 24). Jesus said to the demon, "Deaf and dumb spirit, I command you, come out of him and enter him no more." Mark 9:25. The spirit came out of him, the son looked lifeless, and Jesus took him by the hand and helped the healed boy up (Mark 9:27).

Once a Canaanite woman from Tyre and Sidon came to Jesus and said, "Have mercy on me, O Lord, Son of David!" She was upset because her daughter was severely tormented by a demon. The disciples of Jesus wanted Him to send the woman away. Jesus explained to them that He had not responded to her because He had been sent to minister only to the lost sheep of Israel not to Gentiles (Matthew 15:22, 24). The woman pleaded with Him, "Lord, help me" (Matthew 15:2.

Jesus told her, "It is not good to take the children's bread and throw it to the little dogs." Matthew 15: 26. The woman replied, "Yes, Lord, yet even the little dogs eat the crumbs which fall from their masters' table" (Matthew 15:27). Jesus replied, "O Woman, great is your faith! Let it be to you as you desire" (Matthew 15:28). The woman's daughter was healed from that very hour.

Jesus and His disciples crossed the Sea of Galilee to the country of the Gadarenes and met a man possessed by an unclean spirit. The man lived in the tombs in caves and no one could tame or bind him no matter how hard they tried. Twenty-four hours a day, he would be in the mountains and tombs, crying and cutting himself with sharp stones (Mark 5:4-5). When the man saw Jesus he ran to him shouting, "What have I to do with You, Jesus, Son of the Most High God? I implore You by God that You do not torment me." Mark 5:7. Jesus said, "Come out of the man, unclean spirit!" (Mark 5:8). The demons asked Jesus to send them into a herd of about 2,000 pigs that were feeding in the nearby mountains. The unclean spirits left the man and entered the pigs who ran into the water and drown. When the owners of the pigs arrived to see what had happened, they were surprised to see the man with the demon sitting calmly and in his right mind. The people in the area were afraid to have such a powerful person as Jesus in the area so they asked Jesus to leave. The man who was now free of the demon went home to Decapolis and began to tell everything that Jesus had done for him" (Mark 5: 20).[591]

---

[591] Ronald E. Showers. The Love and Mercy of God. Part 6. *Israel My Glory*, July-August 2012. 39.

Tomb of Jesus at the Church of Holy Sepulcher

No one knows for sure where the tomb of Jesus is but it does not matter. The only important thing is that Jesus died for our sins as a sacrifice and if we believe in him and love him we will belong to him.

God's Faithfulness to Israel

God used Moses to tell the people of Israel what would happen if they obeyed him and what would happen if they disobeyed. Deuteronomy 28 explains the covenant blessings and curses. God is faithful in following through with His curses and will be equally faithful in bringing forth his blessings. In Lamentations the city of Jerusalem and Solomon's Temple were in ruins. In the middle of the ruins, the prophet, Jeremiah saw a ray of hope. Even in times of stern discipline, God has been faithful to preserve His people. Every time someone has tried to destroy the Jewish people, the Jewish people have added a holiday. The Pharaoh tried and the Jewish people received

Passover. Haman's, Book of Esther, attempt failed and the Jewish people received Purim. The anger of Antiochus IV gave the Jewish people the Feast of Lights or Hanukkah. Hitler's hatred led to the founding of the modern state of Israel on May 14, 1948.

God has been faithful to Israel. In spite of many deportations, the Jewish people remained distinct even in the last deportation that has lasted for 1,900 years in 70 countries.[592]

Camel Owner helps Harold to get on the Camel

We had to hold on tightly to the saddle horn to keep from falling off when the camel stood up.

God's Faithfulness to Israel continued

The formation of modern Israel against all odds, Miracle of the Mediterranean, may be the greatest miracle of the twentieth century. Randall Price, an archaeologist and president of World of the Bible Ministries, wrote,

"The fact of the Jewish people's continuity is even more remarkable in light of the testimony of history to exile and return. In all of human history there have been less than ten deportations of a people group from their native land. These people groups disappeared in

[592] Mark Hitchcock, God's Faithfulness to Israel. *Israel My Glory*, May-June 2013. p. 16-18.

history because they assimilated into the nations to which they were exiled. However, the Jewish people did not simply experience a single exile but multiple exiles. The contrast here with other historical exiles should not be overlooked. While other people groups were exiled to one country, the Jews were dispersed to many different countries, and in fact were scattered to every part of the earth. Moreover, the Jewish people are the only people to have returned en-masse to their ancient homeland and to have restored their national independence, by re-establishing their former state. Anyone of these facts of Israel's survival would be remarkable, but taken together they are miraculous."[593]

God's Faithfulness to Israel continued

The building of modern Israel is very good, but the fact that the country is surviving and thriving for sixty-five years in the middle of many enemies is a testimony to God's faithfulness to His promise, "He who keeps Israel shall neither slumber nor sleep" (Psalm 121:4). God may be setting the stage for the events of the end-times and His people's final restoration to the Promised Land. Most people enter Israel through Ben Gurion International Airport in Tel Aviv. There is a big welcome sign with a tapestry with masses of people walking in through the gates of Jerusalem. On it in Hebrew is a prophetic text from the book of Jeremiah that speaks about the ingathering of the exiles. "So there is hope for your future," declares the Lord. "Your children will return to their own land." (Jeremiah 31:17).

If God was and is faithful to Israel, then we have faith that He will be faithful to all who trust His Son. "The same God who made His promises to Israel and faithfully fulfilled them will keep His Word to all of us who trust in Him to save us and see us through to the end" (Philippians 1:6). "Now may the God of peace Himself sanctify you completely; and may your whole spirit, soul, and body be preserved blameless at the coming of our Lord Jesus Christ. He who calls you is faithful, who also will do it." (1 Thessalonians 5:23-24).[594]

---

[593] Ibid., 16-18.

[594] Mark Hitchcock, God's Faithfulness to Israel. *Israel My Glory*, May-June 2013. 16-18.

Monday January 14

Dead Sea Scrolls Museum, the Old City, and the Western Wall

We visited the Yad Vashem Memorial that tells the history and personal experiences of thousands of Jews relating to the German concentration camps and the cruel treatment of the German Jews. Winkie thought of the German prisoner that worked on her Daddy's farm in south Georgia during World War II. It was a very tearful experience to see what happened to the German Jews.

Yad Vashem Holocaust History Museum

Israel Today Magazine reports on Monday, January 14, 2013, states trouble with Syria in an article. Syrian dictator, Bashar Assad has ordered his military chiefs to launch ballistic missiles at Israel if he is killed by rebel forces.

Walking on the streets of Old Jerusalem

The Seven Keys to History Key 7 Consummation

The next event on God's agenda is the Rapture which will bring the Church Age to an end. Born-again Christians will be changed in an instant, meet Jesus in the air, and be with Him in glory. Everyone who has belonged to Jesus and trusted Him as Savior since Pentecost (Acts 2) with be caught up to be with Him in the air (1 Thessalonians 4:16-17). This event will end the Church Age and begin the 70th week of Daniel when God resumes His program for the nations and Israel.

The 70th week of Daniel comes from Daniel 9:24-27. The prophet Jeremiah referred to the same period as the "time of Jacob's trouble" (Jeremiah 30:7). Jesus called this same time as "great tribulation" (Matthew 24:21). All of these scriptures refer to the Tribulation seven years dominated by the Antichrist. At the end of this awful period of time, the world will finally have true and lasting peace.

Earth will have the 70th week of Daniel when the Antichrist, the man of sin, is revealed. 2 Thessalonians 2:3. This will end "the times of the Gentiles" which began when God gave Judah's King Jehoiakim into Nebuchadnezzar's hand (605 BC) and Nebuchadnezzar destroyed Solomon's Temple (586 BC) Luke 21:24 and Ezekiel 30:3. God denoted Israel from prominence in the days of King Nebuchadnezzar to servitude and insignificance for failing to be faithful to Him. The 70th week of Daniel will end Gentile world domination.

Daniel 9:27 describes that in the middle of the 70th week of Daniel (three and a half years) the Antichrist will break a peace treaty and try to destroy the Jewish people. "Then he shall confirm a covenant with many for one week; but in the middle of the week he shall bring an end to sacrifice and offering. And on the wing of abominations shall be one who makes desolate, even until the consummation, which is determined, is poured out on the desolate.[595]

Part of the Old Jerusalem Model Display

The Seven Keys to History: Key 7: Consummation continued

Jesus mentioned this teaching of abomination of desolation spoken by Daniel the Prophet. "When you see the abomination of desolation, spoken of by Daniel the prophet, then run for the hills, for then there will be great tribulation, such as has not been since the beginning of the world until this time, no nor ever shall be" (Matthew 24:15,21).

Revelations 6-18 describes three sets of divine judgments such as seals, trumpets, and bowls. In the beginning of the 70th week, Jesus breaks the first seal, calling the first of the four horsemen of the apocalypse. The Antichrist is the rider on the white horse. Revelations 6:2. The seal judgments destroy 25 percent of the world's population. Revelations 6:8. Then 144,000 Jewish men are sealed probably as

---

595   Richard D. Emmons, The Seven Keys to History. Key 7: Consummation. *Israel My Glory*, May-June 2013. 32-35.

evangelists for the Kingdom of God. There are 12,000 from each of the twelve tribes of Israel. Revelations 7:4-8. These 144,000 are protected supernaturally through the first half of the 70th week. In Revelations 14:1-5, the men are on Mount Zion in heaven working to bring about Israel's reconciliation to the Messiah.[596]

Looking at the Model of Old Jerusalem

The Seven Keys to History: Key 7: Consummation continued.

After the seal judgments come the trumpet judgments (Revelations 8 and 9). These judgments destroy another 25 percent of Earth's population (Revelations 9:18) just as Daniel 9:27 and Matthew 24 predicted.

We reach the midpoint of the tribulation in Revelations 11-13. The Antichrist's covenant with Israel is broken. "But leave out the court which is outside the temple, and do not measure it, for it has been given to the Gentiles. And they will tread the holy city underfoot for forty-two months" (Revelations 11:2).

God sends two witnesses to take the place of the 144,000 for a testimony during the second half of the 70th week (Revelations 11:3). The dragon (Satan) goes after the Jewish people trying to destroy them (Revelations 12:3-17). God protects them at this time. The Bible says "the wings of a great eagle were given to them, and they flee into the

---

[596]   Richard D. Emmons, The Seven Keys to History. Key 7: Consummation. *Israel My Glory*, May-June 2013. 32-35.

wilderness where God protects them for a time and times and half a time. (42 months) (Revelations 12:14).[597]

Walking in old Jerusalem

The Seven Keys to History Key 7: Consummation (continued)

When the bowl judgments are poured out, an unspecified percentage of Earth's population is destroyed (Revelations chapters 15 and 16). God's wrath intensifies on the gentile nations. God preserves and protects the Jewish people guiding them away from the Antichrist who is trying to kill them. God judges the economic and political systems of the world that is represented by a woman and the city of Babylon.

The wedding of the Lamb takes place in heaven with Christ and His raptured church (Revelation 19:7-9). Jesus returns with the armies of heaven to defeat the Antichrist, rescue the Jewish people and establish His Kingdom on earth. "And I saw the beast, the kings of the earth, and their armies, gathered together to make war against Him who sat on the horse and against His army. Then the beast was captured, and with him the false prophet. These two were cast alive into the lake of fire burning with brimstone. And the rest were killed with the sword which proceeded from the mouth of Him who sat on the horse" (Revelations 19:19-21).

---

[597] Richard D. Emmons, The Seven Keys to History. Key 7: Consummation. *Israel My Glory*, May-June 2013. 32-35.

The beast is the Antichrist (Revelations 13:1-10). He and his false prophet are thrown alive into the Lake of Fire. There is no additional judgment for them. This is the fulfillment of Daniel 9:27, "And on the wing of abominations shall be one who makes desolate, even until the consummation, which is determined, is poured out on the desolate." The Antichrist who makes desolate will be destroyed.

The kings and the Gentile armies "will perish with the sword which proceeded from the mouth of Him who sat on the horse. And all the birds were filled with their flesh." (Revelations 19:21). Satan is bound and imprisoned for 1,000 years for the duration of the Messianic Kingdom. "He laid hold of the dragon, that serpent of old, who is the Devil and Satan, and bound him for a thousand years; and he cast him into the bottomless pit, and shut him up, and set a seal on him, so that he should deceive the nations no more till the thousand years were finished. But after these things he must be released for a little while" (Revelations 20:2-3).[598]

Narrow Streets in Old Jerusalem

The streets are very narrow with people and cars to bring merchandise to the shops and for taxis to take people to destinations. As we walked, we watched out for cars, yelled "Car, Move over." And the people jumped out of the way. Some people have apartments and living quarters and you see bicycles at their small living quarters.

---

[598] Richard D. Emmons, The Seven Keys to History. Key 7: Consummation. *Israel My Glory*, May-June 2013. 32-35.

Beautiful Churches have been built in Old Jerusalem and most have something to do with the trial and crucifixion of Jesus.

The Seven Keys to History Key 7: Consummation (continued)

Jesus will come in the clouds of heaven (Matthew 24:29-31). He will descend physically and visibly to the Mount of Olives to take His throne as King of the earth. No longer will He be the meek and mild Lamb He was in His First Coming. He will be the Lion of Judah who judges and wages war and rules with a rod of iron (Revelations 19:11). Jesus returns to bring order and righteousness and to reign on the throne of His father, King David of Israel (Luke 1:32).

The Millennial Kingdom is mainly a Jewish kingdom with a Jewish King who is returning. His throne will be in the Jewish city of Jerusalem and a Jewish Temple will be built. At the end of the thousand years, Satan will be turned loose and lead a final rebellion. Then Satan will be thrown into the Lake of Fire and the Kingdom will move into eternity. Church Age believers will not be Kingdom citizens but will reign with Christ (2 Timothy 2:12; Revelations 20:4,6). It is God's calling for the church to help him reign. God's calling for the Jewish people is to occupy the land promised to them forever and to possess the kingdom forever (Daniel 7:18). No longer will they be persecuted and oppressed because Israel will be the head of all nations; and their Messiah will rule the world.[599]

---

[599] Richard D. Emmons, The Seven Keys to History. Key 7: Consummation. *Israel My Glory*, May-June 2013. 32-35

Western Wall

The Western Wall in Jerusalem is the only thing that remains of the Temple destroyed in 70 AD by the Romans. The entire city of Jerusalem was destroyed. Jerusalem was in ruins until 135 AD when Emperor Hadrian rebuilt Jerusalem and named it Aelia Capitolina. Aelia was the family name of Hadrian. Jews were forbidden to enter the city except for the 9th of Av when they gathered to mourn the destruction of the Temple.

Archaeologists have uncovered streets and shops that once lined the main street of Aelia Capitolina known also as the Cardo.[600]

Winkie put a sheet of paper, folded with prayer requests to pray for the people of Israel, world peace and for the peoples of the world to learn to like each other, God's will for Israel and the world, and all of my friends and family. I felt much joy and peace and the presence of God that I have never experienced before. I put the folded sheet in a crack in the Western Wall with all of the other prayer concerns of people worshiping God at that site.

King David bought what became the Temple Mound. (2 Samuel 24:18-25)

18 "And Gad came that day to David and said to him, 'Go up, raise an altar to the Lord on the threshing floor of Araunah the Jebusite.' 19 So David went up at Gad's word, as the Lord commanded. 20 And

---

[600] Barnhart, David R., A look at Eliyahu. *The Vine and the Branches*. Midwinter, 2012. 16.

when Araunah looked down, he saw the king and his servants coming on toward him. 21 And Araunah said, 'Why has my lord the king come to his servant?' David said, 'To buy the threshing floor from you, in order to build an altar to the Lord, that the plague may be averted from the people.' 22 Then Araunah said to David, 'Let my lord the king take and offer up what seems good to him. Here are the oxen for the burnt offering and the threshing sledges and the yokes of the oxen for the wood. 23 All this, O king, Araunah gives to the king.' 24 But the king said to Araunah, 'No, but I will buy it from you for a price. I will not offer burnt offerings to the Lord my God that cost me nothing.' So David bought the threshing floor and the oxen for fifty shekels of silver. 25 And David built there an altar to the Lord and offered burnt offerings and peace offerings. So the Lord responded to the plea for the land, and the plague was averted from Israel."[601]

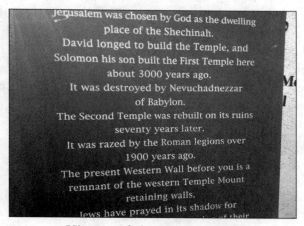

History of the Western Wall

Psalm 122:6-7 states mentions Pray for the peace of Jerusalem. "May they prosper who love you. Peace be within your walls, and security within your towers."

Jerusalem did not fall into the hands of Israel until the time of David. The army under Joab captured Jerusalem and David moved the Ark of the Covenant to a safe place in Jerusalem. King Solomon built

---

[601] 2001 by Crossway Bibles, a division of Good News Publishers and Les Feldick's Through the Bible Ministry.

the temple in Jerusalem and established Jerusalem as an important place in Jewish history. It is believed that the ruins of the Temple and Palace are probably buried beneath the Herodian platform supporting the Dome of the Rock and the Al-Asqa Mosque.

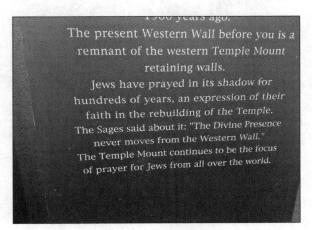

The Western Wall

The Sages said "The Divine Presence never moves from the Western Wall." When Winkie prayed at the Wall she felt the Divine Presence and had a feeling she had never experienced before.

Focus on Israel: The Cardo Then and Now

The Western Wall (Kotel) in Jerusalem is a small part of the retaining wall that held up the Temple Mount at the time of Jesus. Archaeologists have dug below the 2nd century street and uncovered remnants and artifacts dating to the first Temple period including a four room house. Jewish seals used to stamp documents and correspondence from the 8th and 6th centuries BC were found. Some archaeologists believe the house may have been destroyed in 586 BC by King Nebuchadnezzar of Babylon. The street was twenty-six feet wide with raised sidewalks five feet wide on both sides and paved with limestone slabs laid diagonally. Below the street was an elaborate sewage and drainage system.[602]

---

[602]   Focus on Israel. Abiding Word Ministries: The Vine and Branches. Volume 27. Mid Winter 2012. 16.

Tuesday, January 15, 2013

Masada and the Dead Sea

Qumran, in the Judean Desert,
where the Dead Sea Scrolls were found in a Cave

This is the Judean Desert we passed by in our tour bus. Another name for it is wilderness of Judea. In one of those caves, the Bedouin boys found the Dead Sea Scrolls. In Israel, a person can make a cave by digging it out of the limestone in the mountain. Caves could be lived in by people or as a place to keep sheep, goats, and other animals.

We passed by En Gedi in the Judean Desert and the landscape is mountainous with many caves a person can see from our tour bus. There is only a little bit of desert bushes but not much for sheep to eat. David was hiding from King Saul and discovered that he was in the same huge cave as Saul. David sneaked up on the king while he was sleeping and cut off part of his robe and left it to let King Saul know he had been there and spared his life.

Jesus was tempted for forty days in the Wilderness of Judea. As we passed by it in the bus I thought of Jesus and what it must have been like for him.

The Funicular at Masada

We call this a cable car in the United States and in Israel it is called a Funicular. Many people stand in the Funicular and hold on to a pole if you are near one. There were only four seats on a bench in the Funicular and our group insisted that Harold and I sit down. Cable Cars have many cars and only a few ride in it at a time. The Funicular has one car and you crowd as many people in it as standing room allows. The view is fabulous as you ride to the top. Years ago the only way to get to the top of Masada was to walk up the steep path and steps. From the Funicular we could see the path and a few people who chose to walk up it.

Christ's Incarnation: 1 John 1: 1-4

By the time the apostle John wrote 1 John, he had lived through the inception, expansion and persecution of the first-century church. John was on the Jerusalem council that worked on issues such as whether gentiles could be saved if they were not circumcised (Acts 15:1). John began with a statement about the Incarnation of Jesus Christ which is the cornerstone of Christian belief. David Levy, author of this article states, "John proved three truths about the incarnate Christ: (1) Christ is God, coequal with and of the same substance and essence as God the Father; (2) Christ possesses the attributes of omnipresence, omniscience, omnipotence, immutability, and eternality that belong only to God; (3) Christ is the eternal Son of God who took on human flesh and now exists as the God-man." The gospel message of mankind's redemption and reconciliation to God began with the Incarnation of Jesus Christ.

John explained in 1 John 1: 1-4 that (1) John personally experienced Christ in the flesh, (2) Jesus came from God the Father to declare eternal life, and (3) all Christians can have the same fellowship with Jesus that he and the other apostles possessed.

John was not proving the deity of Christ as he did in his Gospel (John 1:1). John was assuming Christ's deity and proving the divine Christ is totally human. John and the other apostles were eye-witnesses to the humanity of Jesus. They ministered with Him for more than three years and knew He had come in the flesh (1 John 4:2-3). The disciples saw the suffering, death, and resurrection of Jesus. John spoke of hearing, seeing, and touching the Lord. Jesus is the Preacher of God's message and the Message of Life and both resides in Him. John and the disciples received a revelation from Jesus that He was the Messiah, the Son of God who became flesh. The disciples handled the dead body of Jesus. The body of the resurrected Jesus proved His Incarnation. John called Jesus the Word of God the One who brings forth the truth of and about God and that eternal life resides in Him. Jesus is the source of life and the light of man's salvation (John 1:4).[603]

On Top of Masada

---

[603] David M. Levy. Christ's Incarnation. *Israel My Glory*, May-June 2013. 36-37.

View from the Top of Masada

Christ's Incarnation continued

In 1 John 1:2 John explains the meaning of life in the phrase Word of life. John affirmed with apostolic authority that Jesus is the eternal life who is coequal and coeternal with God the Father (John 14:6). John explained that Jesus gives eternal life to all who believe. Jesus raised people from the dead giving physical life back to the daughter of Jarius, the son of the widow of Nain, and Lazarus. He also promised to give eternal life to all who believed. John's personal experience with Jesus, his authoritative proclamation of the message given to him by the risen Christ (Matthew 28:18-20) are proof enough that Jesus Christ is the God-Man.[604]

John said in 1 John 3, "That which we have seen and heard we declare to you, that you also may have fellowship with us; and truly our fellowship is with the Father and with His Son Jesus Christ."

The Grace of God Part 4

The New Testament Greek noun related to grace is *charis* which means gracious care, help, and goodwill. Grace brings joy, pleasure, and delight. It is kindness given to a person that does not deserve it. An example is God giving grace to mankind. The following are

---

[604]   David M. Levy. Christ's Incarnation. *Israel My Glory*, May-June 2013. 36-37.

examples of grace. "And if by grace, then it is no longer of works; otherwise grace is no longer grace. But if it is of works, it is no longer grace; otherwise work is no longer work" (Romans 11:6).

"Now we have received, not the spirit of the world, but the Spirit who is from God, that we might know the things that have been freely given to us by God" (1 Corinthians 2:12).

"For if the inheritance is of the law, it is no longer of promise; but God gave it to Abraham by promise" (Galatians 3:18).

Mary, the mother of Jesus, was given special grace. God sent the angel Gabriel "to a virgin betrothed to a man whose name was Joseph, of the house of David. The virgin's name was Mary" (Luke 1:27). Gabriel said to her, "Rejoice, highly favored one, the Lord is with you; blessed are you among women" (Luke 1:28). "Do not be afraid, Mary, for you have found favor with God" (Luke 1:30). The words "highly favored" and "found favor" are part of the Greek noun *charis*. As a result of God's grace, Mary became His chosen vessel through who His eternal Son would become incarnated as the promised Messiah who will rule from the throne of His ancestor David forever (Luke 1:31-33).

As a child in his humanity, Jesus 'grew and became strong in spirit, filled with wisdom; and the grace of God was upon Him" (Luke 2:40). As a boy, "Jesus increased in favor with God and men" (Luke 2:52). Jesus spoke gracious words in the synagogue of Nazareth (Luke 4:22). John the Baptist told the Jewish people that Jesus, "whom God has sent speaks the words of God" (John 3:34). Jesus claimed His words were the Father's words: "For I have not spoken on My own authority; but the Father who sent Me gave Me a command, what I should say and what I should speak. And I know that His command is everlasting life. Therefore, whatever I speak, just as the Father has told Me, so I speak" (John 12: 49-50).[605]

---

[605] Renald E. Showers. Foundation of Faith. The Grace of God. Part 4. *Israel My Glory*, May-June 2013. p. 38-39

Masada View

The Grace of God Part 4 (continued)

Speaking to God concerning His apostles, Jesus said, "I have given to them the words which You have given Me; and they have received them, and have known surely that I came forth from You; and they have believed that You sent Me. I have given them Your word (John 17:8,14).

During His First Coming, Jesus brought grace as God's new way for administering His moral absolutes. Scripture says, "For the law was given through Moses, but grace and truth came through Jesus Christ" (John 17:17). When Jesus came in His First Coming, the enlarged God's grace by adding a new form of it to those already in existence. In Romans 4:1-16, Paul taught that both Abraham who lived before the Mosaic Law and David who lived under that Law were justified from the penalty of sin by grace.

The Mosaic Law never functioned as a means of eternal salvation. No person has ever been justified through the Law. The apostle Paul wrote, "Therefore we conclude that a man is justified by faith apart from the deeds of the law. Or is He the God of the Jews only? Is He not also the God of the Gentiles? Yes, of the Gentiles also, since there is one God who will justify the circumcised by faith and the uncircumcised through faith" (Romans 3:28-30).

In Galatians 2:15-16, 21; 3:11, we learn: "We who are Jews by nature, and not sinners of the Gentiles, knowing that a man is not justified by the works of the law but by faith in Jesus Christ, even we have believed in Christ Jesus, that we might be justified by faith in Christ and not by the works of the law, for by the works of the law; for by the works of the law no flesh shall be justified. I do not set aside the grace of God; for if righteousness comes through the law, then Christ died in vain. But that no one is justified by the law in the sight of God is evident, for the just shall live by faith."

Instead of saving people, the Mosaic Law was "the ministry of death, written and engraved on stones," (2 Corinthians 3:7), "the ministry of condemnation" (2 Corinthians 3:9), and "brings about wrath to those who are under it" (Romans 4:15).

In John 1:17 we learn that God established the Law through Moses as a way of administering His eternal moral rules over mankind.[606]

Masada Ruins

Editorial

Tourists stand atop the fortress Masada in the Judean wilderness and look down 1,000 feet to the desert floor, and think about the Roman invasion in 70 AD. The ancient wall is the remains of the Roman siege camps and the huge ramp built to get the Jewish rebellion leaders. For centuries the winds above the summit seemed to whisper the words,

---

[606] Ronald E. Showers. Foundation of Faith. The Grace of God. Part 4. *Israel My Glory*, May-June 2013. 38-39.

"never again." Now it seems the Romans are back. They do not use catapults, stones, swords and spears. They use rockets, explosives, and automatic weapons and are hostile regimes wanting to finish what their ancient compatriots started.

Egypt is in the hands of terrorists tied to Hamas fanatics. Reckless Western leaders are giving Iran time it needs to get the bomb with its announced first drop on Tel Aviv, Israel. Because of the Syrian rebellion, Israel built another wall to circumvent the attacks that will come if jihadist forces there take over the government.

The good news is that Israel is alive and well. That fact will not change and is the eternal message for all pretenders with bad intentions. When they are gone and forgotten, meaningless footnotes to history, little Israel will be standing. It is written in the Book (Bible).[607]

Forever Changed by the Changeless Christ

Ever since the moment the Holy Spirit descended upon 120 believers at Pentecost, there has been an unending line of people testifying about the change in their lives after Jesus Christ entered their hearts.

Jesus the Savior still has the power to break the chains of sin if a person will believe Him and accept His free gift of grace. People whose lives are caught up in alcohol, drugs, and sexual perversions can experience salvation and a change in lifestyle.

Counterfeit messengers are telling people they have been born with inclinations and lifestyles that can never be changed. These messengers preach that these lifestyles should be accepted and celebrated even though the Bible warns against adopting perverted lifestyles and engaging in sinful practices.

Paul declared, "Do you not know that the unrighteous will not inherit the kingdom of God. Do not be deceived, neither fornicators, nor idolaters, nor adulterers, nor effeminate, nor thieves, nor the covetous, nor drunkards, nor revilers, nor swindlers, will inherit the kingdom of God. Such were some of you; but you were washed, but you were sanctified, but you were justified in the name of the Lord Jesus Christ and in the Spirit of our God" (1 Corinthians 6:9-11).

---

[607] Editorial, *Israel My Glory*, March- April 2013. 6.

Paul also wrote, "Therefore we have been buried with Him through baptism into death, so that as Christ was raised from the dead through the glory of the Father, so we too might walk in newness of life" (Romans 6:4).

The old nature dies hard and the flesh fights the spirit, the person of faith is empowered by the indwelling presence of the Holy Spirit to overcome the world and all of its evil. Paul speaks of this truth in Galatians 5:16-26. Paul concludes, "Now those who belong to Christ Jesus have crucified the flesh with its passions and desires."[608]

Forever Changed by the Changeless Christ (continued)

Hebrews 13:8 states, "Jesus Christ the same yesterday and today, and forever. 2 Corinthians 5:17 teaches, "Therefore if any man be in Christ, he is a new creation; old things are passed away; behold all things are become new."

Confession is good for the soul. "If we confess our sins, He is faithful and righteous to forgive our sins and to cleanse us from all unrighteousness. If we say we have not sinned, we make Him a liar and His Word is not in us" (1 John 1:9-10). Paul said, "But because of your stubbornness and unrepentant heart you are storing up wrath for yourself in the day of wrath and revelation of the righteous judgment of God" (Romans 2:5).

Some modern churches deny Christ's blood for atonement and the rejection of His power to change and transform lives. In these churches, people are invited to come to Christ, sin and all, with no need for repentance or any change in life styles. Paul warned of false teachers by saying, "I am amazed that you are so quickly deserting Him who called you by the grace of Christ, for a different gospel; which is really not another; only there are some who are disturbing you and want to distort the gospel of Christ. But even if we, or an angel from heaven, should preach to you a gospel contrary to what we have preached to you he is to be accursed!" (Galatians 1:6-8).

The message of salvation taught in the Scriptures is "that Christ died for our sins, according to the Scriptures, and that He was buried, and that He was raised up on the third day according to the Scriptures"

---

[608] David R. Barnhart. Forever Changed by the Changeless Christ. The Vine and Branches, Volume 28, Summer 2013, Issue 3. 4-5.

(1 Corinthians 15:3-4). Paul wrote, "Therefore if any man be in Christ, he is a new creation; old things are passed away; behold all things are become new" (2 Corinthians 5:17).

Peter wrote, "His divine power has granted to us everything pertaining to life and godliness through the true knowledge of Him who called us by His own glory and excellence. For by these He has granted to us His precious and magnificent promises, so that by them you may become partakers of the divine nature, having escaped the corruption that is the world by lust" (2 Peter 1:3-4). And the best change of all will be when you get your new eternal body with no sickness, disease and you will live with Christ for all eternity. The Bible says, "Eye has not seen, nor ear heard, neither have entered into the heart of man, the things which God has prepared for them that love Him" (1 Corinthians 2:9).[609]

Masada

Focus on Israel

Israel is largest exporter of Drones in the world. Drone exports have come to about $4.6 billion over the last eight years and is 10 % of Israel's total defense exports. Source The Times of Israel May 20, 2013.

Syria has powerful Tishrene Missiles from Russia and are aimed at Tel Aviv. Each of the missiles carry an 1100 pound payload which

---

[609] David R. Barnhart. Forever Changed by the Changeless Christ. The Vine and Branches, Volume 28, Summer 2013, Issue 3. 4-5.

can cause damage. Russia has sent about a dozen warships to patrol the waters around Syria. Secretary of State, John Kerry recently traveled to Russia and asked Putin not to arm Syria. Apparently Putin did not listen.[610]

The Temple Mount Institute has built a giant copper laver, 8 feet tall and 9 feet in diameter, which can be used to purify twelve priests at one time. The laver was moved to the new headquarters in Jerusalem's Old City with the hope that soon the laver and the other vessels prepared for the Temple will be moved again soon to the appointed place in the rebuilt Temple. There is a new seven branch gold candelabra which cost nearly $5 million has been set aside for the rebuilt Temple. Isaiah 5:6-7 states, "For My house shall be called a house of prayer for all people."

Gabriel Stone now on Display in Israel Museum

The Gabriel Stone that dates to the time of Jesus was discovered on the shores of the Dead Sea by a Bedouin man in 2000. The Gabriel Stone is three feet high and has 87 lines of writing in Hebrew that mentions mainly the archangel Gabriel. The writing is in ink and not carved into the stone. Only 40% of the lines are legible. This stone is displayed at the Israel Museum in Jerusalem (*Huffington Post* 5-20-13).

Herod the Great Exhibit

Herod the Great is known as the king who tried to kill the baby Jesus and Herod ruled Judea from 37 BC to 4 BC. There is a new Herod exhibition at the Israel Museum in Jerusalem and the display authenticates biblical accounts of King Herod. This exhibition shows the final funeral procession from Herod's palace in Jericho where he died to the mausoleum where he planned to be buried. Most of the artifacts were found at Herod's Tomb in Herodium near Bethlehem. You can view vestiges from the Second Temple and a sarcophagus (stone coffin) which may have the remains of Herod.[611]

---

[610] Y-netnews. com May 21, 2013
[611] Focus on Israel. The Vine and Branches, Volume 28, Summer 2013, Issue 3. 16-17.

Masada Ruins

Masada Ruins

The Rapture

The word rapture comes from the Greek word, harpazo, and means to be "caught up." In 1 Thessalonians 4:17 Paul writes about the mystery of the rapture in three different places: 1 Corinthians 15:51-58, 1 Thessalonians 4:13-18, and 2 Thessalonians 2:1-16. Paul also writes about the rapture in Titus 2:13 and Philippians 3: 20-21.

The Importance of Apostle Paul

God's inspired word tells us twenty times that Paul is the Apostle to the Gentiles. Romans 16:25 (KJV), "In the day when God shall judge the secrets of men by Jesus Christ according to my gospel." Romans 16:25 (KJV), "Now to him that is of power to establish you according to my gospel, and the preaching of Jesus Christ, according to the revelation of the mystery, which was kept secret since the world began." 2 Timothy 2-8 (KJV), "Remember that Jesus Christ of the seed of David was raised from the dead according to my gospel." During Paul's conversion in Damascus and for three years, Jesus gave Paul the message He wanted Paul to take to the Gentiles to form the Church that is the Body of Christ.[612]

Masada Ruins

Ground Zero Jerusalem

For years one American husband and wife have battled the United States government over their son's passport because it lists his birth place as Jerusalem. The parents argued that it should be listed as Israel because it is a country. Since the 1948 creation of the country of Israel, the United States government has not recognized any country

---

[612] Source: Les Feldick Ministries, "Through the Bible" Newsletter, July-August-September 2013 Faith plus Nothing.

as sovereignty over Jerusalem. The United States government made the rule that any American child born in Jerusalem lists only Jerusalem for place of birth.

In the 1967 Six Day War, Israeli soldiers stormed the gates of the old city of Jerusalem and stood before the large wall of the Temple Mount and claimed a birthright given to them by God. The problem is that Arab Muslims claim the same area that also has sacred Islamic sites and consider it a birthright to them by God. Both groups assert ancient rights to ownership. So the United States Department Congress, Justice Department and President all debate Who are the citizens of Jerusalem? Is it Israelis or Palestinians, they debate to find an answer to the question.

The biblical prophet, Ezekiel wrote, "Thus says the Lord God; This is Jerusalem; I have set her in the midst of the nations and the countries all around her" (Ezekiel 5:5).

Jerusalem has been a focal point of history that it is sometimes called the center of the world. It is thought to be holy by three major religions such as Christianity, Judaism, and Islam. And Jerusalem has been known for centuries of religious strife and bloodshed. The terrible clashes between Israeli soldiers and Arab youths, United States soldiers dying in Afghanistan, the Western world's dependence on Arab oil, the fear of Islamic terrorism are all links to the religious and political strife in Jerusalem and the Middle East.[613]

Ground Zero Jerusalem

Now the top of the Temple Mount in Jerusalem is dominated by the Islamic Dome of the Rock and the Al-Aqsa Mosque and under Islamic control. The Temple Mount is also the location of King Herod's Temple visited by Jesus. That temple was destroyed by the Romans in 70 AD. The Bible declares that King David reigned from Jerusalem. On this plot, David's son, Solomon, built a beautiful temple to God. Some Islamic writers are trying to rewrite this history. In July 2000 during the second Camp David meeting, the delegations of the United States and Israel were shocked to hear Palestinian Authority leader, Yasser Arafat state that the Temple Mount was not the site of

[613] Gary Petty, Ground Zero Jerusalem. The Good News. July-August 2013. 20-22.

477

Solomon's temple. More and more Islamic leaders are declaring that Solomon never built a temple in Jerusalem.

In a 2009 *Wall Street Journal* story, it was reported that the chief Islamic judge of the Palestinian Authority claimed that Solomon's temple has no historical roots. He added that the Jews are engaged in "an attack on history, theft of culture, falsification of facts, erasure of the truth, and Judaization of the place."

In the same article these rewritten history stories are taught in Palestinian primary-school textbooks and printed in official news-papers according to Palestinian Leaders Deny Jerusalem's Past, September 25, 2009.

The Bible describes Solomon's temple as a beautiful building serving as the place for the worship of the God of Abraham, Isaac and Jacob. The temple contained an inner room, the Holy of Holies or Most Holy Place, and housed the Ark of the Covenant containing the Ten Commandments. The Bible mentions when Solomon finished his prayer of dedication, fire came from heaven and consumed Solomon's sacrifice. God's presence filled the room. [614]

Ground Zero Jerusalem (continued)

Palestinian clerics are trying to discredit the biblical prophecies foretell that God's Messiah will reign from Jerusalem. Isaiah 2:2-3 states, "Now it shall come to pass in the latter days that the mountain of the Lord's house shall be established on top of the mountains, and shall be exalted above the hills; and all nations shall flow to it. Many people shall come and say, "Come, and let us go to the mountain of the Lord, to the house of the God of Jacob; He will teach us His ways, and we shall walk in His paths; For out of Zion shall go forth the law, and the word of the Lord from Jerusalem."

The prophet Zechariah wrote: "Thus says the Lord of hosts: "Peoples shall yet come, inhabitants of many cities; the inhabitants of one city shall go to another, saying, "Let us continue to go and pray before the Lord, and seek the Lord of hosts. I myself will go also. Yes, many peoples and strong nations shall come to seek the Lord of host in Jerusalem and to pray before the Lord. In those days ten men from

---

[614]   Ibid., 20-22.

every language of the nations shall grasp the sleeve of a Jewish man, saying Let us go with you, for we have heard that God is with you" (Zechariah 8:20-23).

In modern times, there is no temple standing dedicated to the God of Israel. Many people believe that Bible prophecy foretells of a future temple when Jerusalem becomes ground zero of biblical prophecy.

When the Roman army destroyed Jerusalem in 70 AD, the Jewish temple caught fire and burned. Roman emperor, Titus built an arch as a tribute to his victory. That arch stands today in Jerusalem and is proof of the existence of the temple. The Roman soldiers carried off the large golden menorah, silver trumpets and the table of showbread.[615]

Roman Bath House Ruins in Masada

---

[615] Gary Petty, Ground Zero Jerusalem. The Good News. July-August 2013. 20-22.

Masada Ruins

Ground Zero- Jerusalem continued

In Daniel 12 there is a prophecy of "the time of the end." Daniel is writing of the time when the Messiah is sent to rule from Jerusalem. Israel's ancient laws say the daily sacrifice can only be conducted by authorized Levitical priests at an authorized site such as the temple. Daniel's prophecy tells us that before the second coming of Jesus Christ, there must be animal sacrifices taking place in Jerusalem. When international pressure and violence stops those sacrifices, the world enters a time of violence so bad that Jesus intervenes to keep earth from being destroyed (Daniel 12: 1-13 and Matthew 24: 21-22).

The controversy over the temple mount will intensify. Prophesy will be fulfilled.[616]

Exploring God's Word

People cannot imagine all that God has prepared for them. Apostle Paul wrote in 1 Corinthians 2:9 Contemporary English Version, "What God has planned is more than eyes have seen or ears have heard. It has never entered our minds."

What God intends seems preposterous to those who have not opened their minds to understand it. Paul wrote, "But the natural

---

[616] Gary Petty, Ground Zero Jerusalem. The Good News. July-August 2013. 20-22.

man does not receive the things of the Spirit of God, for they are foolishness to him; nor can he know them, because they are spiritually discerned" (1 Corinthians 2:14).

Most people concentrate on temporary, physical concerns and their interests. God's thinking is on what is spiritual and eternal. Isaiah 55:9 states, "For as the heavens are higher than the earth, so are My ways higher than your ways and My thoughts than your thoughts."

"He who overcomes shall inherit all things, and I will be his God and he shall be My son." Revelation 21:7. Does it really mean inherit all things? It is taken from the original Greek word, *panta*, and "all things" means the totality of the creation (John 1:3, Genesis 1:28 and Hebrews 2:6-8).

The author, John LaBissoniere, believes all those who love and obey Him, our eternal Father offers opportunity to live, create and flourish with Him in His divine family for all eternity (1 Peter 1:4, Romans 6:23). But to experience that future, each person has to be changed from Mortal life to immortality at the time of the resurrection of the dead (John 10:28, 1 Corinthians 15: 50-52). 1 John 3:2 states that at that moment those who are God's children will be transformed to be like Him.[617]

Arrival at the Dead Sea

---

[617] John LaBissoniere. Exploring God's Word. The Good News. July-August 2013. 23-25.

Exploring God's Word continued

Moses wanted to know what God looked like in Exodus. Moses said, "Please, show me Your glory" (Exodus 33:18). God told Moses, "You cannot see My face; for no man shall see Me and live" (Exodus 33:20). God allowed Moses to see His back, after which Moses' face glowed so much that he had to keep it covered in order not to scare the Israelites (Exodus 33:23, 34:29-35).

In chapter 1 of Revelation, Jesus gave apostle John a look at His form through a vision. "His head and his hair were white like wool, as white as snow. And his eyes were bright like flames of fire. His feet were as bright as bronze refined in a furnace, and his voice thundered like mighty ocean waves and his face was as bright as the sun in all its brilliance" (Revelation 1:14-16 NIV).

God's faithful saints will take on His appearance at the time they are granted everlasting life at the resurrection of the dead or at the rapture (Colossians 1:12, Daniel 12:2). Jesus Christ "will transform our lowly body that it may be conformed to His glorious body." (Philippians 3:21). Revelations 21:4 teaches us, "For those given this fabulous, new spiritual existence, death, sorrow, crying and pain will forever be a thing of the past. King David described it as enjoying "pleasures forever" (Psalms 16:11). All of these wonderful things are a gift of grace.[618]

What did God plan "Before Time Began"

Until the last century, scientists believed time was eternal and absolute. Isaac Newton (1642-1727) believed time was eternal. Only the Bible claims there was a second when time as we know it did not exist. The Old and New Testaments of the Bible refers to God's activities before the beginning of time (Proverbs 8:22-23, John 1: 1-3, 1 Corinthians 2: 7, and 2 Timothy 1:9). God inhabits eternity (Isaiah 57:15). Eternity is God's dwelling and He can intervene at will in the universe (Isaiah 46:10). The Bible tells us that God has always existed and He made great plans before time began.

The Bible tells us of "the hope of eternal life, which God who cannot lie promised before time began" (Titus 1:2). Hebrews 2:10

---

[618] The Good News. July-August 2013. 20-22.

tells us that the reason people were created was to have an unending relationship with God the Father, His son, Jesus Christ, and all of the people whom They would bring to a glorified state. 1 John 4:8 points out that the main characteristic of love that the Godhead desires to share with people. John 3:1-2 says, "Behold what manner of love the Father has bestowed on us, that we should be called children of God! Beloved, now we are children of God; and it has not yet been revealed what we shall be, but we know that when He is revealed, we shall be like Him, for we shall see Him as He is."

Eternal life means we will no longer be constrained by time. All people have a beginning and if a person is faithful to God and believe in the cross of Jesus, we are promised a resurrected body and an everlasting life in a glorious spirit body.

Even the grace of God which is His underserved favor toward us is something God planned before time began. This would be the calling of people, leading them to repentance and forgiving all people who accepted the sacrifice of Jesus Christ for their sins.[619]

What Did God Plan Before Time Began (continued)

2 Timothy 1:8-9 teaches us, "God has saved us and called us with a holy calling, not according to our works, but according to His own purpose and grace." According to John 1:1-3 and John 1:14 God, the Father and the Word who became Jesus Christ were willing to pay the ultimate price of having Jesus, the beloved Son of the Father, sacrificed in suffering and death as a substitute for our sins.

"And if you call on the Father, who without partiality judges according to each one's work, conduct yourselves throughout the time of your stay here in fear knowing that you were not redeemed with corruptible things but with the precious blood of Christ, a lamb without blemish and without spot. He indeed was foreordained before the foundation of the world, but was manifest in these last times for you" (1 Peter 1:18-20).

God has not planned the universe and our existence in a random way. He carefully designed everything to specific details and has

---

[619] Mario Seiglie. What Did God Plan Before Time Began. The Good News. July-August 2013. 26-27.

revealed much about his plan through his prophets and apostles. Matthew 10:30. The apostle Paul wrote, "Bur we speak the wisdom of God in a mystery, the hidden wisdom which God ordained before the ages for our glory" (1 Corinthians 2:7).

The Bible Knowledge Commentary writes about the plan for salvation outlined by the festivals of God laid out in the Bible and reveals seven important steps. It begins with the Passover, which symbolizes Jesus Christ as a substitute for our sins. Remember the Passover took place in Egypt with the Israelite slaves being instructed to slay a lamb, put the blood of the lamb on their doors, and the angel of death would pass over the house. The lamb's blood was a symbol of the blood of Jesus.

The second feast, the Days of Unleavened Bread, picture God's people accepting the sacrifice of sin. The third step is Pentecost when God's Spirit was sent to the disciples so Jesus Christ and the Spirit can make a dwelling place in us (John 14:23). Step number four is the Feast of the Trumpets which symbolizes the Second Coming of Jesus Christ when He returns to rule as King of Kings. The fifth step is the Day of Atonement when Satan will be removed from deceiving people. The sixth step is the Feast of Tabernacles symbolizing the thousand-year rule of Jesus. The seventh step is the Eighth Day where people have a last chance to accept.[620]

The Grace of God Part 5

The apostle John taught that the Mosaic Law was a way to administer His eternal, moral absolutes over His chosen nation of Israel. John 1:17 says, "Grace and truth came through Jesus Christ. "

In Romans 6: 14 we learn that, "For sin shall not have dominion over you, for you are not under law but under grace." Paul makes it clear that Christians are not under the Mosaic Law. Paul teaches that the Mosaic Law was never a means of salvation. People can be free from the Mosaic Law without being lawless because the grace administration does not encourage sinful behavior.

In Romans 8:3 states, "For what the law could not do in that it was weak through the flesh, God did by sending His own Son in the

---

[620]   Ibid., 26-27.

likeness of sinful flesh, on account of sin; He condemned sin in the flesh." In Romans 6:15 Paul stresses "What then? Shall we sin because we are not under law but under grace? Certainly not!"

In Romans 7:1-4, Paul illustrates a marriage analogy to explain his teachings in Romans 6:14. Marriage works with a woman being bound in marriage to her husband until he dies. But death terminates the marriage and frees her to marry another man. Paul used this analogy to teach that Jewish Christians were freed from the binding Mosaic Law and free to accept the doctrine of grace. Paul uses the word *sin* twenty-five times in association with the death of Christ in Romans 6:1through Romans 7:13. But only once does it refer to actual sin (Romans 6: 15). "Shall we sin because we are not under law but under grace. Certainly not." Psalm 51:5 refers to the sin nature a person inherits at the moment of conception. The sin nature is a disposition of enmity toward God. Romans 8:7 says, "The carnal mind is enmity against God; for it is not subject to the law of God, nor indeed can be."[621]

Kalia Beach Restaurant

---

[621]   Renald E. Showers. *The Grace of God*. Part 5. *Israel My Glory*. July- August 2013. 38-39.

The Grace of God Part 5

Paul described the sin nature to the relationship to the unregenerate person as a master to a slave. Paul refers to sin in Romans 8:16 as, "Do you not know that to whom you present yourselves slaves to obey, you are that one's slaves whom you obey, whether of sin leading to death, or of obedience leading to righteousness?" Romans 6: 1-13 tells us that when an unregenerate person becomes a Christian, he is identified with the death, burial, and resurrection of Christ. In Romans 6:6, Paul writes, "Knowing this, that our old man was crucified with Him, that the body of sin might be done away with, that we should no longer be slaves of sin." In Galatians 2:20, Paul writes, "I have been crucified with Christ." Through a person's death with Christ, he lost completely the master-slave relationship that he had with his sinful nature when he was in his unregenerate state.

Paul teaches us the purposes of the death of Christ. One purpose is that the body of sin will be done away with. Body of sin means the unregenerate person's body that is controlled by the sinful nature. Done away with means to dissolve relationships. When an unregenerate person dies spiritually with Christ, his physical body terminates its function as an instrument of sin and stops being a body of sin. In Romans 6:4, Paul writes, "Therefore we were buried with Him through baptism into death, that just as Christ was raised from the dead by the glory of the father, even so we also should walk in newness of life."

Romans 6:8-14 teaches us, "Now if we died with Christ, we believe that we shall also live with Him, knowing that Christ, having been raised from the dead, dies no more. Death no longer has dominion over Him. For the death that He died, He died to sin once for all; but the life that He lives, He lives to God. Likewise you also, reckon yourselves to be dead indeed to sin but alive to God in Christ Jesus our Lord. Therefore do not let sin reign in your mortal body, that you should obey it in its lusts. And do not present your members as instruments of unrighteousness to sin, but present yourselves to God as being alive from the dead, and your members as instruments of righteousness to God. For sin shall not have dominion over you, for you are not under law but under grace."[622]

---

[622] Renald E. Showers. The Grace of God. Part 5. *Israel My Glory*. July- August 2013. 38-39.

Lovers at Kalia Beach

Bible Study with Tony W. Cartledge Luke 19: 28-40

In Luke's version of Palm Sunday, Jesus travels from the valley town of Jericho up the mountainous road to Jerusalem. Jesus told the parable about a king who had high expectations of his servants (Luke 19:11-27). The followers of Jesus expected the kingdom of God to come immediately. Jesus rode into Jerusalem like a king but one clothed in humility instead of pride (Zechariah 14:4-5). Jesus told the disciples where to find the donkey for Him to ride. Jesus usually referred to Himself as "Son of Man." This time He told His disciples to tell the animal's owner if he objected to say, "The Lord needs it." Jesus insisted that the colt be previously unridden. Hebrews believed only animals that had never been used as beasts of burden could be used for sacred events. Luke does not mention people waving palms as Matthew and Mark does.

Luke tells us, "The whole multitude of the disciples began to praise God joyfully with a loud voice for all the deeds of power that they had seen" (Luke 19:37).

John 12:17-18 teaches us, "So the crowd that had been with him when he called Lazarus out of the tomb and raised him from the dead continued to testify. It was also because they heard that he had performed this sign that the crowd went to meet him."

The people wanted Jesus to be a military messiah, stand up to Rome, and make Israel as a leading nation on the earth and then become king. Luke includes a tradition that the Pharisees tried to stop Jesus and the disciples due to their fear of the people accepting Jesus as Messiah. Luke 19:39 states, "Teacher, rebuke your disciples" (NET Version). The Pharisees wanted Jesus to openly retract any claim to being the longed-for messiah or any kind of king. In Luke 19:40, Jesus said, "I tell you, if these were silent, the stones would shout out." The image of stones shouting praise to Jesus suggested that dumb rocks could recognize Jesus while the intelligent Pharisees could not.[623]

Trying to walk in Sinking Mud

Only Ten Minutes of Fun Allowed due to Salt Content

---

[623] Tony W. Cartledge. Bible Study with Tony W. Cartledge. Baptists Today News Journal. February, 2013. 26-27.

Importance of knowing the Modern Names of Ancient Places

In the past Abraham lived in Mesopotamia and journeyed into Canaan. In modern times the correct sentence should be, "Abraham left Iraq and journeyed to Israel and Lebanon. Understanding this helps us to know where Abraham lived and where he journeyed as Abraham obeyed God's command of leaving his home in Iraq to go to an unknown area that God wanted to show him. By faith he obeyed God and God made him the Father of many nations and the religions of Judaism, Christian, and Muslim.[624]

The Biblical World

The Middle East, Europe and Asia have been drawn and redrawn since biblical times. Mesopotamia, Goshen, and Canaan no longer exist. New nations take their places. The land that both the Muslims and Jews both claim as promised from God was mainly in Canaan. Canaan now lies between Syria and Egypt and are now the modern countries of Lebanon, Jordan, Israel and the West Bank.

The twelve tribes of Israel from Solomon's kingdom was divided into Israel in the north and Judah in the south. In New Testament times, Nazareth and the Galilean territory where the ministry of Jesus began was in the north. Judaea and Jerusalem were to the south and the Judaean wilderness between the north and the south.[625]

The Tanakh

The Tanakh is the oldest document written about two or three millennia ago and is the holy scripture of Judaism. It consists of Torah or Law or Pentateuch, Prophets or Nevi'im and Writings or Ketuvim. Some biblical scholars call this book "the Hebrew Bible" and think this is a neutral name for the parts common to Christians and Jews. Some Jews objected to the name because the word "Bible" which comes from the Greek word, Biblia which means "the Books) does not have a precise translation in Hebrew. The narratives and teachings in the Tanakh are very similar to the Old

---

[624]   Robert Sullivan, editor. *Life: Places of the Bible*. Time Inc. July, 2013. 7-8
[625]   Robert Sullivan, editor. *Life: Places of the Bible*. Time Inc. July, 2013. 10-11.

Testament of Protestant Christians. The Roman Catholic and Orthodox Bibles have material found nowhere in the Tanakh. Both the Christian Old Testament and the Jewish Tanakh tell the stories of creation, the Lord's covenant with Israel, the Exodus from Egypt and the Hebrew people's coming to the Promised Land of Israel. Abraham and Moses are both considered heroes. Prophets recounts the history of Israel and has prophecies with heroes and wars especially David. Writings include meditations on evil and death and psalms and praises of Israel's covenant with God.[626]

Dead Sea Lotion and Make-Up Factory

They use mud and the minerals from the Dead Sea to make expensive beauty products.

Noah on Mount Ararat

Noah was the son of Lamech and the father of Shem, Ham and Japheth. The people on earth were very sinful and cruel and God decided to destroy the world. Then he saw Noah, a "just man" and reconsidered. Noah followed the exact instructions of God and built an ark although it took a long time. And Noah and his family plus two of every kind of animals went into the Ark. When the flood was over, God made a wind to pass over the earth and caused the ark to settle on the mountains of Ararat. Noah lived 350 years after the flood.

---

[626]   Ibid., 12-13.

These snow-capped peaks are Mount Ararat and Little Ararat. Ararat is a volcano dormant for 167 years and is located in eastern Turkey near the Armenian and Iranian borders. Around 70 AD, historian Josephus reported the remains of the Ark were easily seen. In 1300 visitors reported seeing the remains of the Ark.

In modern times there is a mosque built in the 18th century by Kurdish chieftain, Ishak, Pasha. Islam considers Noah to be important. The Koran has an account of a son or grandson of Noah named Nu who refused to go inside the Ark. Nu landed on Al Judi, "the Heights.

Through the years, pilgrims and adventurers, including Robert Ballard who discovered the Titanic. In 1959 a pilot on a NATO mapping mission photographed a shape of a boat fifteen miles from Mt. Ararat. Expeditions did not find Noah's Ark.[627]

Ahava Beauty Products from the Dead Sea

Abraham, a Patriarch's Journey

Abraham was a tenth-generation descendant of Noah in the Mesopotamian city of Ur of the Chaldees. The ruins of Ur are at a site about 200 miles southeast of Baghdad. Abraham's name means "father love" or exaltation of the father. Most of Ur worshiped a moon god named Sin. The Hebrew Bible, the Tanakha, the Christian Bible and the Koran all agree that Abraham was a believer in one god, the God,

---

[627] Ibid., 18-21.

and was given the job of traveling far and wide to a new land. "Now the Lord had said unto Abram, Get thee out of thy country, and from thy kindred, and from thy father's house, unto a land that I will shew thee; And I will make of thee a great nation" (Genesis 12:1-2).

Abraham and his caravan stopped in Haran and stayed there until his father, Terah, died at age 205. Haran is between the Tigris and Euphrates Rivers in Turkey and was known for its sun worship. Haran in Hebrew means parched. Even in modern times people use earth-en-mound dwellings that the design has not been changed in 3,500 years. Haran is about 600 miles northwest of Ur and was an important east-west caravan route. It was in Haran that God spoke to Abraham and asked him to go to a land to start a great nation. God said, "I will bless them that bless thee, and curse him that curseth thee; and in thee shall all families of the earth be blessed. So Abram departed, as the Lord had spoken unto him; and Lot went with him; and Abram was seventy-five years old when he departed out of Haran."

Romans 4:16 teaches us, "Abraham who is the father of us all." Lot went to live in Sodom but was saved when God destroyed Sodom with brimstone and fire. Lot's wife was not spared because she disobeyed and looked back at Sodom. Sodom and Gomorrah were located at the southern tip of the Dead Sea and lies on the Israeli-Jordanian border.

Sarah became impatient with God's promise of a child, so she gave Hagar her maid to Abraham to have a child with her. Ishmael was born to them. Later when Abraham was 99 years old when God told him, Sarah would have a baby. A year later, Isaac was born. Abraham died at age 175 and is buried beside his wife in the Cave of Machpelah east of Mamre. In the West Bank at Hebron's Tomb of the Patriarchs where Abraham, Sarah, Isaac and Jacob are buried.[628]

---

[628] Ibid., 22-23.

Political Sign in Israel

Landscape on the Way to the Dead Sea

Modern shepherds take small herds of a dozen or so goats and sheep on these sloping hills to find a little bit of grass bushes to eat. It is amazing that shepherds still walk with their sheep to find food in modern times.

Isaac on Mount Moriah

Genesis 22: 2 teaches us, "Take thy son, thine only son Isaac, whom thou lovest, and get thee into the land of Moriah; and offer him there."

Abraham obeyed and journeyed to Mount Moriah in Jerusalem, bound Isaac, and was about to kill him, when God interrupted and said, "Saith the Lord, for because thou hast done this thing, and hast not withheld thy son, thine only son: That in blessing I will multiply thy seed as the stars of the heaven, and as the sand which is upon the sea shore, and thy seed shall possess the gate of his enemies. And in thy seed shall all the nations of the earth be blessed; because thou hast obeyed my voice." This prophecy led to Isaac's son, Jacob, and then to Israel and in the Christian version to Jesus. Jerusalem is to be God's city of special purpose. Mount Moriah is a slope that now leads to a summit with the gold-roofed Dome of the Rock Mosque. There is a huge rock 58 by 51 feet and has scars that may be the rock where Abraham killed the ram for the sacrifice.[629]

Wednesday, January 16, 2013

We had no tours today and each person chose what to do. We joined two ladies and walked to the Old City of Jerusalem. We were trying to find some of the VIA Dolorosa that we missed seeing.

Antique Store in Old Jerusalem

This is the store the cab driver stopped and found us guide number 1. There were many expensive items of Biblical antiques.

---

[629] Ibid., 32-33

Jacob at Penuel

Jacob tricked his twin brother, Esau, into giving him his birthright for food. Jacob also tricked Esau out of his first-born blessing. Jacob fled Canaan for Mesopotamia to stay with his Uncle Laban and while there he worked for Laban for fourteen years for the marriage of Leah and Rachel. Jacob had twelve sons and one daughter from his two wives and two concubines. Jacob became a rich man after fourteen years of labor when he was paid for it. Laban's sons were jealous of Jacob so Jacob left Laban and traveled back to Canaan toward Esau and his 400-man army. Jacob and his family stopped by the Jordan River. That night Jacob wrestled with "a man" until dawn. Some people believe this "man" was Esau's guardian angel. The angel declared, "Thy name shall be called no more Jacob, but Israel; for as a prince hast thou power with God and with men and hast prevailed." Jacob called this spot, Penuel, saying, 'for I have seen God face to face, and my life is preserved." Jacob's life was preserved and he reunited peacefully with Esau.[630]

Joseph into Egypt

"Now Israel loved Joseph more than all his children, because he was the son of his old age: and he made him a coat of many colors" (Genesis 37:3). Joseph's beautiful coat of many colors caused terrible discord in the house of Jacob because of the jealousy the brothers of Joseph felt. "And when his brethren saw their father loved him more than all his brethren, they hated him, and could not speak peaceable unto him." The brothers discussed killing Joseph but then they played a dirty trick on Joseph instead. "They stript Joseph out of his coat, his coat of many colors that was on him, and cast him into a pit and the pit was empty, there was no water in it. And they sat down to eat bread, and behold, a company of Ishmelites came from Gilead with their camels bearing spices and balm and myrrh, going to carry it down to Egypt. And Judah said unto his brethren, What profit is it if we slay our brother, and conceal his blood? Come and let us sell him to the Ishmaelites."

---

[630] Ibid., 34-35

Their plot was spoiled because a group of Midianites picked Joseph from the pit first and sold him to the Ishmaelites for twenty pieces of silver. The Ishmaelites "sold him into Egypt unto Potiphar, an officer of Pharoah's and captain of the guard."

The brothers took the coat of Joseph and "killed a kid of the goats, and dipped the coat in the blood; And they sent the coat of many colors, and they brought it to their father and said, This have we found: know now whether it be thy son's coat or no. Jacob "rent his clothes, and put sackcloth upon his loins, and mourned for his son many days."

Joseph's luck changed in Egypt when "his master saw that the Lord was with him, and that the Lord made all that he did to prosper in his hand. And Joseph found grace in his sight, and he served him; and he made him overseer over his house, and all that he had he put into his hand."

Joseph had a big problem with his master's wife who had a liking for him. She became angry when Joseph refused her advances and later accused Joseph of attacking her. Joseph was thrown into prison and stayed until Pharaoh's dream. Joseph deciphered the dream and predicted a long famine in Egypt. Pharaoh freed Joseph and made him governor over all of Egypt. Genesis 41:30 teaches us, "And Pharaoh said unto Joseph, Forasmuch as God hath shewed thee all this, there is none so discreet and wise as thou art."

Later Joseph's brothers came to Egypt to purchase food because Canaan had none. Joseph's brothers did not recognize him and Joseph pretended he did not know them. He put a special cup in one of the brother's bags and returned their money in the bag. He sent someone to stop them and search their bags. When the "stolen items" were found one brother was taken hostage and the others sent home with the grain. The brothers were told to bring the younger brother back and the other brother would be released and more grain purchased. At the proper time Joseph identified himself and asked them to bring Jacob and the entire family to Egypt to live. Joseph told his brothers, "So now it was not you that sent me hither, but God: and he hath made me a father to Pharaoh, and lord of all his house, and a ruler throughout the land of Egypt" (Genesis 45:8).

Jacob and his clan was settled in Goshen in Egypt. Joseph would die in Egypt at age 110 and before he died he requested his remains to be returned to Canaan one day and four hundred years later his wish was granted. A new Pharaoh came to power and did not know how Joseph helped Egypt to survive the famine or why the Israelite people were living in Egypt. The Pharaoh made the Israelites slaves that had to work long hard hours for cruel masters.[631]

Interesting Items for Sale in the Antique Shop

Moses Exodus

The Jewish people call Moses, Moshe Rabbenu, which means Moses our teacher, lawgiver, and hero. Christians believe Moses is a model of faith. Muslims call Moses, Musa and believe he is the first prophet connected to Muhammad. Christians have Jesus who modified the teachings of Moses; Muslims have Muhammad who modified the teachings of Moses. Jews are still looking for the Messiah and Moses remains preeminent.

Moses was one of the Hebrews born in Egypt during a time of persecution. Hebrew adults were forced into long hours of daily labor and had to lay mortar and bricks. Pharaoh even feared male infants and so he made a decree that all Hebrew male babies were to be killed and thrown into the Nile river. "And when she could no longer hide him, she took for him an ark of bulrushes, and daubed it with slime

---

[631] Ibid., 36-41.

and with pitch, and put the child therein; and she laid it in the flags by the river's brink" (Exodus 2:3). Brink is land sloping down to the river. Flags are a kind of plant that grows next to rivers. Bulrushes are reed like plants with stems which can be dried and woven into baskets. Slime and pitch were two types of asphalt found in the Bible world. Slime was the paste or solid form of asphalt; pitch was the liquid form. Both slime and pitch were used for water-proofing. An ark is a coffin-shaped container. The ark of Moses contained a three-month-old baby and was used to preserve the deliverer of Israel.

In Exodus 2:1-2, Exodus 6:20 and Numbers 26:59 we learn that Moses's father was named Amram which means high people. He was from the tribe of Levi, married Jochebed, his father's sister, died at age 137 (Exodus 6:16), and they are known to have had three children named Miriam, Aaron, and Moses.

The mother of Moses was Jochebed which means "glory to Jehovah. She was from the tribe of Levi.[632]

Station 4 of the Via Dolorosa where Jesus met his Mother

This is where Jesus met his mother, Mary. John 19: 26 says "When Jesus therefore saw his mother, and the disciple standing by, whom he loved, he saith unto his mother, 'Woman, behold thy son!'"

Moses Exodus continued

---

[632] http://www.learnthebible.org and Ibid., 42-63.

Moses was hidden by faith. (Hebrews 11:23). His parents saw that Moses was a "godly child" (Hebrews 11:1-2 and 2 Corinthians 5:7). Pharaoh's daughter saw the ark among the flags (Exodus 2:3, Job 8:11, and Isaiah 19:6). She sent her maid to check the ark. Pharaoh's daughter checked the ark as the baby Moses cried and filled with compassion she wanted to keep the Hebrew baby. She saw Moses' sister on the bank and asked her to find a nurse for her new baby. Miriam ran home and asked the mother of Moses to be his nurse. Moses grew physically and mentally and learned all the wisdom of the Egyptians (Acts 7:22). Moses became the son of Pharaoh's daughter and knew nothing of his Hebrew heritage. Pharaoh's daughter named her new son Moses because she took him out of the water.

One day Moses saw one of the Hebrew slaves being severely beaten and he killed the Egyptian. He hid in Midian for years, met Zipporah, the daughter of Jethro and they had two sons. Moses looked after the flock of sheep for his father in law, Jethro who was a priest of Midian.

One day when he was tending the sheep by Mount Sinai, he had an experience when "the angel of the Lord appeared unto him in a flame of fire out of the midst of a bush: and he looked, and behold, the bush burned with fire, and the bush was not consumed." Moses said, "I will now turn aside, and see this great sight, why the bush is not burnt."

When the Lord saw that Moses turned his head to look, God called Moses name. Moses replied, "Here am I." God said, Draw not nigh hither; put off the shoes from your feet; for the place whereon thou standest is holy ground. Moreover he said, I am the God of thy father, the God of Abraham, the God of Isaac, and the God of Jacob. And Moses hid his face for he was afraid to look upon God."

The ground where Moses stood has a St. Catherine's Monastery today that was built between 527 and 565 AD by the Byzantine emperor, Justinian. It has a special Chapel of the Burning Bush.[633]

---

[633] Robert Sullivan, editor. *Life: Places of the Bible.* Time Inc. July, 2013. 42-63.

A pair of sandals mark represents the spot where
Jesus met his Mother.

Moses Exodus continued

"And Moses said unto God, Who am I, that I should go unto
Pharaoh and that I should bring forth the children of Israel out of
Egypt?" (Exodus 3:11).

"And afterwardMoses and Aaron went in,and told Pharaoh, Thus
saith the Lord God of Israel, Let my people go." And Pharaoh said,
Who is the Lord, that I should obey his voice to let Israel go? I know
not the Lord, neither will I let Israel go,"

But God led the people about, through the way of the wilderness
of the Red Sea: and the children of Israel went up harnessed out of
the land of Egypt (Exodus 13:18).

"And the Lord went before them by day in a pillar of a cloud, to
lead them the way" (Exodus 13:21).

Exodus tells readers there were about 600,000 men, women, and
children. Bible scholars have been trying for years to figure out the
route the Israelites traveled to Israel. Most scholars think the Israelites
may have taken the most southern route toward the tip of the peninsula. They walked through a barren landscape for three days and the
people were very hungry. When they arrived at the oasis of Marah the
water was bitter but Moses made it taste clean and sweet. The next
stop may have been Elim, a paradise of shade and they rested and

enjoyed the shade and the good water. Then they may have entered another wilderness, the Wilderness of Sin. The people complained to Moses and "Then said the Lord unto Moses, Behold, I will rain bread from heaven for you, and the people shall go out and gather a certain rate every day" (Exodus 16:4).

There is a controversy over which mountain was Mount Sinai. Some scholars believe it was in Saudi Arabia. Moses was associated with Midian and Midian would have been in Saudi Arabia. Paul in Galatians 4:25 wrote of Mt. Sinai being in Saudi Arabia where Paul received instructions from Jesus Christ. Helena, the mother of Emperor Constantine, chose a mountain on the Sinai Peninsula as the "Path of Moses." A Byzantine Monastery was built there and ruins can be seen today. It is not known which place is the real place of Mount Sinai. All that matters is that God delivered the Ten Commandments to the world. The exact place is not that important and modern people can only speculate.[634]

Our Israeli Waitress at the Jerusalem Mall

Moses Exodus

The Lord first called to Moses from the mountain and asked for obedience from the Israelites. Then the Lord appeared to Moses in a thick cloud and promised to sanctify His people. The third morning there was thunder and lightning and the trumpet. And God called

---

[634]   Ibid., 42-63.

Moses up on the mountain and Moses went up. Moses received the stone tablets of law which were to be kept in the Ark of the Covenant. In modern times near Jebel Musa's summit is a chapel built in 1934 on the remains of an earlier church. Some scholars think the chapel is built over the rock used to make the Tablets. There is also a small mosque and the Muslims believe this is the mountain of Moses. No one knows for sure the location of the mountain. Some think Saudi Arabia near Midian and others think it is Jebel Musa on the Sinai Peninsula.

"And Mount Sinai was altogether on a smoke, because the Lord descended upon it in fire" (Exodus 19:18).

Miriam was the sister of Moses who watched baby Moses in the ark. She was a big help to Moses during the exodus out of Egypt. Miriam died in Kadesh where Moses hit the rock and brought forth water for the people.

Aaron, the brother of Moses, helped Moses talk to Pharaoh and demand that the People of Israel be set free. Aaron was made spokesperson for Moses who expressed to God that he had a speech impediment and was sensitive about it. It was Aaron's rod that touched the Nile and turned it red with blood. While Moses was on top of Mt. Sinai, Aaron listened to the people and made them an idol of a golden calf and led the worship of the idol. Aaron died on Mount Hor in Petra and his tomb is located there.

In Kadesh the people needed water so Moses hit a rock and water poured out. Moses made one bad mistake by not giving God the credit for the miracle. Moses would remain the leader of his people during the exodus but God punished Moses for the omission of recognizing God for the miracle by not allowing him to touch the ground of the homeland of Israel. In the mountain region of Moab Moses gazed for the first and last time upon Canaan. Modern scholars think it was at Jebel Nebah, near the northeastern tip of the Dead Sea. Jebel Nebah is a 2,613 foot summit and has a beautiful view of the land. God said to Moses, "This is the land which I sware unto Abraham, unto Isaac, and unto Jacob, saying, I will give it unto thy seed; I have caused thee to see it with thine eyes." Before Moses died he gave Israel advice about obeying God's law and in turn the land would be theres. Moses soon died and was buried in Moab.[635]

---

[635] Ibid., 42-63.

Joshua, the Battle of Jericho

Jericho is located about 10 miles north of the Dead Sea in the Jordan River Valley. Jericho is the lowest city on earth and is 840 feet below sea level and is the oldest city in the world. About 7000 BC a permanent settlement was made when a fort was built by the spring Ain es-Sultan.

Joshua led the crossing of the Jordan and for six days Joshua and his men marched around Jericho. On the seventh day, seven priests marched around Jericho seven times and blew seven trumpets to make the walls fall down.

"So the people shouted when the priests blew with the trumpets: and it came to pass, when the people heard the sound of the trumpet, and the people shouted with a great shout, that the wall fell down flat" (Joshua 6:20).

Later King David had interactions with the Ammonite king, Hanum who had a base in Jericho. Herod the Great, the ruler of Judea at the time of the birth of Christ, had his rival Aristobulus III drowned in a swimming pool in Jericho. Herold built his winter residence near Jericho. Jesus restored sight to a blind man in Jericho. Jesus also went to see Zacchaeus, the tax collector in Jericho. Jesus also used the road from Jericho to Jerusalem as the setting for the parable of the Good Samaritan.[636]

Balloons at the Mall

---

[636]   Ibid., 64-65.

Saul: Into the Promised Land

"Saul, a choice young man, and godly: and there was not among the children of Israel a godlier person than he" (1 Samuel 9:2). Saul of the tribe of Benjamin was anointed ruler over all of the Twelve Tribes at Gilgal. Saul inspired a volunteer army to fight the Philistines. Saul's problem was depression that tormented him.

God told Samuel to go to Bethlehem and fine a man named Jesse and pick out the son that God chose to be a future king after Saul. The chosen one was David, the youngest, who was a shepherd boy. Samuel "took the horn of oil, and anointed him in the midst of his brethren: and the Spirit of the Lord came upon David from that day forward."

David entered the service of Saul as a lyre player retained to help Saul's depression. And then David became a warrior in Saul's army. As David's popularity grew, Saul became jealous, and David had to hide from Saul near the oasis and waterfall of En-gedi on the western shore of the Dead Sea. In the Valley of Jezreel, Saul was having a hard time in a battle with the Philistines. Three of Saul's sons were killed. In despair Saul took a sword and fell upon it.[637]

David in Jerusalem

David's story begins on the hillsides of Bethlehem where shepherds tended their flocks. This is to tie the lineage of David to Jesus, the Messiah, who was born in Bethlehem years later. Christians feel that Jesus is a direct descendant of David and Jews believe that the coming Messiah will be descended from David.

As a young boy, brave David fought the Philistine giant, Goliath with only a sling and stones. David said, "Thou comest to me with a sword and with a spear, and with a shield: but I come to thee in the name of the Lord of hosts." David's first shot sent a stone that knocked the giant down. David took the sword from Goliath and used it to behead him. "And David took the head of the Philistine and brought it to Jerusalem to Saul.

After David became king, he captured Jerusalem and moved the capital from Hebron to Jerusalem that became known as the "city of David." The Ark of the Covenant was traveling with David until he

---

[637]   Ibid., 66=67.

moved it to Jerusalem permanently. David wanted to build a temple but Nathan, the prophet, told him a warrior should not build a temple. David made Israel great.

The prophet Nathan said to David, "Thine house and thy kingdom shall be established for ever." David's tomb is on Mount Zion. Solomon was the king after David.[638]

Making New Friends at the Jerusalem Mall

Solomon: The Temple

Solomon was a philosopher king and he fortified Israel and built up Israel. Solomon turned his attention to the economic, cultural and artistic advancement of the Israeli people.

Solomon believed in arranging a strategic marriage to lessen tensions between rival states. Solomon wed the daughter of Pharaoh to lessen tensions. Solomon established maritime trade with Africa, accomplished agricultural development, created a chariot corps and a cavalry.

Solomon is known for writing 3,000 wise parables and 1,500 poems mostly in Proverbs.

"And behold, I purpose to build an house unto the name of the Lord my God, as the Lord spake unto David my father, saying, Thy son, whom I will set upon thy throne in thy room, he shall build an house unto my name" (1 Kings 5:5).

---

[638]   Ibid., 68-71.

Robert Sullivan, editor. Life: Places of the Bible. Time Inc. July, 2013. 72-73.

The New Testament

"The beginning of the gospel of Jesus Christ, the Son of God" (Mark 1:1). The first four books of the New Testament are called Gospels from the Anglo-Saxon that means "good news." The gospels sketch the life of Jesus, son of a carpenter and his wife. and the son of God. The Old Testament pointed to the coming Messiah and Jesus fulfilled the Old Testament prophecies that pointed to Him. The principal writer of the New Testament is Paul. Before his conversion Paul's name was Saul, a Jewish religious leader, who persecuted the Christians. God chose Paul to be his apostle to the Gentiles. On the road to Damascus to persecute the Christians, Jesus spoke to Paul and converted him. Once converted, Paul was willing to bring the message of Jesus to the world such as Romans, Corinthians, Galatians etc. through preaching sermons and writing epistles. Paul presented a new doctrine of grace which is salvation by faith and not by works.

All of this writing of the New Testament began about twenty-five years after the crucifixion, death, and resurrection of Jesus. By the end of the fourth century AD, Rome had embraced Christianity with the emperor of Rome and a Latin edition of the Bible was ordered with the twenty-seven books of the New Testament. The New Testament is printed in many languages and dialects in modern times.[639]

---

[639]   Ibid., 72-27.

Working at the Mall

Herod, The King's Masada

Solomon and Herod had things in common although they lived in different times. Solomon built the temple and died in 930 BC. Jeroboam led a revolt against the successors of Solomon and the kingdom split in two. Rehoboam, son of Solomon, was made king of Judah. Jeroboam was made ruler of Israel. These two fought with one another and with other nations for centuries. Egypt, Assyria, Babylonia destroyed Solomon's temple, and then by first century BC Rome invaded and installed Herod as ruler. Herod built a temple in Jerusalem.

Herod was paranoid at times and even had his wife and mother-in-law to death. Later he had his two sons killed. But Herod is remembered most for rebuilding Jerusalem's Temple. Herod also built Masada as his out of town retreat.

"Then Herod, when he saw that he was mocked of the wise men, was exceeding wroth, and sent forth, and slew all the children that were in Bethlehem, and in all the coasts thereof, from two years old and under according to the time which he had diligently enquired of the wise men (Matthew 2:16). Herod is remembered for his role in the Nativity narrative of Jesus Christ.[640]

---

[640] Ibid., 76-77.

Back Home in our Hotel Room

John the Baptist: Along the River Jordan

"In those days came John the Baptist, preaching in the wilderness of Judea, And saying, Repent ye: for the kingdom of heaven is at hand" (Matthew 3:1-2).

John the Baptist began to preach, "There cometh one mightier than I after me, the latchet of whose shoes I am not worthy to stoop down and unloose."

John traveled along the Jordan River preaching to the masses and introduced baptism which is a cleansing by water of all sin. Baptism became known as an act of repentance and faith.

Jesus was baptized by John. And a voice from heaven saying, "This is my beloved Son, in whom I am well pleased."[641]

---

[641]   78-79.

The Reason we drink Bottled Water

The water did not have germs but had too many unusual chemicals and minerals. Some days the water was clear but today in the above picture, the water is cloudy and does not look good.

Jesus of Nazareth

When Jesus lived in Nazareth, it was a little village with about 200 families. In modern times Nazareth is an Arab city of about 80,000 and is the largest Arab city in Israel.

In Nazareth Mary received the Holy Ghost and became pregnant. And Joseph was visited by the angel of the Lord who said, "And she shall bring forth a son, and thou shalt call his name Jesus for he shall save his people from their sins." And Joseph did as the angel said and took Mary as his wife.

Before Mary could give birth, the Roman ruler, Caesar Augustus announced that all people must register in the city of their origin. So Mary and Joseph headed for the one-hundred-mile journey to Bethlehem to register. "And Joseph also went up from Galilee, out of the city of Nazareth, into Judaea" (Luke 2:4).

Research by Biblical scholars and archaeologists help us to visualize the route Mary and Joseph took to Bethlehem. By the end of the first day, they would have passed the Sea of Galilee, which would be important to their son's ministry and where thirty years later he would deliver the Sermon on the Mount. On the fifth day of their journey, Mary and Joseph reached the Judaean Desert. There were Bedouin shepherds, mountain lions, scorpions and bandits. As Mary and Joseph approached Jerusalem, they may have seen burned villages and toppled crosses used to crucify rebellious Jews.

Mary and Joseph probably stopped at the Temple and made their sacrifice probably two turtle doves. Then they hiked the short five-mile trip to Bethlehem by nightfall.[642]

Raw Fish for Breakfast

Cooked Salmon is on the green plate on the right and raw fish on the left.

Breads and Pastries for Breakfast

642   Ibid., 80-89.

Jesus of Nazareth continued

The inn was full due to the crowds coming to register. They stayed in a grotto, which is one of many caves used by wandering shepherds for centuries. The precise place where Jesus may have been born is today underneath a church built over the place where Jesus may have been born.

"And she brought forth her firstborn son and wrapped him in swaddling clothes, and laid him in a manger" (Luke 2:7). "And the angel said unto them, Fear not: for, behold, I bring you good tidings of great joy, which shall be to all people. For unto you is born this day in the city of David a Saviour, which is Christ the Lord" (Luke 2:10-11).[643]

Homemade Sachlav for Breakfast

This dish is hot milk thickened by flour and spices and is poured on top of oatmeal. It was delicious and we ate it every morning and miss eating it in the United States.

Jesus the Teacher

The thinking of Jesus was radical for the time. An example is giving your cloak to a needy stranger. Jesus did miracles such as feeding a crowd with small amounts of fish and bread, raising the dead, walking on water etc.

---

[643]   Ibid., 80-89.

Thomas Jefferson took scissors to his Bible, cut out the virgin birth, all miracles and the resurrection and reassembled what was left. Thomas Jefferson considered Jesus a great ethical thinker.

"And Jesus went all about Galilee, teaching in their synagogues, and preaching the gospel of the kingdom, and healing all manner of sickness and all manner of disease among the people from Galilee, and from Decapolis, and from Jerusalem, and from beyond Jordan" (Matthew 4:23, 25).

"The boy Jesus, raised by Mary and Joseph in Nazareth grew and waxed strong in spirit, filled with wisdom: and the grace of God was upon him. Now his parents went to Jerusalem every year at the feast of the Passover. And when he was twelve years old, they went up to Jerusalem after the custom of the feast. And when they had fulfilled the days, as they returned, the child Jesus tarried behind in Jerusalem: and Joseph and his mother knew not of it. But they, supposing him to have been in the company, went a day's journey: and they sought him among their kinsfolk and acquaintance. And when they found him not, they turned back again to Jerusalem, seeking him. There they discovered him in the Temple, listening and questioning. When Mary asked her son how he could have disappeared and upset his parents so, Jesus answered cryptically: wish ye not that I must be about my father's business." And they understood not the saying which he spake unto them."[644]

Jesus the Teacher (continued)

"And it came to pass, that after three days they found him in the temple, sitting in the midst of the doctors, both hearing them, and asking them questions. And all that heard him were astonished at his understanding and answers" (Luke 2:46-47).

"This beginning of miracles did Jesus in Cana of Galilee, and manifested forth his glory; and his disciples believed on him" (John 2:11).

In Cana Jesus and his mother were attending a wedding. When the wine gave out, Mary told Jesus. Jesus ordered, "six water pots of stone filled with water. He promptly changed the water into wine.

---

[644] Ibid., 90-104.

"This beginning of miracles did Jesus in Cana of Galilee, and manifested forth his glory; and his disciples believed in him" (John 2:11).

The Sea of Galilee is a sixty-four square mile lake in a depression of the Jordan River. It is the lowest fresh water lake in the world. In the time of Jesus Capernaum and Bethsaida had more than 15,000 people. Most of the miracles of Jesus happened along the Sea of Galilee

"Then Jesus six days before the passover came to Bethany, where Lazarus was which had been dead, whom he raised from the dead" (John 12:1).

Bethany is located on the outskirts of Jerusalem. Jesus visited Mary, Martha and Lazarus often. Jesus told his disciples, "Our friend Lazarus sleepeth: but I go, that I may awake him out of sleep." Jesus did go and raised Lazarus from the dead. "Then many of the Jews which came to Mary, and had seen the things which Jesus did, believed on him. But some of them went their way to the Pharisees, and told them what things Jesus had done. If we let him thus alone, all men will believe on him: and the Romans shall come and take away both our place and nation."

In modern times Bethany is known by the Arabic name el-Azariyeh meaning "place of Lazarus."[645]

Salad and Cheeses Breakfast Bar

---

[645] Ibid., 90-99.

The chef knew how to turn over the omelet by tossing it up into the air in a flip and catching it in the pan. There was a big choice of items to put in your specialized omelet.

Jesus the Teacher (continued)

"And after six days Jesus taketh with him Peter, and James, and John, and leadeth them up into an high mountain apart by themselves; and he was transfigured before them. And his raiment became shining, exceeding white as snow; so as no fuller on earth can white them" (Mark 9:2-3).

Jesus took Peter, James, and John on a mountaintop close to Capernaum. Some scholars believe it might be Mount Tabor. They prayed on top of the mountain and Jesus was transfigured which was the glowing of Jesus and the appearance of Moses and Elijah who talked to Jesus. Then a cloud appeared and a voice announced, "This is my beloved Son: hear him." Jesus asked Peter, James and John to keep it a secret until the "Son of man" had risen from the dead.

On the way to Jerusalem for the Passover, Jesus and his disciples passed through Jericho. "And they came to Jericho: and as he went out of Jericho with his disciples and a great number of people, blind Bartimaeus, the son of Timaeus, sat by the highway side begging" (Mark 10:46).

The blind man believed in Jesus and Jesus said, "Thy faith hath made thee whole." Jesus said, "Go thy way." Instead Bartimaeus got in line behind the disciples and journeyed to Jerusalem with them.[646]

---

[646]   Ibid., 90-99.

A Plate of Breakfast

Notice the bright color of the fruit. All fruit and vegetables had bright vivid colors and tasted delicious.

Jesus the Passion

"And when he was come into Jerusalem, all the city was moved, saying, Who is this?" (Matthew 21:10).

Many rushed out to meet Jesus and cried," Hosanna: Blessed is the King of Israel that cometh in the name of the Lord." Jesus seeing the glorious city of Jerusalem wept.

"And they came to Jerusalem: and Jesus went into the temple, and began to cast out them that sold and bought in the temple, and overthrew the tables of the moneychangers, and the seats of them that sold doves; And would not suffer that any man should carry any vessel through the temple. And he taught, saying unto them. Is it not written. My house shall be called of all nations the house of prayer? but ye have made it a den of thieves."

Joseph Caiaphas, the High Priest in Jerusalem, decided Jesus must go and was watching events unfolding.

During Passover supper, Jesus told his disciples that one of them would betray him. When Judas asked, "Is it I?" Jesus replied, "Thou hast said." When the supper was finished, Jesus and His disciples went to the Garden of Gethsemane to pray. "And they came to a place which was named Gethsemane and he saith to his disciples, Sit ye here, while I shall pray" (Mark 14:32).

Jesus prayed, "that it it were possible, the hour might pass from him. "And he said, Abba, Father, all things are possible unto thee: take away this cup from me; nevertheless not what I will, but what thou wilt."

Jesus woke His disciples saying, "Rise up, let us go, lo, he that betrayeth me is at hand. And immediately while he yet spake, cometh Judas, one of the twelve, and with him a great multitude with swords and staves, from the chief priests and the scribes and the elders."

Judas had an agreement with the guards that the one he kissed was the one to be arrested. And Judas immediately betrayed Jesus.

In modern times in Jerusalem there is a ridge called the Mount of Olives and on one of the slopes is the Garden of Gethsemane. There is the convent church of St. Mary Magdalene built in 1885 by Czar Alexander III and today houses White Russian nuns.

Jesus was taken before Pilate who asked, "Art thou the King of the Jews?" Jesus answered, "Thou sayest it."

We had a quick breakfast, loaded up the tour bus, and drove about eighty-one miles to Tel Aviv. We said our tearful good-by's to our Jewish bus driver of ten days and our Christian Arab guide who had made walking in the footsteps of Jesus come alive and meaningful for us.

In Tel Aviv, Pastor Greg, guided us through security, picking up tickets, and getting on the plane. One of our bags set off an alarm, and Harold had to go to special line and have the bag checked. The culprit items were Winkie's hand warmers and a special magnet. Harold had to explain that hand warmers were to warm up cold hands. This time we checked in all four bags and only had to keep up with bright red bag with computer.

This was the longest day with 26 hours instead of 24. Half was spent on Israeli time and the other half on United States time. We dozed but never went into deep sleep. We followed doctor orders and walked on schedule and ate and drank every time it was offered.

We changed planes in Newark, New Jersey and headed for Atlanta. We were relieved not to see the predicted snow on the ground. We flew to Charlotte North Carolina because of our airplane schedule. Our First Baptist bus picked us up and we arrived sleepily around two a.m. in Augusta, Georgia.

It took about eight days to get over jet lag. There had been seven hours difference in the Israeli time and Augusta time. I was not sleepy when night came in Augusta because that was day in Israel. It took time for my stomach to adjust back to the Augusta diet instead of the Israeli Mediterranean diet.

Interesting Magazine Articles

An Appeal to All Americans in the Light of Christ's Return, by David R. Barnhart: The Vine and the Branches, Fall 2012, p.6-9.

Jerusalem-Why it Matters. The Vine and Branches Magazine by Abiding Word Ministries. Fall 2012 issue. Page 15.

Pray for the Shalom of Jerusalem. The Vine and Branches Magazine by Abiding Word Ministries. Fall 2012 issue. Page 16-17,

Major Discoveries in Israel:

Seal of Samson: A stone seal dating to the 11th century BC with a long-haired man killing a lion with a long tail has been found. This is during the time period of the Judges in Israel and the seal discovered was found near the Sorek River a few miles west of Jerusalem. This area was the border between the Israelites and the Philistines at that time. Judges 14:6.

Seal of Bethlehem: Zachi Zweig, an Israeli archaeology student, discovered the "Bethlehem" seal dating back 2,700 years to King Hezekiah. In Hebrew was these words on the seal, "In the seventh year of the king's reign, taxes from the city of Bethlehem for the king." This is the oldest reference to Bethlehem ever found outside the Bible.

When God steps in Elwood McQuaid. Israel My Glory Magazine. November/December 2012. p. 10-12.

Awaiting the Bridegroom. Patrick Neff. Israel My Glory. September and October 2012. p.18-20.

The Rapture versus the Second Coming of Jesus. Thomas C. Simcox. Israel My Glory Magazine. September and October 2012. page 22-23.

The Seven Keys to History. Key 3: Catastrophe: Richard D. Emmons. Israel My Glory Magazine, September-October, 2012. 30-32.

Conclusion

*T*HANK YOU FOR COMING WITH US ON OUR TOUR OF ISRAEL. TOGETHER WE SAW MANY PLACES WHERE JESUS WALKED. AND, WE SAW PLACES TODAY WHERE WE MET PEOPLE, SHOPPED, ATE REALLY GOOD FOOD, AND DISCOVERED MANY THINGS ABOUT THE HOLY LAND OF ISRAEL.

WE PRAY THAT YOU WALK WITH JESUS EVERY DAY OF YOUR LIFE AND TRUST HIM AS YOUR LORD AND SAVIOR. WE ARE PRAYING THAT JESUS WILL BE CLOSE TO YOU EVERY MOMENT OF YOUR LIFE AND THAT HE WILL PROTECT AND PROVIDE FOR YOUR EVERY NEED.

WE WOULD LOVE TO HEAR FROM YOU. SEND US A LETTER TO:

PO Box 2115
Evans, GA 30809.